Angus Bethune Reach

**Leonard Lindsay**

The Story of a Buccaneer

Angus Bethune Reach

**Leonard Lindsay**
*The Story of a Buccaneer*

ISBN/EAN: 9783744659017

Printed in Europe, USA, Canada, Australia, Japan

Cover: Foto ©Thomas Meinert / pixelio.de

More available books at **www.hansebooks.com**

# LEONARD LINDSAY

OR

## *THE STORY OF A BUCCANEER*

BY

## ANGUS B. REACH

"No Peace beyond the Line."—*Old Sailor's Proverb*

LONDON

GEORGE ROUTLEDGE AND SONS

THE BROADWAY, LUDGATE

NEW YORK: 416 BROOME STREET

# CONTENTS.

# CONTENTS.

# LEONARD LINDSAY;

## OR,

# THE STORY OF A BUCCANEER.

---

### CHAPTER I.

#### OF MY BOYHOOD, AND HOW, BEING CAST AWAY AT SEA, I AM CARRIED TO THE WEST INDIES AGAINST MY WILL.

It was in the fair sunlight of a May morning, in the year of Grace 1672, that that great brave ship, the Golden Grove of Leith, hoisted her broad sails, with many a fluttering pendant and streamer above them, and stood proudly down the Firth of Forth, designing to reach the open ocean, not far from the hill, well known to mariners by the name of the North Berwick Law. On board of the Golden Grove, I, LEONARD LINDSAY, then in my twenty-second year, was, you must know, a sailor, and I hope a bold one. My father was a fisherman, and, as I may say, his coble was my cradle. Many a rough rocking in truth it bestowed upon me, for it was his use even before I could go alone, to carry me with him a fishing, wrapped up, it may be, in a tattered sail, while my mother, with a creel upon her back, journeyed through the landward towns, and to the houses of the gentry, to sell the spoil of hook and net.

We fared hard and worked hard; for no more industrious folk lived in the fisher-town of Kirk Leslie, a pleasant and goodly spot, lying not far from the East Neuk of Fife, than old Davie Lindsay and Jess, his wife

B

and my mother. Many a weary night and day have
come and gone since I beheld that beach whereon I was
born ; but I can yet shut my eyes and see our cottage
and our boat—called the "Royal Thistle"—rocking at
the lee of the long rough pier of unhewn whinstone,
gathered from the wild muirs around, which ran into the
sea and sheltered the little fisher harbour, formed by the
burn of Balwearie, where it joins the waters of its black
pools to the salt brine. Opposite our house was a pretty
green bourock, as we called it, that is to say, a little hill,
mostly of bright green turf, with bunches of bent and
long grass, which rustled with a sharp sad sound when
the east wind blew snell, and creeping cosily into the
chimney neuk, we would listen to the roaring of the
sea. But the bourock was oftentimes brown with nets
or with wet sails stretched there to dry, and below it
there lay half-buried in the sand, old boats, mouldering
away and masts and oars all shivered, bleaching like big
bones in the sun and the rain.

I remember old Davie Lindsay my father well.
He was a stern, big man, with a grisly grey beard,
shaved but once a month. No fisher on the coast had a
surer hand for the tiller, or a firmer gripe to haul aft
the sheet of the lugsail in a fresh breeze and a gathering
sea. Often when we were rising and falling on the
easterly swell, half-a-score miles from Kirk Leslie pier,
he loved to tell me old-world tales and sing old-world
songs of the sea. Then would he recount how the Rover
sunk the bell which good abbot Ignatius, of Aberbroth-
wick, caused to be placed upon the wild Bell Rock, as a
guide to poor mariners ; and how the pirate dreed the
weird—that is, underwent the fate—he had prepared for
himself, and was lost with ship and crew on that very
reef. Sometimes, too, he would drop his voice, and when
I came close to him, he would speak of great monsters in
the sea ; of the ocean snake, whose head looked up at the
bridge of Stirling, and whose tail went nine times round
the Bass ; of singing mermaids, who come upon the
yellow sands at night, and beguile men with their false

lays, till they leave house and home, being bewitched by
the glamour of elfin palaces under the brine; and, most
terrible of all, of phantom ships with crews of ghosts,
which sailors see by the pale glimmerings of the moon,
when it shines through the driving scud, upon a mirk
midnight and a roaring sea. But, then, if I was frightened and cried, my father would straightway change the
theme, and burst out with a strong clear voice into some
loud fishing-song, or, what I loved better still, into some
brave, ancient ballad, about the fair kingdom of Scotland,
and its gallant kings and stalwart knights; and of such,
my favourite was the lay of Sir Patrick Spens, for he was
both a knight and a sailor.

> " The king sits in Dunfermline town,
>   Drinking the blude-red wine,
> O whare will I get a skeely skipper
>   To sail this ship of mine?

> " Then up and spake an eldern knight,
>   Sat at the king's right knee,
> Sir Patrick Spens is the best sailor
>   That ever sailed the sea."

Oh, I can yet hear my father's strong voice rising over
the dash of the water and the moan of the wind, as he
sung the brave voyage of Sir Patrick to Norroway, to
bring home the king's daughter; but his tones would
sink and grow hoarse and low, when he chanted the
storm, and the perishing of all the fair company on the
voyage home.

> " O forty mile off Aberdeen
>   'Tis fifty fathom deep,
> And there lies gude Sir Patrick Spens,
>   Wi' the Scots lords at his feet."

My father's long home was also the bottom of the sea.
One wild March day, the coble left Kirk Leslie pier
without me. I staid at home mending a dredge-net with
my mother. The easterly har was on the coast, that is
to say, thick cold mists and a keen wind. As the sun
rose high so did the tempest; we could see nought sea-

ward, for the grey fog was out upon the water, but every
wave came white, over and over the pier, from end to
end.   My mother went to and fro, wan, and praying to
herself; as indeed did many another fisher-wife, for they
had great cause.   The night was awful.   I sat cowering
beside my mother, who was rocking herself on a settle
with her apron over her head; or now and then stole
down to the beach, to where men stood with lanterns
upon masts to show the harbour mouth to the poor folks
at sea.   Three boats, with crews pale and worn, made
the land before the day; an hour after dawn our coble
came tossing to the outside belt of the surf—but she
was bottom upwards.

In a month after this, my mother and I went to her
father's, a very old man, and a reverend elder of the kirk.
He sent me to school to Dominie Buchanan, a learned
carle, who by his own account behoved to be of the race
of the great Geordie Buchanan, of whom they tell merry
tales, which surely are idle and false, for he was a severe,
grave man, and handled the tawse unmercifully, as his
royal pupil, gentle King Jamie, could in his time well
testify.   At school I was diligent, and pleased master
and friends.

Afterwards, up to my sixteenth year, I went much a
fishing in the boat of Saunders Drauggletute, my maternal
uncle, when desiring to see more of my country than
could be descried in our furthest voyages between Kirk
Leslie pier and the deep-sea fisheries at the back of the
Isle of May, I made many coasting trips, for the space of
near five years, in the stout brig Jean Livingstone, belonging to Kirkaldy, during which time I twice visited
the Thames and the city of London; plying also once
each year with a great cargo of herrings to Antwerp, in
the Low Countries.   But still I wished to see the world
further from home, and to this intent preferred rather to
go on board the Golden Grove of Leith, as a common
sailor, than to be mate of the Jean Livingstone, a promo-
tion which was offered me by John Swanson, skipper and
part owner of the brig.

The reason of my coming to think of the Golden Grove was, that the Jean Livingstone having a cargo of goods from Yarmouth to Edinburgh, lay while they were delivered close by the great ship, then preparing at the foot of Leith Wynd for a voyage to Italy, and from thence to divers ports on the Moorish side of the Mediterranean sea. Now Italy was a land which I had long wished to behold, as being once the seat of that great people the Romans, some knowledge of the poetry and philosophy of whom, the worthy Dominie Buchanan had not failed to instil into me, but which I ofttimes felt with pain to be fast fading from my mind. Indeed, I must tell you that it is to the exertions of that learned man that this narrative is altogether owing, for he, seeing, as he was pleased to say, a more congenial soil in my mind for the seeds of his instructions than was presented by the other fisher-boys, took great pains to imbue me with a love for the humanities, which has not deserted me entirely unto this day. After much pondering upon my prospects, I therefore finally made up my mind to offer myself on board of the Golden Grove, which I did, and was accepted without more ado. My friends would have me pause and think of the dangers of unknown coasts, and pirates and robbers of the sea, but I knew Captain John Coxon, of the Golden Grove, to be a stout and experienced seaman, and one who was readily trusted with rich freights— while as to freebooters, when I looked upon the array of culverins, demi-culverins, and falconets ranged upon the decks, and also the show of carabines and patterreroes placed about the masts, with many stout fellows to man and wield them, I felt we could bid defiance to any rover who ever sailed out of Sallee.

Therefore, to make a long story short, we completed our cargo, took in provisions and water, and, as has been said, on a fine May morning, I do not remember the exact day, sailed. The wind was so fair that by even-fall we saw St. Abb's Head.

And here at the outset of what was to me so adventurous a voyage, I would describe my captain and my shipmates, as well as the stout vessel herself, the latter being indeed a brave craft, with top-gallant forecastle and high poop, surmounted by three great lanterns; but, as the reader will shortly perceive, the Golden Grove and I soon parted company, and I never saw either her or any of her crew again.

We carried the fair north wind with us all along the English coast, until passing through the straits of Dover, we bade farewell to the white cliffs. Then in two days' time we saw upon the larboard bow great rocks which form the cape called La Hogue, in France, and passing to the westward of the island of Guernsey, sighted the little isle of Ushant lying off the port of Brest, where the French maintain fleets and great naval stores. Hereabouts the wind changed, veering round to the westward, and speedily rolling in upon us billows so vast that we could well discern that we were no longer in the narrow seas, but exposed to the great strength and fierceness of the Atlantic or Western ocean. Notwithstanding, however, we made good progress; the breeze was not steady but blew in squalls, making it often necessary to hand topsails, and raising great seething seas around us, over which the Golden Grove rode very gallantly. At night-fall, on the eighth day of our voyage, we lost sight of Ushant and entered into the great Bay of Biscay. The sea here runs exceedingly high, tumbling in to the shore in great ridges of blue water; but with a stout ship, well manned, the nature of the waves is not so dangerous as that of the short, boiling surges in the North Sea. And now I come to the accident which so sadly determined my lot for many a day.

On the morning of either the 13th or the 14th of May the weather was squally and unsettled, and the sea irregular and high. About eight o'clock, looking forth to windward, I saw a great blackness in the sky, which I took to be the prelude of a gust of no common strength. At the same moment, the mate of the watch ordered the topmen aloft to hand the topsails, we carrying at the moment no higher canvas. My station was upon the leeward fore-topsail yardarm, and as I clung by the man-ropes to the great creaking pieces of timber, grasping the fluttering canvas of the sail, I thought I had never seen a finer sight than the great rolling ship below, wallowing and labouring in the white foaming seas, which would sometimes strike her and pour heavy masses of clear green water in a flood over the decks. When we were securing the sail, the motion aloft was very great, we being violently swung from side to side in such wise as might well make giddy even the grizzled head of an old mariner. Meantime, the gust to windward was coming fast; the blackness increased, and a rushing sound, as of the chariot wheels of a host, rose above the rude clamour of the sea. Then, amid great showers of flying brine, which it drove before it, the fierce wind struck the Golden Grove bodily over upon her side. At the same instant, I heard a hoarse voice below summoning the men from the yards down upon deck; but as I was about to obey, the tempest grew terrible. There were great clouds of mist above me, through which I could see nought below but the white patches of waves breaking over the strong bulwarks of the ship. Suddenly the canvas, which had not been quite secured, was torn open, as it were, with a loud screech by the wind, and flapped and banged so that I felt the very mast shake and quiver violently, while I received rude blows from the loose and flying ropes, insomuch as, being half blinded by that and the pelting of the brine, I shut my eyes, and bending down my head grasped the yard firmly in my arms. I might have remained thus three or four seconds, when I heard the loud howl of the wind suddenly increase to a sort of eldritch scream. In a moment, the mast gave two violent jerks, and with the third I heard five or six sounding twangs like the breaking of harp-strings, and immediately a crashing of wood. Then, still clinging to the yard, I was hurried with a mighty rush through the air, and suddenly plunged down into the choking brine, which rose all gurgling over my head, and I knew at the same time that the Golden Grove had carried away her fore-topmast, and that I was overboard in the boiling sea.

By instinct, I suppose, I struggled so to climb upon the floating wreck as to get my head and shoulders above water. Then I saw that I was alone in my misery. I have said that my station was at the outer end of the yard, and I conceive that my shipmates must have gained the top, and from thence, I hoped, the deck. But as for me, I saw nought but speedy drowning for my fate. The seas rose in great foaming peaks and pyramids around me, and the wind drove drenching showers from the crests of the waves down into the hollows. All around gloomy clouds passed swiftly, torn by the squall, but the pitchy darkness which showed where its strength lay, was far down to leeward, and looking thereat as I rose upon a higher sea than common, I faintly descried the ship in a crippled plight, but having managed to put her helm up so as to scud before the storm. She was already near a league away, and leaving me fast; so that the bitterness of death rose up in my very heart. For a moment I thought I might as well die at once, and letting go my hold of the spars, I allowed myself to sink backward into the sea. But God has wisely made man to love life with a clinging love, and to grapple with death as with a grim enemy. Therefore, as the water closed above me, and I felt suffocating, I could not help making a struggle, which soon replaced me on my desolate seat on the floating wreck. I looked at the spars, and saw that the topmast had broken only about a foot beneath the place to which the yard had been lowered. Nearly the whole of the foretop and the top-gallant masts of the Golden Grove, with the fragments of the foretopsail, which had been rent almost into ribbons, and the yard to which they were fastened lay therefore in the sea. I clambered in from the end of the yard, and took up my position where the mast and it crossed each other; making myself fast thereto with one of the numerous ends of broken rope which abounded, and for near an hour sat dismal and almost broken-hearted, un-

heedful of how the waves tossed me to and fro, or how
they sometimes burst over and almost stifled me. I was
somewhat roused by a feeling of warmth, and looking
abroad saw that the clouds had broken, and that the sun
was shining brightly on the sea. The wind was also
abated, and the waves not combing so violently, I was
more at ease. Then I heard that terrible sound—the
sound of the sea alone—which no one who has listened
to save he who has swam far from any vessel, or who,
like myself, has clung to a driving spar. On the beach
you hear the surf, where the waves burst upon rock or
sand; on shipboard you hear the dashing of the billows
on counter and prow; and, above them all, the sigh of
the wind and the groaning of timbers and masts. But to
hear the sea alone, you must be alone upon the sea. I
will tell you of the noise: it is as of a great multitudinous
hiss, rising universally about you—the buzz of the
fermenting and yeasty waves. There are no deep, hollow
rumblings; except for that hissing, seething sound, the
great billows rise and sink in silence; and you look over
a tumbling waste of blue or green water, all laced, and
dashed, and variegated with a thousand stripes, and
streaks, and veins of white glancing froth, which embroider,
as it were with lace, the dark masses of heaving and
falling ocean. Hearing this sound, and seeing this sight,
I tossed until the sun got high and warm. I felt no very
poignant anguish, for my soul was clothed, as it were, in
a species of lethargy—the livery of despair. Sometimes
only I tried to pray, but thoughts and tongue would
grow benumbed together.

Once, indeed, I was for a time aroused. I heard a
sharp little dash in the water, and a soft quackle, as of a
sea-fowl. Looking up, I descried beside me two ducks of
that species which we, in the Scottish seas, called marrots;
they are white on the breast and neck, and brown above,
and have very bright, glancing, yellow eyes. Moreover,
they dive, and use their short wings under water, as other
fowls do theirs in flying. By the appearance of these
creatures I knew that land was, at farthest, within two

days' sail.  There—tilting gaily over each sea—they swam for hours, seeming to look at me ; sometimes they would dive, but they never went far from the wreck, always coming up and riding head to wind, with their keen yellow eyes fixed as I thought upon the poor drowning mariner.  They seemed tame and fearless—for, indeed, what should they dread from me ?  Once, in a sort of melancholy mirth, I raised my arm threateningly, but they stirred neither wing nor leg to flee, lifting over seas which would make a great man-of-war work and groan to her very keel, but which these feathered ships, built by God, could outride without a film of down being washed aside from their white breasts.

The sun having attained its zenith began to descend the westerly skies, and the afternoon was fair and warm, the wind now blowing but a summer breeze.  Sometimes, when on the crest of the swell, I looked anxiously for a sail, but I saw nought save the bright horizon, against which the sharp outlines of the waves rose and fell in varying curves and ridges ;  so that now again I resigned myself to death, and covering my face with my hands, I, as it were, moaned, rather than sung inwardly to myself, many verses of psalms, which, when I was but a little child, I had repeated at my mother's knee. Meantime, I began to feel a stiffening and a heavy drowsiness over all my limbs and upon my soul.  When I opened my eyes the heaving waters turned into divers colours before my sight, so that I knew that my brain was wandering, and that my soul was departing.  Howbeit, a holy tranquillity came down upon me.  The blue sea appeared to melt away, and I saw—but dimly—the green bourock and the sweet soft swarded links of the Balwearie burn, with the brown herring nets drying on the windy grass.  The place seemed holy and still ; the sun was hot, and none were stirring, and presently I knew it was a summer's sabbath day, for from out the open windows of the grey old kirk there came a low sound of psalmody, and I heard, as it were, in my brain, the voices of the congregation, as they sang—

"In Judah's land God is well known,
His name in Israel's great,
In Salem is his tabernacle,
In Zion is his seat."

After this, there came on me silence and darkness, I having gradually fallen into a fit or trance.

I was roused by rude shocks and pulls, and a confused clamour of voices. Opening my eyes with effort, I saw surging upon the broken water, close to the spars, a ship's boat with men, one of whom—he who rowed the boat oar—had grasped the collar of my sea doublet, and was hauling me into the pinnace, in which effort he succeeded, ere I could well make out whereabouts I was. At the same time several voices asked, in two different languages, what was my name and country, and how I came there. Now, of both of these tongues I had some smattering, the one being French and the other Low Dutch, of which I had heard and picked up somewhat in my several voyages up the river Scheldt to Antwerp.

I therefore, trying to muster my senses, replied truthfully that my name was Leonard Lindsay—that I was a Scotsman, a mariner of the ship Golden Grove, of Leith, wherefrom I had fallen overboard, the spar to which I clung having been, as, indeed, they might perceive, blown away in tempestuous weather.

At this they consulted in a low tone amongst themselves. They were all seafaring men, mostly very swarthy, and tanned by the sun and the wind. They wore long black hair, and silver and gold earrings, which glanced amid their greasy curls. Only two were fair and blue-eyed—namely, the men who first addressed me in Flemish or Dutch. After remaining for a brief time beside the spars, and seeming to consult as to whether they were worthy to be made a prize of, they decided in the negative, and dipping their oars into the water, rowed away, the steersman narrowly watching the run of the seas, so as to avoid being broached-to and swamped. In the meantime, I had clambered from the bottom of the boat, and looking over the bows, saw, not more than a third of a mile from us, a bark, which appeared to be both small and frail to contend with such a sea. The manner of her rig was new and strange to me, for she carried two masts, both very stout and short, and above them were two great supple yards, upon which was spread a good show of canvas, each sail being of that triangular form, called by the seamen who use them, lateen. In fine, the ship belonged to a port on the Mediterranean coast of France, and was of the class named feluccas.

It was necessary to approach the vessel with great caution, inasmuch as she rolled and surged excessively. We therefore came slowly up, under her lee-quarter, and a man, of very dark complexion, and the fieryest eyes I ever saw, jumped up upon the gunwale, and hailed the boat in French, but talking so rapidly, that I could make nothing of it. Then, a line having been thrown on board, it was made fast to me, and without more ado, I was soused into the sea, and dragged on board the felucca, where I lay panting on the deck, while the crew —very wild and fierce-looking sailors—amused themselves with my wretched appearance. Presently, however, the man who had hailed the boat, and who seemed to have great authority on board, came up to me, and putting the rest aside, said more deliberately than before, but still in French, and with a peculiar accent—

' You are not, then, a Spaniard ?'

I mustered my few words of French, and answered, that—' I was not, but a Scotsman.'

Without more ado, he stooped over me, and searched my pockets. They contained some small English coins, being groats and silver pennies, and also a letter, which Captain Swanson, of the Jean Livingstone, had written to me to Leith. The sight of these things appeared to satisfy his doubts, for he spoke a few words in a kinder tone to those about him, and presently leaving me, a man dressed in a tarnished livery, like a lackey, brought me a great cup of hot distilled waters, which I greedily swallowed, and found myself comforted and refreshed.

Being, however, much exhausted from the length of time which I had passed in the water, I laid me down upon a heap of sails in the forecastle, and being taken but little notice of, thanked God, inwardly, for my deliverance, and began to drop off to sleep. Only beforehand, like a sailor, I observed the course of the ship. The wind being westerly, and she being close hauled, and labouring heavily to windward, I deemed, and with truth, that her destination must be across the Atlantic. But whithersoever she went, with my then feelings, mattered little ; I was saved from an early death, and grateful for my escape, I fell into a deep and dreamless sleep.

When I wakened it was dark night, and the first watch was set. As the wind, however, was now very steady, and the sea not only lower but regular, the men were mostly lying and dozing about the deck, except he that conned and he that steered. Seeing me stirring, a sailor presently came to me with a lantern in his hand, and, to my great joy, addressed me in English, asking me from whence I came, and the particulars of my disaster. Having shortly informed him, I requested that he would tell me what the ship was, which had rescued me, and what manner of treatment I might expect at the hands of the captain and crew. At first, he made as if he would put off talking of these matters, but as I was importunate, he asked me in turn, whether I had not heard of the great association of men of all nations, but principally Englishmen, Frenchmen, and Hollanders, who carried on a constant warfare with the Spaniards among the islands of the West Indies, and along the coast of Darien, sometimes even crossing that narrow neck of land, and descending with fire and sword upon Panama and other towns of the South Sea. To this I replied, that certainly I had heard of these companies, but only very partially and nothing distinctly, that they were, I supposed, the adventurers called Flibustiers or Buccaneers, and more anciently the 'Brethren of the Coast.' My new friend made answer moodily, that I should most probably have ample means of learning more of these Freebooters ere I put my foot on British ground again—'That is,' says he, 'after you have either escaped or served your time.'

These phrases naturally threw me into great trouble, and I earnestly asked what he signified by them.

'Why,' he replied, 'that you will be sold as an apprentice, or in other words, as a slave, to the French West India company, in the Isle of Tortugas, on the northern coast of Hispaniola, whither we are bound.'

At these words I grew sick at heart. 'Better,' I said, 'to have allowed me drown in that sea than to have rescued me only to sell me into slavery.'

'Not so,' answered my companion, something sternly. 'You are young, and have a thousand hopes before you. The Hand that miraculously preserved you this day is ever stretched out in wisdom and mercy, readier to help than to chastise.'

At this I could not avoid looking steadfastly at my Englishman; such phrases being little apt to fall from the lips of sailors. By the light of the lantern, I saw that he was a tall and stout old man, with something of great grandeur, as I thought, in his high brow and serene eyes. He could not have been much younger than sixty-five, but he was still a very strong great man, with a presence and bearing not like those of a wild sailor who has lived, as I may say, all his life with his hands in the tar-bucket. After some pause he went on to inform me, that besides himself there was no Englishman amongst the crew, and that he counted upon being safely put ashore at Tortugas, from whence he could get to Jamaica ; for, as he said, he was not unknown to the hunters and privateers who frequented the former island. In reply to my entreaties, that he would endeavour to take me with him, he said it was not possible ; for although the captain might consent, yet that many of the crew were greedy low fellows, who would not render up a maravedi of the profits, to which, by the articles of the voyage, it seems that they were all in some sort and in different proportions entitled.

'But be thankful,' said my comrade, 'that you are not

a Spaniard; for had you but a drop of the blood of that people in your veins, a speedy death would be the best fate you could hope for on board a ship commanded by Louis Montbars.'

'Why,' said I, 'is he so inveterate against the people of Spain?'

'I find,' returned the Englishman, 'that you do indeed know little of the adventurers of the West Indies, if you have never heard of one of the most noted captains of them all. He is a gentleman of good birth, of Languedoc in France. In his early manhood, having taken great interest in reading various relations of the barbarities committed by the Spaniards upon the ancient and inoffensive Indians, the inhabitants of the islands and the main discovered by Christopher Columbus and his coadjutors and successors, Montbars, being, like many in the South of France, a man of warm and fierce passions and feelings, made a solemn vow to God and the Virgin, that the whole of his future life should be devoted to the task of revenging upon every Spaniard who might be placed in his power the injuries received at the hands of their fathers, alike by the fierce Charibs of the islands, and the gentle Peruvians of the main. To this intent, he spent all his patrimony in fitting out a ship, in which he sailed to the West Indies, and speedily made his name so famous, and so terrible to the Spaniards, that they call him in their language, 'The Exterminator,' and know that they can hope for not one moment's life after they come into his power. In general,' pursued my informant, 'he is grave, staid, and courteous, unless his mind run upon what I cannot but think the sort of bloody madness wherewith he is afflicted. And then, indeed, and more especially when in action with the Spaniards, he demeans himself more like a raging demon than a Christian man. He has lately had occasion to visit his native land, and I being also in Paris on my own business, and hearing that he proposed to set forth again, joined him as a mariner, but to be put ashore after the voyage at the island of Tortugas.'

This was the substance of our conversation that night After which the quarter-master came to me, and saying, he understood that I had been a fisherman in my youth, and so must needs know how to make nets; and that they were in want of some seine nets for use in the keys or small islands of the Indies, I might therefore, by making them, pay my passage. To this arrangement I very willingly acceded, and the next day had a hammock assigned to me, and set about my task of net-making, which was pleasant enough, pursued in fine weather upon the deck; although, indeed, my heart was heavy and sore with thinking of what was before me.

I soon discovered that my Englishman's appellation, by which he was known, was Richard Wright, although that was not, indeed, as I afterwards found, his proper name. The crew were now reasonably kind to me, and the more so because Wright, whom they seemed to respect, took me in some sort under his protection, and upon the whole I found myself not ill off. The Captain mixed very familiarly with the men, as is common on board of privateers, and sometimes he would recite to them tales of the cruelties of the Spaniards to the Indians; how in Hispaniola the numbers of these latter were reduced in fifteen years from a million to sixty thousand; how the Spaniards worked them to a miserable death in the gold mines, or hunted them with bloodhounds through the mountains, feeding the dogs only upon the victims' flesh; how the Spaniards would often kill these miserable people for mere diversion, or for wagers, or to keep their hands in, as they called it; and how many of these white savages had made a vow—ay, and kept it—that, for a certain time, they would destroy thirteen Indians every morning before breakfast, in honour of our Saviour and the twelve apostles! With such relations, and all of them I believe to be true, would Montbars seek to stir up the deadly wrath of the ship's company against the Spaniards. But, in truth, this was a flame which required but little fanning, it being my opinion that had the Spaniards behaved like angels rather than demons, still the great body of ordinary Buccaneers would be content to treat them as the latter, so long as they possessed fair towns and rich mines ashore, and many treasure-ships and galleons at sea. Notwithstanding, however, it must be confessed that there never being a nation more proud, cruel, and arrogant than these Spanish—at least, in all that refers to their American dominions—so there never was a people more justly to be despoiled of their ill-gotten gains.

But these are considerations apart from my narrative. Our voyage was reasonably prosperous, the west wind having soon given place to more favourable breezes, and at length, but not until after many teasing calms, which delayed our progress, the first welcome fannings of the trade wind caught our sails, and we glided swiftly towards the setting sun, over the great heaving ocean swells and undulations, from whose shining sides flying fishes would leap briskly forth, and within which, the water being wondrously clear, we usually saw, on looking over the low bulwarks of the bark, swift dolphins, which swam round and round us, even when our ship was sailing three leagues an hour, and many smaller fishes, one individual of which, called by sailors a bonetta, about a foot long and of a reddish colour, swam for three days and three nights just before our cutwater, so that the men began, as it were, to know that fish, and used to feed it with crumbs from the end of the bowsprit.

About the 6th of June, the weather being then very hot, with light breezes, we crossed the line, as it is called, not of course the true equator or equinox, but the tropic of Cancer. This was, according to the custom of the sea, a great festival on board, those who had not passed that way before being obliged to submit to the ceremony of baptism, as they call it, which was performed after the manner then in use amongst French ships, as follows :—

The master's mate dressed himself in a strange sort of garment, fashioned so as to be ridiculous and burlesque, and reaching to his heels, with a hat or cap made to match. In his right hand he held a great clumsy wooden

c

sword ; in his left a pot of ink. His face he had besmirched with soot, and he wore an uncouth necklace
made of strings of blocks or pulleys, such as are used in
the rigging for ropes to pass through. Thus accoutred,
all the novices knelt down before him, while he favoured
the shoulders of each with a smart slap of the sword,
smearing also a great cross upon his brows, or sometimes
over all his face with the ink. Immediately after, the
novice was drenched with dozens of buckets of water, and
the ceremony ended by his depositing his offering, as they
call it, of a bottle of brandy, which must be placed in perfect silence at the foot of the mainmast. For myself,
I underwent the mummery with the rest, and had, fortunately, sufficient in my pocket to contribute my bottle of
brandy. One of the Hollanders on board told me that
their mode of baptism was different; they either insisting
upon a ransom, according to the station of the novice, or
hoisting him to the main yard and from thence dropping
him into the sea three several times. 'If, however,' said
my informant, a simple man, 'he be hoisted a fourth time in
the name of the Prince of Orange, or of the master of the
vessel, his honour is reckoned more than ordinary.' In
case of the ship—I speak still of the Hollanders—never
having passed that place before, the captain is bound to
give the mariners a small runlet of wine, which if he
neglect to do, they maintain that they may cut the stem
off the vessel. But in French and in Dutch ships, the
profits accruing from the ceremony are kept by the
master's mate, and spent upon the arrival in port, in a
general debauch by all the seamen.

---

## CHAPTER II.

### OF MY ESCAPE FROM THE FRENCH SHIP, AND MY LANDING IN HISPANIOLA.

AND now, being fairly within the grasp of the trade wind,
we sped swiftly on towards those western islands whither
we were bound, experiencing, however, as we approached

the Indies, some of the squally weather common in these
latitudes.   Such gusts soon blow over, but are troublesome
and fatiguing to mariners, and wearing to ship and rigging.
First comes a black cloud on the horizon, then the waves
to windward become tipped with whitish foam.   Presently
the gust strikes with great force, the firmament being
very dark and threatening : at the time of its greatest
strength there will be a flash of lightning and a thunder-
clap or two, after which a pelt of rain and a sudden clearing of the sky, the squall being for that time over.

Meanwhile, I often discussed with Wright the question
of my deliverance.   He said that there was now so much
jealousy between the French and the English, in the West
Indies, that I could possibly look for no other fate than
being sold to serve my time as a slave in Tortugas ; where
I would be employed in field labour, such as the cultiva-
tion of tobacco, great crops of which are grown in that
island.   Wright's opinion was, that I ought, in some
way or other, to attempt an escape before being landed
at Tortugas ; but this was easier talked of than done.
While all was still unsettled between us, ' Land ' was one
day proclaimed from the mast-head.   This announcement
surprised us all, for we had not expected to see any land
until we came in sight of the mountains of Hispaniola,
which still lay well to the westward.   However, we soon
found that, either through currents or errors in the
reckoning, we were further to the south than we had calculated, and that the island we saw was one of the Virgin
Isles, forming a cluster just where the long line of windward islands which stretch northward from the mainland,
trend away to the west.   This discovery necessitated a
change in our steering—we hauling up two or three points
more to the northward.   The next day we saw, at a very
great distance to leeward, a long faint blue ridge rising out
of the water, which was the mountain line of the high
ground of Porto Rico.   Towards evening, the trade wind
abated, being influenced, as we conjectured, by the distant
land-breeze, which blows at night off the shore, in and
near these islands ; and before the setting of the sun the

weather grew wellnigh calm. It was then that one of the crew discovered a bottle floating not far from the felucca, and pointed it out to the Captain, who straightway commanded it to be brought aboard; inasmuch as mariners in distress often fling such into the sea, with letters and papers relating their sad condition. Now, on board the felucca were two boats—the pinnace, in which I had been rescued, and a little skiff, not bigger than a canoe, which, being hoisted out and manned by two hands, brought in the bottle. It turned out to be empty and of no account. Still the finding of it was a lucky accident for me, inasmuch as the skiff was not again hoisted on board, but—the weather being exceedingly fine, and we soon expecting to use her to help in mooring ship—left towing astern.

That same night, Wright came to me and pointed her out as a means of escape.

'Look you,' says he, ' your business is to get ashore on some island where you will find Englishmen, and which is not entirely under French or Spanish influence. Now, on the coast of Hispaniola are not a few of your countrymen and mine, sometimes cruizing, sometimes hunting and slaughtering cattle. By the course we are now lying, we shall have to run all along the northern coast of Hispaniola, which we will probably approach close to, for the benefit of the land-breeze at night, and because the shore is bold and the sea deep. Provided the skiff be left towing astern, it will not be difficult for you to smuggle yourself into it in the night-time, and so escape ashore.'

This advice appeared to me admirable, and threw me quite into a fever of eagerness and anxiety. I was in the middle watch that night, and how often I gazed upon the little boat—the expected ark of my deliverance—as she tossed upon the smooth ridges of swell, which glanced like silver in the bright moonlight! About nine o'clock in the morning the trade wind resumed its powers, and we soon saw rising out of the ocean, upon our lee bow, the blue-peaked-mountains of Hispaniola. All day, you may be sure, I very eagerly watched the weather, fearing

lest the approach of a squall would cause Montbars to
order the skiff to be taken on deck, but the sky continued
quite cloudless, the sun was burning hot, and the sea
breeze—for such amid the Western Indies they call the
regular daily trade wind—blew most refreshingly upon
our starboard quarter, urging the felucca gloriously along.
We were now fast closing in with the coast, which
stretched in a long high range under the lee; and as we
approached an exceeding bold promontory, called Le
Vieux Cap François, I saw how delicious was the land,
with its bright green forests—its rocks, rising from thick
bushes and brushwood—and the great blue mountain
peaks in the distance. Besides ourselves the ocean was
solitary. No sail scudded before the breeze—no fishing-
boat rode head to sea, surrounded by the buoys of her nets
and lines. All above was a sky of dazzling and lustrous
brightness—beneath was a limpid and foaming sea, from
which arose the groves and rocks, the deep ravines and
the green savannahs of an isle which seemed Paradise. I
stood in the bows of the felucca, and stretched forth my
arms, and prayed for the moment when I should set foot
on shore.

When I was in this kind of rapture, Wright came to
me privately, and asked whether I was determined to
make the attempt. I replied, I only longed for night to
come. Then at his request I went below with him to
his berth, when he showed me, all else being on deck, a
short-barrelled musket, hid in the bedding, with a flask
of fine glazed powder and a small bag of balls. There
was also a leathern bottle, called a broc, well stoppered
and full of water, and some biscuits. 'These things,'
says he, 'will be necessary for you, so that you may not
want, until you pick up some comrade along shore.
Should you not succeed at first, you must trust to your
gun for food, and you will soon find water, of which
there is abundance, fresh and clear.'

I thanked him heartily for his goodness and foresight,
for I had thought of nothing but how I should get ashore,
not even how I should satisfy my hunger and thirst when

I landed.  But Wright was my good genius, and, taking
advantage of our being now alone, for the deck was so
much the more pleasant that all were there, he made me
put on a couple of stout linen shirts which he gave me,
as also a good jacket, such as sailors wear, and a pair of
strong yet light shoes, like pumps.  I was quite overpowered with such goodness, and could scarce refrain
from weeping.  What a poor forlorn miserable creature
I should have been had Wright not been on board ! and
although I was nothing to him, yet had I been his son,
the old man could not have used me with more grave
and simple kindness.  I told him that when he first
spoke to me I was in great desolation and despair of
spirit, but that now my heart was cheery and buoyant,
and that I well trusted to see my own land again.  At
this his face darkened, and he heaved a great sigh.  I
went on, and said that he, too, I hoped, would end his
days, not in these burning climes, but in the green valley
of Hertfordshire, where he told me he was born.

'No, no,' says he, 'never—never !  I shall see England no more.  I am but a wanderer and an outcast,
even like Cain of old, and the place that once knew me,
shall know me no more for ever.'

With this he sat himself down on a great sea-chest,
and putting his hands to his face, sobbed aloud, so that
all his great frame was shaken.  I was much moved, and
strove to take his hand.  Then he looked at me with his
large grey eyes, all dry, and, as I thought, somewhat
bloodshot, for he could not weep, and said, 'In a churchyard there, lie my fathers and my kindred, also the wife
of my bosom and the two children of my loins, but my
dust must not mingle with theirs.  I shall sleep my last
sleep in some desert wilderness, or amid the weeds under
the sea.'

Observing me much astonished, and, perhaps, somewhat frightened, for I thought he must have committed
some great and horrible crime, he grasped my hand in
his, till I thought the blood came, and said, in a low
voice—

'Young man, I know not your soul, whether it loveth the gauds and the pomps of the world which are but vanity, or whether it would walk in the paths which are narrow and thorny, but which lead upwards. Yet I do believe you to be in spirit true and leal; and wherefore then should I dissemble, that if I am an outcast, it is in a holy and a just cause—ay, and a cause which will triumph, when the blood of the saints which crieth aloud is justified and avenged! Leonard Lindsay, I am one of those who by voice and hand did to death the man Charles Stuart.'

This, then, was one of the regicides whom I had often heard were wandering about the world, being driven from their land by this great and justifiable deed, for so my parents taught me to esteem it, of the putting to death of the king. I would have told my friend somewhat to this effect, but he stopped me, saying, applause or disapprobation were alike to him; that he would help and comfort all his fellow-men, but that he cared not for their opinion on what he had done, always looking for judgment inwards to his own soul, and thence upwards to his God.

Shortly after this we went on deck, and my first glance was astern, where the skiff was still towing, although the waves raised by the sea-breeze ran so gaily, that sometimes as they chased us, the boat, rising on the crest of the following sea, would seem as though she would be hove bodily on deck. The land was now quite close, not more than a mile under the lee, so that we could see a great succession of bays and little headlands with bushes of many sorts, and rich tangled underwood, creeping among and clothing the knolls and banks even to the water's edge. Over these, high palms bended and waved in the sea-breeze, these seeming to issue from every crevice in the rocks; and sometimes, where a rivulet came down into the sea, the banks thereof being flat and soft, grew great thickets of the mangrove bush, a shrub which rises on bare grey stems out of the water, supporting whole beds of tangled and intertwisting foliage above, thus raising, as it were, a sort of canopy above the water. Between such places and the rocky headlands were often little bays, with narrow strips of white glittering beach, running like crescents from cliff to cliff, the sea breaking in flashing surf upon the shingle, and often sending its spray pelting among the bushes. Never, indeed, had I seen a more glorious coast, one so teeming with beauty and the riches of an overflowing nature. Involuntarily after every long and ardent gaze I turned my eyes upon my skiff, praying within my heart that nought might come to make my adventure miscarry.

As the evening approached, I was so impatient that I disposed of the biscuits, the powder, and the ball about my person, and was for ever going below to the berth to see that the musket was safe. The mariners, however, being excited and joyful, that the end of the voyage was nigh, gave little heed to me, otherwise my continued movements and feverish demeanour could not have but raised suspicion. In those low latitudes there is but little twilight, and half an hour after the sun went down into the sea ahead of us, the stars were shining out through the night. Meantime the sea-breeze had died away, and for an hour or longer we were left heaving upon the glassy swell, the land showing in vast dusky masses which, as it were, cut great spaces out of the firmament twinkling with stars, and the roar of the surf coming heavy and loud over the sea. Presently, after divers faint puffs, which caused the canvas to flap, shaking down on the deck great showers of dew, the land-wind, or *terral*, arose in its turn, balmy and sweet with the smell of the forests, and our lateen sails being dipped, we glided along, leaning over to seaward. The mid-watch came at last, and it had not been set for more than half an hour, ere the men dropped to sleep, under the lee of the bulwarks, excepting the steersman, and he leaned heavily and drowsily over the tiller. Then I brought on deck the musket and the broc, depositing them in safe places. But the question was how to get on board the skiff so as to elude the notice of the sailor who steered. Having soon devised a plan, I communicated it to Wright, who did not hesitate to put it into execution. Going aft, he stood beside the helmsman, and after some time, looking astern, remarked how the land-wind broke the usual heave of the sea into wild disorderly waves, and then observing that the skiff might be injured by being flung under our counter by the jumble of the water, he took the rope and hauled the boat ahead—the steersman thinking no harm—until he made it fast alongside, and screened from sight by the mainsail. In five minutes after, with a strong gripe of the hand, and a fervent 'God speed you,' I swung myself noiselessly aboard, and placed the gun and the broc in the bottom of the boat. Wright, so I must still call him, then undid the rope. My hand was at that moment upon the smooth side of the felucca, which I suddenly felt slip by me; I was adrift! Holding my breath, and my hand still against the planking of the vessel, she glided fast and faster by me, eluding as it were my clutch, when her shape melted away into the run. A minute after and I saw the small dusky hull and white stretching canvas becoming indistinct in the darkness ahead. I was alone, but I was free. For near an hour I remained almost motionless, fearing every moment to hear an alarum-gun fire; but the night continued silent, and then with a good heart I took up my oars, and using two as sculls, rowed towards the coast. The land-breeze blew steadily, so I had to tug long and hard. At last, seeing the dusky bank close ahead, I paused to look for a landing-place, but none could I see. The nature of the coast seemed to have changed, the land hereabout being a long smooth wall of perpendicular rock, sinking sheerly into the sea, which rose and fell at the base, with a loud hissing, pouring, gurgling sound—not like the deep thunder of surf. I therefore set myself to pull eastwardly, in search of a creek or bay. I knew that the moon would presently rise over the land, and in sooth, in about an hour, I noticed the glow of her broad disc peeping over the edge of the cliff ahead of me, and showing it, fringed, as it were, with a line of bushes and brushwood, which curled over the precipice, surmounted now and then by one of the tall, bending palmetto trees. In about an hour I had moonlight sufficient to see pretty distinctly the great limestone ledges along which I was cautiously coasting—pausing on my oars, now and then, to hear the great buzz of insects and the forlorn cries of night-birds which floated from the land. It must have been near three o'clock, when I saw a black-like opening in the wall of cliff, and very cautiously I pulled my boat inwards. For some time I was in great doubt as to whether I had found a creek, but presently I beheld the two portals of rock between which I was, fairly astern of the boat, and saw and heard the white gleam of the surf breaking on the beach. But the former was too high for me to risk a landing, and I would have pulled out to sea again, but seeing another dark shadowy space upon the left, I made for it, hoping it might turn out an oblique channel leading from the main cove. I was not deceived, and presently the boat glided along a sort of dusky canal, with great rocks on either hand, clothed with rich creeping herbage ; trees hanging over either ledge, and, as the channel narrowed, meeting, and by their intertwining boughs shutting out the blue sky. Below me the water showed as black as tar, yet sparkling, when the undulations from the outer creek caused it to rise and sink upon the bushy banks. Now and then a flutter of wings would echo in the narrow passage, and the loud shriek of a night-bird would drown the noise. Anon a scrambling, walloping sound, followed by a splash, as of a great animal scuttling from a ledge into the water, would ensue, and again, for a time, there would be deep silence. In about a quarter of an hour, the heave of the sea was no longer felt, owing, as I concluded, to the shallowing of the creek ; and then, making fast the skiff to a great protruding branch, which I struck my head against, I rolled myself in a blanket which I found Wright had flung into the boat, and was soon asleep, being thus, as it were, safely anchored to the New World !

## CHAPTER III.

#### I JOIN A BROTHERHOOD OF HUNTERS AND ADVENTURERS ON THE COAST.

I DID not wake until the sun was reasonably high, although but few rays found their way into the curious cove, which by such a lucky chance I had hit. It was, indeed, a sort of natural corridor or aisle : rocks covered with plants and bushes forming great green walls, with tangled trees bending from side to side, and meeting and interlacing above, like a roof, while the floor was limpid water. The air within this natural alcove was of a greenish hue, and the reflection from the water the same. Great numbers of gay-coloured birds fluttered and screamed, rather than sang, amid the boughs; and on almost every projecting stone by the edge of the water stood a great grey crane or heron, watching for the small fish which form its prey. After I had looked my fill, I began to think of breakfast; for, in order to eke out my store, I had gone supperless to bed. So I munched a couple of biscuits, and took a great pull at the sweet, fresh water. There were fruits and vegetables of many kinds growing near, which I feared to meddle with, not knowing their properties. After breakfast, I cast off from my bough, and paddled to and fro in the channel to seek a landing-place. This I was not long in discovering, at the spot where a little runnel of the most transparent water I ever saw in my life came trickling down in a small hollow, or what, in Scotland, we would call a scaur. The sides of the ravine were, it is true, very steep, but they were clothed with matted grass and vegetation, so that I could clamber up without much difficulty. I therefore made my boat fast very carefully, for I knew not what use she might be to me afterwards, and also loaded my gun and hammered the flint, after which I addressed myself to climb to the top of the bank. I found this tolerably hard work; the heat of the sun was excessive, and here there was no sea-breeze to refresh one.

Moreover, I did not much like the infinity of creeping and crawling things which, as I made my way upwards, I startled amid the coarse grass and underwood. Great beetles, shining and speckled—writhing creatures, like grey worms, with numberless legs—horrible hairy spiders —and one or two small snakes, all mottled and brindled. Besides, there flew about me, making a tiny buzz, as if they blew small hairy trumpets, hosts of that accursed fly called by the French maranguinnes, and by the English mosquitos, which stung me until I was almost mad, —slapping my face and my hands, and thrashing the air with a leafy branch, but all in vain. At length, after great toil, I stood upon the top of the bank, and felt, to my joy, the cool blast of the strong sea-breeze, which rustled in the bushes, and soon blew away my insect enemies far to leeward. Then, mounting a moderate-sized eminence, I set myself to reconnoitre ; and truly I might have deemed that I was in a desert and unpeopled land. Behind me rose great swelling ridges, extending above one another as far as my eye could reach, and all covered with bright green brushwood, with here and there one of the long feathery palm-trees standing up like a steeple over houses. Not many paces in front ran a long fringe, as it were, of waving trees and bushes, marking the extreme edge of the cliff, which sank into the ocean ; while beyond this there stretched out the great blue expanse of the sea, speckled here and there with white, as the waves broke, but sailless, and as lonely as the land. The great mountains which we had seen from on board were here invisible, and even the ridges around, as I gazed on them, seemed to move and quiver in the great heat. Notwithstanding pretty humming-birds, less than Jenny Wrens, fluttered about, and there was a mighty chattering, as of armies of parrots and parroquets, which whooped and called to each other from grove to grove.

At first, I felt a kind of sinking at being alone in this great wilderness, but plucking up courage, I set off to trudge along the coast to the eastward. The journey was toilsome in the extreme, for the stunted shrubs were tangled so, that I was ofttimes compelled to cut a passage with my clasp-knife, and the heat made my temples throb and ache strangely. At length, seeing great trees of prodigious size, the skirts of a forest, on my right hand, I made for them, and entering their shade, found better walking, for here was a canopy of leaves which warded off the sun, and also prevented the growth of underwood, the ground being clear, and the air cool, between the vast trunks of these glorious trees. However, I kept upon the edge of the wood, for fear of losing myself, not designing to stray far from the sea. Having marched thus near two hours, I heard a noise, which, as I came nearer, I took to be the yellings of wild animals; so that, somewhat startled, I looked to the priming of my gun, and also gazed around for a tree into which it might be convenient to climb. Meantime, the tumult came nearer, and I imagined it to be of dogs, yet it was rather a savage yelping than the deep bay of hounds. Next I heard a great crashing of branches on the edge of the wood, and making my way there, and mounting a tree, I speedily saw a huge wild boar, as I judged, with great tusks, and his jaws covered with flakes of foam, closely chased by a pack of dogs. These latter were fawn-coloured, with black muzzles; their legs were short, but very brawny; and as I heard no sound or shout of hunters, I concluded, with reason, that the pack before me were descendants of those ferocious bloodhounds brought by the Spaniards into Hispaniola, and other islands, to hunt down the inoffensive Indians, and which, being deserted by their masters, ran wild and multiplied, so that flocks of them assemble, and hunt the cattle and boars for their own support. Meantime, however, the quarry had turned to bay underneath a tree not far from me, and the dogs stood round in a semicircle, yelping at him. At length, one bolder than the rest made a spring, and drove his great jaws, as it seemed to me, into the animal's flank. This was the signal for a general onset, and, in a moment, the boar, grunting and squeeling

hideously, was tumbled on the ground, the ferocious
dogs, with jaws and muzzles all blood and froth, tearing
and riving its living flesh, so that, in the space of a very
few minutes, the creature was not only killed, but well-
nigh pulled into morsels. Then the dogs, several of which
were hurt, and limped and whined, fell to and ate their
fill, after which having gorged themselves to their very
throats, they lay down to sleep. Seeing this, I concluded
that I could with safety pursue my journey, and accordingly got down from the tree and did so, none of the
bloodhounds molesting me.

I walked until the afternoon, still seeing no sign of
human life, and then feeling very hungry, and moreover
wishing for something more savoury than bread and
water, I looked about for game. Many green lizards or
guanos were to be seen in the branches, and these the
Frenchmen on board the felucca had assured me were
good food, but I could not bring my stomach to them,
and at length, after several unsuccessful shots, I secured
a bird, nearly double the size of our pigeon, on which I
determined to dine. Coming to a little rivulet of clear
water, with pretty pools, nourishing the most luscious
profusion of water-plants, I sat me down, and presently
discovered a large duck quackling and nibbling in the
herbage. Now, the flesh of a duck I knew, but the bird
I had already killed was a stranger to me; so taking a
very careful aim at the poor fellow, I fired and sent the
bullet—I had no small shot—right through him. But
immediately there rose such a loud rustling of wings,
and quacking, and screaming, that I was confounded, until,
making a few steps in advance, I saw that the rivulet a
little above spread into a good-sized weedy pond, which
harboured thousands of ducks, and teal, and widgeon, all
of which flew away on hearing the report of my piece.
Having recovered my game from the water, I set to
work, plucked him, and, kindling a fire of dry sticks and
leaves, broiled him thereon. The cookery was rough,
but I thought the fare capital, only the want of salt
annoyed me. Having dined, I jogged on as before, and

as evening approached found myself exceedingly fatigued
and dispirited at having seen no human being. When
the sun went down and the short tropical twilight gave
way to night, through which the stars blazed with a fiery
lustre, unknown to me until I had crossed the Atlantic,
I even began to ponder as to whether I had done well in
leaving the ship at all; but speedily shaking off this idle
despondency, I wrapped myself up in my blanket, which,
in spite of its weight, I had carried strapped tightly on
my shoulders, and seasoning my biscuit with a piece of
tobacco to chew, made my supper, and slept in the fork
of a tree, lying back not uncomfortably among the
branches. I awoke once or twice and listened to the
low hum and drone of insects, in addition to which a
bird, as I judged, uttered from time to time a long
mournful cry, sounding like ' Weep, poor weel,' which
was very melancholy, echoing through that great midnight wilderness. Around me gleamed the little lights
of glow-worms, called by the Spaniards *Moscas del Fuego*.
But these extinguished their lamps in the latter part of
the night.

I was awake with the sun, at the rising of which a
great white fog which lay upon the earth and drenched
me, lifted and dispersed. The heat soon dried my
clothes, and about nine o'clock, when the sea-breeze
whistled through the herbage, I began again my weary
march. Not long after, having a good view of the sea
from a promontory, I descried almost beneath me, a ship
under sail, lying along shore, which, the coast here tending southerly, she could do very well, and yet keep her
sails full. She was a two-masted vessel, seemingly very
quick, and, plunging over the breasting waves gallantly,
soon passed me, steering to the east and keeping fear-
lessly along the rocks. I found no wild ducks to-day,
but, urged by hunger, I shot a monkey; and although
the poor creature looked horrible when skinned, his flesh
was not unpalatable. Towards the afternoon, I perceived
that I was approaching an indented part of the coast, and
I saw many ravines down which I could have gone to the

sea. Now and then, too, I would get a glimpse of such
pretty, shingly and bushy bays as I descried from the
felucca, while on the other hand, between the hills, there
opened up vistas of great flat green fields, here called
savannahs. I had hopes that I was approaching some
inhabited place, and ere long I heard faint shouts before me and nearer to the sea. This made me push on
vigorously, yet not without caution; and at length,
forcing my way through a forest of stunted trees, I
caught a glimpse of the figure of a man through the
boughs. His back was to me, and I thought he was
standing in a low tree, when suddenly a great gust of
the sea-breeze came rattling in the wood, and the man
swang to and fro with a slow motion, among the waving
branches. Immediately a horrid thought seized me, and
looking up as I heard a croaking, I saw two great carrion
vultures circling in the air. Manning myself, I ran
forward, and there, sure enough, was the body of a man
hanging from a horizontal branch of a tree, his feet not
many inches from the tops of the Guinea grass. I was
overpowered with horror; but turning away from the
terrible sight, what were my feelings to see two other
bodies hanging in a similar manner! Having a little
recovered my first natural fright, I looked attentively at
these unfortunates. They were all three dressed in the
same fashion, with coarse shirts, great jackets or doublets, cut in a square fashion, like the coats of the water-
men on the Thames, and pantaloons. What surprised
me, however, was the red filthy hue of the garments, as
though they had been soaked in blood, and never cleaned
or scoured. But then I called to mind what Wright
had told me of the hunting dresses of the Buccaneers,
and how they took a sort of pride in being disorderly and
neglectful of their attire, never washing it from the
blood-stains which their occupation plenteously bedaubs
them with. The hair and beards of these men were long
and matted, and they wore buskins of untanned hide. I
looked attentively, but could see no gun or weapon, and
the whole matter was a mystery to me. However, it

was not a pleasant locality to linger in, so I continued
my way, and presently saw a fine wooded bay, with
winding shores, lying beneath me, the forest sometimes
reaching into the very surf, but in other places leaving
beaches of sand, carpeted as it were with a sort of
creeping grass of the kind, as I afterwards heard, called
Bahama.

Along this bay I skirted, often stopping to look keenly
about. At length I saw a boat or canoe, pulled by
several persons, paddling across the smooth surface; and
observing it disappear beyond a green headland on the
opposite side of the bay, my attention was directed
thither, and presently I noticed several columns of thin
blue smoke rising up above the trees at that very point.
I was still gazing at them when the sound of voices
smote my ear distinctly, and I had scarce time to conceal
myself among the thick brushwood, when near a score of
men, some of whom wore gold-laced doublets and seemed
officers, came scrambling down towards the water from a
point higher up the bay than I had attained. I saw at
a glance that they were not Englishmen, being much too
swarthy; and as they passed at no great distance, and
talked and laughed loudly, I perceived that their language was Spanish, the sound and accent whereof I knew
very well. All these men were armed, each with a great
bell-mouthed short-barrelled gun, but I observed that
three carried, each of them, in addition, a musket of
quite another shape. Seeing that they were Spaniards, I
was in mortal dread that they might have bloodhounds
with them, fiercer even than the wild dogs I had seen,
and I drew my strong clasp-knife, determined that, at
least, there should be a weasen or so cut before I was
worried. Happily, however, the party had no dogs whatever. I held my breath as they were passing, but what
was my consternation when the whole body stopped not
ten paces from me, while one pointed out to the others
the smoke on the other side of the bay. At this, two or
three other of the fellows made gestures, by jerking their
heads aside and pointing to their necks, as though there

D

were halters round them, and then all laughed. But he who seemed the principal officer restrained them, and taking out a pocket compass, appeared to set, as mariners call it, the direction in which the smoke appeared. Then they all went on together, I cautiously following at a very respectful distance. Their course was to the outer part of the bay, and they proceeded hastily down a steep wooded glen, in which I lost sight of them. Presently, however, I heard them hailing a ship, as I conjectured; and I was right, for having got a little further, I heard the ripple of water, and saw over the trees the rigging and masts of a vessel, which I recognised as the same I had descried at sea early in the morning; and, getting a good vantage-ground, I at last looked down upon her deck, and saw a well-armed ship, full of men. Putting all these circumstances together, I soon concluded that the craft was a Spanish Guarda Costa. Then I thought of the men pointing to the distant smoke, and making motions as though they would hang the people there. In a moment I saw it all. The three executed Buccaneers—the three guns different from the rest carried by the Spaniards—their gestures at sight of the smoke of a little settlement! Doubtless the party belonged to a ship which had come upon the coast to make the usual attacks on the French and English settlers, and they, having caught these three unfortunates in the woods, had hanged them out of hand, and meant to attack the people on the opposite side of the bay, taking them by surprise. This last I inferred from the care with which a sheltering cove had been found to conceal their vessel.

It was now my clear duty to make my way to the opposite side of the bay, to warn the people there, who, being enemies of the Spaniards, must necessarily, by the rule of these seas, be friends of mine. But how to get to them? I knew not how far up the country the bay, or lagoon, extended; to swim across would not have been difficult, but I thought of caymans and sharks, and my heart failed me. Notwithstanding, I made my way to the seaside, and sat down on a large rock. What would

I have given now for the skiff I had abandoned! But then, if I had come along the coast in her, I should have been picked up and murdered by the Guarda Costa. So in cruel perplexity I sat until it grew dark. All at once I thought that if the three unhappy Buccaneers who were put to death belonged to the settlement opposite, that they would have brought a canoe to waft them over, which I might find along the shore. This idea gave me fresh vigour, and I ran eagerly along the shingle, climbing from time to time over points of rock which jutted out. Near two hours were wasted in fruitless search, wading through little creeks, and tracing small channels amid the bushes into which the rising tide was flowing, when at length, just as I was despairing, I happily found the object of my search. In a narrow cove, alongside a ledge of rock, floated a light canoe, scooped out of a single tree. I immediately stepped on board, and using the paddle alternately on either side, managed, though I was awkward at first, to make the canoe move in the direction I wished. Crossing the bay, I had enough to do to keep the land wind from blowing me out of my course, and by the time I was two-thirds over, every muscle in my body ached with the unwonted exercise. Paddling on, however, I suddenly saw on the dusky shore a cluster of red dim lights, by which I knew that I had opened the headland behind which the smoke rose, and almost at the same moment I heard behind a faint plash, and the rattle as of arms. I saw at once that I had no time to lose, if, as I guessed, the boats of the Guarda Costa were not far astern. Immediately I redoubled my efforts, making for the lights, and at the same time hailed, ' Ho ! the shore, ahoy.' Immediately a voice replied, ' Is that you, Benjamin ?' When I heard the sounds of my own language, my heart leaped to my mouth ; and, catching up my musket, I fired it off, shouting, ' Look out ! look out! the Spaniards! the Guarda Costa !' In an instant there gleamed a great many little lights, as of lanterns carried by people running about on the beach, and I heard the clash of arms and loud halloo-

ings; then the voice I had heard sang out again, ' Where
are they ?—who are you ?'   But before I could reply
the Spaniards suddenly fired two volleys in my direction,
the flashes showing two great boats, full of men, and
rowing fast.   The water near me was torn up by the
balls, but none touched the canoe, and the fire was
promptly answered by a small piece of artillery ashore,
which echoed grandly in the hills, and caused a harsh
concert of the wakened birds.   Not willing to be between
two fires, I paddled hard, and presently ran the canoe
on the beach ; when I leaped out and found myself in the
midst of a group of men, all shouting and cheering in
English and French, running to and fro, and fetching
and making ready arms,—their muskets, and hangers,
and pikeheads gleaming in the sparkle of the lanterns.
Directly I splashed through the surf, I shouted that I
was a friend and a Scottish sailor, and that the Spaniards
were upon us ; whereon they gave a loud shout in my
honour, and in defiance of the enemy, and fired a straggling volley.   This the boats returned briskly, and the
Buccaneers, rushing up to their middles in the sea, cried
out with desperate imprecations to the Spaniards to come
on, swearing they would roast them alive on their *grilles
de bois*, and taunting them with every infamous name,
keeping up a spattering irregular fire all the time.   However, Jack Spaniard, seeing a warm reception before him,
hung off, keeping in the shadow of the little headland.
Then two or three canoes were promptly manned, but
the men in their eagerness over-crowded them, and fought
amongst themselves who should go ; so that time was
lost, and meantime we heard the dash of oars, as the
boats, having failed in their purpose of surprise, pulled
away.

When the hubbub was a little abated, I was asked by
a dozen persons at once what I was ; whereon I recounted
that having left, I did not say escaped, from a French
ship on the coast, I had travelled hither, and on my way
saw the Spaniards, and guessed their intentions.   Then I
told them of the bodies I had passed hanging from trees,

at which they raised a great clamour of cursing; for these, as I had guessed, were their comrades, who had crossed the bay to hunt the day before. Then there was a proposal to man all the canoes, and go and attack the Spaniards; but just as this was acceded to with a loud shout, a light pirogue, which it seems had been fishing down the bay, ran in with the news that the ship had weighed anchor directly her boats returned, and made all sail to sea. On this there was a great groan given for the cowardice of the Don, and the crowd began to disperse.

At this moment a young Englishman came up to me, and asked, with great solicitude, if one of the Buccaneers I had seen hanging was light haired with yellow moustaches. I replied in the affirmative; on which, in words of strong passion and feeling, he swore that he would bitterly revenge on the Spaniards the death of Benjamin, his ' partner,' as he called him, and, in short, broke out into a great paroxysm of grief and rage. Meantime, several of the Buccaneers offered me the hospitality of their huts, but my Englishman declared I must go to his, as he was now alone, which the rest consenting to, very cordially shook hands with me, and thanked me in French and English, and then I followed my new friend along the beach to his hut. There were a good many of these, irregularly placed, and beside several there smouldered a slow fire, making the lights I had seen in the bay. Over these fires there were gratings or hurdles of wood, and on them lumps of beef, rudely cut, drying and cooking little by little; great bales and heaps of hides lay about, the perfume exhaling from them not being by any means pleasant, and numbers of dogs howled and barked without ceasing. My conductor led me into a hut built like the others, of wood and clay, and thatched with some sort of thick leaf. The inside was lighted by a smoky lamp, showing two beds of hide with dirty blankets, and a clumsy table. There were shelves all round, whereon were ranged several guns, hangers, and long Spanish knives, with fish and boar-spears, and other weapons. Also I saw a mariner's compass and some

instruments for taking the latitude, so that I rightly
guessed my host to be a sailor as well as a hunter.
Besides these, there were strewn about, bits of net, canvas, bullock horns, and one or two panthers' skins were
arranged as coverlets for the beds.

My host asked many questions about the Spaniards,
while he produced for supper a piece of dried beef, prepared over the slow fire which I had seen, and which
being called ' boucan ' gave to those who make it the
name of ' Buccaneers.' I found it somewhat tough, but
relishing and wholesome. After supper, we had brandy
and rum, tempered by water, and while drinking it very
sociably, my comrade informed me that he was a native
of Cornwall, and that his name was Treveltham ; but
that here, following a custom which was universal among
the Buccaneers, he had changed it for a nickname, or
*nomme de guerre*, by which only he was known to the
generality of his comrades. His Christian appellation
being Nicholas, he was called Nicky Hamstring, a whim-
sical appellation, which set me laughing heartily. He
had been on the coast since the end of the last rainy
season, and liked the life well. The bay on the banks of
which we were, he told me, was the estuary of a river
called Le Marmousette, and about it there were much
wild cattle. The English and the French Buccaneers
lived here generally good friends. ' Not but,' said he,
' that sometimes when the rum has gone round, there is
not a brawl, and it may be a stick with a knife ; but after
all the island is big enough for all, and the cattle are
many enough for all, and so we love each other, and hate
Jack Spaniard ' While we were talking, we heard loud
shouting and singing without, great roaring choruses
both in French and English, and ofttimes a Lingua
Franca, which was a compound of the two, but the
burden of all being words of hatred and contempt of the
Spaniards. Once or twice I thought the singers would
have entered our hut, for the door had neither lock nor
bar, but they did not, and as the night wore on, everything became silent except the dogs, who, having been

unloosed from their kennels to act as sentinels, growled hoarsely along the beach. Having drunk and talked as much as we chose, we went to bed, I having, indeed, been asleep all through several long stories which Nicky recounted of the exploits and bravery of the Buccaneers, my drowsiness being easily excused to my companion by the long journey I had come that day.

---

## CHAPTER IV.

### OF THE LIFE OF A BUCCANEER.

NEXT morning Nicky asked me to accompany him, with two others to guide them to the spot where their comrades had suffered, in order that they might bury the bodies; we accordingly set off in the canoe, our companions being one Jonas, as he was called, an Englishman, and Pierre le Noir, or Black Peter, a Frenchman from the coast of Normandy. Jonas was so called, owing to the great ill-luck which he had met with in cruising, having been twice taken, and once very nearly hanged by the Spaniards on the coast of Porto Rico; while once upon the Mosquito coast, in the expedition in which l'Olonais, a famous French Buccaneer, was killed, he had been left for some months in a small quay or island near the Mosquito shore, eating what wild fruit he could get, and what birds he could catch with his hands. We landed in the same creek in which I found the canoe, and after less troublous walking than I expected, my comrades knowing the country, found the bodies still hanging, but already defaced by the hideous vultures, so as to present a horrid spectacle. Nevertheless, having brought shovels and pickaxes with us, we performed our task, and over the grave, for they all three were laid in one, we put a rude cross made of withies, or willow wands, and so left them to take their long sleep in the wilderness.

Being returned to the opposite side, I rambled through

the village, for such it was, to note the appearance of the place, and its inhabitants.

The huts were built upon a green bank, rising pleasantly from the sea, the little headland of which I spoke sheltering it. Behind some lofty ridges, partly covered with luxuriant wood, which here and there had been cleared, certain small fields were marked out, these last being planted with a brown herb, like overgrown rhubarb, which they told me was tobacco. At the water's edge was a rude wharf, made of wood called shingles—and several canoes and European-built boats lay there. While I was sauntering about, one of the former put off, navigated by two Indians, who spoke both French and English reasonably well. These Indians were better and more neatly attired than the whites ; they were of a sallow-brown hue, had long, lank black hair, and very bright eyes. In person they were tall, raw-boned, and muscular. In the canoe they carried an assortment, as it were, of spears, called fizgigs and harpoons, for striking fish ; at which exercise they are inconceivably expert, often killing in a forenoon what will form a good dinner for a hundred men. The Mosquito men, for so are these Indians called, are therefore very highly prized by the whites, who give them good wages to go on board their ships, or to stay at their settlements on shore, to provide turtle or manatee for the company. While I was looking at them, Nicky came up to me, and we walked through the village together, he bringing me into many of the cabins, all of which were similar to his own. Those of the men who were not in the mountains or savannahs hunting, were attending to their boucans, or fires, for the drying of the meat, and I thought as I saw them, working like butchers and cooks, that I would rather take the huntsman's part of the business. All around lay the quarters of slaughtered beeves and hogs, while the Buccaneers, armed with long knives, cut the flesh from the bones. These lumps were then carefully salted in open sheds used for that purpose, and after being well steeped in brine, were placed on the boucan—that is to say, upon the grille of wood above a slow fire, which gradually dried and cooked the meat, giving it at the same time a sort of smoky taste, which however is not without an aroma to the palate. This method of preserving meat may be called national in these islands, for so did the original Charibs dress their food, whether fish or flesh. These savages were so fond of this cookery, and of such endurance, that an Indian returning from the chase, fatigued and hungry, would often wait patiently by the boucan, or as they called it, the *barbecu*, the best part of a day, until a fish or slice of hog, or beeve, was well cooked, the morsel being suspended almost two feet above a little and slow fire. The Charibs, being cannibals, were often in use to treat their prisoners just as they treated their game, and I know many who, visiting some of the smaller windward islands, and also the Brazilian coast, saw great flitches of human flesh, smoked and barbecued, hanging in the huts. The meat, when sufficiently preserved in the manner which I have described, the Buccaneers placed in storehouses, built so that both land and sea winds may play well around them. The hides are also prepared in a rude fashion, and the tallow, the whole being periodically sold, either for money or goods, to the captains of privateers for their crews, or to certain planters in those islands in which cattle do not abound. The latter are the best customers, making regular contracts with the Buccaneers for the supply of a certain quantity of meat and hides for a fixed sum, the stipulations on both sides being honourably adhered to. Many of the Buccaneers have servants and hired assistants, who are chiefly employed in conveying the cattle from the spot where they are killed to the boucan, and afterwards in helping to stow away the food. Although this appeared to be a regular settlement, its inhabitants led but a roving life. Many of them intended to go to sea for a change at the first opportunity, and others, conceiving that there were more cattle and fewer hunters to the eastward, spoke of shifting their quarters. This I heard while wandering about with Nicky, from boucan to boucan, and hut to hut. The scene indeed was a new one to me. Such groups of wild-looking blood-stained men ; such slashing and cutting of meat, as though one were in the shambles ; such shouting and singing in different tongues, mixed with the clamour of dogs and the screams of parrots, and other birds from the neighbouring groves ; such quaffing of bumpers of brandy and constant smoking of tobacco ; such an appearance indeed of rude plenty and coarse health and enjoyment—all this made a curious impression on me, and I returned to the hut pondering on it.

'Well,' says Nicky, 'will you stay with us, and be my comrade, in lieu of poor Benjamin? Here is his stock in trade,' pointing to two good guns and a little assortment of household stuff. 'By the rules of the coast, as you know, we all work in couples. Each man has his comrade, with whom he shares all : and when one dies, the survivor is entitled to his partner's wealth and implements—the last of which I will very willingly bestow upon you, should you deem it meet to join me.'

We talked for some time about the matter. My own mind was naturally buoyant, and my spirits easily fitted themselves to circumstances ; and so, concluding that I would lead an adventurous life, and see much well worthy of being beheld, we in the end concluded a bargain ; and then putting on a doublet which had belonged to poor Benjamin, and which being almost new, was but slightly smirched with blood, my partner summoned in several of the chief men to the hut ; and they being accommodated with great goblets of brandy, admitted me by acclamation into the body of the brave Huntsmen and Buccaneers, and the ancient order of Brethren of the Coast, baptizing me in brandy, with various mummeries, by the nick-name of Will Thistle, as showing my Scottish nativity. Then Jonas, who was there, would fain have had a carouse, but they persuaded him not, saying that there was ample work to do, and little time to do it in, before the ships would arrive from Jamaica and Nevis for boucan.

Behold me now, therefore, a Buccaneer on the coast of Hispaniola! I let my beard and moustache grow, and they and my hair, which was naturally luxuriant, mingling, I speedily looked as grim and grisly as any of them. My comrade, Nicky, was a good man and true ; he had really felt the death of Benjamin his partner, and so had been at first more grave and more reserved than usual. But as this natural feeling wore away, he became truly a merry madcap, with a jest, sometimes of the coarsest, or a lusty sea-song, or a tale of brave privateersmen, ever in his mouth. Under his tuition, I soon became a good shot, and learned to break up a bull or cow most scienti- fically with the knife. Also I became acquainted with the various trees and shrubs, birds and beasts of the coast. I knew how to fell the mountain cabbage, and to roast the savoury plantain in the hot cinders. I could bake the mealy cassava cake, and I knew how to bore the Frank palm for the luscious sap which flows from the wounded bark. Besides, these great forests and fair beaches teem with infinite food. We turned the lazy turtles which we found upon the shore, or hunted for their eggs in the hot sand. We intercepted and roasted the land-crab in his annual journey from the mountains ; we shot the guano or yellow lizard, as he whimpered in the boughs, and prejudice being set aside, found his flesh like that of a barn-door fowl ; while the racoon and the monkey both formed good roasts when we tired of pork and beef. Then on every pond bred flocks of fat ducks, and, in the season, the delicious ortolan fed amid the guinea grass. Great hosts of pigeons built in the high trees and the rocks, and the bright-coloured woodpeckers afforded us many a savoury dish. For the sea, the mosquito men kept us well supplied. Standing in the bows of the canoe, with their barbed spears poised and ready, and their keen eyes fixed upon the water beneath, there was hardly a fish at which they darted their harpoons which the next moment lay not quivering and bleeding in the bottom of the boat.

## CHAPTER V.

### HOW WE ENCOUNTER GREAT DANGERS, THE SPANIARDS ATTACKING US.

I HAVE said that the bay on which we lived was part of
the mouth or estuary of the river Marmousette, which,
rising in distant mountains, falls into the sea, between
Port Plate, a great land-bound gulf, and a high cape
called Point de Cas Rouge. A mile or so further up the
country than the Buccaneer settlement, the coast was
low and marshy; the mangroves here grew in great
abundance, and divers deep channels of salt water ran
away from the main branch of the sea, and led, some of
them, to great open savannahs, covered with rich grass,
where the wild cattle loved to come and feed. One day,
five of us started in a small pirogue, which could barely
contain such a crew, to seek for bulls and cows in these
swampy prairies—a Buccaneer called Walshe, who perfectly knew the mangrove canals, acting as pilot. We
paddled up alongside of the bank, and having come to the
swampy ground, directed the canoe through certain intricate channels in the forest of mangroves, with the intent
of coming to a bit of the savannah favourable for our sport,
which Walshe knew. It was curious, thus rowing, as it
were, through a submerged forest. The water beneath us
was very deep—for we were obliged to keep in the channels
by reason of the mangroves growing on the muddy banks
—and quite transparent, so long as the fat black slime
remained undisturbed. Over head, the mangroves formed
a complete canopy, so that we paddled in a hot green
twilight, looking through long vistas of this natural
alcove, or else trying in vain to make our eyesight penetrate more than a few yards athwart the infinity of grey,
slimy stems. At this time, the tide was flowing inward,
floating alongside of us broad layers of thick, rich scum,
which gradually, as it were, clung to the trees on either
side, leaving the mid-passage clear.

I, happening to be in the bow of the canoe as look-out

man, amused myself by gazing down into the green, translucent sea, ahead of the ripples caused by the progress of the canoe. The channel could not have been less than three fathoms deep, yet I saw, as clearly as though there were nothing but air beneath me, the broad, moving leaves of great plants at the bottom, and the heaps, and coils, and meshes of twisted stalks, and long, serpent-like withes springing from the fat mud, and which waved with a slow and sickly motion as the passing tide stirred them. There were also great shoals of fish of divers kinds, which fled away on all sides as we advanced; but what fascinated my gaze was the appearance of a huge blue shark, which I could distinctly see cleaving the water about half way between the boat's keel and the bottom, and keeping pace with us very exactly. I was in the very act of raising my head to tell what I had seen, when I heard a loud exclamation from Walshe, who was steering, and who exclaimed that there was a rope stretched across the passage. The words were hardly out of his mouth, when the canoe struck the obstacle, broached to with the swing of the tide, and in an instant turned over, tilting us all, with a huge splash, into the water. As I went souse into the sea, the vision of the horrible monster which I had just seen shot through my very heart and brain, and striking out with convulsive strokes, in a moment I clutched a mangrove stem, and then, almost unknowing how I did it, I swung myself into the tree. Turning round, I looked for my companions; two were clinging to the canoe, which was drifting rapidly away with the tide. Nicky, my comrade, was in a similar position to myself, but on the opposite side of the creek; but poor Walshe was struggling in mid-channel, vainly trying, in his flurry, to swim against tide. We both shouted to him to sheer to one side; but just as he was attempting to do so, I saw a bluish white glimmer shoot through the troubled water beneath him, and at that moment, the poor fellow gave such an unearthly yell, that the woods echoed, flinging his arms about, and dashing the water into a foam, in the midst of which he disappeared, his cry ending in a loud, choking gurgle. Then there rose and rolled a great smooth, boiling wave, tinged with blood, as the shark, having secured his prey, turned again on his belly, and dived into the deep water. Nicky and I sat looking at each other for near the space of ten minutes without uttering a syllable. Then we began, I know not why, to talk in low whispers, and to consult upon our own situation. Our hope was, that the two hunters, who had stuck by the canoe, would be able to right it, and return for us, and so, joining our voices, we shouted loud and long, but the only answer which came back was the clamour of parrots and other birds, and the hissing sound of the water pouring between the slimy mangrove stems. We had no fire-arms, they having gone to the bottom when the canoe upset ; so, having shouted ourselves hoarse, we had nothing for it but painfully to converse with each other. Our discourse turned upon the cause of our mishap. The rope was, by this time, far beneath the water, but we could observe the tremor of the two stout mangroves to which it was attached. It was Nicky's opinion that there were Spaniards upon the coast, and that we had fallen into one of their traps— they being aware that we sometimes used these canals to paddle to the savannahs, and return with the ebb of the tide. 'If so,' said my comrade, 'we shall not be left long here, and shall come by a fate not much better than that of poor Sam Walshe.' I inquired if there was no hope of escape at low water, when we might wade through the water to firm ground ; but my comrade replied, that unless we were giants, we could hope nothing from that. Neither would it be practicable to clamber shorewards from tree to tree, on account of the great multiplicity of canals and passages which traverse the mangroves, the smaller of which harboured caymans in their muddy depths. 'No, no,' concluded Nicky, 'we can do nothing ; we must wait and take our chance.'

Presently the tide began silently to ebb, and in due time it left the marsh bare. But, oh ! what a dismal spectacle that was! Everywhere fat banks of black mud, nourishing everlasting mangroves, the obscene slime here piled up in great rotting masses, there smooth in beds, from which bubbles of impure air would come bursting to the surface, and sending up hideous smells of putrefaction. The air, indeed, became as the air of a pesthouse. Dank vapours began to roll amid the trees, a sort of seething steam boiled up from the pools and canals, and by night-time a wet grey fog, which was as the very breath of fever, brooded all through the marsh. The night wind was hardly felt amid these woody solitudes; and if a gust sometimes swept by us, it only brought the unwholesome vapour in fresh supplies. From time to time, we called to each other. Nicky recommended me to keep the collar of my doublet between my teeth, so as to breathe through the stuff, but we suffered terribly from hunger. With the morning, the fog lifted, and the tide, which had of course flowed and ebbed during the night, began to flow again. Still, there was no appearance of relief. We would even have welcomed the arrival of the Spaniards, but not an oar or paddle-splash broke the terrible silence. We were both, I think, falling into a sort of stupor, when Nicky suddenly shouted to me.

'There—see, there!' he cried; 'down the channel!'

I looked, and lo! our canoe, still floating on her side and full of water, was coming drifting up, rubbing the mangrove stems, on my side of the channel.

'Now or never, Will Thistle!' cried Nicky. 'This is life or death! Catch her as she passes!'

I roused all my strength, and slipped down from the fork, where I had been sitting, until my legs were in the water. The canoe drifted close in, and I had no difficulty in catching the rope, which yet hung from her bow, and making it fast to a tree. At this Nicky gave a great hurrah, and slipping from his perch, swam boldly across the deep water, having grasped my hand before I was aware of his proximity. 'Here,' says he, 'let me right the boat, a Mosquito man taught me the art.' And,

sure enough, in a minute or two the canoe was swimming
properly, only still half full of water. This, however, we
speedily baled with our hats, and getting into the canoe,
found it none the worse. By good chance a couple of
spare paddles had been secured in the boat, with a piece
of spun-yarn. We, being so far fortunate, shook hands
with each other very heartily; and after bestowing a few
sorrowful words upon our unhappy comrades, all of whom
were indeed lost, we set ourselves to consider what was
our best course to return again to the settlement. We
could either have gone on with the flowing tide, and
landed upon the savannah, as we originally purposed,
from whence we could have made our way by land,
although the journey would be toilsome, or we might
return into the open lagoon in the canoe, and so paddle
down the coast. This last plan we determined upon, even
although to follow it there would be a necessity for waiting some hours, until the force of the flood tide had spent
itself. But to wait in hope is another matter from
remaining in despair ; and so, making ourselves as comfortable in the canoe_as we could, we tarried patiently. At
length, the stream beginning to slacken, we pushed off, and
paddled cautiously seaward. Coming to the spot where the
rope had been stretched across the channel, we paused,
and after some search, having found it, we managed to
cast loose either end, although it was then near two feet
under water, with the intention of carrying it away as a
memorial of our escape. Hardly, however, had we got
it into the canoe, when we heard the sound of oars and
voices rapidly approaching, as if from the landward side.
We paused to listen, hoping it might be our comrades
coming in search of us; but presently the sound approached so near as to enable us to distinguish the
Spanish accent of the speakers.

‘ Give way for the love of God !’ I exclaimed, tossing
the rope aside. We both seized the paddles, but ere the
canoe had got headway, a large boat, full of men, suddenly appeared behind us at a winding of the channel.
At sight of the canoe they set up a great shout, called

upon us in Spanish, French, and English, to surrender. But we only plied our paddles the harder, working fast to seaward.

Oh, thought I, that we had not removed the rope, and then the Spaniards, in their eagerness, would have been caught in their own snare; but a minute's reflection told me that the tide was then too high for the line to have stopped the pursuing boat. The chase was now a most eager one. True, we were tired and faint; but the sight of our deadly enemies nerved our arms; the paddles bent and cracked and the light canoe flew over the water with a speed which the heavy boat astern could not hope long to cope with. At this moment the Spaniards fired at us, the bullet flashed in the water alongside, and Nicky cried to zig-zag the canoe—that is, to pull her by jerks from side to side, out of her true course, so as to make the object a more difficult one to hit. We accordingly paddled in this fashion, and it was completely effectual: not a shot struck us. Now a ball would sing overhead; now one would tear up the still water alongside of us; but neither the canoe nor ourselves were hit, although the Spaniards must have fired a score of shots. Still the efforts we were making were too severe to be long continued; and, in spite of our exertions, our muscles began to flag. It was then that, ahead of us, we saw a bend in the channel, on the right of which grew a huge mangrove, with dozens of long cord-like withes depending into the water. 'Thank God, we shall do yet,' said Nicky, who knew the channel well. 'Pull for the other side of that big mangrove!' And in a moment the canoe glanced round the corner in question, and we were shut out from the view of the Spaniards. Here a small muddy creek almost covered with foliage, diverged from the main channel.

'I know not where it leads,' said my comrade, 'but we must take it. The strait is too narrow to row in, so we cannot be followed.'

The advice was good, and the canoe speedily flew up the tributary creek, urged on, not only by our paddles,

E

but a favouring current. This last circumstance gave us good heart, for the tide being now ebbing, and the current along the passage in our favour, it was evident that it led to the open sea. The Spanish boat had, no doubt, passed the outlet of the small creek without observing it, for as we sat silently to listen, we heard the dash of the oars and the shouts of our pursuers to the left, but could see nothing through the thicket of mangrove stems. We were about to resume our paddles again when the distant sound of musquetry struck our ears. We both listened reathlessly; volley after volley was fired, and mingling with it came the deep roar of culverins and other heavy ordnance. In a moment the crew of the boat near us, as though they had also heard the noise of conflict, gave a great shout of 'Death to the Pirates!' for so they called the Buccaneers, and shot off their pieces in a loud straggling volley.

'The settlement is beset,' said Nicky; 'the Spaniards are on us in great force, and they must have been lurking in the lagoon for days; this explains the cowardly treachery of the rope,' and he broke into loud invectives against our enemies, to all of which I most heartily said 'Amen.' For was not this attack most wanton? Here were we, living in a wilderness belonging to no man, killing those wild animals which God hath appointed to be human food, and so far surely performing a service to our fellows, when down come the Spaniards upon us out of pure arrogance and ill-blood, hanging and shooting our defenceless hunters, and, as we had no doubt, now attempting to destroy our huts and the property, for the accumulation of which we had honestly sweated and toiled. But such it has been ever since any flag but that of Spain floated in these seas. The mariners of many nations came naturally to enrich themselves with the produce of the new-discovered lands; but Spain arrogantly desired to squeeze in her greedy gripe the whole New World! Therefore, is it wonderful that we—the sailors of England, Scotland, France, Holland, and Portugal—should give the Spaniards fierce and eager battle?

It **was they** who began the warfare; and such being the case, we paid them back in their own coin—usually, indeed, giving them the worst of the bargain.

Such were the natural thoughts which passed through my head as we sat listening to the roar of battle, which we could hear but faintly, being more than a league distant from home. Presently, without speaking, we addressed ourselves steadily to our paddles, and it was not long before, to our great joy, we shot out of the dreary forest of mangroves, and found ourselves in the clear water of the lagoon. The boat which had given us chase was not anywhere to be seen; but we now heard the firing distinctly, for it was kept up very hot and constant. By this time the tide was running out like a mill stream, and the canoe was swept down with great rapidity before it. There was no wind, and the current had a glassy look; the air, too, was inexpressibly sultry. Great wreaths of dense vapour hung upon the hills, and the firmament was one louring sea of black clouds piled one above another, as though climbing up on each other's vapoury shoulders from the horizon to the zenith. Presently the gloom increased to a foreboding blackness, which hung upon land and sea. The sounds of the birds and the insects were hushed, and in the intervals of the firing we heard only the low continuous rush of the turbid tide washing amid the mangroves. All at once a great flash of lightning tore, as it were, the black firmament into a blue gulf of flame, and at the same instant the thunder came, not rumbling or pealing, as I have heard it in Britain, but exploding with a splitting crash which seemed right above us, and which went through and through our ears. A quick succession of flashes and peals followed, so that I was almost blinded and deafened, for I had never seen or heard such terrible thunder or lightning; and then, at the recommendation of Nicky, who said that the storm would probably clear up with a squall, which we were ill prepared to face in the open lagoon, we paddled into a little opening in the amphibious forest, and made the canoe fast amid the

trees. Here we abode for more than half-an-hour, the
thunder and lightning continuing to be fearful; and the
effect of each flash, gleaming down through the thick
leaves and branches of the network of boughs above us,
and lighting up with a grim glare the unwholesome
marsh, with its slimy stake-like boles of trees, its long
twisting withes, and its black oily pools and channels,—
the effect of all this was, I say, very fearfully grand.
But at length the rain began to fall; the gloom deepened,
so that under the mangroves it was as murk as midnight;
but gazing from beneath them to the opposite side of the
lagoon, we saw dimly a sort of moving and rending of
the vapoury clouds, and then a sudden and perpendicular
descent upon the hills of what appeared to be countless streaks of mist or vapour, binding, as it were, the
green earth by webs of watery thread to the firmament.
This, Nicky said, was the rain, and truly we found it so;
for the misty appearance spread fast and far, and we
heard a mighty rustling sound, which became louder and
louder, until the windows of heaven above us were
opened, and down, not in mere drops, as it appeared to
me, but in opaque sheets and masses of falling water,
tumbled that blinding rain, lashing the sea as though it
were smitten by rods into churning foam, and beating
with a continuous assault our leafy canopy, until it poured
through the drenched branches in tiny waterfalls.
Meanwhile we cowered in the canoe dripping from every
limb, and watching the weather over the lagoon. Before
long, there was a sudden rift or opening torn through
the veiling fog, and the perpendicular lines of the rain
became slanting, or were broken and dispersed. At the
same moment, we saw distant ridges which were hid and
lost before in the vapour, now standing out clearly and
rigidly in the thinning air, and Nicky whispered to me
to note how the feathery palms were bending and shaking,
as though great airy hands were seeking to drag them up
by the roots. It was the clearing squall, and a few
moments only passed away ere heavy dank puffs sighed
through the mangroves with a wet, warm, unwholesome

savour, as the steams of a caldron where masses of putrid
vegetation were simmering, and then, driving before it a
broad belt of tumbling foam, and whistling and hurtling
through the air with a sound as of rushing wings and
blowing trumpets, the blast came down from the far-off
mountains and fell upon the sea. I have often seen more
violent squalls since, I have also been afloat and ashore
during a hurricane or tornado, but this was the first West
Indian tempest I encountered, and I did not soon forget
the great grandeur of the elements—the torn clouds flying in misty fragments—the blast whizzing through the
trees, with a long loud eldritch cry—the foam gathered
up from the sea, like the drift from the great wreaths of
snow at Christmas on a Scottish muir—the rustling hosts
of leaves, and rent and riven foliage scattered through the
air—all the confusion of wild noises, the dash of the
troubled sea, and the constant crackling and smashing of
boughs and branches, torn out and blown fast away to leeward.

In the midst of the elemental strife there shone upon
the waving and dripping woods, and the torn and tumbling sea, a pale watery ray of sunlight. This was the
indication that the fury of the storm was over. The
broken clouds showed patches of deep azure here and
there; the mists had been rolled away to sea in the impe-
tuous currents of air; presently the gust lulled; the
foam flew no longer about the water; and the birds began
to cry from out the thickets. Nicky therefore counselled that we should again put to sea.

'The squall,' he said, 'must have put an end to the
fight, and if the Spaniards be attacking our huts from
their ships, which is most likely, they may well have
been either driven ashore upon the bluff, or blown out
to sea.'

So we paddled cautiously along the edge of the mangroves, listening for any sound of the renewal of the
combat, but heard none. It was obvious that, one way
or another, the matter was decided—either that our comrades had been overpowered, or that the Spaniards had

been forced by the weather to discontinue the attack. At length, we approached a point in the shore where the character of the bank changed—the ground heaving itself boldly above the high-water mark, and the mangroves ceasing to grow; a little further on, a bluff of limestone rock, overgrown with brush and creeping trees, and its base green with tangled and slippery sea-weeds, stretched out into the water, and from the top of this we knew our settlement was visible. Having, therefore, made fast the canoe in a suitable place, we clambered through the dripping grass and leaves to the summit, and there saw a piteous sight. The rock being high, we overlooked several small capes and bays which stretched between us and our late habitation, and saw plainly the green bank upon which our huts stood, and the pretty clear bay, with its crescent of white sand and shingle beneath. In this bay —with her top-gallant-masts struck, and top-masts and yards lowered—there lay a great Spanish ship, carrying not less than thirty guns, with immensely high forecastle and poop. Moored somewhat nearer the beach was the smaller Spanish ship which had already attacked us, riding also very snugly with her top hamper lowered; and astern of them, and ashore upon the rocky bluff which formed the seaward horn of our bay, was a small sloop, which, as we conjectured, had been driven from her moorings by the force of the tempest, and now lay bodily upon the rocks, the sea beating and breaking over her. But the piteous sight was our huts and storehouses —some lay in ruins on the ground, torn and shattered by cannon-balls, others had been set on fire, but the rain, having so plenteously descended, had extinguished the flames, which, however, still smouldered in the blackened ashes and amid the charred timber, sending up thin volumes of bluish-grey smoke. All over the beach were scattered the bales and casks in which we had been used to store the provisions we made; and the principal of these the Spanish robbers were removing into the great ship; but, saddest sight of all, round the burning huts, and upon the shingle down to the water's edge, were strewn the corpses of our late comrades, they having evidently sold their lives dear, for many Spanish soldiers and seamen were stretched out starkly among them.

We long remained crouched amid the brushwood, regarding this sad spectacle as though fascinated by its horrors. Who had escaped? we thought; and, if any, where, and how? Not a man in our company but who was brave as the steel he wielded; but what could a handful of undisciplined hunters and sailors do against the broadsides of two Spanish men-of-war?

Nicky and I looked at each other mournfully—unarmed, and fainting with hunger and thirst, what were we to do. Under the torments of the latter infliction, however, we found that we need not long suffer. In the hollows of the rocks, and the reservoirs of the large green leaves of divers plants, the heavy rain had left abundance of water, of which we drank and were refreshed. After this, we sat down in a sheltered nook to hold a council of war. The Spaniards were still busy upon the beach, and occasionally straggling into the woods. Boats were continually passing from the ships to our shingle wharf, and we saw preparations being made to warp the sloop off the rocks, from which we concluded that she had not been much damaged. Nicky and I had hardly begun to consult upon our condition, when we suddenly heard the voices of men in a suppressed tone, not far from us in the thick underwood. As the speakers might be Spanish, we ceased to talk, and lay close, burying our persons, as it were, in the long coarse grass, and listening with all our ears. The distant talking continued, but in what tongue we could not tell, for the wind still blew in gusts, and ever and anon carried away the sound. At length, just as we were despairing of making out who our neighbours were, I felt something wet and cold glide from under my bare leg, and turning sharply round, I saw the grass moving, and the green glistening skin of a snake gliding over my flesh. Involuntarily, and with a great shout, I started up. 'It is all over,' said Nicky; 'we are discovered.' But in a moment a gruff voice hallooed—

' Who goes there ? '

And we both joyfully cried out in reply, that we were friends and comrades. Immediately there was a great rustling in the boughs, and running up thither we presently found a remnant of our own company, who grasped our hands, and could scarce speak for joy at seeing us. The men who thus joined us were five in number: Ezra Hoskins, an English seaman of Dover, called by us Stout Jem, not only for his size and muscle, which were prodigious, but because of his boldness and fearlessness of heart; then there was another Englishman, from Newcastle, whose real name I know not, because I never heard him called by any appellation but that of Black Diamond; and a Hollander, a sturdy slow-witted fellow, from Helvoetsluys, near the Brill, whom we called Meinheer; the other two persons were the Mosquito Indians, Blue Peter and Jack, skilful strikers of fish and manatee, and very attached, faithful fellows.

You may be sure that we had much to tell each other of our adventures. First, Nicky narrated our mischance in the Mangrove Creek, from the devil-like snares of the crafty and cowardly Spaniards. And then, Stout Jem told how, in the evening of the previous day, the Indians being fishing towards the open sea, saw the sloop working up with the last of the sea-breeze, but considered her to be a friend, from one of the windward islands, come to load; and how the Buccaneers, being thus thrown off their guard, had hoisted lights upon the headland, to guide her after it fell dark. It had certainly surprised them to see answering lights, as it appeared, further up the lagoon, and they had set a good watch, and were wakeful in consequence, not well knowing what to expect. As the night wore on, and our canoe did not make its appearance, their anxiety increased, and towards morning a Mosquito man, who had been hunting manatee in the sedgy banks of the savannahs, came into the settlement, and reported that he had heard the oars of boats pulling in the Mangrove Channels, and that he had seen lights glimmering amid the night-fog. It was now evident that there was something in the wind, but they never reckoned on being attacked by such a force as came against them. Besides, the strangers might be all French from Tortugas, or St. Christopher's, or Dutch from Cura-çoa, and might not exactly know how the old settlers would relish an intrusion in their hunting-grounds. It was not until almost day, that our comrades saw a great ship coming into the bay, being towed against the land-wind or *terral*, which was then waxing faint, by her boats. A pirogue went off to her, but not returning, those on shore concluded that the arrival was friendly, and that their comrades had stayed on board to carouse, and they were only undeceived upon the rising of the sun, when they saw two Spanish men-of-war, besides the sloop, lying in the bay, and were saluted with hot salvos of artillery. Seeing their mistake, the Buccaneers, fol-lowing their usual tactics, leaped into their canoes and tried to board. But the Spaniards hove great stones and cold shot into the boats, keeping up at the same time a sharp discharge of musketry, so that the canoes being broken and swamped, those who were not maimed or killed of their crews, were fain to swim to land, where they were again attacked by a body of Spaniards, who, with loud shouts, issued from the woods, proving how skilfully the whole position had been invested. The Buc-caneers, being thus sorely discomfited, retreated into the cover of the brushwood and trees, and maintained a distant fight, aiming chiefly at the Spaniards who showed them-selves on board the ships, and those who emerged from the seaward-side of the huts. This lasted nearly all the morning, when the weather becoming threatening, the Spaniards, who were until then held as it were in check, determined to make a great effort, and calling to their men ashore to take care of themselves, opened a great fire upon the huts, the balls crashing through and through them, and, at the same time, flinging fire-balls and other combustibles, so that presently one-half of the settle-ment was in flames, and the other demolished. Then the Dons landed in great force, and were met by the remnant

of our comrades, who fought desperately. But the
Spaniards having overwhelming numbers, finally routed
them, and drove them by small parties into the woods.
It was at the conclusion of this affray that the storm
came on, and since its abatement our comrades had been
roving along the shore, seeking any other survivors of the
fight, but hitherto finding none.

---

## CHAPTER VI.

### HOW THE DEADLY FEVER OF THE COAST FASTENS ON ME.

SUCH was the history of the treacherous Spanish attack
which destroyed the settlement of the Marmousette.
Our first care was to learn how the party we had met in
with were armed, and great was our delight to find that
the Indians carried two guns apiece, nearly all the muskets in the village having been brought into the woods.
Besides there was abundance of ammunition. After
a short consultation, it was determined to take the canoe,
and although our number would somewhat overload her,
to cross to the other side of the bay, where we had more
security against being molested. Having therefore carefully looked to our pieces, we clambered down the bank,
and standing by the canoe, unanimously invested Stout
Jem with the command of the expedition. As the
Indians used the paddles most dexterously, they were set
to work to propel us, and with Stout Jem for steersman,
we set out. On our way I began to experience a drowsiness, which I had before felt, but immediately checked.
Now, however, the sensation, amounting indeed to one of
impending stupor, began again to overpower me. My
chin fell upon my chest, and I had little snatches of disturbed sleep, in which curious confused ideas, and odd
combinations of words and things, seemed to float into
my brain, and which, when I started up again, which I
would do every minute, fled away like phantoms, so that
I could not for my life remember what I had been dream-

ing of the moment before. All this time I was inwardly urged to speak, I seemed to have nothing to say, but still something forced my tongue and lips to move, and all at once I called out—

'Is that a black corby on the thorn-bush near the boat's grapnel?'

At this extraordinary speech, the Englishmen in the canoe turned sharp round to me, and Stout Jem asked what I meant. At his voice all the dreamy sensations left me, and I felt myself blushing up to the roots of my hair, and wondering what I had said, for I remembered not a word.

'Here,' said Stout Jem, kindly, 'swallow this, my good boy;' and he held me a great flask of spirits. 'You have been breathing over-much marsh fog on an empty stomach, but you'll live to pay off Jack Spaniard yet.'

I took the flask and held it to my head, when suddenly the greasy leathern bottle appeared to swell and lengthen, until it seemed a puncheon which I held. A curious nervous feeling came crawling over my limbs, and my breath grew thick, and my eyes dim. The first taste of the brandy banished these sensations, and the cordial marvellously restored me.

'You must eat somewhat when we go ashore,' said Nicky. 'I am ravenous; and then we will consult on what we can do to take our revenge.'

'No, no; no eat,' said Blue Peter, the Mosquito Indian; 'sleep mosh, sleep good, smoke pipe, and sleep cool and long.'

But I felt so much better that I fully intended to make a good dinner. We landed in one of the bushy coves which abound in the frith of the Marmousette, and which could not be seen by the Spaniards on the other bank. Stout Jem then despatched the Indians to hunt, and ordered the rest of the party to aid in building a hut. Nicky and myself, however, were so weak from want of food, that we were excused; and the Dutchman having some biscuits and smoked beef in his pocket, generously

gave us enough to make a good meal. Meantime, Stout
Jem, Black Diamond, and Meinheer, were actively at
work. They had two hatchets, and their long knives,
and with these they felled and prepared sufficient wood
for their purpose, driving stakes into the earth, and in-
terweaving leafy branches, with the skill of experienced
foresters. Nicky and I were then set to work to pull a
quantity of coarse long grass, which grew upon the beach,
for beds ; and one of the Mosquito men returning, he
kindled a fire, and began to cook the hind quarter of a
fine boar which he had shot in the wood. Meantime, I
was plucking the grass, sometimes sitting by the seaside,
for I felt weak and ill. The food I had eaten was no
refreshment. My temples throbbed strangely and my
skin was fevered and dry. Then these horrible wandering
thoughts began to come again, and I squeezed my head
with my hands, as though I could thus drive them out.
Sometimes I thought I felt again the hot marsh vapour
sickening the air ; then the sea-breeze fanning me, I
would tear the clothes from my chest, and put back my
long dank hair to let the blessed cool wind play freely on
me, and cool my seething blood.

All at once I saw, under the shade of a genipa tree, a
tall stout man, who stood motionless, and watched me.
Deeming him a Spaniard, I would have shouted out, but
my tongue refused to obey me, and turning hot and dry,
rattled as it were against my teeth, while no sound but a
low hiss could I form. Still the figure stood there ; and
now I saw a glimmer as of a naked weapon which it held.
The sun being now setting, his rays came slanting down,
and one of these quivering through the trees fell full
upon the face of the stranger, and I saw that it was
Walshe, with his great eyes glaring at me, just as they
glared when the shark rose in the mangrove canal, and
pulled him down beneath his crunching teeth. I stood
trembling, and trying to pray. The features were livid
and blue, and the eyes sunk and expressionless, yet
horribly bright. Just at this moment one of the last
puffs of the sea-breeze shook the trees around, and the

sunlight falling in a different stream, and chequered by other branches upon the appearance, the face gradually seemed to change. Feature after feature melted away, until the agonized countenance of the unfortunate seaman was gone, and, instead of it, there remained the massive features and pensive gravity of my preserver on board the Frenchman—Wright. Just then the weapon, which I had formerly observed to glitter, moved, and I saw the figure heave up a great broad axe on one hand, and point to it with the other. It was, indeed, the regicide, with the emblem and the instrument of his deed.

Making a sudden effort, I burst the leaden bonds which seemed to confine me, and with a strange courage rushed forward. As I did the phantom grew dim and dimmer, and when I placed my hand upon its breast, I felt but the gnarled bark of the genipa tree, whilst the axe, at the same instant, seemed to become a branch with clustering foliage dancing in the wind. I grew directly sick and faint.

'Oh, my God!' I murmured, 'I am going mad! My brain is whirling, and my eyes make me see things which are not!' and so I sank upon the ground, and sobbed. Presently, I was somewhat better, and I manned myself. 'It is but a feverish attack,' I thought. 'I will return and try to sleep.' It was, however, with some difficulty that I arrived at the hut. My limbs felt as if loaded with lead, and the pain of an intense headache went like hot iron wires into my brain. When I reached our half-finished abode, I saw everything through a sort of haze, and the voices at my ear appeared to come from miles away. I was soon placed, lying upon bundles of grass, in the windward side of the hut, and after that I remember little more of what happened during three nights and three days. Only I know that my sufferings were very great; that my mind appeared to ramble as though it were a disturbed spirit or ghost flitting all over the world. Now, I would seem to be far away on the pleasant coast of Fife. The sun would shine, and the corn rustle and the yellow broom by the burnie's banks

smell sweet in the summer's breath. But I could enjoy
nought. I was as it were seared, and the sources of
pleasure dried up. I saw the forms of people I loved,
but I could speak to none. I saw my mother sitting on
a sandy knowe, resting her head upon her hand, and
looking over the blue sea. But when I would embrace
her, there came darkness and pain, and the vision vanished.
Then, perhaps, in my delirium, I would fancy I was at
sea; sometimes it was in the old fisher-boat, the Royal
Thistle. No wind would stir, the sky would be glowing
like a heated copper globe, and the boat would lie move-
less as though nailed to the unstirring sea. Suddenly my
father's eyes would look into mine with a long wan stare,
and so would we sit glaring at each other, like famishing
and despairing beasts, while months, and years, and ages,
would appear to come and go and bring no change.
Anon, the mood would alter. Then I was on board the
old brig, Jean Livingstone, with a merry breeze and a
blithesome crew. The bonny crags of St. Andrew's
Bay would seem under our lee, with the ruined towers
of abbeys and churches rising over the green links, and
fading from our sight, as we worked gallantly seawards.
But the scene would straightway change to a furious
storm in a mid-winter night, with the foam of the sea and
the snow-flakes flying together. Then round the light of
the binnacle there would crowd ghastly faces, staring
into mine—faces with shaggy antique beards like the
ancient sailors of Sir Patrick Spens, long, long sleeping
in the wild North Sea; and so surrounded by these fishy
eyes of hapless drowned mariners, I would feel the good
brig seem to founder beneath my feet, so that I would
start struggling up from my bed of grass, crying out that
I was drowning—that the boiling waves were choking me !

This was my seasoning fever, as they called it; and,
though it did not last long—thanks to the good treatment and the medicinal herbs of the Mosquito men—it
left me passing weak and helpless. I recovered my reason
all at once, as one waking from the stupor of deep sleep.
My hair had been cut close, and my head was tied round

with freshly-plucked plantain leaves, constantly drenched with water. I lay upon blankets, none of which we possessed when I was taken ill, and my linen was reasonably clean and fresh. The wattled hut was open to the breeze on every side, and as it contained but one bed more, I guessed that it had been given up for my use and that of my partner, Nicky, as indeed it had. Looking around, I saw several pots, pans, baskets, and boxes scattered about, from which I concluded that the Spaniards had departed, and that my comrades had been able to recover some of the wreck of their property from the ruins of their habitations. And this, indeed, I found afterwards to be the case.

I was too weak at first to call out, and so remained in silence, enjoying a delicious languor, and cool and moist from head to foot. The fever had thoroughly left me, and I felt thankful and devoutly glad. Presently I distinguished the well-known smell of the smouldering fire of the boucan floating into the hut, and soon afterwards, Nicky, with bare arms and grimed hands, entered; his eyes sparkled when he saw me so much recovered, and presently calling the rest together, they all shook hands with me, and told me to be of good cheer, for I had forereached on the marsh fever, and would soon be quite hearty. And so, indeed, it was. I grew very hungry, and, being well fed, regained my strength fast, so that, two or three days after the fever left my blood, I was abroad sniffing the cool breezes of the sea.

Except two men—both French—who had joined when I was ill, none of the survivors of our original party had turned up; some of them had no doubt been made prisoners by the Spaniards, others might have started off along the coast to the eastward, as, indeed, many previously intended; but we feared that upwards of one half of our comrades were either captives, who would be forced to labour in the mines of Cuba, or had already —and the fate of these latter was more to be envied— died with their wounds, in front, giving battle to the Spanish robbers.

Being little able to work for some time after my reco-
very, and the rest of the party being engaged in the
usual toil of hunting wild cattle, and preserving the meat
by the boucan, it was often my habit to take the canoe
and proceed in her down towards the mouth of the bay,
so as to enjoy the fresh and briny breeze which came
from the north-west across the ocean. To make these
expeditions more pleasant, I prepared a mast with a small
lug sail, such as the canoe could bear, and I could manage
with ease. Almost my first trip, when thus provided,
was to the scene of the late contest. I found nearly
every trace of a settlement destroyed. The rude jetty
was all but demolished, and over the ruins of the shattered huts, great crops of luxuriant herbage had grown,
from which I often started snakes and venomous insects,
such as centipedes and scorpions, who delighted to make
their nests in the holes and crevices which they found in
abundance amidst the ruins of our huts. On a sweet
spot of green-sward, under the shadow of a great spreading tree, there were rows of little mounds, very green.
Here our poor comrades lay buried. The Spaniards, it
seems, had interred their dead, and on their departure,
which happened on the day after I was attacked with
fever, all our party had gone across the bay, and laid the
dead Buccaneers beneath the mould. Upon the bark of
the great tree I was at pains to carve a deep cross; for,
though the symbol in Europe be the mark of a corrupt
and idolatrous church, still I felt that in the wilderness
it might bear a truer and a wider meaning, and point out
to future strangers that the mounds beneath the tree
covered the graves of Christian men.

---

## CHAPTER VII.

### THE BUCCANEERS TIRE OF THE LIFE ON SHORE, AND DETERMINE TO GO AGAIN TO SEA.

SEARCHING about the place I often discovered little
tters, which I stored in the canoe and brought to our
settlement, such as axes and hammers, harpoons for

striking fish, fragments of cordage, rope and canvas; and twice I dug up from the ruins, boxes containing seamen's clothes, which were very welcome to us all; in one of these trunks I discovered some Spanish books, including a grammar and dictionary, and of these I hastened to avail myself, inasmuch as I saw that a knowledge of this language might soon be of the greatest service to me. Neither did my companions grudge that I thus applied much of my time to study, for none of them knew more than a few words of Spanish, and they were quite aware of the advantage of having one at least of that party conversant with that tongue.

Thus, time passed away tolerably pleasantly. The season for the arrival of the ships expected to load with the boucan prepared for them at the village on the east side of the bay, having passed, and none of them appearing, we concluded that stragglers from our old company had succeeded in making their way to Jamaica, Tortugas, and other islands, and had informed the merchants and planters there of the attacks of the Spaniards, and the utter ruin of the settlement, adding, very probably, that they were the sole survivors of the massacre. It, therefore, became a question with us what to do. The Frenchmen were for journeying along the coast to the westward, and then watching an opportunity to go across to Tortugas; but Stout Jem told them they might do so if they pleased, but he would prefer an island where his own countrymen had something to say in matters, an opinion which the rest of the English, as well as the Dutchmen and the Indians, who do not love the French, joined in very cordially. The Frenchmen, who, to do them justice, were very good fellows, on this gave up their proposition and swore that they would follow Stout Jem to the death.

'Say you so, my boys?' cried the Dover mariner. 'Then so be it; and what I propose is this. Here be nine stout men of us, for I count the Indians as good as white blood. Our peaceful trade in beef and hides, hath been ruined by these accursed Spaniards, so I vote for the sea again.'

F

This proposal meeting with a clamour of approbation, Stout Jem flung aloft his hat.

'We have had enough of the shore this bout, mates,' quoth he. 'I want to hear the wind whistle through tarry ropes again, and feel a stout ship dancing under my feet.'

'Yah, yah,' said the Hollander. 'We zaal be Zee Roovers once more;' and all the company flung up their hats like our leader, and swore that they would take deep vengeance on Jack Spaniard. For my part, I was well pleased, for I felt I was a sailor, and that I had no business to be following a hunter's life ashore. I had not very much taste for shooting bullocks, and still less for breaking them up, cooking and storing them; and, although I had always cheerfully taken my turn to watch the boucan fire, my mind would often stray away upon the ocean, and I would pant for the fresh sea-breeze, and the dash of the foaming brine. As for my comrade, Nicky, he was that easy kind of going man, that he seemed to care very little whether he was on land or sea. He worked, ate, drank, sang and slept, and then rose merrily next day to go through the same routine. But Stout Jem, who was the life and soul, as well as the captain of our party, was a sailor all over. He had been many years in the Caribbean sea, was a good pilot, understood every current, and every indication of the weather; and moreover, knew by heart every buccaneering trick for easing of their cargoes the treasure-ships of the Dons.

But before we could go to sea, we must have a vessel; and saving the canoe, which was hardly fit for a cruiser, we were as unprovided as though we lived on the top of a mountain. There was nothing therefore for it, as we could not go in a ship to the Spaniards, but to wait until the Spaniards should come in a ship to us, that is to say, in such a small ship as we could master, and afterwards manage. We might indeed have not found much difficulty in entering an English privateer, many of whom we knew were hovering on the coast; but being acquainted with each other well, we preferred in the first place to

capture such a small craft as we could man, afterwards
making such additions to our crew as might from time to
time be resolved on.  In the meanwhile, we continued to
hunt and prepare the flesh of wild cattle and boars, so
that we should have a good stock of provisions when we
were ready to go to sea.

Being, as I have said, always fonder of water than land,
I often induced the Mosquito Indians to allow me to go
with them in their canoe, when they went to strike fish
and manatee.  Generally the Indians permit no one to
accompany them in these expeditions, and if they are
forced to allow a white man into the canoe, they will
purposely miss their aim at every fish or animal they
strike, and so return empty handed.  However, I being
a great favourite with Blue Peter, who had indeed saved
my life in the fever; and losing no opportunity, by such
petty gifts as I had it in my power to make, of showing
my gratitude, he made no objections to my accompanying
him and his comrade in many of their expeditions.

We used to start before sunrise, Blue Peter in the
bows of the canoe, and Jack in the stern, both paddling
quickly, while I sat amidships in the bottom.  No
Europeans I ever saw can paddle so silently, swiftly,
and surely as the Indians on the Mosquito coast.  They
hold the shaft of the paddle almost upright, never touching the gunwale therewith, or splashing rudely in the
water.  On the contrary, the broad part of the paddle
dips as clean as a knife, and the canoe glides with a perfectly smooth and rapid motion, so that, did you not observe how fast the water ripples by, you would hardly think
you were moving at all.  When pursuing the manatee,
our usual game, the head of the canoe was turned up the
creek, to the higher banks, where the shore was sedgy
and low, where the mangroves reared their dismal groves,
and where, the water gradually becoming brackish and
muddy, there is found floating and waving from the
banks, the long narrow-bladed grass on which the manatee loves to feed.  The creature we hunted is a harmless
beast, like a great seal.  It is a misfortune for himself

F 2

that he has tender white flesh, tasting like veal, and that his skin makes very good thongs and straps, which the Buccaneers use for divers purposes. Were it not so, he might float unmolested in the warm muddy water, nibbling the streaming grass, as the lazy current carries his heavy form slowly up and down the mangrove canals, twinkling his little pig-like eyes, and anxiously jerking his great stupid-looking head, if a cayman rolls with a splash from the muddy bank into the river, or a squatting flock of wild-ducks rise with a whirr from the sedgy surface of a neighbouring pool.

But the poor manatee, being good to eat, must submit to be harpooned and eaten. When we came to the feeding-ground which he loves, the Indians would paddle with double caution, and Blue Peter, who was the striker, would carefully examine his harpoon, and see that it lay convenient to his hand. The spear used for capturing the manatee is about eight feet long. The iron barb, a heavy and sharp piece of metal, is attached to the thicker end, and to the other is fastened a circular knob called the bobwood, round which is wound a strong line, one end of which is fast to the bobwood, the other to the iron of the harpoon. When the weapon is flung, the barb alone sinks into the creature's flesh, the staff coming unloosed from the iron, and the line rapidly unwinding from the bobwood, as the stricken creature dives in its agony and fear. The Indians then paddle after the staff, and having seized it, gradually wear out the strength of the game, and kill it.

I shall not soon forget the first manatee hunt I saw. We embarked at early dawn, and glided silently along the green shore, from which the mist of the night was lifting and rolling in white clouds far up the mountains. After long skirting the mangrove wood, we turned from the main channel into a narrow creek, slipping along in perfect silence. Listen as I would, I could not even hear the water at the canoe's bow, her mould was so perfect, and so steady the strokes which propelled her. The drip of the water from the paddles, as they were lifted, alone made a slight tinkling sound. The sea-breeze had not yet begun to blow, and the sun came down scorchingly upon the tangled wood and the green water, the surface of which glanced like bright, clear oil. Presently Blue Peter laid his paddle noiselessly down, and took up the harpoon. I looked anxiously ahead. Clustered round the trunk of a vast mangrove, which rose up out of the water, there was a tangled heap of soaking grass and weeds. The kneeling Indian crouched as if he were a graven image of ebony or bronze, and I saw the floating weeds move, and heard a grinding, spluttering sound, as of a cow grazing. Then the Indian moved a finger of his left hand, which he had kept outstretched; his comrade at the stern saw the sign, and a peculiar sweep of the paddle sent the canoe slantingly towards the weeds. As she diverged from her course, Blue Peter stood erect, and raising his right arm, with all the muscles swelling out like knots and lumps of iron, darted the harpoon, as it appeared to me, into the centre of the moving weeds. Instantly there was a great splash and plunge, and the canoe rocked upon a wave, which scattered the floating herbage, so that I saw disappearing in the water the broad brown back of a creature as large as a cow. Blue Peter, the instant he struck, sank again upon his knees, and snatching up the paddle, prepared to move. Meantime I could see nothing of the harpoon, for it had been carried under water. The Mosquito men then talked to each other in their own tongue, pointing to the direction in which the manatee appeared to have dived, and then began to paddle lustily. About five minutes might have elapsed, when Blue Peter exclaimed, ' Ho!—there!' and pointed. I, looking in the same direction, descried the staff of the harpoon seeming to fly along the surface of the water, the round bobwood throwing up a foam two feet high. Then the Mosquito-men pulled hard in chase. I could never have thought that their gaunt, brown bodies had so much strength in them. The muscles of their naked arms and chests strained and swelled, the paddle-shafts cracked, and the canoe seemed at every

stroke to be lifted out of the water.  Still they did not
gain upon the harpoon towed by the manatee, but, on
the contrary, rather lost, so that I began to fear that we
would never see either harpoon or quarry; but, on a
sudden, the motion of the former stopped, and it floated
tranquilly upon the water.  The manatee, being fatigued,
had sunk to the bottom, and lay there.  We now paddled
carefully up, and Blue Peter caught the staff, and began
to pull upon the line.  Immediately that the wounded
creature felt the smart, it started again.  I saw the line
vibrate and stretch out in a direction abeam of the canoe;
but, in a moment, Jack, who held the steering-paddle,
swept the bows round in the direction taken by the
manatee, while Blue Peter fastened the line to the prow
of the canoe.  There was a jerk or two, though not so
much as I expected, and straightway we began to move
ahead, Peter crouching in the bows, signing to Jack how
to steer.  For near a quarter of an hour did the wounded
beast drag us through the water, sometimes so swiftly
that the foam whizzed past us—anon changing his course
so suddenly, that had not the canoe been steered with
perfect skill, he would have dragged us under water.
Then, his strength beginning to ebb from him fast, we
hauled upon the line, and gradually closed with our prey,
whose blood was now reddening the water.  I pitied the
poor creature, as he put his head above the surface, and
grunted and moaned after his fashion, but he was soon
out of his pain.  Slipping alongside of the carcass, Blue
Peter passed his long knife around its throat, and after
one or two struggles and plunges, the manatee turned
over upon its back, dead.  We towed him ashore, and
securing him to a tree, presently paddled off in search of
more game of the same sort.

But upon the whole, I better loved our fishing expeditions than the hunt of the manatee.  The poor
defenceless brute always inspired me with pity.  There
is a meekness about his face which moves one.  He makes
no attempt to turn to bay or show fight, but is slaughtered
as unresistingly as a calf, and the haunts he loves are the

muddy and unwholesome canals among the mangrove swamps. But in spearing fish we often rowed down the bay to the rocky points and ledges of reef which formed the outermost horns of the lagoon. There the clear, blue sea, white spangled by the merry strength of the sea-breeze, stretched illimitably out, and the everlasting surf flung aloft its clouds of sparkling spray, high up among the rocks, now and then giving the bushes a taste of the savour of brine. It was in the still pools and channels, formed by breakwaters of rock, that the canoe was then navigated. Let the sea-breeze be blowing, and the surging swells be tossing in, as hard and fast as they might, there was always calm water behind the reefs—so calm and so clear! I might think that I was looking into the swirlings of our trout-pool in the Balwearie Burn, but for the bright, jagged coral, and the strange sea-weeds at the bottom, and the still stranger fishes floating, as it were, in pure mid air, but a fathom down beneath the keel of the canoe. Gliding over these translucent waters, sometimes scraping the battered side of our skiff against the rough coral edges; sometimes receiving a sparkling shower of spray when a bigger wave than ordinary burst upon the outside reef, the Mosquito men were in their glory. Blue Peter stood erect in the bow, his black, flashing eyes fixed on the water as though he would note every scollop in the edge of the jagged sea-weed, or every wavy ridge on the bed of white sand, and his long thin fish-spear darting occasionally down into the flood to be straightway drawn, bending and quivering, back with a noble fish, writhing and floundering, impaled upon the barbs. Always upon these expeditions I kept a good look-out seaward, and often mounted pinnacles of rock that I might have the better view. Once or twice I saw a sail, apparently set on board a small vessel, slipping quickly down to the westward, or beating painfully to windward; but the barks were too far at sea for me to make out aught of their character or country.

During this period of my sojourn in Hispaniola it was our custom to spend the evenings together in the principal hut—that which was first constructed, and which was of an ample bigness. Here, seated round a great chest, which served for a table, we smoked our pipes, drank pretty deep draughts of the rich palm wine, and told in turn stories of our lives and adventures. The hut being only wattled, and that very imperfectly, the strong land breeze blew through and through it, causing the flame of our solitary lamp to waver and flicker, and not unfrequently putting it out altogether. We sat upon bundles made of our clothes, or heaps of dried grass, and must, in sooth, have appeared a parcel of strange ragamuffins, with our faces burnt to mahogany colour by the sun ; our hair and beards long, tangled, and matted ; and our clothes, being coarse doublets and short jackets, cut in uncouth shapes, and often red and greasy with the blood and fat of the animals which it was our business to kill. Stout Jem, being reckoned the head and commander of our party, sat on a kind of settle for a throne, and the rest of us crowded as near the great chest as we could, the two Mosquito men excepted, who commonly sat apart squatted on their hams, and speaking to each other softly in their own tongue. Sometimes we would play dice on these evenings, not for money, of which we had none, but for the carcasses of the cattle which we had killed and flayed ; but as the play was always fair and the dice true, it was generally found that no one either lost or gained much in the long run. It was, however, the story-telling nights I loved the best. Many of the tales then told were indeed very vulgar and common, and unworthy of being recorded, turning solely upon butcheries of the Spaniards at sea, and upon great seasons of debauch, after a successful cruise, in Tortugas or Jamaica. Not a few tales were also told of ghosts and omens, and such extravagances, which the superstitious nature of sailors causes them to believe and to hearken greedily to. I heard many such histories both at this time and afterwards, and I design to insert one here, not because I think it at all credible, but because it is a very good specimen of the histories of ghosts, phantoms, and other supernatural appearances which were current among the Buccaneers. This story was told by Stout Jem very solemnly, and listened to with no less eagerness; and in recounting it I will endeavour to put the matter into the narrator's words, of which, for an uncultivated seaman, he had a good flow. Stout Jem called his history 'The Legend of Foul-Weather Don,' and to it I will devote the next chapter.

## CHAPTER VIII.

### THE LEGEND OF FOUL-WEATHER DON.

STOUT Jem told it thus :—

'My story, mates, is a strange one, and I say not whether it be true or false. I heard it in the middle watch, one fine night, slipping down the coast of Porto Rico, and the seaman who told it to us, said, that when he was a boy he sailed with the man to whom the thing happened, in a big ship which hailed from Bristol. That the spirits of the dead walk the world—ay, and sail the seas—is a thing I cannot say nay to. I cannot tell you that I ever saw anything of the sort myself, but credible mariners and grave and sober men have assured me of things which have made my marrow creep, and the hair stand up, all bristling out of my flesh. Well, then, about this story. The man to whom the adventure happened, was by name Ned Purvis, a mariner. It must be nigh sixty years ago since he sailed out of the port of London, on a trading voyage to the coast of Guinea. Purvis was then a younker, there being little better than a year since he had followed the sea, and this was his first voyage abroad; he having undertaken it in the ship of his uncle, a good old man, of a mild disposition, and well loved of the crew. As for Ned Purvis, he was a reckless, ruffling blade, that cared neither for man nor devil, when his blood was up, and who thought but little of the glimmer of a drawn cutlass, or the flash of a pistol, in a quarrel. But as I told you, mates, the old man, the captain, was mild of speech and of heart, and greatly loved his nephew, and thought much of the lad's spunk and wild spirit. So they sailed southerly, as became navigators, bound as they were to traffic for spices and rich oils and gold with the blacks of Africa.

'Having lost sight of England, they had prosperous winds and pleasant weather, and nought occurred until the seventh day from that in which they saw the last of the white cliffs. Then they were just moving through the water and no more, for the breeze was but a puff, and the sun going down, when all of a sudden they saw a boat with a man in it, so close aboard that you might toss a biscuit into her. It was curious, mates, that almost all the men on deck saw her at once, when she was, as it might be, alongside; and yet no one had seen her approaching. But strange as that was, comrades, it was not so strange as the cut of the boat, and, for that matter, the cut of the man in her. The stem and stern of the craft were very high, and ended in curled bits of carved wood. Her gunwale, too, was all carved and sculptured, in such a way as you may have seen the pulpits and choirs of cathedrals and abbeys, and such buildings in England and France, and the Low Countries, being very artificial work done with gravers and chisels.

'Ned Purvis remembered afterwards, when he saw a great Spanish painting of Christopher Columbus, landing on his second voyage upon the island of Hispaniola, that the admiral sailed in a barge, carved and ornamented after the fashion of that of which I am now telling you. And the man, mates, looked as old as his boat. He had on a high, conical hat, with a feather in it, and he wore a grave coloured doublet, of an old fashion, with slashes in the arms, and brocaded flowers embroidered thereon. Round his neck was a stiff ruff. He had red stockings, and great bunches of ribbon in his shoes. The face of this strange person was severe and grave. He had no moustachoes, but a thin peaked beard which fell over his frill. Every now and then he smiled with a strange, wild expression, which was that of a bitter sneer; and his eyes shot a sparkling light, which was stony and cold, and from which men turned their heads, as if by instinct. Well, then, the captain, when he saw this queer cruizer, seemed fascinated, and gazed upon him, as you may have seen small birds on the boughs gaze at snakes, whose eyes glitter out of the grass beneath, and presently the man in the boat waved his arm, as a signal to those on board to take him in. Well, no one stirred but Ned Purvis, and before the old captain could prevent him, Ned flung a rope to the stranger, who straightway caught hold of it and mounted on deck.

' " Where is your captain?" says he, in a hollow harsh voice.

' The old man comes forward, as pale as a corpse, and, quoth he—

' " In the name of God, what want ye on board my ship ?"

' Now, at the name of God, Ned Purvis thought that the strange man started and shook : but he replied not, only taking the old captain by the hand, pointed to his boat, which was towing astern.

' " Men," said the old mariner, faintly, " he will not be denied; get his boat aboard."

' But the crew slunk together in a body, and murmured to each other, but put not a hand to rope or tackle. Then Ned Purvis stood forward.

' " Who are you?" said he, " and why should we take you or your boat aboard?"

' " You yourself asked me," quoth the strange man; " you flung the rope; but for that I should have floated past you. I never come, but where some one welcomes me."

' Now, at this, Ned Purvis confessed that he felt like a great sinner, and all the men turned round and looked first at him and then at the stranger. But Ned plucked up courage, and determined to give them all bold words. So he walked up to the stranger, and said—

' " Well, I did heave you a rope; no true-hearted mariner would see a man adrift upon the ocean, and not

offer him rescue. I care little what you be. If you aro
our fellow-creature, we have done but our duty in saving
you ; if you be not, why, we are honest men here, having
no crime upon our consciences, and we defy the devil and
all his works. Come, shipmates, lend a hand, and heave
the old gentleman's barge aboard. It's the captain's
orders, and orders must be obeyed.''

'And so, after a little grumbling and murmuring, the
boat was hove aboard and placed between the masts.
There was neither food nor water in her, and her bottom
was as foul with barnacles and sea-weed as if she had
drifted ten times round the world. Meantime, the
stranger and the captain went below, and the men stood
in a group round the cabin, but they could hear nought
of what took place there, and presently they retired to
their usual posts. Well, Ned Purvis was in the first
watch, and when it got dark he was standing leaning
against the main-chains, wondering at the strange event of
the day, when the captain touched him on the shoulder.

'"Nevvy!" says the old man, "know you whom you
have brought aboard into this ship?"

'"Why, uncle," answered Ned, somewhat taken aback
at this address, "ought we not to take aboard any man
we find starving in a boat upon the ocean, more than a
week's sail from land?"

'"Ay, nevvy," quoth the old captain, "any man, but
not any phantom ; it is more than a hundred years since
the passenger you brought on board this unhappy ship
was a man!"

'"Do you know him, then, uncle?" says Ned ; "have
you ever seen him before?"

'"Ay, boy," replied the old mariner ; "once, when I
was a youth, he boarded a ship in which I sailed, as he
did ours to-day."

'"And what did he?" asked the young sailor, his
heart fluttering within him.

'"Raised storms," said the elder Purvis, solemnly ;
"raised a tempest such as I never saw before, and had
hoped, until now, never to see again."

' " Then, in the name of God," says Ned, clenching his fists, " as I brought him on board, I'll pitch him overboard, and I'll begin with his boat first." And so saying, he began to make fast a tackle to the curled prow.

' " Hold, hold !" said Captain Purvis ; " he must go by his own free will, or he will not go at all."

' " But who—who, in the devil's name, is he, uncle ?" shouted Ned.

' " He is a restless phantom—a wandering, unquiet spirit," says the old seaman, with his voice trembling, and his grey hair all dank with the cold sweat. " He was a cruel captain of Spain, who, holding a high command in Hispaniola, wrought great cruelties to the natives, and even to his fellow-countrymen, amassing thus a great treasure, which he buried in one of the small keys or desert islands of the Western Indies, to wait an opportunity of conveying it to Spain : at length this seemed to have arrived, and in a stout vessel he set sail for the treasure island ; but on the voyage a terrible fever fixed upon him, and having partially recovered, he found his memory so gone that he could not recal to his mind any signs by which he knew either the island, or the part of it where the treasure lay. · Notwithstanding, however, he would continue to cruize for weeks and weeks among the cluster called the Virgin Isles, to the east of Porto Rico,—never sleeping, so they said who sailed with him, but always standing on the highest yard, gazing wistfully for his treasure he had buried. At length his crew lost patience, and insisted upon returning to Hispaniola ; at this he fell into furious fits of rage, but at last, they being obstinate, he swore a solemn oath that, dead or alive, he would sail the sea until his treasure was either found and spent, or placed for ever beyond the reach of men. And then, ordering them to put out a boat, stepped on board, and they left him floating, an hundred years ago, just as we found him this afternoon."

' " But he has been seen since," quoth Ned, after a pause, for he did not know what to think of this story.

' " Twice that I know of," said his uncle, " and once, I tell you, I saw him, and he came on board and brought tempest with him; they called him ' Foul-Weather Don,' and learned men say he must keep his oath, in the spirit, if not in the body, and that he will have no rest till the terms of it be fulfilled."

' " So he brought bad weather, did he ?" said Ned, musing.

' " For the three weeks he was on board," says the old man, " the blast never lulled, and the sea ran higher than the mainyard."

' " And what did he do all that time ?" cries Ned, again.

' " He sat in the great cabin," replied the uncle, " with his back against the rudder-case, and never spoke word nor broke bread."

' " How did he leave you ?" was Ned's next question.

' " He rose one evening, just in the twilight, and ordered the captain to put his boat into the water, though none of us thought a boat would live in such a sea, and none built by man's hand could. But that one"—and the old sailor pointed to the sea-worn craft, with her bottom one bed of weed and barnacles—" but that one floated like a duck upon the great breaking seas; and presently, with grave courtesy and farewell gesture, Foul-Weather Don stepped to the gangway, and from thence on board his skiff. We saw him once or twice rising on the tops of the great seas, and standing up in the boat with his hands clasped, as one praying; then boat and all disappeared, and we saw him no more. The next hour the gale broke, the sea went down, and we were again enabled to lay our proper course."

' " And what is Foul-Weather Don doing in the cabin just now ?" says Ned.

' " Sitting with his back against the rudder-case," answered Captain Purvis; " and see—look there !" the old man added, and he pointed to the east, " look at that bank of clouds rising from the ocean—there's the gale coming. Before midnight Foul-Weather Don will have all his winds blowing about him."

' With this, mates, Ned Purvis walked away forward, and pondered long and deeply. The rest of the crew were whispering in groups upon the forecastle, and the poor old captain was standing wringing his hands beside the magic boat. So presently Ned spoke to two or three of the men, and they shook hands with him and promised to stand by him. Then he went down to his berth and took out a great pistol, and carefully examined the lock and cleaned it ; afterwards he opened his chest, and produced from it a bright Spanish dollar; this he hammered into a round ball, and with it, instead of a leaden bullet, he loaded the pistol. So presently, armed in this fashion, he came on deck, the men following him by ones and twos, and marched right to the door of the great cabin. His uncle met him at the door. " What do you want here ?" quoth the old man ; " take my advice, and let him alone."

' " No," says Ned, " I brought him here, and I'll make you rid of him ;" and so saying, he put the old man aside, and entered the cabin. It was almost dark, but the light from the binnacle came down through the sky-light, and showed the strange passenger sitting there, as the captain had described, with his back to the rudder-case.

' Ned Purvis marched heavily in, and the phantom, or whatever it was, looked up at him, and so they remained for more than a minute staring into each other's eyes. The men were watching them over each other's shoulders at the door.

' " Foul-Weather Don," says Ned at last, as bold as steel, " you're more free than welcome."

The spectre took no notice.

' " I hove the rope to you," says Ned, " and I thought I was doing an act of duty by my fellow-creature. But now, I hear, that there's no living blood in your veins, and that you roam the ocean, bringing bad weather on the mariners you fall in with. That may be true, or it may not. If not, say so, and say who you are. If you be a shipwrecked man, you are welcome here ; but if not, men have told me that a silver bullet can wound even a

ghost, and if you do not speak in time, by God, there is
a rare chance now of testing the truth of the saying.
Answer !"

'And Ned cocked the great pistol and levelled at the
strange passenger.  The figure never moved a muscle of
its wan stern face.

'"Take the dollar and my blessing with it, then,"
shouted Ned, and he drew the trigger.

'The pistol exploded, and for a moment the cabin was
so full of smoke, that they could not see what execution
had been done.  When the vapour cleared a little off,
Foul-Weather Don was standing up, his stony eyes
giving out their cold sparkle, more horribly than ever.

'"You gave me your benison," he screeched out, " I
give you my malison ; and the executors and the tokens
of it will follow you night and day, until either my fate
or yours be accomplished.  If you do not believe me, go
on deck, look over either quarter, and see if I do not
speak sooth."

'These, mates, were the very words of Foul-Weather
Don ; for I have got all the conversations which relate
to the matter by heart, as they were told to me.  And so
Ned and the rest of them being terribly startled, tumbled
up on deck, one tripping up the other in their hurry ;
and the first thing they did was to stare into the sea,
where the phantom had told them to look, when sure
enough they saw the fins of two great blue sharks, awful
monsters in size, keeping way steadily with the ship ; and
just as Ned came on deck, they gave a sort of frisky
plunge in the water, as much as to say, " There you are—
very good ; and here we are."

'To make a long story short, mates, before midnight,
such a gale was blowing from the eastward, that there
was nothing for it but to put the ship before the wind ;
and not only that day, but that week, and for three
weeks after that, did the hurricane, for it was little else,
continue, blowing the ship entirely out of her course,
until at length, the captain and crew knew that they had
sailed from near the coast of Africa to the coast of

America, and that if the wind did not soon take off, they would be run plump ashore, either on the continent or one of the islands. Meanwhile Foul-Weather Don, as before, never rose from the cabin, nor broke bread nor spoke word. Indeed, if he were talkative, he had no one but himself to hold converse with; for captain, quarter-master, mates, and all, lived forward, and gave up the cabin to the phantom passenger. But Foul-Weather Don was not the only thing which stuck to the ship. The sharks kept way with her as steadily in the thunder-ing gale as in the light breeze. The crew could see them occasionally, ploughing along in the troughs of the sea, one on each quarter, and keeping their places as exactly as if they were towing after the ship. Well, all hands got low and mopish. The old captain was fairly unmanned; and even Ned Purvis, dare-devil as he was, began to quail. At last, they knew by their reckoning, and by the look of the sky towards sundown, that they were approaching the land, and that one way or the other their fate would soon be settled. So one evening, the men were gathered in groups, watching the signs of the sky, and pointing out to each other right ahead the warm coloured clouds which sailors know hang over the land. The weather looked as wild as ever; the scud above flew even faster than the waves below; and you should have seen the battered look of the craft as she went staggering along, under a rag of canvas, which was becalmed every moment in the troughs of the sea. Indeed the ship looked almost a wreck. Her bulwarks had been washed away long ago, the hatchways were all battened down. Out of three boats she had carried, only one was left, being strongly lashed to the deck, while the sea-battered skiff of Foul-Weather Don, although there was not so much as a rope yarn to make it fast, had never budged for all the great seas, which had been for weeks rolling over and over the decks, so that the men were obliged to lash themselves to ringbolts, and to the masts, and never could light a fire, or wear a stitch of dry clothing.

'Well, as I was saying, the poor fellows were holding

G

on as well as they could, and wondering where the ship
and they themselves would be to-morrow by that time,
when the two seamen, who were taking their turn at the
helm ropes, gave a loud shout, and the rest turning about,
saw Foul-Weather Don standing upon the deck.

'"He's going—he's going," whispered old Captain
Purvis. "The Lord hath preserved us in his great goodness."

'Well, Foul-Weather Don looked eagerly about as if
he expected to find his treasure island, and then he
mounted the rigging—all the crew holding their breath
and watching him—and gazed from the maintop long
and sadly. At length, he made a sort of motion of despair, and came down to the deck, where he stood wringing
his hands. All at once he turned to Captain Purvis, and
motioned for his boat to be hoisted into the sea. In a
minute, mates, the tackles were manned, and they let the
skiff go smash into the water, with a surge that would
have burst another boat into staves. But only the devil,
mates, could swamp a craft like that; she floated alongside as light as a well-corked bottle.

'"Haul your wind, when the elements will allow you,"
says the Don, quite solemnly.

'"Thank you for nothing," quoth Ned Purvis. "I
should think we would, when you have brought us across
the ocean against our will."

'But the spectre replied not a word, and seemed to
glide rather than to clamber over the ship's side into the
boat. When he was fairly aboard, Ned Purvis bellowed
out, "Take your sharks with you, Foul-Weather Don,
they are fitter companions for you than for Christians."

'But there was no reply, and in a minute the phantom
and his boat glanced away from the ship's side, and the
last the crew saw of her was a black speck with a figure
in it, in the very crest of a breaking wave. Just as this
happened, and they were beginning to breathe freely, one
of the men shouted "Land!" and sure enough the next
time they rose upon a sea, they saw right in the glare of
the setting sun the dusky coast line of an island. In an

hour after, the gale broke, lulling fast, so that before midnight they had courses and stay-sails on the ship, she lying-to with her head to the eastward. You know, mates, that in hot countries it is up wind, up sea, down wind, down sea, so that by sunrise the next day there was nothing but a great smooth swell to show that a gale had just swept across the wide Atlantic. The first thing Ned Purvis did when he came on deck to take the morning watch, was to look over the quarter, and he confessed afterwards that his heart felt sick when he saw the two blue sharks still alongside swimming close to the surface. The other seamen saw the creatures too, and they looked at Ned, and whispered among themselves.

'Well, you may be sure that, after such a run as the ship had had across the Atlantic, she wanted refitting, and the crew wanted vegetable food, and rest; so that when the usual trade wind came to blow, and they found from one or two fishing canoes that they were amongst the most northern of the Windward islands, they cruised about, looking for a convenient beach to land at, and to refresh themselves. All this time, mates, the sharks kept their places as steadily as the very masts. Ned fished for them in vain. He even baited the hook with the choicest pieces of pork and beef aboard, but they would not as much as push the morsel with their snouts. "No, no," said the men, when they saw this; "the creatures have their orders, and they obey them." Then Ned tried the harpoon, but though he had often speared porpoises and dolphins, he could not make a hit at the sharks; either the ship lifted or lurched, or the ravenous animals glided aside, or the water made the spear glance; but, however it was, Ned confessed that he could not even scratch their dingy backs.

'Upon this, there was little but black looks and murmuring words in the ship. Poor old Captain Purvis was at his wit's end, and the crew, although they used to love poor Ned, now began to look at nim as though he were a Jonas, and Ned knew it.

'"The curse," said the men, "is following us in a

G 2

visible shape. There can be no good luck for ship, or
crew, or cargo, with such a couple of attendants swimming astern."

' Well, Ned tried hard to laugh it off, but he could
not succeed, and his arguments were of as little avail.
" Why," he would say, "they can't jump aboard, messmates; the ocean is theirs as well as ours, and if a cat
may look at a king, I don't see why a shark may not
look at a ship."

' But though he spoke in this tone, I can tell you that
Ned was but ill at ease himself. Well, this lasted three
days, and all that time they were cruising about among
the islands, looking for a place which would be snug to
anchor in, and out of the way of Spanish ships. On the
third day, when the ship was about a league from a small
sandy isle or key, the men noticed that the sharks came
closer to her than ever, as if they were getting more and
more watchful of their prey. This made the pot boil
over, and the boatswain and three-fourths of the crew
went to the captain in a body, and said that Ned must
leave the ship that hour, for that he was a doomed man,
and that a doomed man made a doomed ship. There was
land close to, they said. Mr. Purvis would get plenty of
water and provisions, and he might soon get his passage
off in another ship, but whether he did or not, he must
go ashore now. Old Purvis tried to argue the thing,
but the men would not hear his words, and in the
middle of the hubbub, Ned comes forward, frankly, and
says —

' " Messmates, I have brought misfortune on the ship,
and spoiled the voyage ; I am willing to land."

' On hearing this, Captain Purvis wished to follow his
nephew, but they would not let him because he was the
only good navigator they would have, after Ned went
away, in the ship. So, presently, the remaining boat
was launched, and beef, and biscuit, and water, sufficient
for two months at least, were put in her, with a musket,
and ammunition, and a shovel, that Ned might have the
means of digging for water. When the boat shoved off,

the sharks followed, on which Ned, pointing to them, shouted to his uncle to be of good cheer, for they would meet again, and that the ship was now free of bad omens. The boat landed in a little cove, and Ned stepped on shore with his gun in his hand. The men placed his provisions and the shovel upon the beach, and shook hands with him; and as they rowed back to the ship, they gave him a cheer for his stout heart. Well, when they were gone, Ned began to look around him, and truly he was alone in a desolate place. Most of the island appeared to be sand, upon which, in some places, there were great banks of Bahama grass growing, and about a rood from him there was a little hill, with bushes in it, and one very old tree at the top. What rejoiced Ned, however, was to see plenty of turtles sleeping on the sand, and numerous birds. Well, he lived here nigh a fortnight, sleeping under a rock in a sort of cave, which was cool and pleasant, and looking out in vain for a ship. All this time the sharks kept cruising along the shore, and Ned used to amuse himself by flinging great stones on them from the top of rocks rising out of the sea. One day, however, having climbed the little hill, and sat down under the tree, he observed a curious thing. The tree, which must have been dead near a century, and which was all covered with moss, had several withered branches, to which cross pieces of wood had been rudely fastened, but in such a way that, unless you looked very closely, you would have thought that such was the natural growth of the tree. But at two hours, or thereby, after noon every day, these branches cast shadows as of six crosses, all in a circle on the sand. It was after Ned observed this that he climbed the tree, and found that the crosses were artificial. Then all at once it struck him that they were meant for marks, and then he thought that something might be buried there. Well, mates, off he goes for his shovel, and sets to work at once. It was hot work digging in that climate, but he very soon scraped the lid of a great chest made of ironwood, and bound with hasps and clasps of metal.

' "By all the stars," quoth Ned, "who knows but this is Foul-Weather Don's treasure-chest."

'Mates, I believe it was. Ned soon wrenched the lid off, and there he saw great ingots and rough lumps of gold, and precious stones, just as they were dug up from the mines in Cuba and Hispaniola by the Indians for the Spaniards. There they had lain for a hundred years, and no man the wiser or the better.

' "Aha," says Ned, "I would fain have you in England, but what am I to do with you here?"

'However, he made shift to carry the wealth, lump by lump, down to his cave near the sea; then he brought the box, and stowed the gold as before, covering all over with loose sand. The very next morning, mates, Ned, on awaking, saw a small bark—he did not know what she was—becalmed, not a mile from the shore, waiting for the sea-breeze. So he mounted a rock, fired his gun, waved a handkerchief, and shouted. Presently, a boat pulled off from the bark, and Ned went down to the cove to meet her. There were a couple of men in the boat, of what nation I know not, but the vessel to which they belonged was a turtler, from one of the large windward islands—Martinico, I believe. So Ned told them that he had been marooned for striking the quartermaster of the ship in which he sailed, and asked them if they would give him a passage to any port where he could ship for England. So the turtlers consulted together, and asked him if he had wherewithal to pay his passage. Upon which Ned, who cared nothing at all for money, took them into his cave, and showed them the treasure-chest. At the sight of it the turtlers stared, as well they might, and most readily agreed to take off Ned and his gold at once. The three set to work, and presently the boat was loaded almost to the water's edge with riches. The turtlers went about like men in a dream, and they were only roused from a sort of stupid bewilderment when they had rowed the boat out of the cove and found her so heavy that they feared she should be swamped by the heave of the sea.

' " Lord!" says one of them, "see there ; if the boat were to fill and go down. Did you ever see more fearful monsters?"

' And sure enough there were Ned's old friends swimming on each side of the boat, as though they were appointed the guardians of the treasure. However, no accident happened, and as they neared the turtling ship, the sailors cried out tnat they were coming on board with treasure enough to buy a kingdom.

' You may think for yourselves, mates, how the entire crew of the bark, which carried about half-a-dozen men, received their freight. Ned told the simple truth as to how he had got it, and the turtler, immediately that the sea-breeze came, stood away for Martinico, the two sharks following as usual. Gold, mates, is a thing that makes demons out of men. The big chest stood upon the deck, and the crew hung round it, and would hardly work the ship. Presently they began to handle and weigh the lumps, and dispute about their value. Ned saw that a storm was brewing, and fearing that he would be stabbed or flung overboard to the sharks astern, so as to be no bar to a distribution of the wealth, stood forward and said that they were as much entitled to the gold as he, for if he had found it, they had given him the means of turning it to use. Well, at this speech they professed great satisfaction, and swore that Ned was an honest man and a good comrade, and that as he said, so it would be done. But it was clear that they all distrusted each other. Ned saw them whispering and caballing, and once or twice he observed a man concealing a knife in his garment, so that the haft came handy to his grasp. All this time the sharks were following steadily in the wake, and Ned did not like the look of the weather, for great black clouds were gathering in the sky. Still the men were looking sourer and sourer at each other, and gradually drawing off into two parties, one on each side of the chest, the twain watching each other warily. Ned tried to remonstrate with them, and told them that they ought to take in sail, for the weather looked threat--

ening. But they ordered him to mind his own business, and said, they had not taken him on board to be captain over them. So Ned sat on the weather-bulwark, looking very uneasily to windward. Mates, you have all seen a squall in these seas, and you know how it comes. The weather getting very thick, the men forming each group began to whisper, and then, all at once, as if they had made up their minds, they gave a loud shout, and made a rush at the box ; as they did so, they drew knives and snicker-snees, and cut and chopped at each other, struggling and cursing over the chest. Ned saw the blood splash down on the gold, and he rushed forward to separate them, crying out, "Madmen that you are—look out for the squall first and fight afterwards."

' But it was too late, mates. The sky got black, and with a loud roar the squall came, tearing up the sea before it, and in the very centre of the flying foam Ned swore he saw Foul-Weather Don, with his arms stretched forth, as if in triumph. In an instant the blast struck the sails, heaving the turtler bodily on her broadside, and as she lurched over, the heavy box of gold fetched away with a mighty surge, and went crashing through and through the frail bulwark, and then with a great plunge down to the bottom of the ocean, there to lie, mates, even until the day when the sea shall give up its dead ! All this passed in a moment, and the next instant the ship, as though relieved by having cast forth the guilty gold, righted with a heavy roll, which sent the seamen sprawling across the deck, with their knives in their hands, and bloody gashes in their faces and limbs. The squall was over, and the sun burst out ; Ned rushed to the lee-beam, and saw, just where the gold had fallen into the sea, the bottom of a boat all covered with barnacles and sea-weed, which he knew well. She seemed now saturated and rotten with water, for the charm was off her, mates ; and while Ned gazed at her, she went gradually down into the great depths of the sea, and the sharks sunk out of sight with her. As they disappeared, Ned felt a heavy load leave his heart, and he

thought that he had got cheaply rid of it, even at the
expense of the gold. The curse was taken off him, and
he rather surprised the turtlers, who were standing looking very like fools, by cutting a set of capers on the
deck. The first thing they did was to try for soundings,
but the line ran out every fathom, and the lead touched
no bottom. So they lengthened the cord with every
piece of loose rope in the ship, but the sea appeared un-
fathomable. The gold was sunk in a gulf from which no
power of man could raise it; and so at length, mutually
cursing and blaming each other, they wore the ship
round, and stood back to pursue their turtling cruise.
From that time to this, mates, no mariner has ever seen
Foul-Weather Don. Ned Purvis got safely back to
England, and, as I informed you already, he told this
tale, aboard the Bristol ship, to him who made it known
to me. Regarding its truth, I leave every man to judge
for himself.'

---

## CHAPTER IX.

THE AUTHOR, WITH SUNDRY OF HIS COMRADES, SET OUT FOR THE
CREEK WHERE HE LEFT HIS BARK, AND THERE BRAVELY
CAPTURE A SPANISH SCHOONER.

NEARLY a month passed away since the evening on which
I listened to the story of Foul-Weather Don, and no
ship had yet passed within a dozen miles of the mouth of
the bay. So all hands began to grow very impatient,
and divers schemes were proposed, such as shifting our
quarters to some other point of the coast, where we
might have better luck. It was then that I, for the first
time, called to mind the boat which I had left in the
creek, where I first landed on the island. Now, as I had
heard many stories of buccaneers putting to sea in boats
or canoes, and boarding and capturing Spanish vessels, it
occurred to me, that if we could get possession of the
Frenchman's skiff, we could divide our party between it
and the canoe, leaving ample room for the stowage of
provisions and water for a cruise. This scheme I im-

parted to Stout Jem, by whom it was received with approbation. We were nine in number, well armed, and therefore of quite sufficent force to capture any Spaniard, not a man of war, which we were likely to fall in with. It was therefore resolved that Le Picard, one of our Frenchmen, Blue Peter, and Nicky, should start, under my guidance, for the cove to the westward, and if we found the boat, should navigate her round the coast to the bay, where the rest of the party would be prepared with provisions and water, ready to stow on board, so that, in company with the canoe, we could put to sea at once. No time was lost in putting the scheme into execution. Meinheer, who knew something of sail-making, cut out a small square sail or lug, which we were to carry with us, and which would suit the boat, it being easy for us to cut and fashion a mast and yard after we had found her. We also carried a good-sized keg for water, and a small quantity of beef and cassava bread, trusting chiefly, however, to our guns for our subsistence.

We set out by moonlight, intending to sleep during the heat of the day; and after an hour's trudge through the wet grass and bushes, which were quite drenched with the copious dews, passed the spot where lay the Buccaneers who had been hanged by the Spaniards. Truly our poor comrades slept in a tranquil resting-place —a spot of greenest grass, with feathery palms overhead, bending and rustling in the night wind. We stopped to rest, when the sun rose, until the sea-breeze should set in, watching its coming from beneath a thick mango-tree, whence we could look down upon the blue sea beneath. After the land-breeze flickered and failed, there was a pause, during which the sun shone with blistering power. Then, far off, on the glassy surface of the sea, came the dark belt of roughened water, streaked with white, which proclaims the daily return of the brisk north-westerly trade, and in half an hour more, it was whistling through the bushes in half a gale of wind. We dined this day by the little runnel where I had killed the duck, and then travelled until sunset, when we encamped

in our blankets, well worn out by our long day's march.
The journey to the cove was fatiguing, but performed
without any particular adventure. We sometimes saw
wild cattle, and heard the cry of wild dogs, and I observed,
when we got glimpses of the sea, numerous great brown
pelicans, flapping heavily over the water, somewhat like
the cranes on our own coasts, and often diving down with
a splash into the sea after the fish, which they mark from
a great height. In the afternoon of the second day, I
reckoned that we could not be far from the cove, but the
exact spot was difficult to hit, as the general appearance
of the coast hereabouts was very similar, and the tangled
growth of underwood prevented us from always keeping
so close to the edge of the sea-cliff as we otherwise should
have done. We had trudged along all the afternoon,
keeping a sharp look-out, and sometimes forcing our way
with our great knives through the creepers and brushwood, so as to be able to gaze down the iron-bound sea
wall to where the great driving swells were rising and
sinking upon the rock, and foaming furiously over every
projecting peak and pinnacle of stone; when, having
stopped to hold a consultation—for I was now becoming
very fearful that we had overshot our mark—we all suddenly heard the report of a musket or fowling-piece, fired
not far off. This terribly disconcerted us, for we knew
that the cove could not be distant, and we feared that the
secret of its existence was not known to me alone. However, we withdrew into the thicket, where we could not
well be discovered, and lay close. In the course of the
next hour, we heard three shots fired from different points
around us, and discoursed eagerly as to whether they
were probably Buccaneers, or Spaniards who were hunting in the neighbourhood. At all events, we now
despaired of recovering the boat, inasmuch as the great
chance was that the hunters had landed in my cove, as
I called it, and would, of course, appropriate the skiff, if
she still lay there, to their own purposes.

While we were talking lowly among ourselves, Blue
Peter, the Mosquito-man, suddenly started up on his

knees, and told us to listen. We did so, very intently, and presently heard a rustling and a snapping of dry twigs in the wood, but although we looked with all our eyes, we could see nothing.

'Tush!' says Nicky; 'you are a fool, Peter! and take a wild pig for a Spaniard.'

But the Indian seized his piece, cocked it, and suddenly levelling it, fired, before we could prevent him.

'Hush!' quoth he, very earnestly—'hush! and we will be safe.'

'Safe!' said Nicky. 'Why, if they are Spaniards, they will be down upon us in a twinkling.'

'No,' replied the Mosquito-man — 'no, no! They shooting all round: think my gun one of their camarados—eh?'

'The man is right,' said Le Picard. 'But what, in the name of the diable, have you fired at?'

'Me show you!' said Blue Peter; and he crawled into the underwood so circumspectly, that one scarcely heard a rustle, and presently, returning, flung the body of a huge dog among us.

'A Spanish blood-hound!' exclaimed Nicky; and we all recognized the fawn colour, with grim, black muzzle, and the great muscular limbs of the animal. But to put all question aside, the creature wore a leather collar, with a brass plate, on which was inscribed the name, 'Manuel G. Alcansas,' so it was quite clear, that we were surrounded by a hunting party of the enemy, and that, had it not been for the keen eye of the Indian, who observed the blood-hound, and shot it almost when it was in the act of giving tongue, we should probably have been massacred. We were all tolerably startled, and, after a hurried consultation, agreed that we might as well lie close where we were, as attempt to shift to less dangerous quarters, as by moving we might unwittingly run into the very jaws of death. At last we decided to climb up certain trees, the branches whereof interlaced, Blue Peter having first cut the throat of the dog, and scattered the blood copiously around, so that it would embarrass and destroy the scent of any other hound which might pass that way. He then flung the body up into the branches of a tree. Not long after we heard a voice hallooing loudly, as we supposed for the slain dog, and some other shots were fired at a distance. However, the sun sank and the stars shone down through the leaves, and we still remained unmolested. Making ourselves as comfortable as our position would permit, we munched our supper, of which, however, we could eat but little, for we suffered much from thirst. Fortunately, there was water enough in the keg to afford us a few mouthfuls a piece, but we were afraid to straggle abroad in search of more. With the grey dawn we were afoot, cautiously exploring the locality, and I had much ado to restrain a sudden burst of exclamation when I recognised the little hill, to the top of which I had climbed to look around, after scrambling up the precipitous banks of the cove. I now knew whereabouts we were, almost to a yard, and carefully guiding the rest, and taking great heed to make no noise, we made our way to the top of the very scaur or ravine, up which I had crept from the water. It was not easy, however, to make out whether the cove was empty, for the morning was yet dim and grey, and the trees grew thick below. We proceeded, however, moving in single file along the edge of the rock, which, as the reader remembers, was thickly covered with wood, such as bushes and parasitical plants, with great trees growing out of the rifts and cracks in the cliff, and bending over the water so that the branches of those on both sides interlacing, quite canopied the still deep sea beneath. As we clambered on by the edge of the precipice, a sound suddenly struck my ear with which I was too well acquainted to be easily deceived—it was the flap of canvas. Nicky heard it as well as myself, and we all paused. The land wind was just beginning to die out, and only came in heavy dank puffs down from the hills. We waited for the next gust; it shook the dew from the branches in a great sparkling shower, and gave a great rustle, as it were, down the ravine, in the middle of which, we again heard the

flap of canvas, and a rattle as of reef points against a sail.
Being guided by the sound, we proceeded a few paces
onwards, and then coming to a comparatively clear bit of
ground, we crawled upon our bellies to the edge of the
cliff, and through the trees and boughs saw a small vessel
with two masts, of the class called schooners, beneath.
She was moored in the very centre of the cove, very
snugly, being made fast by four hawsers, two a-head and
two astern, to the trunks of trees growing near the water
on either bank.    She had two boats in the water, floating
by her main chains, and one of them I immediately recognised to be the object of our journey.    Here, then, was
the vessel to whom the hunters, whose guns we had
heard, evidently belonged : and, indeed, without other
evidence, Nicky and Le Picard knew enough about the
fashion of those seas to be sure that the schooner was
Spanish built, she being, possibly, a fishing vessel from
Cuba, although what she did on the coast here, we could
not well imagine.    The question now, however, was how
we were to act ?    Thinking themselves, no doubt, in
security, there was not a single man awake upon deck ;
but several stout fellows were lying asleep under canvas
and tarpaulins upon the forecastle.    Presently, after we
had gazed our fill upon the schooner, Nicky asked our
opinion as to whether it would be possible to clamber
down to the water's edge, and make off with both boats
before the crew awoke.    But Le Picard thought the risk
too great.    Besides, he argued, when they miss the boats,
they can chase us out to sea in the schooner, where we
would infallibly be taken.    While they were talking, I
was turning over another plan in my own mind.

'Instead of taking the boats,' quoth I, 'why should we
not take the ship ?'

At this they all started, and reminded me that we
were but four men, whereas the Spaniards might well be
a dozen ; and they had dogs, too, fierce bloodhounds, of
which Le Picard, in particular, professed a great horror.

'Look you,' quoth I, 'this is my plan.    Yesterday the
Spaniards were hunting ashore, and to-day it is very like

that they will renew their pastime, leaving, perhaps, only
one man, or perhaps not even that to take charge of the
schooner; for you see that she is moored very safely, and
with her bows pointing down the creek so as to be ready
for a start. Now, look at her rigging; see, her jib can
be hoisted in a moment, and her fore and mainsails can
be set merely by letting go the brails, and running aft
the sheets; for you observe that the gaffs are already
hoisted, therefore the schooner is ready for sea. Now I
know, in a general manner, the direction of the cove
below. It runs for a little way parallel to the coast, and
then turns to the right, and so opens up into the sea.
What is there to prevent us boarding the schooner when
she is left almost, if not quite, undefended, and so carrying her away?'

They all applauded this design, and the more we
talked of it the better it seemed to be. The schooner
was a trim-looking vessel, such as the Spaniards can
build very well, and we judged from her shape that she
was exceeding fast as well as easy to manage. Besides,
the greater length of the cove running westward, what
puffs of sea-breeze traversed it would be in our favour,
and although there would necessarily be some risk when
we had passed the elbow, and came to get the ship out in
face of the swell, yet we determined at all events to
make the experiment. Nothing venture nothing have,
so we shook hands gaily, and thanked our stars for such
a slice of good luck.

As in many other adventures, the first and most difficult duty which we had to perform was to wait, so we
ensconced ourselves in thick bushes, where we could see
without being easily discerned, and watched the Spaniards
as keenly as hawks do larks. The sun was above the
horizon about half-an-hour, when a man issued from the
cabin, and tapped the deck loudly with a handspike. At
this summons the sluggards on the forecastle began to
stir themselves, and to crawl forth, one by one, yawning
from under the sails, and presently three or four bloodhounds, who seemed to have been sleeping among them,

came whining and stretching themselves from their warm
nests. The man who had wakened the rest, then went
round the schooner, and appeared to examine the state
of the moorings. The aspect of things seemed to satisfy
him, for he went below, and presently the crew had their
breakfast, which they ate on deck—a couple of bowls of
cocoa, or some such beverage, being carried aft to the
cabin. Soon after this, we observed, with great delight,
a number of muskets and pistols brought on deck, at the
sight of which, the grim bloodhounds yelped and bayed.
The captain, as we called him then, appeared again; and
after a long discourse, carried on with a great deal of
gesticulation, the whole crew gathering round and hand-
ling the arms, the bloodhounds were fed, and the skiff—
my skiff—hauled alongside, no doubt to convey the
hunters on shore. The captain then seemed to be giving
orders to one of the crew, a stout fellow, who wore a
great striped woollen cap and had a long unsheathed
knife in his girdle, and then the whole party, excepting
the fellow with the knife and cap, tumbled into the
boat, the bloodhounds leaping in along with them, and
rowed towards the extreme head of the creek. The
Spaniards numbered about a dozen, without including a
boy whom they had with them, and of course weighed
down the skiff until her gunwale was almost at the
water's edge. We were for a little time in some
perturbation, lest they should chance to come our way.
We heard them shouting, and laughing, and crashing
through the boughs, as they made their way up the steep
banks of the creek, and then the boat came floating down
again to the schooner, with the boy paddling her. Meantime, the man with the striped cap had disappeared in a
little cook-house or caboose, from the funnel of which a
smoke began to rise; and the boy, having made fast the
boat, went aft to the cabin, and presently returned with
the bowls, which we had seen carried thither, empty.
Now, as we had seen but one man come out of this cabin,
and as breakfast had been served there for two, we considered that there were three persons left in charge of

the ship, but that one of these was probably sick or disabled. While we were making these observations, the reader may be sure that we also listened attentively, in order to find out in what direction the hunting party had proceeded; and presently, hearing shouts and the reports of guns very faintly, and gradually becoming more so, until they were no longer audible, we congratulated ourselves that the hunters were out of the way, and that so far, our task would be easy.

The next point was, how to get on board the schooner so suddenly and so quietly as to leave those in charge of her no opportunity of giving an alarm. First we thought of swimming, but Le Picard was not skilful at this exercise; and, besides, we saw the backs and snouts of several caymans, moving about in the water. Then Nicky proposed to swing ourselves aboard, by means of the warps, fixed to the trees; but on close examination, we found the banks so precipitous, that it would be very difficult to make our way to the ropes, without giving an alarm. We were thus in considerable perplexity, fearing our scheme would miscarry in the very outset, when I observed a means whereby we might, although at some risk, accomplish our end. I have said that the cove or creek was so narrow that the branches of the great trees, growing in the refts of the rock on either side, met and interlaced, and from these branches hung perpendicularly, like great ropes, many long tendrils or withes, very tough and strong. Now, as it chanced, one of these depending from a stout branch, swung close by the foretop-mast head of the schooner, dangling indeed to the cross-trees. I pointed this out to my comrades, and they all agreed that it would be very possible to clamber out upon the bough, and slide down the withe into the rigging; but that the deck must be clear when we made the attempt, otherwise we could not fail of being discovered. It was fortunate, therefore, that the man with the striped cap continued in the cook-house, where we heard him clattering amongst pots and pans, and concluded that he was preparing a meal for the men ashore. But,

H

as Nicky said, when one cooks a dinner, one never knows who may eat it. The boy remained about the deck for some time, but at length went into the cabin, and, staying there, we concluded to make the venture. Fastening our guns across our shoulders, we again shook hands, and vowed to stand by each other to the death. Then we crept cautiously along, until we came to the tree, from which sprang the great branch, which we looked to be the first stage of our journey to the schooner's deck. This tree grew about a fathom beneath the edge of the rock, but it was easy to swing ourselves down to it, by the matted vegetation, which clung to the face of the stone. Then, one after another, we crawled out upon the bough, which shook a little, but bore us bravely. The schooner was now right below, and not a living thing stirring on her decks. I was the first man, and Nicky was at my heels. The Indian came next, and the Frenchman brought up the rear. All of us whites being sailors, the feat was not difficult; and as for the Mosquito man, he could climb like a cat. Having satisfied myself that the withe was well attached to the bough, I first twined my legs round the former, and then grasping it, slid easily down, until my feet touched the cross-trees of the Spanish schooner, and in a moment my comrades were clustering around me, no alarm being as yet excited. After pausing a moment, to get firm grips of the stays, I gave the word, and the whole four slid like lightning down the ropes, hand over hand, as sailors say, and came with a great bounce upon deck together. Le Picard instantly leaped to the cook-house, and the Spaniard coming out at the same moment, the Frenchman dealt him a blow with the butt-end of a heavy pistol, which flung him backwards, quite stunned upon the deck, while Nicky and I ran to the cabin, meeting at the threshold, the boy, and a comely woman, very dark, and with the blackest eyes I ever saw, who directly set up a great shriek of dismay.

But Nicky and I, pointing to the cabin and drawing forth pistols, made them understand that they must go below and be silent, as they valued their lives. The boy slunk back directly, and the woman turned to a livid paleness, and, swooning away, would have fallen down the ladder, but we supported her and laid her on the cabin floor ; then, directly running on deck, we shut down the hatch. All this hardly occupied a moment ; and, seeing Le Picard and Blue Peter cutting the warps forward, we drew our knives, and, working with good will, soon severed the tough piles of hemp, aft, and the schooner was unmoored. We waited a moment with great impatience, to see if she would drift, but, remaining stationary, we ran up the jib, and slackened the brails of the mainsail, so as, without actually setting the sail, to expose a good breadth of canvas, but it hung idly; the sea breeze had not yet set in, or if it had it did not reach us in the depths of the creek. We therefore flung a long line into the lightest of the two boats alongside, and Blue Peter and Nicky leaping into it, pulled with all their strength for the elbow at which the creek tended seawards, and made the line fast to a tree there, while Le Picard and I hauled upon the warp, and soon saw that the schooner was obeying the impulse thus given to her, and slowly moving through the water. In a twinkling, our comrades leaped on board again, and added their strength to ours, all of us working with clenched teeth and breathless eagerness. Just then, turning to look at the wounded Spaniard, who was sprawling upon the deck, I felt a breath of cool air on my face, the jib-sheet rattled, the light canvas swelled out, and in a moment the mainsail moved out of its sleepy folds, and the warp upon which we were hauling slackened. The schooner felt the puff, and I ran aft and took the helm, steering her in close by the starboard shore, which, when we turned seawards, would be the weather side of the cove. The mingled trees and rocks seemed to glide away from us. I looked over the side, and saw the bubbles rippling in the transparent water ; and as I lifted my head again, I started with delight to feel the first heaving of the schooner, as she began to meet the lazy

swell. The elbow, or turn of the creek, was not more
than the length of the schooner ahead of us, and my
three comrades all ran to the bows to watch the depth of
water, and shouted that we might graze the rocks.
Therefore I ported my helm, so as to send the vessel
close in, and just as we slowly opened the corner I put
the tiller hard down, and being fortunately a very handy
craft for steering, she gradually swung round, and we all
uttered a shout together as we saw, at the end of a short
rocky passage, the open sea, streaked with the white bars
of breaking waves.  But we were not out yet: almost
immediately on rounding the point of the creek a gust of
the sea breeze struck us on the starboard bows, making
the jib rattle and flap like thunder, and directly the head
of the schooner fell off towards the rocks on the leeward
side.  The Frenchman exclaimed that we must take to the
boats after all, but Nicky answered him, " Yes—but only
to carry a warp to the rocks at the mouth of the creek !"
No sooner said than done.  Another line was flung into
the skiff, and Nicky and the Indian went with three strokes
to the weather extremity of the creek.  Here the surf was
beating violently, coming with great lashing surges round
the corner of the cliff, and causing the water to rise and
fall more than a fathom with every undulation of the sea.
Here was a jagged pinnacle of rock beaten by the waves,
which every now and then burst right above it ; over
this the Indian with great dexterity cast a loose hitch of
the line, while we on board, running to the schooner's
bows, hauled upon it as before.  It was lucky for us that
the sea-breeze only blew up the ravine in uncertain puffs,
and that the place was full of counter-currents, and
eddies of air, which first filled our sails one way and then
another, as we heaved and rolled upon the broken swells
which dashed from side to side of the channel.  We
worked at the warp like desperate men, as, indeed, we
were.  Every now and then a sudden toss of the water
would fling us back ; but then the counter reflection of the
seas from the opposite wall of rock would jerk us forward,
and we soon found that we were gradually making our

way towards the mouth of the cove, keeping so close to
the weather side, that every now and then the masts,
when flung over to starboard, rattled among the bushes
overhead, and sent down showers of leaves, which would
fly in uncertain whirls and dives amongst the rigging.
At last, the decisive moment came. In a minute we
would be hove upon the leeward entrance of the cove, or
be out clear at sea. I ran again to take the helm. Le
Picard and the Indian, running to the weather fore-
chains, gave a last surge upon the line by way of a launch.
The schooner's head plunged into the trough of the sea,
not a fathom from the rocks, and as she rose—her bows
drew beyond the shelter of the cove—the full blast of
the sea-breeze caught her jib—and her head swung gain
to leeward.

' Help her with the foresail, comrades !' I shouted.
They had anticipated me—the Indian letting go the
brails, and then helping the whites to draw aft the sheet.
The sail surged and flapped so as to shake the schooner
to her very keel, and the great sheet-block jerked madly
to and fro with bounds which would have dashed through
a strong wall. But still, though they could not yet
master the canvas, the schooner was not insensible to its
lifting power, and I felt her, as she rose with her broadside to a great clear sea, gather way, and start as it were
from under me. There was just a moment of terrible
suspense. The masts bent to leeward until their trucks
were within a couple of fathoms of the lee promontory.
You could almost leap on the great rough masses of wet
stone, which lay close a-beam, and then in a moment the
schooner rose to another sea, all three sails now bellying
to the wind, and once more hove clear of the land,
although I saw through the clear water a glimpse of reef
under our counter, which the keel must have scraped,
and although the head of the mainmast actually tore away
the projecting branch of a great prickly bush which was
waving and dancing in the wind.

We were drawing our first deep breath after our peril
when I heard a great shout above me, and starting round,

I saw between me and the sky the figure of a man standing with a gun upon the very verge of the precipice
which formed the line of coast.  He directly fired his
piece, and set up a loud outcry to his comrades, three or
four of whom directly joined him, and fired a volley at us
which did no damage.  So we jumped up on the taffrail
rail, and waving our hats, gave them a loud cheer, and
told them that if they wanted their schooner, they might
swim after us, and then we would consider the matter.
They made violent gestures, but the sea-breeze blowing
so freshly, carried back their voices, and we knew not
what they said.  Carrying on as we best could with our
ill-set sails, until we had made a good half mile offing, we
luffed the schooner up into the wind, and with some
trouble, got the canvas properly extended; then pulling
the helm hard down, we got the jib-sheet to windward,
and so lay to, dancing and surging merrily upon the sea.

And now we shook hands again, and embraced each
other cordially.  Here we stood on the deck of a fine
schooner—our own by lawful capture from our enemies—
and we thought of the surprise we would give our
comrades in the bay.  But the first thing to be settled
was the fate of our prisoners, and we determined very
unanimously that they must be put on board one of the
boats, and left to find their way to the shore, Nicky only
stipulating that if the lady should take a fancy to him,
she should be allowed to remain on board.  With some
laughing at this proposition, we opened the cabin door,
and called to our captives to come on deck, which they
did, pale and trembling, for they seemed to expect no
less than instant death.  Nicky would be gallant to the
lady, and to that end made her profound salutes, and
spoke some gibberish, which he said was very good
Spanish, for an expression of his admiration of her
charms; but she never ceased crying out for 'her husband
—her husband,' and begging, in the name of all the
saints, to be put ashore.  The boy, being more collected,
managed to inform us—I, with my scanty knowledge of
Spanish forming but a poor interpreter—that the schooner

was called Nostra Senora del Carmine—that she had come
to catch tortoise and to hunt wild cattle along the coast,
it being the opinion of the citizens of Havannah, to
which she belonged, that the late expedition had routed
out all the privateersmen and hunters on the northern
shore of Hispaniola.   We then directed our attention to
the man who had been acting as cook, and who, having
partially recovered from his blow, was sitting up and
looking very scared and foolish.   However, his wits—if
he had any—were still abroad, and we could not make
him understand any of our questions; only when he was
shown the boat with a couple of oars, and we pointed to
the shore, and made as though we would push him over
the side, he comprehended fast enough, and presently he
and the boy got into the skiff belonging to the ship, and
the lady, who had somewhat recovered her spirits, followed them, taking some clothing with her, and hiding
her face as much as she could in a black veil.   Although
the sea was rough, they had a good boat and a favourable
breeze, and we did not stand on our way until we saw
them fairly into the shelter of the cove.   Then we
shifted the helm, let go the weather jib-sheet, and so
began to plough our way to the eastward against wind
and sea.

## CHAPTER X.

### THEY RETURN WITH THE PRIZE TO THE MARMOUSETTES, AND NICKY HAMSTRING SHORTLY RELATES HIS HISTORY.

THE wind blowing steady, the ship was easy to manage,
so we speedily set to rummage our prize.   Going into
the hold, we found that she had little aboard save some
campeachy-wood and some cocoa-nuts, and a couple of
old brass guns, of about six pounds calibre, which seemed
to have been put there for ballast.   In the cabin was
a good store of powder and lead for casting bullets, which
was exceedingly valuable to us, and several long-barrelled
muskets in good condition.   The best part of the prize,

however, was her storeroom, as it contained a great
quantity of rope, canvas, and other things appertaining
to the use of a ship.   We also found a tool chest and a
medicine chest, both of which were very welcome to us.
In navigating the schooner, we, of course, divided ourselves into two watches—the larboard and the starboard
watch, Nicky and I having the one, and Le Picard and
the Indian the other.   We also reefed our sails so as to
have the ship snugger, and the better prepared for squalls
should any happen.   We made good progress that night
when the land-breeze blew, and hoped next day, by
evening, to observe the headlands of the Marmousettes.
Catching sight, however, soon after sunrise, of a sail close
in shore, and not wishing, in our weak condition, to be
overhauled, we stood away directly to sea, so that, by
noon, only the blue mountain ridges of Hispaniola were
visible.   In the afternoon we put about ship, and made
again for the land.   This long stretch caused us to lose
much time, so that we had another night's navigation
before us ere we could work up to our bay.   Nicky and
I had the midwatch.   It was a glorious night.   We were
running five or six knots, with the cool land-breeze
sighing in our sails.   The heaven was one vault of stars,
and, lying on deck wrapped up in folds of old canvas,
while Nicky held the tiller beside me, I fixed my gaze
upon the Southern Cross, that beautiful cluster of stars
which shines only in the tropics, and which, appearing in
the solemn and thoughtful night, always caused me to
feel that I was in a strange part of the world, even more
than the curious animals, and plants, and men, which one
sees daily and ordinarily about one, when abroad.   And
yet, beautiful as the constellation was, methought it had
less charms than the Plough, and the bright belt of Orion
circling about the polar star, which I used to gaze upon
in the long night-watches at home.   As I thought of
these, I thought of the old fisher-boat tossing upon the
wild bay of St. Andrew's, or lying stilly at her grapnel in
the mouth of the Baiwearie burn, while my mother and I
sat with our palms mending nets upon the sand-hill in

the sun. I think I would have been a great day-dreamer
had I not led such a stirring life as kept my muscles
busier than my brain; but on these quiet clear nights,
aboard ship, when all was still, save the steady murmur of
the wind, and the monotonous plunge of the vessel, as
she breasted the ever-rolling seas—in these nights there
is a witchery upon me, and I love to let my fancy carry
me away, and surround me with old faces and old times.
So now, being in this mood, I dreamed and dreamed with
my eyes open, persuading myself that I was on board the
Jean Livingstone again, and that we were jogging along
the rocky coast of Forfar, until I actually started up,
and looking at the shore to windward, thought that I
could discover in the shimmer of the moon the tall white
rock we called the Lady of Arbroath.

'Nicky,' says I, being in this mood, 'do you ever
think of home?'

'That do I,' he responded, 'and hug myself that I am
not there.'

'But is there no old place,' quoth I—'no old face you
would wish to look on again?'

'Not a bit of it,' he replied, 'I am too happy here.
We have a good ship, we have staunch comrades, we have
prospect of wresting plenty of doubloons and pieces of
eight from those rascally Spaniards. We have Jamaica,
with all its taverns, and its dice, and its wenches, to help
us to spend them; and besides all these, why, we have at
this moment a steady land-breeze, which is sending us
along at five knots, and a glass of good brandy, after a
good supper, to keep out the marsh fever. What more
can any man want?'

'Perhaps,' quoth I, 'you were not happy at home?'

'You have hit it there,' replied my comrade. 'No.
My father was a stout king's man—why he was so, I
know not, for I am sure the king never did much for
him. But poor dad got what brains he had knocked out
at Naseby, and some time after my mother married old
Ephraim Crotch, as bitter a Puritan as ever wore cropped
hair and ass's ears. Now I, being a youth of spirit, did

in no ways take to my father-in-law—on the contrary.
Well, I mocked his slang, and mimicked his snuffle.
Many a time did he lay his staff across these shoulders—
augh! they ache even now! The old frump—I hate the
thought of him!—often hath he turned me out of doors,
to sleep in the fields. Then have I peeped in at the
lattice, and seen old square-toes snug in the chimney
ingle. "Ha!" thought I, "my father's bones would rattle
in their grave could he but look in, and see you in his old
oaken chair, whelp of the Barebones breed!" So you
may believe that our house was a pretty place for
bickering. I loved all that my stepfather hated. He
said that music was devil's screeching—ergo, I played the
viol and the tabor till they were broken on my head. He
denounced all diversion, swore that rope-dancing was a
subtle device of the evil one, and that the bowling-alley
was the highway to hell—ergo, did I frequent fairs and
jovial meetings, where the bowls trundled, and wrestled
many a fall, and grinned through many a horse collar. I
promise thee, Will, I was not made for a Puritan, and so,
at length, they having, by an ordinance of old Noll,
hewed down our Maypole, I e'en laid a good thick splinter
thereof across the back of my reverend stepfather, and
marched from Cornwall for ever and a day.'

'To London, no doubt?' quoth I.

'Even so,' he said, 'but there I found neither gold
nor silver in the streets, and I lived for some months a
very unedifying vagabond sort of life, knees and elbows
being generally very bare, and stomach generally very
hungry. At length, being hard driven, I e'en enlisted,
though it went hard against my conscience, under Old
Noll. Such drilling, such fighting, and such psalm-
singing. The sergeant's ratan was never off our
shoulders, except when he was exhorting us in the pulpit,
or standing on a horseblock, calling the royalists sons of
Agag. So, this going on for some time, and I trying in
vain to become a saint, for which I had not sufficient bad
qualities, I e'en took leave to desert; and because the
land was too hot to hold me, I became a mariner and

went to sea. But at sea, Will, I saw one great sight, I saw the king land on the beach of Dover, and having long observed that seasons of rejoicing are seasons of hospitality, I treated my ship as I had done my regiment, and followed the royal train up to London. That was indeed a march. All the country flocked to the road to see the king come back to his own again. It was nothing but eating and drinking, and up caps, "Huzza for King Charles, and to the devil with the Rump!" Well, on Blackheath, near London, was drawn up my own old regiment. 'Gad, the sun was on my side of the hedge now, for there stood our sergeant as grim as Beelzebub in the sulks, and I having many pottles of wine in me, gave a tug to his grizzled moustache, and asked what he thought of me for a son of Agag now. I warrant you Old Ironside used his halberd with very little discretion by way of reply, and so I came away with a bloody cockscomb. But all was one for that. Wine was a great balm, and I applied it plenteously; being indeed in a very loyal state of drunkenness for certain days, I know not how many, until, having a little recovered, I found myself in the filthy hold of a ship with other ragamuffins; some sober and weeping, some drunk and singing, and some ill with the small-pox and jail fever, raving and dying. Then I presently understood that all this goodly company was bound on a voyage to the plantations in Barbadoes—we having, it seems, signed articles to that effect, in consideration of certain small sums of money, which they told us we had received, and spent in drink very jovially, and as became stout-hearted fellows. I made a bold attempt to escape by knocking down the sentry at the hatchway, but all I gained by the proceeding was a pair of very heavy irons, which were put on near the Tower, and which were not knocked off until we were three days' sail from Barbadoes. There I landed, and, being duly sold, was set to labour with sundry other companions in misfortune amongst the sugar-canes. In a few months I was one of a very few survivors, but being very weak and sickly from two fevers which I had, I was not very sharply looked after, and so I managed, without much difficulty, to smuggle myself on board a small bark bound for Jamaica, where I joined the " Brethren of the Coast," and have lived a reasonably jolly life ever since.'

This was Nicky's story, and an adventurous one it was. While I was thinking of it, he began again—

'No, no—no England for me, while there are Spaniards to fight, good ships to sail in, and stout fellows to drink with in these bright Indian seas.' And therewith, having taken a good draught of brandy, he burst out singing:

'Take comfort, pretty Margery, and swab away your tears,
Your sweetheart, Tom, has sailed among the gallant Buccaneers,
So dry your eyes, my Margery, your Tom is true and bold,
And he'll come again to see you, lass, with glory and with gold,
For his comrades are the stoutest and the bravest in the land,
And there's ne'er a Don came out of Spain will meet them hand to hand.

So-ho! for pike and sabre cut, and balls about your ears,
'Tis little he must care for these, would join the Buccaneers!

'The man who lies at home at ease, a craven heart has he,
While there's wild boars on the hills to hunt, and Spaniards on the sea;
So look alive my stately Don, for spite your thundering guns,
Your shining gold we'll make our own, and eke your pretty nuns.
We'll spend the first, and love the last, and when we tire ashore,
'Tis but another cruise my boys, and back we come with more.

So-ho! for pike and sabre cut, and balls about your ears,
'Tis little he must care for these, would join the Buccaneers!'

'Silence, silence, Nicky!' said I, laughing; 'you will awaken the watch below.'

'So be it,' quoth he; 'to listen to such a song is better than sleep. 'Tis a rare good one, and a rare fellow made it in Tortugas, one night when we were melting the last pieces of eight remaining after a cruise on shore. But you put me out. Hear the last verse—

What though to peace in Europe, the Dons and we incline,
The treaty seldom has much force—to the south'ard of the line.
Here's wassailing and fighting, the merriest of lives,
With staunch and jovial comrades, with sweethearts and with wives.

We sweep the green savannahs, we storm the Spanish walls,
And we're kings upon the water, by the grace of cannon balls.

Then ho! for pike and sabre cut, and bullets round your ears,
'Tis little he must care for these, would head the Buccaneers!'

Next morning, after being becalmed as usual in the interval between the land breeze and the regular trade wind, we kept pretty close in with the coast, looking anxiously for our bay, and we even feared that we had overshot our mark; but about noon the well-known rocks became visible, and presently thereafter we dashed up the Marmousettes, wondering what our comrades would take us for. There was no English flag aboard; but thinking that the folks ashore would recognise the cut of the boat sail which we carried along with us, we hoisted that to the mainmast head, and with this strange standard flying approached the beach. We could see no change in the bay, and hoped to find our friends all well. Presently, as we were rounding a wooded point, and just opening the huts, a musket was fired ashore among the trees, and we heard the loud, hoarse voice of Meinheer shouting that a strange ship was in the bay. At this moment, doubling the little cape I speak of, and furling up our sails as well as we could, we descried the whole of our party running about in great commotion upon the beach, shouting to each other, loading their pieces, and hammering their flints. Thereon, we all gave a great cheer together, and showed ourselves conspicuously above the bulwarks; on which, we being immediately recognised, they answered our cheer with loud exclamations, and, running to the canoe, came alongside just as our anchor fell three fathoms deep upon the white sand.

'What ship is this?' exclaimed Stout Jem, who was the first to leap upon deck.

'She was the schooner Nostra Senora del Carmine,' I replied; 'but now she is a bold privateer, and will, I hope, never bear a Spanish name again.

Then we related all the particulars of the schooner's capture, and informed our comrades what a clever sea-boat she was, and how we thought that, were she well manned, we could not have a more proper ship for our purpose. And then we moored the schooner carefully, and Stout Jem inspected her both below and aloft very minutely, being exceedingly well pleased at the quantity of stores which were on board, and also at the smart appearance and weatherly look of our prize. So all the company being in high spirits, we set to work at once to victual the schooner, having ample supplies of provisions at hand, and into her we of course transferred what clothes and property of the kind we had saved from the attack upon the first settlement; and having finished our task by nightfall, the whole party embarked, and we towed the schooner to the middle of the bay, where we anchored, and Stout Jem then proclaimed that he meant to hold a grand sailing council upon deck. This is a ceremony always in use amongst the buccaneers, and at these consultations they settle the articles of the voyage, and assign to every man what his share shall be of the total amount of booty which may be captured.

## CHAPTER XI.

THE BUCCANEERS PRESENTLY SET SAIL IN THE SCHOONER FOR JAMAICA, WITH A RELATION OF THE EVENTS WHICH HAPPENED THERE.

BEHOLD us, then, seated in great conclave under an awning, which it was Stout Jem's first precaution to have spread, as, the berths in the schooner being close and stifling, we desired to sleep in the open air. In such a case, the stretching of an awning preserves a crew from the fall of the unwholesome dews, and from the rays of. the moon, which, mild and beautiful as they are, yet, by some hidden power, swell and distort the features of such as sleep with their faces unprotected from the baneful light. A sea-box put upon deck served as a table, and we sat on chests and coils of rope round it. The night was beautiful and serene. The land-breeze just murmured aloft, the sleeping water of the bay was dotted with the twinkling images of the stars, and all

around the dusky hills flung their forest ridges high into
the balmy air—wreaths of mist and vapour, like broad
white ribbons, showing where the rich alluvial valleys
and ravines clove the sweep of the wooded uplands.

Two or three lanterns stood upon the chest, glimmering on the pans and pipkins wherein we held our punch,
and the fiery red sparks beneath every man's face gave
note that we all loved to fortify our frames against night
air by wholesome pipes and tobacco. So, presently,
Stout Jem addressed us pretty nearly in this fashion :

'Well, mates, we sit on the deck of our own craft,
lawfully won from those misbegotten Spaniards, by four
brave men of our own party. Now, as the capture was
made before we are afloat, the vessel, by the laws of the
coast, belongs to our comrades who took her, and of
course they must be paid duly, when the prize-money
comes to be overhauled. Meantime, the question is,
shall we straightway go to sea ?'

On this we all shouted—'Yes, yes ; a cruize, a cruize!'

'Good,' continued Stout Jem, 'I say, with you, a
cruize. That being settled, there are other matters to
consider. Here are no guns, either calivers, arquebusses,
culverins, or falconets. To make booty of the rich
Spanish galleons without cannon, is like trying to eat a
lump of bull-beef without teeth. The two brass guns
below may do in their way. For these we have, however,
no carriages ; and besides, we want a piece of far heavier
metal. Another matter is, that on board here we have
neither a surgeon nor a carpenter, although both we and
our ship are likely to meet with plenty of hard knocks ;
and furthermore, to make a cruize successful—and as the
old falconers were wont to say—to fly at game of the
first head, we must have more men. Jack Spaniard does
not always leave his ships defenceless, and his galleons
have rows of teeth which bite sharply. My counsel
therefore is, that we stand for Port Royal in Jamaica.
On the way we may chance upon a something worth
picking up, and once arrived there, we can fit out in
good style, and take on board what men we please.

Besides, there we can have a French commission, or
Letter of Marque, the French being now at war with the
Spanish.   I know that the Dons have hung many of our
brave comrades with their commissions about their necks,
but still I approve of doing all things regularly and in
order.   Now, then, you have heard my advice—what do
you say to it?'

We replied, with great acclamations, that he had
spoken very justly ; that we had all confidence in his
counsels, and that we created him captain of the expedition. After some further discussion, I was named quarter-
master, I being a more experienced sailor than many
older men ; and to Stout Jem, or, as we now called him,
Captain Jem, was given the charge of the larboard, and
to me the charge of the starboard watch.   This done, we
re-christened the schooner—dashing a bottle of spirits
upon her bows—and calling her the ' Will-o'-the-Wisp.'
We lay quietly at anchor that night, and weighing before
dawn, the last of the land-wind carried us clear of the
bay, and when the sea-breeze struck us next morning,
we up helm, veered away the sheets, and stood away
along the coast bound for Jamaica.

How vast is the difference between beating to windward in a small vessel against a rough sea, and flying
gaily on before wind and waves! Cape and headland,
and bay and creek, appeared and disappeared, as the
nimble Will-o'-the-Wisp went bounding on, kicked as
it were by every foaming sea which rolled behind her.
You may be sure that we kept a good look-out for
the former owners of the schooner, as we ran just past
the entrance to the cove, but no human form could we
descry among the rocks and woods.   Not very far to
leeward, we however observed a boat, with a small
clumsy sail, making her way along the coast ; and, approaching a little nearer, I soon guessed that she was
the boat of the Spaniards, which we had given up to
them, and that they were probably risking the chances
of a run to Cuba.   To satisfy our curiosity, however, we
kept slightly away and very soon overhauled the little

craft. She had but four men in her, including he who seemed to have been the captain, and the woman. Their sail was a clumsy thing, made of hides and scraps of canvas, and useless for any other purpose than to drive before the wind. As we approached them, the captain got up and hailed us very vehemently in Spanish. The purport of his discourse, as I gathered it, being whether, after robbing him of his ship, we meant to run down and sink the boat. A movement of the tiller soon made him easy on that point, and he sat down doggedly, with his teeth clenched, scowling at us. The woman clung to him convulsively, and the three men lay stretched in the bottom of the boat, only showing their tangled hair and black eyes above the gunwale. Captain Jem, who as he was a brave man, was a kind one, told me to ask whether they needed any food or water, which I did; but the Spaniard only waved his hand impatiently, muttered somewhat about ' *Perros Inglesos,*' English dogs; and one or two of the men clenched their fists at us over the side of the boat. All this, however, we could well afford to take in good humour.

'Well,' quoth Captain Jem, 'if they are well victualled, so are we; and if they won't say aught to us, we have little that I know of to say to them. So, cast loose your brails, my sons, and let's be jogging.'

The sails, which had been partially furled, were accordingly reset, and in half an hour the boat was a speck on the horizon to windward. We ran through the strait which separates Hispaniola from Tortugas, near enough to the latter coast to see that there were long stretches of flat rich land washed by the sea, and high mountains beyond. We also saw a great many sails of small boats and barks coasting along, and innumerable canoes fishing. That same night we passed the north-eastern part of Hispaniola, and, directing our course towards the south-east, sailed straight for Jamaica. In the afternoon of the next day we sighted at a great distance the longest outlying point of Hispaniola, and in twenty-four hours thereafter, descried Cape Morant, in Jamaica; and coast

I

ing along the southern shore, which lies hereabouts, very
rich and flat, with great peaks, called the Blue Mountains, in the distance, we descried at nightfall the glimmer of distant lights, which we knew to be those of Port
Royal. Here is the principal harbour in the island—a
very commodious and safe one—formed by a deep indentation in the land, like a gulf, and sheltered by a long
spit or bank of sand, called the Palisades, on which
the surf beats vehemently, while within the water is
like a mill-pond. There is but one entrance, and
that well fortified; and the town of Port Royal is built
just beyond the inlet or passage from the sea. Although
it was near midnight when we anchored outside, resolving not to enter until we had daylight to help our pilot,
a canoe presently came alongside of us, manned by a
couple of negroes, who were fishermen and pilots, and
who offered us abundance of fish and fruit very cheap.
These men managed their canoe like thorough seamen,
and one of them we retained to take us in as soon as the
sea-breeze should blow next morning.

This fellow wore coarse canvas trousers, a striped shirt,
and a great straw hat, and grinned and showed his white
teeth, and rolled his eyes, and clattered in his gibberish
fashion to all on board.

'Oh, me de best pilot in all Port Royal,' he would
say; 'take in a king's ship, big enough to put dis
schooner in him pocket, and never rub him keel. No,
no, massa, Dick Canoe,' for so he called himself, 'de
best pilot in all de island, and bery much esteem and
respect by all de merchants, officers, and gentlemen privateers.'

On asking him for news, he told us that many privateers were in the harbour, and that their crews having had reasonably good luck in an expedition to the
main, were spending their money in the usual fashion
ashore; information which pleased us the more, as we
would probably have our pick and choice of good men.
So next day we ran in among very intricate sand-banks,
which lie at the mouth of the harbour, and presently

saw the houses of Port Royal, with hundreds of artificers labouring to construct forts and bastions and such works around them, disposed so as to command the entrance to the harbour completely. Inside, in the smooth water, rode many brave merchant ships and certain smaller barks, which, I believe, had often brought destruction upon the Spanish towns of the main; but these last seemed empty, except a negro or two left in charge of them, all hands being carousing on shore. We dropped our anchor in a suitable place, and cast lots who should remain on board to take charge of the schooner, while the rest went into the town. The die fell upon Black Diamond, and the Mosquito men stayed on board voluntarily, intending, however, to put off in a canoe during the day to strike fish upon the sand-banks and the little islands near the Palisades. Captain Jem, Nicky, and myself went ashore in the pilot's canoe, meaning to make the necessary arrangements for the further prosecution of our voyage. We found Port Royal very bustling and busy. As I have said, the people were occupied in building great fortifications, under the direction of officers in the English uniform, some of the workmen being, as we heard, criminals, others negro slaves, and the rest free labourers, either white or black. On the beach, great crowds of negroes were rolling down casks to the water's edge, or along the wharfs, where the boats of the ships in the harbour were awaiting them; these labourers being generally naked except a pair of light drawers and a tattered shirt, and shouting, and chattering, and laughing to each other, while the white drivers, who walked amongst them with great broad-brimmed hats, very often interrupted their conversations with a smart crack of the whip, and a harsh order to labour on. Passing through these busy crowds, and amongst great heaps of goods, such as bales and casks just landed from England, and masses of shipping stores, over which grave merchants and supercargoes were busy with pen and ink, comparing invoices, bills of lading, and what not, and wrangling about qualities and freights, we emerged among the houses of the town, which were in general mean, and but of one story, built indeed commonly of wood, with shingle roofs, which rattled in the sea-breeze, and often sheltered by orange trees covered at once with fruit and bright flowers, and mangoes with their heavy foliage, and tamarinds, with branching feathery leaves, and long waving pods.    The houses had great open casements and covered galleries, called jalousies, with pillars, round which many gaudy creeping plants clung.    Here there were great stores, with all manner of commodities, and there, vast taverns, from the open windows of which we could hear loud roaring songs in French and English, and a great clatter of glasses ; and now and then, when the noise somewhat lulled, the rattle of dice.    The streets, which were very narrow, dusty, and irregular, were crowded with groups of half-drunken seamen and their trulls, gangs of negroes carrying great baskets of fruit and vegetables on their heads down to the harbour, with planters upon horseback, who rode along scattering the crowd right and left, and bullock-carts, which creaked and rumbled by, laden with kegs of sugar or rum, and drawn by oxen, all slavering at the mouth, and seeming half dead with dust and heat.    Through these crowded and smothering streets, Captain Jem, who was our leader, pushed along with the air of a man who knew his business and could do it.    He was often stopped and accosted by his acquaintances, many of whom professed themselves surprised to see him, as they heard that he had been murdered by the Spaniards in Hispaniola.

'What! Stout Jem, still in the land of the living ?' said one man, a very tall personage, burnt almost black by the sun, wearing great moustaches, and having a hanger fixed to a broad leathern belt—' what! Stout Jem again!    Why, my lad, we drank a rousing glass to thy memory no later than the night before last, at Nance Finlayson's on the quay.    We heard that the Spaniards had sent thee from Hispaniola to a hotter place still.'

'No, no, Captain Archemboe,' quoth our commander ;

'they tried, but having failed, we mean to have our revenge.'

'What! and you have left the wild bulls and are for the sea again? It doth thee honour, man. Hunters are but gentlemen butchers after all. The sea, sir—the sea, with a tight ship, and tight lads for a crew, and reasonable good luck among the galleons—that, sir, is the field, and these be the chances for gentlemen! They tell me that Davis hath come in from the main after a very good cruise, so now I am bound shoreward to see my ancient friend, who, I warrant thee, will screw gold out of the Spaniards, though he squeeze them till it distil at each pore. I give you good day—I give you good day!'

And so, calling to an attendant negro, this formidable gentleman passed on. Captain Jem told us that his name was Crashaw, and that he had been a valiant buccaneer under Mansueldt, but was now retired from the sea, and very rich. He cultivated considerable plantations, and had shares in many privateers. Our object was, however, first to see a person of Captain Jem's acquaintance, who was an old man, a money-lender and usurer, and a sort of agent for many of the buccaneers, as it was necessary that we should obtain certain stores upon credit before setting out upon our voyage, and this old man was in use to serve privateers in such matters. Accordingly, we presently came to a long, rambling sort of house, in which was a great open store, full of goods of all kinds, while vast masses of ship furniture and implements, such as stones, anchors, boats, and the like, lay under sheds around. There were many seafaring people viewing the property, and chaffering with the clerks and workmen who sold the goods. But Captain Jem passing through them into the store, amid the bows and congratulations of many there, we followed him through a small door and sundry passages into a distant room, within which we heard a rustling of paper, and presently, Captain Jem pushing open the door, we found ourselves in the company of an aged man, with long white hair, a thin face, and very bright grey eyes, who was seated at a desk, he

wearing a dirty, greasy doublet, all ink-stains, and loose
pantouffles, or breeches, much too big for him. Upon
sight of Captain Jem, he got up hurriedly and shook
him very cordially by the hand, saying, like the other,
that he never thought to have seen him again, for that
the Spaniards were reported to have made but short
work of all the English and French hunters on the
northern coast of Hispaniola. Upon this Captain Jem
told him how we had captured a very fine Spanish vessel,
and designed to put to sea again directly; but that in
the meantime he must furnish us with sufficient stores
and ammunition, and so become a partner in the enterprise. The old man at first shook his head.

'Look ye,' said he, 'little is done now-a-days save by
fleets. My good friend Captain Morgan, a very brave
man, and wise in those things, ever recommends union.
The Spaniards' treasure-ships commonly sail in squadrons, and heavily armed; and their towns along the
coast are very securely guarded, so that there is usually
hard fighting before these be come at. However,' quoth
he, 'I have great confidence in you, Ezra Hoskins—or
Stout Jem, as I hear they call you—and provided your
crew be such as I approve of, why I will stand the risk of
loss in the venture, being well assured that you and your
men will do their best for me and for themselves.'

At this, Captain Jem re-assured the old gentleman
very warmly, and then it was settled that he should
come aboard the ship that evening, to see what might be
wanting, and how many guns we could stow. After
this he ordered refreshments of spirits and tobacco, and
while we were smoking, he called a young clerk, and
writing a short letter, gave it him, with instructions that
he was to carry it at once to the jailor of the town prison, who would thereupon bring Alonzo Peres before us.
The old man, observing that we looked inquiringly at
each other, told us that a vessel, in which he had no
mean share, being cruising in the Gulf of Darien, had
fallen in with and captured a Spanish Barco del Aviso,
or packet-boat, which had, however, as usual, thrown her

despatches overboard in a sealed leaden case. But the captain of this barco proving, when made a prisoner, a cowardly fellow who would reveal all he knew of the movements of the richly laden ships belonging to his countrymen, the English had kept this man a prisoner on board, while they dismissed his comrades in a piragua, intending to get all the information they could out of him.

'Therefore,' quoth our old gentleman, who I found was called Pratt—'therefore, we will have him here, and examine him. The bark which took him has gone to the Pearl Islands on the Mosquito shore, and perhaps he can give some information which may guide you on your cruise.'

So presently the Spaniard was brought in pinioned, and led by two men. He was a very big man, but with scowling and mean features ; and by his air and complexion, he seemed to have been lying weeping in the straw of his dungeon. On seeing us, he immediately began, in the Spanish language, to pray, in the name of all things holy, that we should dismiss him, and let him go back to the mainland to his daughter Paquitta, whom he loved very dearly, pitiably exclaiming that he was a poor man, who had been ruined ; still that he wished the English no harm, and would pray for them for ever, if they would only let him go.

But Pratt cut him short in his lamentings, and proceeded to ask, in Spanish, which he spoke very fluently, a great number of questions, as to the trade between Carthagena and Old Spain, and as to when certain richly-laden ships — the names whereof Pratt had at hand in a great register—would sail out of that port. To all this the Spaniard replied very amply and humbly, and said, in particular, that a large ship, in which was embarked a considerable quantity of pieces of eight, and silver plate to a much greater amount, but he could not say exactly how much, would probably be ready for sea, and put out in about two months' time. This ship carried, he informed us, a private venture, and would not have con-

voy. Moreover, she was old, and a very slow sailer, and
that the merchant who freighted her was the more confident that she would escape, inasmuch as it was reported
and believed in Carthagena, that all the buccaneers were
upon the point of joining their strength in Jamaica, and
landing about Porto Bello, with the intention of crossing
the isthmus, and making a descent upon Panama and
the shores of the South Sea. This account the traitor
confirmed with abundance of oaths, calling upon us to
believe him the more, inasmuch as, quoth he, ' I have
now no reason to tell you a lie ; I stand in your power,
and if you hear more certain news, which is likely, and
it contradict what I have said, why I am in your hands
to work your will on !' And with that the pitiful-
hearted creature began to sob and weep again. Truly, I
had never seen so small a soul in so big, lusty, and goodly
a body.

Having made his disclosures, Pratt told the Spaniard
that he should no more go to prison, but live there in his
house, and if all turned out to be true as he had stated,
that he would have his liberty, and, it might be, a reward
beside. So he being dismissed, we talked the thing over,
and determined to propose to the crew a cruise on the
Darien coast, and perhaps to look into the Gulf of
Venezuela. We then took leave of Mr. Pratt with many
courtesies, and returned towards the beach. On our way
hither, we heard a great tumult and clamour, and, turning
down a narrow lane into the street from whence it proceeded, saw, what was to me a new and strange sight.
In an open space, which partially commanded the
sea, and backed by a great tavern with verandahs and
galleries, was assembled a crowd of people, men and
women, white, brown, and black, drinking, smoking,
dicing, and swearing. There were tables and huge
benches scattered about, and sitting on these in every
attitude, or lying on the ground, not being able either to
sit or stand, were the people of this strange company. In
the centre of the carousing place, was a great cask with
the head knocked out, and from it a half-drunken seaman,

with a face of leering shyness, was drawing forth wine in a broken bucket, and pouring it into the glasses, mugs, and pipkins, held out to him on all sides. Most of the men were white seamen, and they sprawled over the tables and benches, with tobacco pipes in their mouths, and waved their glasses, and sang loud catches and songs, in which the shrill screaming voices of the women rose above their hoarse bawling. Most of these women seemed of the sort which frequent the streets in Wapping, and rob the seamen; others were half-bloods, being mulattos; or mustafees—that is to say, three-parts Indian; or quadroons—that is to say, three-parts white. But they were all dressed in flaunting gauds, and the sparkle of jewellery flashed upon their brown skins, as they flung their arms about, and rattled dice, or swallowed liquor like the men. Every now and then a brawl would arise, and knives would straightway glitter in the air, and loud thick voices would shout out oaths and exclamations in English, and French, and Low Dutch. But the general feeling of the revellers being pacific, the combatants would be straightway torn asunder, and perhaps flung upon the ground, to the danger of their bones; after which, the orgies would proceed as before; the men would rush in staggering groups up to the cask, or would produce their dice again, or greasy packs of cards—a species of gambling we learned from the French—and set themselves to play, some with great gravity and in silence, others shouting and yelling as luck turned for or against them, and all of them tossing about handfuls of gold and silver, such as dollars and doubloons, as though the money had been dirt; until, perhaps, a party would break out into a loud roaring song, all curses of the Spaniards, which heating them to the highest pitch, they would start up, the women with them, hallooing and screaming like fiends, and capering and jumping, tossing over benches and tables upon the ground, and at last drawing forth, and brandishing their hangers, and firing their pistols in the air!

In the very midst of this riotous assemblage, a man,

not very sober, but not very drunk, got upon the top of
an empty cask, he being supported at the legs by the
same Crashaw we had met, and bawled out in a thundering voice that he was going to sell certain commissions
to cruise against and capture Spanish vessels, and that
those gentlemen privateers who designed shortly to go to
sea again, would do well to hearken, and if possible
purchase, as the commissions would be sold very cheap,
and their product would be spent in wine, to be drunk
out at that present sitting by all the honourable company.
At this announcement there was a general uproar of approbation, and Captain Jem, plucking my sleeve, said,
that here might be matter which concerned us, and,
having whispered that the man on the cask was Captain
Davis, of whom Crashaw had spoken, we made our way
through the throng, who indeed received us very cordially,
everywhere holding up full glasses of wine and brandy,
and pressing us to drink. Meanwhile Davis recognised
Captain Jem, and, jumping down from the cask, bade him
welcome. Seats were immediately procured for us, by
the summary process of flinging their former occupants
on the ground, and we lit pipes and jingled glasses, like
the rest; although I do not know a more disgusting
thing than when a sober man comes into the company of
many who are drunken, and has yet, in a certain degree,
to conform to the humour of those about him. From
Davis, Captain Jem at once procured such a commission
as he thought we wanted. I did not see what mighty
good the document could do us; but it seems to have
been a fancy of our commander's, and for the paper
we agreed to pay a couple of doubloons, for which we
gave an order upon Mr. Pratt, which was immediately
sent into the tavern, and shortly re-appeared in the
shape of an additional keg of wine, although that in the
cask was not yet, by any means, consumed. But when
the Buccaneers saw the fresh liquor, they flung their
lighted tobacco-pipes into the old cask, and then, with
drunken glee, drew forth great mugs and glassfuls, with
which they besprinkled each other, and at last upset the

cask, treading, trampling, and dancing in the spilt wine, until they had churned it into red mud.

You may be sure that we were anxious enough to get away from these mad revellers, who, after the foolish fashion of too many sailors, both abroad and at home, were spending, in a few hours or days of insane debauchery, the money which they had risked their lives for months to obtain. At first, they were not willing to let us go, insisting that since we had paid for the additional keg of wine, we should bide the drinking of it out; but upon our telling them that we were busily engaged in fitting out a privateer, and that the Blue Peter would speedily be hoisted at the fore, they consented to let us depart—first drinking success to our cruise in great bumpers, with cheering and firing of pistols, and almost every man shouting out some advice, as to whither we ought to proceed. Here was one bawling out in favour of the Mosquito Coast; and there another screaming that most booty would be found to the eastward of the Gulf of Venezuela. At length, we got free, and devoted ourselves for some days to preparing the schooner, internally, for the accommodation of a larger crew than she had ever before carried.

There was no lack of hands, for Captain Jem was known as a commander, and as soon as we hoisted the Blue Peter, seamen came off in great numbers and applied to ship with us. Captain Jem personally examined all claimants, and when they passed his scrutiny successfully, it was for those who already formed the crew to receive or reject them. In this way, in a couple of days we were well manned by thirty-six stout seamen, including our original party. Except two Frenchmen and one Dutchman, all the new part of the crew was English. Our boatswain was a short, square-shouldered, powerful man, who had once commanded a ship, and was a good West-Indian pilot. His name was John Clink. We had also a good carpenter, and what was of almost as great importance, a surgeon, esteemed very skilful, a young Scotsman, like myself, bred in the University of Glasgow,

and very eager in prosecuting researches into the natural
history and productions of the teeming islands and con-
tinents of the West. The surgeon's name was Wood.
Meantime, Old Pratt had come on board, and after
inspecting the schooner, presently sent four guns, with a
great quantity of ammunition, and near sixty stand of
musketry, with boarding-pikes, cutlasses, and hangers in
proportion. We also carried a great boat which took up
almost all the space between the masts, and we slightly
altered the rigging of the schooner, setting up square fore-
topsails and foresails, so as to make her handier going before the wind. Our victualling being now completed, and
all things ready for sea, we had, as is usual among Buccaneers, a general meeting of the crew to determine and sign
articles. A paper of indenture was drawn up by Mr.
Pratt, and to it we all affixed our names, or our marks.
First, the indenture stipulated that the terms upon which
the voyage was to be undertaken, were ' no prey, no pay.'
Then it was provided, that all the booty obtained, of
whatsoever nature, should be flung into one general stock,
nobody whatsoever keeping anything back for himself,
but acting fairly and honourably to his comrades ; out of
this common fund all were to be paid in due proportion,
considering their station on board, or their share in the
venture. First came the proprietors of the ship, who
were three—being Le Picard, Nicky, and myself, for they
did not count the Indian. A certain proportion was
awarded to us, in the capacity which I have mentioned,
and another proportion to Mr. Pratt, calculated by the
value of the sea-stock, &c., wherewith he had supplied us.
Then the salaries of the captain, the quartermaster, the
boatswain, the carpenter, and the surgeon were fixed,
and certain sums were determined upon, to be given in
compensation for the different species of wounds which
we might receive. These compensations were upon the
following scale, and they applied alike to all the ship's
company. The loss of a right arm, six hundred pieces of
eight, or six slaves ; of a left arm, five hundred pieces, or
five slaves ; for a right leg the same ; for a left leg, four

hundred pieces of eight, or four slaves ; for an eye one hundred pieces of eight, or one slave ; and for a finger the like sum. As for the proportion of pay, the captain had as much as five ordinary seamen, and the quartermaster, or master's mate, which was my station, that of two. The rest of the crew shared equally, and two boys whom we had on board drew the pay of one able-bodied man. Furthermore, it was stipulated, that each mariner, without any distinction of rank, should be daily entitled to two full meals of the ship's stores, besides what game or fresh meat we might fall in with, and the indenture concluded by reciting that all those who signed it by name or mark, did thereby take a solemn oath, not to hide or conceal from their comrades the slightest article of value which they might become possessed of, but to fling all, without let or drawback, into the common fund. This document was committed to the care of Mr. Pratt, and a copy made by one of his clerks, which was deposited in the main cabin, and of free access to all. It was then proclaimed that next morning, on the setting in of the sea-breeze, which, on the southern side of the island, is favourable for leaving the coast, we would weigh anchor and stand off upon our voyage—so all was bustle and hurry—the schooner being surrounded by fleets of canoes, selling vegetables, fruit, and such wares, to be added to the sea stock of all who were minded to purchase them.

---

## CHAPTER XII.

### OF THE DEATH OF AN OLD FRIEND.

ABOUT sunset, Captain Jem came up to me, and inquired whether I had any final business to settle ashore, in which case he could spare me a couple of hours, but no more. I replied, that I had no reason for quitting the vessel, when all at once, the thought of my preserver on board the French felucca, Wright, flashed upon me. I remembered how he had told me, that he lived in Jamaica, at Port Royal in all probability, and I reproached myself for not having before thought of inquiring after him. So I proceeded on shore at once, and went straight to Mr. Pratt's, who I imagined would be likely to give me the information of which I stood in need. Nor was I disappointed. Mr. Pratt, indeed, knew no person of the name of Wright, but he had frequently seen the man to whom my description must apply, and whose real name was Blagrove. 'He lives,' said Mr. Pratt, 'in great retirement, dwelling in a small hut on the outskirts of the town, and cultivating, with two or three negroes, such a small plantation, as suffices to supply him with the necessaries of life.'

Mr. Pratt then, at my request, called a negro lad, and ordered him to be my guide to Blagrove's dwelling; adding, however, that the old Cromwellian lived in such solitude, and hated the faces of strangers so cordially, that he doubted whether I should be admitted. Determined, however, to make the experiment, I set off, the negro preceding me with a lantern. After clearing the town we had a rough and rugged walk, through trees and plantations, and deep Guinea grass, already drenched with dew. Fire-flies sparkled in every bush, and the hum of innumerable insects, and the harsh croaking of frogs in the swamps and ditches, made a melancholy music. At length we descried a distant light gleaming amid trees; at the sight of it, the negro stopped, and pointing, said, 'Dat Massa Blagrove's house!' at the same time making as though he would return.

'Well,' said I, 'do you not intend to come on and light me to the door?'

The negro suddenly fell upon his knees. 'Oh, Massa, please not insist; let Juba go back, now. Massa Blagrove terrible man, Obeah man, no like oder white buccra; live all alone by himself, wid Fetish. Oh, most great heaps of Fetish.'

Now, at this time I did not understand the negro at all. I knew not what he meant by Obeah or Fetish, but I afterwards found that the gloomy life and austere manners of the old Republican, had caused the negroes to believe that he was a sorcerer, or being of supernatural powers, and that they dreaded above all things being obliged to enter his grounds after dark. Seeing Mr. Pratt's negro, however, in a state of visible terror, at the idea of proceeding further, but having no time to stay to investigate the cause, I took the lantern from his hand, and told him to remain where he was until I came back. This he promised to do, but I had hardly advanced two paces, when I heard him scampering away through the rustling grass as fast as his legs could carry him. I called after the fugitive, but he gave no reply, so after muttering a curse upon his cowardice, I consoled myself by the reflection that he would be likely to get a sound flogging from Mr. Pratt for returning without the lantern, and then slowly advanced towards the light, which yet glimmered through the trees. I was not long in ascertaining that it shone from the rude window of a wattled hut, over which the branches of a great tree waved and rustled in the land wind. Having found the door, I knocked repeatedly, but received no reply, and as I stood listening, I thought I heard the sound of smothered moans. Thereupon I lifted the latch—the door was not otherwise secured—and entered. The cottage consisted of but one room, very rudely furnished. Hoes and spades, and such like implements, lay in the corners. There was a massive oaken table in the centre of the room, and at one end of it stood the candle, whose light I had seen from without. Hanging from the roof, close to the table, was a sort of rude curtain of canvas, which screened off a portion of the chamber, and from behind this curtain I heard the moaning come again: after hesitating for a moment I stepped forward and removed the drapery. Upon a low bed, without any curtains, his head and chest supported by a bag, such as that in which seamen keep their clothes, lay Wright, or Blagrove—now, alas, a dying man. He was terribly wasted, as though by fever or ague; his grey eyes so sunken that they seemed to gleam from the bottom of dark holes, and his features were shrunk and distorted, for the fingers of Death were

pressing them. The sick man took no notice of me, so
that I could mark a large Bible in which he seemed to
have been reading, and which had fallen from his pithless
hand upon the bed.

'Mr. Wright,' I said. He replied not a word.

'John Blagrove,' I repeated.

He started, and said feebly, 'I am he—who calls ?'

'Leonard Lindsay,' I replied, 'the Scots mariner, whom
you aided to escape from the ship of Montbars.'

'Lindsay—Lindsay !' he muttered, 'I know not that
name.' He paused, and then said loudly and clearly,
'Death—my voice is for death. He hath most foully
betrayed his great trust, and the blood of the saints
crieth against him. By what law, sayest thou, shall we
put him to death ? Even by that which gave Jericho and
its people to the sword of Joshua, the son of Nun.'

Listening to this, I saw that the mind of the dying man
was running upon the great action of his life, and forbore
to disturb him. But presently the delirium fit seemed
to pass away, and he stirred restlessly, and muttered that
he was athirst. I looked round the cottage, and finding
a pitcher of water and a mug, held the latter to his lips ;
when he had drunk he seemed revived, shut his eyes for a
moment, and then, opening them, fixed his gaze upon me,
and smiled faintly.

'I know you now,' he said ; 'how came you here ?'

Feeling that his time was but short, I hurriedly replied,
that having arrived at Jamaica from Hispaniola, I had
heard that he resided here, and had lost no time in coming
to see, and thank him.

'You will see the last of me, then,' he murmured ; 'I
told you I should rest in the wilderness, and I am fast
going to that long home.'

I asked him if he had not had proper medicines and
help in his fever.

'No,' he replied, 'none ; I did not wish to live. I left
myself in the hands of God. He has called my soul, and
I obey the summons as firmly as I can.'

'But surely,' quoth I, 'you require help—attendance ?'

'None,' says he—' a man can die alone. When I felt the delirium coming on, yesterday, and knew that my hour was at hand, I called together my four slaves and gave them their liberty. They went singing and shouting away, and I remained here waiting for the last moment with contrition, and prayer, and praise.'

After this he was silent for a long time. Then he said, ' Once I was a judge at a great trial, now I go to be judged for my judgment. Then, I did that which I believed to be right and good. I am of the same mind still. Before an hour, I shall know whether my voice spoke justly or no.'

A very dismal silence succeeded. Blagrove was sinking very fast. When I took his hand it was cold and wet, and his breath began to come in flutterings and gaspings. While I watched him, the light, which burned in a rude iron candlestick, suddenly flickered and went out; and, except for the glimmer of my lantern, we were in darkness. Indeed, it was very terrible. The great branches of the tree overhead groaned as they swayed with the night wind, and sometimes hit the roof with a loud rattle ; the dismal croak of the frog sounded incessantly ; and the goat-sucker whooped his loud hollow note from the forest. As I watched the dying, I suddenly heard the lattice of the window shake, and, turning round with a start, saw a hideous black face, crowned with a curly mass of grey hair, laid close against the coarse thick glass. My heart beat, and my blood curdled as I gazed. In a moment, however, the face was withdrawn, and I was vainly attempting to persuade myself that the vision I had seen was fancy, when, by the uncertain light of the lantern, I observed the latch of the door move. The cold sweat came out upon me again as the door opened, and a hideous apparition entered. It was that of a very aged negro woman. Her face had that peculiar blackness which marks those negroes actually born on the Guinea coast ; and it was, so to speak, a perfect mass of huge wrinkles and skinny folds, through which her white teeth appeared with a ghastly conspicuousness. The

K

principal part of her dress was an old dingy blanket; and round her neck was hung a cord, upon which shreds of cloth, birds' feathers, pellets of clay and stones with holes in them—the shells of eggs, and fragments of broken bottles were strung. This uncouth being advanced slowly into the hut, holding up in both hands a sort of graven image, or idol, made of a block of wood roughly carved, and stuck over with such scraps of offal and filth as composed her own rude necklace. I was so absorbed in a sort of compassionate horror, that I had no power to prevent her approach, but rather shrank from her—the hag looked so fearful and witch-like. So she proceeded to the very side of the bed—Blagrove, meanwhile, having his eyes shut and his hands clasped, as though in secret prayer—and then suddenly dropping on her knees, she raised her hideous idol before the face of the dying, and said, in a harsh grating voice:

'Buccra dying—buccra pray to Obi.'

Coming to myself at these words, I dashed forwards, wrenched the idol from the hands of the idolatress, and flung the hag back towards the door. She turned upon me with the fury of a wild cat.

'What for you here?' she said; 'he is Obeah man, me is Obeah woman. Obeah men and women pray to Obi. It is one great Fetish.'

For reply I walked to the door, and, opening it, flung the idol forth into the night. When I turned again, the hag was affixing a bunch of parrot feathers to the bed.

'I set Obi for him,' she cried; 'I set Obi for you. De Fetish hab kill him—de Fetish will kill you.'

Blagrove at this started up in bed—'I am getting blind,' he said, faintly; 'what voice is that?'

'De voice of Mammy Koromantee—of de Obeah woman,' said the hag; 'de moder of Paul, your negro, dat you set free. Paul say you die; I bring Obi for you to pray to—Obi great.'

'Lindsay, Leonard Lindsay,' gasped Blagrove, 'come close to me—quick!—I am choking. Keep her away, fling down the strange god—fling Dagon from the high places.'

I now supported his head, and saw that the great change was at hand.

'Mary, Mary,' he said faintly; 'I come, Mary, my wife.'

There passed a spasm over his face, and then his head hung heavy and dead across my arm. Immediately, the negress raised her voice, tremulous with age, and began to chant a sort of song—perhaps it was a dirge, in her own tongue.

'Go,' said I, interrupting her lament—'go to Mr. Pratt's, and tell them that Blagrove is dead; they will return with you, and I will give you money.'

'You gib me money,' said the negress, quickly; 'oh, den I go to Massa Pratt's, and I find Obi when do daylight come.'

With this the hag bustled out as speedily as her old limbs would bear her, and in less than an hour Mr. Pratt and some of his people arrived. I paid the old woman her guerdon, and was glad to be relieved from my melancholy post—Mr. Pratt assuring me that all needful attention would be bestowed upon the dead. As for the woman, he said that she was more than half crazed with age and infirmity; but that in coming to the hut he believed that, after her own fashion, she had meant kindly. She was reputed by the negroes to be an Obeah woman, or witch, and the scraps of feathers, rags and egg-shells wherewith she had adorned herself were the means by which she wrought her spells and incantations.

---

## CHAPTER XIII.

### THE BUCCANEERS SAIL FOR THE SPANISH MAIN, AND ARE CHASED BY A GREAT SHIP OF WAR.

In an hour after these events, I was on board the 'Will o' the Wisp,' greatly to the relief of Captain Jem, who feared, from my long stay, that some evil had befallen me; and with the first puff of sea-breeze in the morning, we were gliding past the point of the Pallisades out into the open ocean, on my first buccaneering voyage. As the sun rose into a cloudless sky, the merry trade-wind freshened until it tore up the tops of the long swells into ridges of rolling foam, and caused the schooner to careen gaily over, so that the water buzzed, and gushed, and gurgled in the lee-scupper holes. Then my spirits, which all night long had been heavy and depressed, rose with every mile of sea which rolled between us and the land, and I felt as elated and merry, bound upon a wild and venturesome expedition to an unhealthy and little known coast, as when the 'Golden Grove' raised her anchor from the sands of Leith, and I expected in due time to see the hills of Italy and Greece.

We had a fierce and wild-looking crew, wearing in their dress the fashions of many lands; some were clad in jackets cut out of rich brocades and stuffs captured from the Spaniards. Others had doublets of hide. All wore moustachioes and beards, and carried great broad-bladed knives stuck into girdles of leather, or neatly twisted yarn. The experience of a few days showed us that we were manned by active and skilful seamen, one or two who turned out inferior in this respect being set to duties fitted for them, such as cooking, serving out the provisions from the casks, and helping the carpenter or sail-maker. Moreover, the men seemed tractable as well as handy fellows, and were on very good terms with each other, and quite delighted with the captain and the ship. To this there was but one exception—a sailor from London, called Bell. This man was sullen, sulky, and lazy, and Captain Jem having found him skulking from work, upon one occasion, when the wind blew very fresh, and the whole crew were on deck taking in sail, gave him so strong a hint with the flat of his cutlass, that for some time, at least, there was no repetition of the offence.

On the third day, after losing sight of Jamaica, soon after sunrise, we descried a great sail to windward. The weather was then almost calm, and the swell trifling. Still the appearance of the sky was, as we thought, threatening. The sun had risen of a fiery red, and huge fleecy banks of vapour brooded over the ocean. The sail must have been for some time in sight ere we had distinguished it from the wreaths of white morning mist which here and there floated over the water; but having made it out, we knew that so great a spread of canvas must arise from a stately ship. Now, if she were an Englishman, a Frenchman, or a Dutchman, we had nothing to say to her, whereas if she were a Spaniard, she must be either an exceeding rich merchantman, in which case it was our business to speak her as fast as possible, or she was a man-of war, in which case, we could hardly pack too much canvas upon the schooner to get her out of such a dangerous neighbourhood. However, the ship had the weather-guage of us; she would bring down the sea-breeze with her, and all we could do was to lie idly upon the swell, watching her motions. For myself, I climbed to the schooner's main-topmast, with the best perspective glass we had on board; and I had not been long there before I could plainly perceive that our big neighbour had felt the power of the sea-breeze, for she rose fast, spreading her great sheets of canvas out, like wings, and coming directly down upon us.

Captain Jem then hailed me eagerly from the deck, asking whether she looked like a merchant ship or a frigate. At first, I could give little satisfaction to his questions, as the stranger was coming directly towards us; but presently, whether from bad steering or not I am unaware, she gave a sheer to starboard, and lifting that moment upon a swell, I saw that she carried a great broadside of heavy guns, with a very high poop, rising I am sure forty feet above the water, and all encrusted, as it were, with galleries and carved windows, after the fashion in which the Spaniards build their men-of-war. Upon this intelligence, we prepared for immediate flight. We were to leeward, and so had nothing for it but to run before the wind. As yet, however, only those little puffs or airs called by sailors cat's-paws, the precursors of the coming wind, were stealing over the great shiny

backs of the smooth lazy swells, whereas the Spanish
frigate, for such we doubted her not to be, was in the
midst of roughened water, and rolling two great ridges of
white foam, from beneath her bows.  How we cursed the
chance which condemned us to lie idle on the ocean,
when a formidable enemy was swooping down upon us,
with a wind which made his heaviest canvas surge, and
his stout masts bend and creak.  Meantime, however,
we prepared to set studding-sails, and indeed hoisted
them to be ready for the first of the coming breeze, at
the same time, by the help of a sweep or great oar
swinging round the head of the schooner in the direction
which circumstances compelled us to take.  This manœuvre
was instantly observed on board the great ship, for she
straightway fired a cannon, and hauled up the gorgeous
ensign of Spain to her main-topmast head, where it
streamed forth in all its red and yellow glory.  The next
moment a bright spout of flame flashed from the Spaniard's
bows, and the ball came skipping along the sea, making
its last plunge not a quarter of a mile from us.  But
almost at the same moment our sails flapped and surged,
then steadily swelling out, the schooner began to slip
through the water.  Seeing this, the Spaniards fired again
and again; but without effect.  Meantime, we were hard
at work, setting every stitch of canvas we could get to
draw, and presently we had quite enough of wind for the
safety of our spars, the breeze driving before it that
heavy pelting shower, which often falls soon after sunrise,
and which sailors call the Pride of the Morning.  The
' Will-o'-the-Wisp ' was now careering along at her full
speed, rolling heavily before the great following surges,
which would often rise in white foam, hissing and glancing
round her stern, and then melting, as it were, from
beneath her, would sweep on, while the schooner plunged
heavily down into the trough, her sails flapping like
thunder in the lull, and then tearing and struggling, as
though they would drag the masts out of the keel as the
vessel was hove high again on the crest of the next
following wave.  Still the large ship was gaining upon us

fast. A schooner is a species of vessel unfitted to scud before a brisk gale, like a square rigged ship, although in beating up to windward, we would most likely have the advantage. However, we spread every inch of canvas we could stretch out, and Captain Jem and myself both stood by the tiller. In an hour from the commencement of the chase, the Spaniard was not a mile astern of us; and truly, if the great ship had been a friend, she would have been a gay and a gallant sight—with her brave tall masts, and great sheets of canvas, which rolled from side to side, like a tower which totters in an earthquake, and her vast bows, all carved and encrusted with ornaments and devices, which would now plunge deeply into the brine, and then rise with the sea water pouring and flashing down, amid the sculptures and images of saints and long moulded and fretted ledges and serpentine projections of carved wood, which extended in gracious undulations on either side of the cut-water. But we had little mind to admire the cunning work of the Spanish artificers, although, unhappily, every moment we saw it plainer and plainer. Our men began to look pale and troubled, and spoke in whispers to each other, and some of them lay sullenly down upon the deck. Meanwhile, Captain Jem and I consulted together in a low voice, and presently hit upon a plan which would give us, at all events, a last chance.

'Nicky Hamstring,' said Captain Jem, 'show the Don a sight of the flag which Sir Francis Drake carried against the great Armada.'

At this bold speech, the men seemed to pluck up a little.

'What, boys!' quoth brave Jem; 'you do not mean to stretch out your throats to the Spaniard's whittles?'

'Where is the use of preaching?' cries one of the men. 'If we don't strike and heave-to, he will give us the stem, run his ship crash over us, and send us to the bottom before we can say a prayer.'

Captain Jem pulled out a great pistol and cocked it.

'That was George Bell's voice!' he shouted. 'Hark ye, you snivelling cur, say but another syllable of striking or heaving-to, and I'll send you to hell with the word upon your lips. Comrades,' continued the captain, raising his voice, 'is it fit that brave men and staunch should listen to a hen-hearted skulk like the man who spoke ?'

'No, no!' cried the whole of the crew, 'no striking; let the Dons do their worst.' And at that moment the ensign of St. George fluttering up to the main-topmast head, we greeted it with a cheer, the echo of which came back from the broad sails of the Spaniard.

'Now, men,' said Captain Jem, 'be steady and sharp, and in ten minutes we shall have the big ship's weather-guage.'

Several moments passed in perfect silence, broken only by the roar of the sea around us, and the great plunges of the Spanish ship, as she came careering and wallowing over the waves. We looked back, and saw her bows clustered with men, and standing upon the bowsprit, with his arm round a stay, we could discern the figure of an officer, with a very brave uniform, and holding a trumpet in his hand. Presently this officer passed his trumpet to a man who stood by him, and who at once hailed in good English. We all heard his words, for they echoed loudly between the sails of the two ships.

'Surrender,' he said, 'or we will run the frigate over you.'

'Stand by your sheets, men,' said Captain Jem, softly ; 'and never fear for all I do, that we are going to run our necks into Spanish hemp this cruise.'

'Do you surrender ?' hailed the Spaniard once more.

There was now not a hundred feet between the man-of-war's jib and our taffrail rail. It was fearful to see the great ship, like a moving steeple, rushing down upon us, and, despite of myself, I felt my teeth grinding against each other. I looked back once more, there was the mighty prow, clustered with men, frowning above us, and ploughing the sea into a great furrow of foam. That ship could crush our schooner as a rock would smash a pipkin.

Yet no muscle quivered in Captain Jem's face. All at once he sung out, sharp and quick—

'Nicky, strike the flag.'

The Spanish man-of-war rose upon a great sea, heaving her bows out of the water almost to her keel. The next moment she would be crushing down bodily upon our deck. Just then the red-cross ensign disappeared from the mast-head, and Captain Jem, turning round, took off his hat. The officer on the bowsprit of the great ship immediately shouted, and as he spoke the vast bows gave a sudden sweep to the port or larboard side, almost shaving our taffrail as they grazed past.

'Now, then!' roared Captain Jem, ramming down the tiller hard a port. 'Sheets, boys, mind your sheets—in with them—in with the larboard sheets. Hurrah, boys, hurrah! show the Don that he must shut his claws quick, or we will slip through his fingers.'

The words had not been spoken when the Will-o'-the Whisp flew round like a top, in the opposite direction to that of the Spaniard, plunging down into one tremendous sea, taking tons upon tons of the glancing green water over her weather bow, and then lying over to the wind, until the washing seas rose up to the very centre of her deck. Of course the studding-sail-booms snapped like pipe-stems, and the sails they supported burst away and floated down to leeward. But for this we cared very little.

'If the spars stand it we're safe,' shouted the Captain to me.

I looked aloft, the schooner was almost on her broadside, the sea pouring over and over us in great curling volumes of blinding spray, flashing up high into the rigging, and drenching the surging, tearing canvas. This lasted but for a moment. There was a lull, the schooner righted in the water, plunged heavily at one or two seas, and then, although carrying a fearful press of sail, shot gaily away to windward. We looked astern. The Spaniard had been utterly discomfited by our manœuvre. After diverging from her course just enough,

as she thought, to save us from being run down, she had
been obliged to keep before the wind, being afraid, with
all her sail, to try the desperate experiment of luffing up,
and was now a good mile to leeward, her crew busily employed in getting in all her light canvas, evidently with
the intent of following up the chase.

'Now, boys!' called out the captain—'we have not
shaken off the Don yet.   He has had a taste of our quality, but he will be after us again.   So while he is amusing
himself to leeward yonder, let us get in a reef or so, the
schooner will make better way through the water than
when she is dragged down by too great a show of canvas.'

So presently the Will-o'-the-Wisp' was under suitable
sail, working hard to windward.   Captain Jem was right
in saying that the Spaniard meant not to give up his prey
after one baffled swoop, and in a brief space he was close
hauled upon the same tack with ourselves, careening down
to the wind, until we sometimes expected to see him turn
over bodily.   It was lucky for us, that, heeling over so
much, he could not bring his guns to bear upon the
schooner.   Once or twice he fired a cannon, but the ball
must have passed far above us.   Our own pieces were too
small for us to return the compliment, across a mile of sea,
with any chance of hard hitting ; besides, it was our cue
to trust rather to our legs than our teeth, and to mind
our canvas rather than our guns.

All that long and anxious day did the Spaniard stick
to our skirts.   Had the breeze been lighter, we would
have left him hand over hand, but the strong wind, and
great tumbling seas, often bore us bodily to leeward, while
the Spaniard burst through and through them with mighty
plunges.   Such a wind and sea, I repeat, could not but
be of great advantage to the bigger and heavier ship.
Thus it came to pass that when the sun touched the
western waves, the Spaniard still held his position about
a mile to leeward of the schooner.   We had run more
than one hundred miles since we hauled our wind,
and still for all we could see, we had neither lost nor
gained an inch.

The night came on, but the wind still howled una-
batedly over the far-spreading ridges of angry water.
There was no moon, and great patches of dusky clouds
went scudding by between the ocean and the stars.

'Now, my mates,' quoth Captain Jem—'we shall find
out whether Jack Spaniard's eyes mark well in the dark.
Let all lights be extinguished in the ship, except the
binnacle lantern.'

This order was speedily obeyed, and soon afterwards
the binnacle lamp was carefully screened, and at the same
instant we lit a bright lantern, and placed it conspicuously
on our lee quarter. By this manœuvre it is evident
that the Spaniard, if he saw aught, saw but one light, as
though we carried no more. After this we tacked several
times, shifting the lantern so as to allow our pursuer a
good view of it, and make him believe that we were showing the light in bravado. By this time it was nine
o'clock and the wind was sensibly abating. We could
see naught of the Spaniard, although many a pair of eyes
were strained until they ached and throbbed with vain
efforts to make out the secret of his whereabouts. About
ten o'clock, we were upon the starboard tack, the schooner
then laying a course which would have brought her back
to Jamaica. A good-sized cask was then prepared, by
eight twelve-pound balls being cast into it as it stood on
one end on deck. Then a sort of pole or spar, made out
of an oar, was fitted into the cask, being stepped as it
were amongst the cannon balls, and coming up through
the opposite head of the cask, like a mast through the
deck of a ship. This apparatus being well secured by stout
ropes, was hove overboard, and slackening the lines, we
saw that it floated perfectly upright. The machine was
then hauled in again; the lantern which I have already
mentioned, was made fast to the top of the pole, and then
the cask and all were carefully lifted over the bulwark,
and cast adrift upon the sea; while, at the same moment,
the tiller was put down, the schooner tilted gaily round
and filled upon the other tack, and in five minutes we were
half a mile away from the decoy beacon, which glimmered

with an uncertain light, as it rose rocking upon the ridges of the seas. In silence and in darkness we kept our new course. Happily this was the gloomiest period of the night. Lowering banks of cloud lay heavily upon the eastern horizon, and the stars only glimmered occasionally through the scud. The schooner was kept a little from the wind, so as to make her sail her very best, and went careering, as though she bore a light heart, across the waves. We saw or heard nothing of our enemy, and by midnight we trusted that many a league of ocean rolled between our gay schooner and the great Spanish man-of-war.

## CHAPTER XIV.

### THE STRANGE ADVENTURE OF THE UNKNOWN SHOALS AND THE DWARF PILOT.

THAT evening it chanced that I had the mid-watch, and so when the dead of the night came, I took charge of the deck, and Captain Jem, and all who were not upon duty went below. The weather was moderate, with a steady breeze broad upon our larboard beam, as we steered almost due south. I walked the deck for nearly three hours without having occasion to give an order to one of the watch. I was weary and exhausted, for the excitement of the chase had now gone off, and as for the seamen around me, they were stretched out dozing here and there upon the deck, and as we had a clear sea, and the wind held very steady, I was loth to rouse the poor fellows up. There was an old grey-headed sailor, whom we called Bristol Tom, at the helm, and I sometimes listened to him as he crooned over ancient sea ballads, which had been sung by the sailors of Sir Francis Drake, and sometimes conversed with him upon the clever style in which we had shaken off the Spaniard. So the night waned slowly away. Every ten minutes or so I would go forward and cast a long look over the dull sea, stretching away before us like a heaving sheet of lead, save where here and there

it was broken by a dullish white streak, where a wave
rose higher than common, curled, and broke. At length,
it wanted but half an hour to the time of my relief, and I
sat down upon the weather bulwark with my arm round
the stay, and began, according to my frequent custom, to
build very gorgeous castles in the air. I thought of the
happy day when, having made prize-money sufficient in
these far-off seas, I would return to Scotland and hear
again the music which of all others was sweetest to the
ear of my memory—the voices of my kindred, and the
whimpling and gurgling of the Balwearie burn, as it
trickled down the broomy knowes into the clear pools,
where, with a running noose made of horsehair, attached
to the end of a switch, I used to mark and catch the
speckled pars. During my meditations, it struck me
once or twice that the motion of the sea was changing;
that the flow of the waves was not so uniform, and that
they jerked the schooner sharply as though she were
ploughing a cross sea. Thinking, however, that Bristol
Tom might be nodding over the tiller, I called to him to
look sharp and steer fine, to which he promptly replied,
'Ay, ay, sir!' and my spirit fled away again to the bonny
shores of Fife. All at once, a low, dull roaring sound, very
different from the sharp plunges of the schooner, and the
seething, hissing noise of the seas, as they burst in beds
of foam from beneath her bows, came floating on the night
wind.

'Bristol Tom!' I cried, sharply, 'did you hear nothing
like the roar of surf?'

'Lord love ye, sir,' quoth the steersman, 'there be no
surf but where there be land near the top of the sea,
and hereabouts five hundred fathom of line would reach
no bottom.'

'It must have been the wind eddying in the sail above
me,' I thought, but I kept my ears cocked pretty sharply.

Presently, I heard the sound again; there could be no
mistake about it. There was the hollow boom of great
seas breaking over banks of sand. I started up, and
swung myself on the ledge of the bulwarks.

Not a quarter of a mile on our weather bow I could see a great bed of tumbling spray, which gleamed with a pale lustre in the dark.

"Breakers on the weather bow!" I shouted. 'Up, men, up! Keep her away, Tom, keep her away. Call all hands!—stand by sheets and brails—see all clear with the anchor."

In a moment the deck of the schooner was alive with startled men, I leaped forward, and flung myself on the bowspirit.

'Breakers right a-head!' I screamed 'Up with the helm—hard up.'

'Breakers on the lee bow!' sung out two or three voices at once.

We were embayed. The white water tumbled and roared all around us: I thought all was over, when right a-head I saw a space of dark sea. This might be our salvation.

'Hold your luff!' I shouted—'hold your luff! but keep her well in hand. So—steady.'

'Steady!' replied Bristol Tom, and the schooner shot through a narrow channel—so narrow that the drifting foam of a great surge upon our weather bow flew over us in a salt shower. By this time the whole crew had tumbled out of their hammocks, and rushed upon deck half awake, and calling out to know what was the matter?

"Down with your helm—hard down!" I cried again. The schooner swept up into the wind, and a great mass of foam seemed as it were to glide from beneath her bows.

'Breakers a-head!' sung out Nicky Hamstring's voice as the direction of the ship was altered.

'Keep her away again,' cried Captain Jem and myself together. The bows of the manageable little vessel receded fast from the wind, when she sunk in the trough of the tumbling swell, with a jerk and a jar which appeared to shake her very ribs.

'She has struck!' cried half the crew at once. But the

next sea hove the ship buoyantly aloft; the wind came down with a heavy puff; she bent over before its influence, and for near five minutes rushed madly on amid the broken water which flashed and glanced upon either side of us; now, by a sudden twitch of the rudder, and a rapid jibbing of the sails, avoiding a reef, or spit of sand which lay directly across her course—anon, running along a belt of white water, until, mayhap, a sudden bend of the reef caused us to whirl the schooner right into the wind's eye again, and try to beat slowly up the tortuous channels, expecting every moment to be flung with a crash upon a ledge of coral rocks. All this time the men were working to clear the anchor, and just as the schooner was hove into the wind to weather the corner of a long shallow point of breakers, our moorings were let go, our sails sharply brailed up, and we had soon the satisfaction of finding that we rode easily to our anchor in about eight fathom water, with a great labyrinth of sandbanks and low ledges of rock around.

All this appeared to us like a dream; ten minutes before we had been ploughing along the open ocean, not dreaming that there lay land within three hundred miles of us, now we were in the midst of an immense and unknown shoal, and a flaw of wind, or a shift in the set of the currents which must traverse its intricate channels, might fling us on a bank of sand or rock, on which we would leave the bones of ship and men.

Of course, our first business was to make our moorings as secure as possible. The Mosquito men, who have keen eyes, both by night and day, pointed out a dark lump upon our starboard bow, which we soon made out to be a low lying rock, and accordingly manning our light boat, we speedily carried out a warp, which we made shift to secure round a jagged projection of the reef, all clustered over with oysters and sea-weed.

Meantime, Captain Jem, with Bristol Tom, and myself, and sundry of the oldest mariners, retired into the great cabin to examine the maps and charts. We certainly did not know the exact position of the schooner, for in the hurry of yesterday's chase, no observation had been taken, but this we knew that no shoal or island, indeed no sound-ings at all, were laid down in our charts, near which we could possibly be.

'No, comrades,' quoth Captain Jem, 'here be rocks and banks, shoals and sands, which no mariner hath up to this time reported; although, mayhap, many a brave seaman hath found his long home amongst them.'

We looked long and earnestly to the east, before the blessed light came out upon the ocean. At length the dawn grew pale in the sky, then a red, warm glow bright-ened above the waves; the thin night mists rolled away; the sea-birds came shricking and clanging from their nests and holes, and we, truly, saw a lonely and desolate sight. All around the schooner, for miles and miles, was a pale greenish sea, laced, as it were, with bars and streaks of surf, which spread around like open net-work, and dotted here and there with great smooth banks of bright sand, and low, long reefs like jagged walls, rising now and then into a higher point of precipitous rock which showed, per-haps, some eight or ten feet above the level of the surf. The blue sea formed the framing of this dismal picture. As for the Spaniard he was nowhere to be seen, and, sooth to say, we thought or cared little about him. In regard to our own position, it was a miracle how we had by chance attained it; when I mounted the rigging and saw the great chaos of banks and spits of sand, and white belts of tumbling surf, through which we had reeled and staggered, as it were, blindfolded, without in the least knowing our course or the direction of the channels, I felt as if a miracle had been accomplished in our favour. Having got safely in, however, the question was now how to get safely out again, and so having called a council upon the deck, it was determined that the schooner should be made as snug as possible at her moorings, while the shallop, which was our smallest boat, went out to survey the shoal, and if possible hit upon a safe passage to the open sea.

After breakfast, this plan was put into execution, and

the charge of the boat was intrusted to me. The day was fine, the sea-breeze cooled the air. We put into the shallop some beef, biscuit, and a beaker of water, and rowed off in very tolerable spirits. Our first intent was to trace the route by which the schooner had arrived at her present anchorage; but the attempt soon bewildered us; one man was confident that we had passed to windward of this bank, while another maintained that we had run under its lee. Here was a reef which our bowman remembered to have observed perfectly well, while he who pulled at the stroke oar was equally confident that the schooner had never passed within a mile of it. We therefore gave up the idea of taking the ship out as we brought her in, and set to work to discover another passage into blue water. But sure such a hopeless range of shoals, banks, reefs, and dangerous points of rock, never bewildered poor mariners; sometimes we thought that we had hit upon a channel, but just as we were upon the point of finding our way clearly into the open ocean, a few specks of white water only seen when the sea fell into a trough at that place, would stretch across the route, and reveal the fact, that a ledge of pointed and pinnacled reef barred the way. Then the currents and sets of the tide puzzled us greatly, washing up one channel and down another, and boiling round the rocks in such a puzzling whirl of eddies and counter-eddies, that our boat was nigh stove more than once upon the sharp coral reefs. At length, after pulling the best part of the day, and landing upon many of the rocky plots, we made our way, with weary muscles and aching hearts, to the schooner, to report our ill success. We found that they had moored the vessel very snugly—that in case of accidents they had got the launch into the water, and that she lay in a snug little sandy cove, well sheltered from the swell, and, at half ebb, locked up, as it were, in a clear pool, like a shallow caldron.

The afternoon passed away very dully. Captain Jem sent the small boat out again, with a fresh crew, to look for turtle and sea-birds; and it was determined that, next

L

day, both the boats should start upon an exploring expedition. The turtling party soon returned with half-a-dozen fine turtles, and a great quantity of oysters; they had shot several ducks, but the greater quantity of birds they saw were noddies and sea-gulls, which they did not care to disturb.

About an hour before sunset, the men were lounging under the awning which we had set, fore and aft, some of them fishing in the clear water beneath us, when, on a sudden, there was a great cry of astonishment raised; and looking up from the chart which I was studying, I saw a strange little man, so small, he might almost be called a dwarf, deliberately climbing over the taffrail. A dozen of our seamen rushed to lay hold of him, but he waved his hand, as though there was no necessity for violence, and jumped lightly down on deck.

'Where is the captain of this ship?' quoth he, in a strange shrill cracked voice, and speaking English with a slight foreign accent. At this moment, Captain Jem came out of the main cabin and stared heartily, as indeed we all did, to see so unexpected and strange-looking a visitor. The creature—who was so queer and dwarfish a man, that, as I gazed upon him, I thought of old-world stories of Brownies and uncanny men of the moors—could not have been above four feet high. He had very broad shoulders, and such long muscular arms, that they looked like fore legs of an ape. His face was big and broad, but not by any means ugly. He had light blue twinkling eyes and long fair hair, and a beard of a flaxen colour. The little man's dress was as strange as himself. He wore a broad hat, made of great ribbons of strong green sea-weed, very neatly plaited and wrought. He had a linen shirt, not of the cleanest, with a cloth cloak hanging round his loins, and bound with a broad belt of similar sea-weed to that which formed his hat, while on his legs, which were very short and thick, he wore a pair of coarse canvas drawers. His great brown splay feet were bare. When I say that this strange-looking apparition had a sort of necklace of coral, mixed with small pieces of gold and silver money hung round his neck; that his ears were weighed down with big silver rings; and that in his hand he carried a paddle, with a broad blade at each end, I have fully described to the reader the stranger who now advanced towards Captain Jem, pulling off his hat, and making a very polite bow. Not to be behindhand in good breeding, Stout Jem was nothing loth to return the salaam; after which, he asked the little man how the devil he had come on board.

'Look over the side and you will see,' quoth the dwarf. We all rushed to the bulwark, and there sure enough was a light canoe most beautifully constructed, floating, as it appeared, on the very top of the water.

'Well, sir,' quoth Captain Jem, 'you seem a country-man of the most of us here, and you are very welcome. I can't help, however, thinking that you must have dropped from the moon. Mayhap you are the man in it.'

The dwarf waved his hand very impatiently, as who should say, a truce with your idle jeers, and then quoth he very solemnly—'I am a pilot.'

At this we all listened greedily enough.

'Well,' says Captain Jem, 'I can't say that we are not in want of one. But whereabouts may we be? Is there land nigh; and what do you call these rocks and sands?'

'There is no land that I know of nigher than New Providence,' answered the dwarf, 'and it lies a good hundred leagues to the westward and southward; and as for these rocks and sands, I cannot tell you their name, because they have got none.'

'Then what ships come hither that you act as pilot for?' asked I.

'None at all,' replied the little man, very briskly. 'There is nothing to take ships hither, unless it be a few turtle, and these they can get in far less dangerous places.'

At this we all stared at each other, and the men murmured that the dwarf was mad; and Bristol Tom whispered that mayhap the creature had been marooned— that is, deserted—upon these rocks, and that he had lost his reason. After a short pause, however, the dwarf-pilot resumed his discourse.

'There never was a ship,' quoth he, 'which came to these shoals but stayed there. There be plenty of room for a navy to lie on these sands and reefs, and then the first gale of wind that comes, smashes them faster than e'er a ship-breaker in Limehouse.'

Captain Jem now began to lose patience, so he cried very wrathfully.

'If you talk more riddles to us, little man, God smite me! but I will run you up to the yard-arm by the breech of your galligaskins, and so dip you into the brine, as men serve a mangy monkey!'

'Nay,' answered the dwarf, 'I came on board to help you out of a scrape. You are discourteous, so get you to sea as you best can.'

'Well, well!' replied Captain Jem, 'I was in the wrong; but tell us frankly, man, what you are, and how you come to live amongst these accursed shoals?'

'What I will do for you is this,' quoth the dwarf—'and I will do neither more nor less; I will pilot your ship out to sea, and I will ask nothing for it, but that you make me rid of you without loss of time.'

'Why,' quoth I, 'you must be very fond of solitude to propose anything of the sort; and if you obstinately refuse to tell us what you are, or what you do here, how can we trust the ship and all our lives to your management?'

'You will have me on board,' said the dwarf, 'and I give you free leave to hang me up by the neck, not by the breech, if I as much as scrape a barnacle from the bottom of the schooner.

This proposition certainly looked reasonable.

'What will you do, when we get to sea?' asked Bristol Tom.

'What is that to you, old man?' quoth the dwarf; 'go your ways, and leave me to go mine. I warrant I should have had more wit than to come blundering in here against my will.'

" So you landed here on purpose ?' says I.

' Whether I did or no,' says the dwarf, ' is nothing to you.  Do you want a pilot, or do you not ?'

Here, Captain Jem whispered to me that there might be more in this scene than met the eye, and that we should do well to secure the strange pilot who crowed so smugly.  I assenting, the captain tipped the wink to half a dozen of the crew, who thereupon advanced towards the little man.  But he was sharper than we, for, observing what we intended, he made but two jumps, one upon the bulwark, and the other into the canoe below, the bottom of which I thought would be driven out by his weight; but not a bit of it—the little bark-built skiff gave a great surge, and then floated tranquilly a couple of fathoms from the side.

" Call you that seamen's hospitality ?' says the little man, grinning.

Captain Jem flew into a great rage.  ' Get your muskets, men,' he cried ; but directly after, controlling himself, he directed us to give chase in the shallop, and bring back the pilot by force.  Anticipating this order, I leaped into the boat, and calling out for four young men, who were the best rowers and the most muscular and long-winded fellows in the schooner, they jumped into the shallop with great glee, just as the dwarf, thinking he might as well have a start, dipped his paddle into the water and glided away.  We were soon in chase, straining at the oars with right good will, and sending the shallop dancing at a great rate through the sea.  Meantime our shipmates on board the schooner mounted into the rigging that they might observe the race the better, and encouraged us with abundance of cheers and exhortations not to spare our muscles.  We brought the boat gradually to its full speed, the canoe being then only a dozen or so fathoms a-head.  The dwarf was kneeling in the bottom of his craft, striking the water alternately on either side with the broad double blades of his paddle.  Of course he had his back towards us, but he went, as the Spaniards phrase it, ' with his beard upon

his shoulder,' that is to say, constantly looking back, with
a provoking grin upon his face. We soon found that if
we caught the gentleman at all, it would not be until
after a hot chase and a long one. But we gave a shout
and buckled to our work in good earnest. Meantime,
the dwarf seemed to keep ahead almost without an effort
—his light vessel skimming the very surface, while our
heavier shallop was driving the sea into tiny ridges of
foam, and leaving a wake of dancing agitated water. So,
encouraging my men to pull long and strong, and steady
strokes, we flew at a great rate through the intricacies of
the shoal, speedily leaving the schooner far behind. It
must have been a brave sight for a spectator to see—the
light canoe, with its strange rower, spinning along, followed through all its windings and doublings by the shallop, impelled by cracking oars and straining muscles.
Now and then we would cross bays and creeks only
partially sheltered from the swing of the sea, the canoe
jumping as it were, over the broken and sweltering
waves, like a cork upon the parchment of a beaten
drum, while the shallop would plunge, and jerk, and
thrash, amid the cross surges, taking them on board over
the larboard and starboard gunwales at once. Still, I
think we would have caught the dwarf, nervous as was
his arm, and swift as was his boat, had it not been for the
rapidity with which he could wheel her round and round,
following the crooked channels, and threading the narrow
and intricate passages of the shoal, while he managed all
the time to keep the canoe at great speed. Of course our
boat was not so handy. Our utmost endeavours would
not always suffice to keep her clear of a spit of sand, or
to alter her course in time to avail ourselves of a short
cut into which the canoe would suddenly diverge. At
length, my men began to show symptoms of distress ;
they panted at their toil, and, looking over their shoulders,
began to murmur that there was no use in chasing the
devil. All this while, the pilot had never ceased his im-
pudent grin, and he seemed to be as fresh as when he had
started from the side of the schooner. At length, we

found ourselves in a pretty long open passage, with impassable barriers of reefs on either hand. The canoe was not more than a few fathoms ahead, for as we had flagged in our efforts, so had the dwarf relaxed in his. I thought that now was the time for a grand push, and shouting to the men that the game was in our hands, the brave fellows made a great rally—the ashen staves of the oars cracked, the water buzzed and foamed, and in a moment the boats were not more than a few feet apart.

'Huzza, we have him now!' I shouted.

The men pulled like devils, the dwarf worked hard with his paddle; but nothing could keep before us in such a chaise — foot by foot, we overhauled the canoe.

'Three strokes more, comrades, and he is ours.' The men shouted, but the breath had hardly left their lips when—crack!—the bows of the shallop went smash upon a submerged spit of sand. The men were flung higgledy-piggledy, head over heels, sprawling into the bottom of the boat, while a couple of oars snapped like pistol shots. We had run upon a bar which crossed the passage, some six inches under water. The canoe, thanks to her light draught, had floated over it unhurt, and was now lying a few yards a-head—the abominable little dwarf grinning more furiously than ever.

'If we had a musket in the boat, you should laugh on the wrong side of your mouth,' I shouted, gathering myself up and wiping my nose, which was bleeding famously. One of our men caught up a broken shaft of oar and hurled it at the canoe. The little man, who was as quick as light in his movements, parried the missile with the broad blade of his paddle, and called out—

'Ho! ho! pretty fellows to think of taking a ship out to sea without a pilot, when they can't row a boat without running their noses against a post.'

The answer to this was a simultaneous salute from all the fragments of the broken oars, one of which, despite his adroitness, gave the little man a very tolerable thwack across the shoulders, upon which, not choosing to risk the consequences of another broadside, the dwarf called out—

'Good night; you had better pull to the schooner if you don't wan't to sleep among the noddies and the boobies. Ho! ho!—good night.'

He then coolly paddled off, whistling. To have attempted to follow him would be sheer nonsense. We had our wings, as it were, clipped, and if we could not catch the canoe with four fresh men and four oars, there was little chance of overhauling him with four wearied men and two oars, so we addressed ourselves to get back to the schooner. The chase had lasted nearly an hour, and upon looking around we saw the mast of the 'Will o' the Wisp' at a distance which somewhat startled us. There was a flag flying at her main-topmast-head which we supposed was a signal of recall. We therefore began to retrace our course, manning the remaining oars double.

'I hope we may make the schooner, Will Thistle,' said Edward Lanscriffe, one of the boat's crew.

'So do I,' said Paul Williamson, who tugged at the same oar with him; 'it would be ill sleeping among desert rocks and sands, and them haunted too.'

'Haunted?' said I, 'what do you mean? Haunted by whom?'

'By whom but the dwarf who paddled that canoe,' answered the bowman, a sailor from Penzance.

'Why,' quoth I, 'do you think he is anything but a man like ourselves—only, perhaps, for the matter of that, a trifle shorter?'

All the men shook their heads gloomily, and one of them replied—

'No, no; it is no mortal that lives alone amongst these reefs, and refused the help of Christian men to carry him away from the middle of the sea.'

'That is over true,' quoth Paul Williamson, 'and greatly do I fear that his coming boded no good to ship or crew. He ought not to have been allowed on board.'

I tried to laugh at all this, but somehow I was startled and put out of spirits myself, not that I much heeded the fancies of the superstitious sailors, but the whole thing seemed to me so wild, and strange, and uncommon, that I mused and mused hardly knowing what to think of it. Meantime, we were making the best of our way to the ship; of course our progress was slow, for we had to fish out a channel amid the shoals, and the tide being then low, the task was the more difficult. The accursed dwarf seemed to have led us into the most puzzling nook of all the reefs. We rowed and poled, and sometimes waded, dragging the boat along slippery ledges of rock, or smooth banks of fine white sand; but the schooner was still separated from us by a good couple of miles of rock, and sand, and sea, when the sun went down, and in less than half an hour we were groping in the darkness. The ship then fired a gun, and hoisted a light to one of the mast-heads as a signal. The twinkle of this light was, however, so faint, that had we not observed the lantern run up, we might well have taken it for a star, and therefore I kept my eyes steadily fixed upon the tiny spark, intending not to let it get out of sight. Directing the men, therefore, how to row, and continually bumping against points of rock and sand, we jogged on until, just as we rounded a long belt of reef, along which we had been running, the rush of a current of the young flood tide, which had just began to set in, sheered the shallop's bows violently round, bore us some yards away out of our course, and then tossing us into a sort of boiling caldron, or rather slight whirlpool, we were swung round and round until our heads were giddy, and every idea of our proper course gone. Pulling at last clear of this vortex, we tried to discover the signal-light from the schooner, but in vain. The sky was now gemmed with stars down to the very horizon, and we knew not where to look for the guiding ray. It was then that I recollected how easily I might have set the position of the schooner by the constellations, but I had not thought of doing so, and now it was too late. The men began to look startled, and one of them said, in a low voice—

'I told you so; no schooner for us to-night.'

'Why do they not continue firing guns?' I muttered, impatiently. 'Come, boys, let us give them a cheer.'

The night was calm, and I thought our voices might be heard on board the ship, so standing up, and putting our hands trumpet-fashion to our mouths, we gave a long shrill halloo, and then listened intently. For a moment we heard nothing but the surging of the currents as the tide came washing along the channels of the reef, and the low sound of the surf outside. But then was heard distinctly the answering halloo. We shouted again, and shoved off in the direction of the voice, making very good way, for we had struck a tolerably open channel, along which the tide was setting fast. Presently we heard the hail again much closer.

'Come, come,' quoth I, 'Paul Williamson, you will swing in your hammock to-night, for all that is come and gone.'

'Boat ahoy!' said the voice a third time. 'Sheer to port, and keep along that belt of surf on your starboard beam. Have you caught the dwarf?'

'No, confound him!' I shouted; 'and we thought we should never have got to the schooner again. Why did you not keep firing?'

To this no answer was given, and Edward Lanscriffe asked, in a low tone, which of our comrades it was who had hailed. This was a puzzler. We none of us knew the voice.

'Will-o'-the-Wisp, ahoy!' I shouted. 'Halloo!' was the reply. 'Why the devil don't you come aboard? Have you fallen asleep over your oars?'

'We can't see,' we replied, standing up, and peering into the darkness. 'Show a light, man—show a light!'

Immediately a lantern gleamed ahead of us. We pulled towards it. It shone from a dark object. I was in the act of telling the men to lay on their oars, when grit, grit, grit! the boat's keel scrunched upon the sand, and at the same time the lantern was extinguished.

'Ho! ho! Do you want a pilot? I think you do,

indeed,' exclaimed the shrill, cracked voice we knew so well.

'The dwarf, by God!' ejaculated Paul Williamson. 'I told you so. It is a demon, and we are bewitched.'

I was in a great rage. 'You skulking vagabond,' I shouted out, 'wait till daylight to-morrow, and we'll see whether an ounce of lead won't catch that canoe of yours, quick as it is.'

To this there was no answer made, although we sat listening for near ten minutes. What was to be done? We hardly knew; but anything was better than lying idly where we were. The night breeze now struck cold and chill; the men had been overheated at their oars, and their teeth began to chatter. There was a very cordial response of 'Amen,' therefore, as I said, 'I wish we had put a bottle of brandy into the boat.' For half an hour or so we pulled at random, the men whispering and muttering to each other, when I saw a faint flash in the distance, and presently heard the report of a gun. 'There goes the schooner, at length,' I cried. The boat's head was promptly put into the proper direction, and we recommenced our weary pull with something like energy. We must have been near the outward edge of the shoals, for the surf thundered loud, and great broken swells often came rolling past us in a multitude of uneven undulations. All at once the confounded voice of the dwarf hailed us.

'You are going the wrong way, my brave fellows. If you expect to reach the schooner on that course, you must pull the boat round the world, and carry her over Asia.'

'Never mind the spiteful creature,' I said, in a low tone; 'he is but attempting to mislead us. It is his turn to-night; it will be ours to-morrow, when the sun rises.'

Ten minutes more elapsed, then another musket was discharged, almost due ahead. 'See,' I exclaimed, in great triumph; 'we are keeping the exact course; we shall be on board in a jiffey.'

Paul Williamson shook his head. 'The schooner,'

quoth he, 'is anchored near the centre of the shoals, and you hear how heavy and how near the surf is beating.'

I was somewhat troubled at this, I confess, but I saw nothing for it but to pull on. So we did, until having coasted for some time along a succession of rocks, on the opposite side of which the sea was running heavily, we suddenly shot out from beyond their shelter, and imme-diately the boat was hove up upon the crest of so high and long a swell, that we all exclaimed at once, that we were out in the open sea. Just then, the pernicious dwarf hailed again, his voice now seeming to come from astern.

'You are better pilots than I reckoned,' shouted the spiteful atomy, 'only that when you would keep at sea you come ashore ; and when you would hug the land you start off right into the ocean.'

This time, at all events, he was clearly not deceiving us, so we promptly pulled the boat about, and were soon in the comparatively smooth water of the reef. One thing we now knew pretty well—the dwarf was armed, for it must have been he who fired the muskets, and, not doubting but that his optics were far more accustomed to the darkness than ours, we thought it extremely pro-bable that he might amuse himself by plumping a shot or two into the boat. This was not a comfortable idea to cherish, so I hailed at random—·

'Pilot ! pilot—ahoy !' no answer. We repeated the summons a dozen of times, but heard no sound save the heavy beat of the surf and the wild cry of sea-birds.

'Why, the scoundrel has gone home to bed,' quoth I ; 'and, to tell you the truth, comrades, I think we may give up playing at blind man's buff for the night, and wait peaceably until we see the schooner in the morning."

This counsel was followed. We presently found a sandy cove, in which we lay very snugly, and then, after setting a watch, dropped off to sleep, weary, hungry, thirsty, and vexed.

The day dawned, and we speedily discovered the schooner, about as far off as she was when we lost sight

of her after sundown, the evening before.   A pull of an
hour brought us alongside, upon which there was a great
outcry to know whether we had caught the pilot, and
why we had not returned betimes.

' Why,' quoth I, ' we could not see you in the dark.'

' There was a light all night at the main-topmast-head,'
says Captain Jem.

' Yes, but we lost sight of it once, and then we could
not tell your lantern from a star.   Why did you not
fire ?'

' We were clearing away the bow gun,' answered Captain Jem, ' when we heard you fire a musket.'

' We fire ! that was the dwarf.   We had no musket.'

' By the Lord !' says Captain Jem, ' I think we are all
bewitched among these cursed reefs, which no one ever
saw or heard of before.'

---

## CHAPTER XV.

### AT LENGTH THEY CATCH THE DWARF PILOT, AND HEAR STRANGE THINGS TOUCHING A TREASURE.

PREPARATIONS were now again made in order to discover
a way out.   My comrades would have me turn in and go
to sleep, but I was too much excited to hear of it; and,
accordingly, after breakfast I was in the shallop again,
with four fresh men, including Nicky Hamstring and
Bristol Tom.   We carried with us fragments of light
wood and great stones for sinkers, to buoy a passage for
the schooner.   There was no need of lead or line, for we
could see to the bottom of the crystal water, even where
it was many fathoms deep.   We were thus engaged great
part of the day, and being now working with something
like method and regularity, we were making sensible progress in discovering a channel, when, just as I was setting
one of our buoys, Nicky Hamstring grasped my arm,
and whispered with a sort of gasp, ' There—look there !'

I followed his eye, and started up with delight.   A
long bank of sand, with ridges of coral, along which we

had been skirting for some time, terminated in one of
the largest and highest rocks we had seen. Indeed,
when the tide was out, it seemed rather a rocky islet
than a rock; but what directed our attention to it was a
deep cleft, into which the sea ran, and in which, as in a
cistern of water, floated the bark canoe of the dwarf pilot.
The shallop was close alongside the sand-bank when we
made this discovery, and Nicky and I leaped out of her
into the shallow water like a couple of madmen, and
screaming to our comrades to row for the little creek, we
both scampered along the dry hard sand towards the
rock.

'You secure the canoe,' I called to Nicky; 'the owner
is not far from the nest; so, while Nicky went clambering along the steep shelves to the cove, I climbed up the
ledges of the rock, slipping down now and then into
cracks and hollows, which peeled my shins famously, but
very soon arriving at the summit, from which I caught
sight of the dwarf running with great speed round the
base of the rock, and immediately gave chase, shouting
out to our friend to surrender at discretion. But he
took no notice, making as straight as he could for the
cove, whence, doubtless, he expected to get clear off in
his canoe. I seeing this, thought it unnecessary to risk
my neck in order to intercept him, and so clambered
leisurely down the rock laughing aloud, and calling to
the dwarf that I had told him that our turn would come
with daylight. Meantime, the little man went skipping
over the rocks like a goat, never making a false step,
until suddenly he came in sight of the cove, within which
the shallop by this time lay alongside the canoe. Then
he sent up a shrill cry of surprise, which my comrades
answered with a cheer, and stopping short, appeared to
pause for a moment, after which he made straight for a
projecting shoulder of the rock, round which he speedily
disappeared.

'Never mind,' quoth I; 'take care of the canoe, and
we shall soon find him.' So saying, I called upon Nicky
and Bristol Tom to land, which they did, making their

way to the projection, round which the dwarf had run, while I, following a steep cleft or split in the rock, which ran from near the top of it, down to a white sandy beach on the opposite side from the cove, descended rapidly. All at once, about half-way down, my eye caught the flutter of canvas, and immediately I discerned something like a tent, very snugly pitched in a nook of rock, about a couple of fathoms above high water-mark, with a sort of fence of barrels and boxes round it.

'Ho, ho!' quoth I. 'Here is the hermitage, at last.'

'Stop!' says the shrill voice I had so often heard, 'stop there—as you value your life!'

And thereon I descried the dwarf, with a long-barrelled Spanish gun in his hand, which he was in the act of lifting to his shoulder.

'Stop!' quoth he again; and being unarmed, I had nothing for it, in prudence, but to obey.

'My friend,' says I, 'you may as well uncock that gun. Your canoe is taken, as you saw. My comrades are upon the rock. The schooner is not a mile off, and if you are fool enough to fire at me, hit or miss, I warn you that it will be the last time you will ever pull a trigger.'

The little man paused a moment. 'Let me alone, and I will let you alone,' he said.

'No, no,' quoth I. 'You paid us the first visit, and we must show our good breeding by returning it.'

The pilot considered for a brief space, made a passionate gesture with the air of a man deeply mortified, and then called out, at the same time grounding his musket—

'Come on. I will do you no harm.'

So I descended and joined him, just as Nicky and Bristol Tom made their appearance on the beach below, having run round the islet. By this time we were close to the tent.

'Come in,' says the dwarf; 'I shall be more hospitable than you.' The habitation consisted simply of a dry cleft in the rocks, over which a roof of canvas had been stretched, supported in the centre by a pole. For furniture there was a hammock, not slung, but laid upon

the sandy floor, and a sea-chest, upon which lay a very
complete set of astronomical instruments, with paper,
pens, and ink, and a half-finished chart, which, appearing
to be a plan of the shoals, I laid violent hands on at once.
There was some common household stuff, such as knives,
plates, and pots in a corner, and near them a good-sized
water barrel.

'Well, gentlemen,' says the dwarf, very politely, 'behold you in my dwelling. What may be your pleasure?'

'Our pleasure,' said I, 'is that you shift your dwelling
for a brief space, and sling your hammock on board the
schooner.'

'I protest against being thus unlawfully carried away,'
says the little man.

'You are at perfect liberty to protest,' said I ; 'but
you must go on board all the same.'

The pilot gave a curious sort of grin, but did not seem
disposed to resist our power. Nicky Hamstring then
went to the top of the rock, and hailed our comrades to
bring the canoe and the shallop round, which presently
they did. Meantime I was considering within myself,
whether by a careful overhaul of the little man's dwelling,
I might not be able to light on some clue to the motive—
and it could not be a common one—which seemed to bind
him to these desolate shoals. Resolving to take my own
time and my own way in the search, I directed my comrades to put the pilot into the shallop and row aboard of
the schooner, telling Captain Jem that I would follow in
the canoe, after a careful search of the tent. They
started off accordingly ; the dwarf, who appeared to be in
tolerable good humour, notwithstanding his capture,
taking my place in the stern-sheets, and managing the
tiller.

As soon as they had disappeared, I commenced my
inquisition. The chart of the shoals was very skilfully
constructed, and neatly put upon paper, being very different, indeed, from the rude scrawls which seamen commonly trace, of coasts and islands. No indication, however, was to be observed of any harbour, or secure cove,

the existence of which might make the reefs a place of refuge. I noticed, however, on the north-west corner of the shoals, a cross slightly traced with a pencil. Putting the chart in my pocket, I searched the hut thoroughly, raking up the sand which formed the floor; and also prying into the casks and boxes which surrounded the tent. These appeared to contain nothing save common coarse provisions. The contents of the sea-chest were clothes such as sailors wear, with one suit of a Spanish cut and fashion, in a pocket of which I felt something hard. Examining more closely, I found the object to be a small and old book, in the Spanish language, imprinted at Granada, in the year 1507, and purporting to be the 'Voyages and Perilous Journeyings of one Vincente y Tormes, who sailed on board the Caravel, called the Pinta, with the great Admiral Christopher Colon, or Columbus, for the Discovery of the New World.' Looking over the contents of this volume, I found them to be accounts of divers voyages made between Spain and the West Indies, written in very bad and cramped Spanish, and containing but dry details of little interest.

I was about to lay the volume down, when I noticed that it came very easily open towards the latter portion, as though that part had been peculiarly studied, and looking more closely, I saw that a leaf had been cut out. Towards the foot of the page preceding that which was missing, was a chapter with a title as follows—

HEREIN I DISCOURSE OF THE PERILOUS LOSS OF THE GREAT TREASURE SHIP SANTA FÈ, AND OF MY MIRACULOUS ESCAPE, BEING THE ONLY ONE OF THAT SHIP'S COMPANY WHO, THROUGH THE SPECIAL GRACE OF THE BLESSED VIRGIN, WAS PRESERVED OUT OF A GREAT DANGER.

Then followed the words of the narrative in this wise :—

' Now all things being in readiness, there was a great mass held, with other needful ordinances and prayers to the saints ; and so, on the 14th of June, we loosed from the city of Porto Bello, intending to touch at St. Domingo, in the great Isle of Hispaniola, to receive the

tribute from the caciques, and so thence across the ocean
to Spain.    But, alas, it fell out otherwise!—for being but
six days at sea, with contrary winds, which here do blow
continually from the north-west point of the compass, we
did unhappily——'

This was the last line of the page; the following leaf
being, as I have said, torn out.  The narrative recommenced upon the succeding page with these words :—

'Thus—thus was I—all praise to the holy saints,
particularly to my patron St. Geneviève, and to the
Virgin—rescued from my hopeless and miserable condition, and carried home to Spain, I being very heavy and
desponding in that voyage, on account of the loss of all
my shipmates, so that I vowed never to tempt the seas
again, but rather to live on crusts and water ashore.'

From the remaining chapters, which were few, it would
seem that the author had kept to this resolution, for he
narrated that he became a water-carrier and a servant to
a priest, called Pedro Vronez, to whom he dictated the
book.  The perusal of what I have set down above, the
reader will possibly guess, gave rise to a startling train of
ideas in my mind, and putting the adventures of Vincente
y Tormes in my pocket, I jumped into the canoe, the
Mosquito-men having taught me the management of such
cockle-shells, and was presently alongside the schooner.

Captain Jem was leaning over the side, fishing with a
hook and line.

'Well, what have you found?' quoth he, as if he did
not think that my search could have availed much.

'Found!' I echoed, clambering on board.  'I have
found what may well make our fortunes.'

At these words, our comrades came running from all
sides very eagerly.

"Where is the dwarf?' quoth I.

'Oh, in the great cabin,' replied the captain.  'A
sullen piece of goods, I warrant you.  He refuses to
speak a word.'

'Have him out,' answered I; 'and we will try to make
him find his tongue.'

And so, presently, Master Pilot was hustled forth upon the deck.

'Will you tell us,' quoth I, 'why you choose to live alone amongst these grim rocks?'

The little man grinned, twisted his features, and answered never a word. The crew looked on curiously.

'Once upon a time, there sailed a Spanish treasure-ship from Porto Bello.'

The dwarf pricked up his ears, and all the blood went away from his face.

'In which ship,' I continued, 'there was a mariner named Vincente y Tormes. But the ship had not been six days at sea, going to Hispaniola to receive the tribute of the Caciques, when it was lost upon certain reefs, *with the treasure on board*, and Vincente y Tormes of all the crew was saved, and carried to Spain, where afterwards he became a water-carrier and servant to a priest, named——'

'You need not trouble yourself to recite further,' said the dwarf, with a shrug of the shoulders. 'You guess my secret. I thought none of you had wit enough to pick the marrow out of that bone, but it was all my own fault. I came on board this schooner, and in doing so threw away, by one moment of folly, the fruits of years of labour and danger. Dolt that I was!—what could it matter to me whether you succeeded in blundering out, as you blundered in, or stayed here until the first heavy blow smashed your ship to powder on these coral reefs? It would have been all the same to me.'

Having made this speech with great bitterness, but in a perfectly composed fashion, the dwarf sat down upon a coil of rope, and shrugged his shoulders almost as high as the crown of his head.

The crew were now all in a hubbub, for they comprehended, more or less, that there was the wreck of an ancient galleon upon the reef, and they knew that silver and gold are metals which brine rusts not.

'I suppose,' quoth the dwarf, 'that you will give me a fair share of the booty when we get it?'

This they all proclaimed that they were very ready to do, and one or two of the more eager shook hands with the dwarf, who assumed a very sour smile.

'Now, then,' quoth the captain, when the tumult was a little abated, 'tell us somewhat more about this, and rely upon it we will deal justly by you. Who and what are you?'

'Why,' quoth the dwarf, 'my story is of the shortest; my name is Paul Bedloe, and I was born beneath the Peel of Douglas, in the Isle of Man; my father owning a small craft, which plied to Liverpool—a village on the Lancaster coast—I was brought up a sailor, but I liked better to write and cipher than to handle ropes and furl sails; and having, also, a great liking for geography and astronomy, I became a very good navigator, and going to London, settled at Limehouse, where I kept a school for teaching seamen the art of navigation. Growing somewhat tired of this business, however, I went several voyages to these seas with a captain who had been my scholar; and afterwards, returning to Europe, I wandered through many countries, taking great delight in Spain, where I found several interesting accounts left by the first discoverers of America of their voyages. One day, in the shop of a Jew in Cadiz, I discovered the book which you, sir'—turning to me—'doubtless, found in my chest. One leaf of that work had a very particular interest for me, and from the time I first saw it, I have kept it carefully on my person.'

With that the Manxman produced the missing page from his bosom.

'By the help of this,' continued he, 'I found out how the treasure-ship, Santa Fè, had been stranded upon an exceeding great shoal, and how a storm soon coming on, she had sunk in middling deep water, between two ledges of rock. The ship's company having deserted her in boats, these were speedily swallowed up in the storm, save that one in which Vincente y Tormes sailed, and which survived the tempest, although it was driven far to leeward. The wind then taking off, a calm followed, during which all the seamen in the boat, with only the exception of Vincente y Tormes, perished miserably of hunger and thirst. He was himself nigh dead, when a caravel descried and picked him up; ultimately conveying him to Spain, where he settled, and went no more to sea. You may judge,' continued Paul Bedloe, ' whether I have not given a fair account of the missing page ;' and, hand ing the document to me, he continued as follows :—

' On reading what I have now stated to you, it occurred to me that, in all the maps and charts which I had seen, no mention had ever been made of any such shoals as that upon which the "Santa Fè" was wrecked, and I concluded that no ship had ever fallen in with them, save those which, like the Porto Bello galleon, had never returned to tell the tale. Hence, I concluded, that it was very possible that some fragments of the wreck might yet remain undisturbed, containing boundless wealth. With much ado, and by spending nearly all which I possessed in bribes, I got access to the documents in the archives of the Minister of Marine of Spain, and there I found the loss of the " Santa Fè" fully confirmed. She had sailed from Porto Bello, and had never been heard of again. This entry, mark you, was before the date of Vincente's publication, while he, not having appeared to contemplate the possibility of recovering the foundered wealth, took no steps, and communicated with no one on the subject. After this, I carefully examined Vincente's narrative, and compared with it the records of many voyages from Porto Bello and Carthagena to Hispaniola and Porto Rico, so that, at length, I satisfied myself that the shoals in question must, if they existed at all, be within a circle of fifty miles in diameter. I next communicated with a brother of mine in Bristol, touching the matter, and informing him that I intended to proceed to the West Indies in search of the shoals, and the wreck of the "Santa Fè," conjured him, in case he heard from me again, to have a ship ready fitted out, to sail for the longitude and latitude which I would send him. I embarked at Cadiz, and landed in Porto Rico, which island I suspected of being almost right to windward of the shoals.    Here I made acquaintance with a Welsh seaman, to whom I partly communicated my projects ; and with the help of a negro and two Indians, very faithful attached fellows, we constructed a great " Piragua," victualled her very well, and put off to sea.    We cruised for a month with no success, and then were forced to run for the Samballas Islands, off Darien, for more provisions. Putting to sea again, after a three weeks' voyage, we hit upon the spot we sought for.    The weather was then exceeding calm, and we could see the bottom in the very deepest parts of the reef, so that on the eighth day of our search, we actually descried the remains of a great ship, wedged between two rocks, about five fathoms under water.    Our Indians were brave divers, and speedily brought up pieces of carved wood, and two or three old-fashioned swords, which satisfied me that we had hit upon the wreck of an ancient Spanish vessel ; for when we scoured the blades, we could read on them the word " Bilboa."    At length, after tearing a great deal of the wreck to pieces, the divers reported that they had come to many large chests, with great clamps of rusted iron ; and one of these being wrenched open, a small ingot was seen lying just beneath the lid, which we soon found to be virgin silver.    On this, I stopped further proceedings, and wrote a letter to my brother in cipher, such as we had agreed upon to use.    This letter, my comrades in the " Piragua" started away with, designing to make Jamaica, and send it home by an English ship ; while I, having an ample amount of provisions, and having found great basins in the rocks, which the rain filled with fresh water, determined to remain, until the " Piragua " returned from Jamaica, to watch over my treasure, and to study the best means of recovering it.    In case of accident to the " Piragua," I had a canoe, with which, in moderate weather, I was not afraid of reaching the land.    I had been here just two months and three days, when, on waking one morning, I saw your schooner.    Such, gentlemen, is my story from first to last.'

You may be sure that there was great acclamation at these tidings of a ship-load of riches falling, as it were, into our mouths; but Captain Jem, who appeared to have his doubts of Mr. Bedloe, ordered his person, his chest, and hammock to be very strictly searched. Everything found, however, confirmed the story. There were several books upon navigation, and an old diary in which were entered divers sums in dollars, reals, and marvedis, which appeared to have been expended upon the Spanish officials at the office of marine. Besides this, the draught of a letter, addressed to Master Richard Bedloe, near the church of St. Mary, Redcliffe, in Bristol, corroborated a great portion of the dwarf-pilot's story; so that, upon the whole, we began to believe him firmly. The ingot, he told us, the Welshman had taken to Jamaica to be assayed.

By the time that all these particulars had been ascertained, the day was almost at an end, and it was determined that, with the dawn next morning, both the boats should start to the wreck, provided with due tackle, and having the Indians, who are excellent divers, aboard. Paul Bedloe's hammock was swung in the great cabin, and a watch placed over him all night: but he appeared to sleep soundly, and to be but little affected by the probable downfall of his golden hopes. Indeed, so much was I struck with this, and so composed was the dwarf in confessing the whole matter to us, part of which must at all events be true, that I came to the conclusion that, despite of all his pretended candour and frankness, the fellow intended to play us a slippery trick after all; so that, confiding my suspicions to my comrades, Mr. Bedloe was informed that, five minutes after he had given any symptom of treachery, he would be dangling from the sprit of the main-sail. To this intimation, the only answer he vouchsafed was the old shrug of the shoulders.

The night seemed long to many on board, and with the grey dawn the boats were manned, Bedloe sitting beside the captain in the launch, and directing the steersman. The dwarf told us that he would take the boats to the

place where the wreck lay, which was near the open sea,
by such a channel as the schooner could follow in.  We
therefore laid down buoys as we went along, it being determined that as soon as the launch reached the wreck, I
should pull back in the shallop, and navigate the ship to
the scene of action.

And now, behold us, with shout, and joke, and laugh,
like men who are to be speedily and marvellously enriched, pulling gaily for the sunken El Dorado.  The
morning mist was rising slowly from the ocean; the surf-
ridges sparkled in the first glances of the hot sun-light;
and the white and grey sea-birds wheeled and screamed
joyously over-head.  The very rocks and sands bore a
changed aspect in our eyes; instead of forlorn and dreary
shelves of crag and shingle lying desolately in a far-off
sea, we gazed upon them as the mystic beds of incal-
culable wealth:  'The sea,' we said, joyfully, 'may not
give up her dead, but she keeps a feebler clutch upon
her gold.  Courage, comrades, courage! we shall divide
the ingots which were melted for the treasury of Old
Castile.'

'Why may there not be more than one single cast-
away ship lying hereabouts?' quoth our surgeon.  And
we echoed, 'Why indeed?'

At this juncture I noticed Paul Bedloe start and
turn pale, just as he did when I told him his secret the
day before.  He recovered himself, however, directly,
and it was not until after events had made me connect
that start with the topic of conversation at the moment,
that I realized all its significance and meaning.

A pull of less than an hour brought us to the spot
where Bedloe declared that the treasure of the Santa Fè
lay hid.  The shoal, to the southward extremity, where
we now anchored the boats, split into two long branches
or arms, having deep and sheltered water between them.
It was on the weathermost or eastern of these banks,
among spits of sand and jags of rock, that the remains of
the ill-fated ship lay.  Making fast a grapnel to a point
of coral, we allowed the boats, under the pilot's direction,

to drift five or six fathoms to leeward, until they floated
in a rather deep channel, or hole, well sheltered by the
coral reefs from the motion of the sea.

'Now then,' quoth Bedloe, 'look beneath you.' Immediately, we were all bending over the gunwales of launch
and shallop, and presently, shading off the light with one
hand, we saw, some five fathoms down, wavering and
quivering through the clear cold water, the mouldering
form of a ship of size. There lay the once graceful hull,
bulged and split by the rocks, the bows broken off altogether, the quarter and stern firmly jammed in a crevice
of the reef, and so uninjured that we could distinguish
the quarter galleries and the outlines of the sculptured
figures and medallions and carving. The deck had been
partially broken up, and two or three cannon lay half
upon the bulwarks, half upon the rocks. All three masts
had been broken off close by the board, and their stumps,
like the rest of the wreck, were encrusted with masses of
shell-fish, and heaped, here and there, with wavy bunches
of slimy seaweed. Fish of many sizes and forms glided
tranquilly between us and the foundered ship, and once
or twice we saw a great flat ray rise up from the dark
recesses of the hold, and glide like a plate of burnished
copper along the deck.

'There, gentlemen,' says Paul Bedloe, ' you see I have
dealt fairly by you. You look upon the Santa Fè, which,
more than one hundred and sixty years ago, set sail from
Porto Bello for Old Spain.'

So, rising up, we gave a great shout, which, in a minute,
we heard echoed by our comrades, whom we had left behind in the Will-o'-the-Wisp.

'Will Thistle,' says the captain, ' bring up the schooner
directly, and for heaven's sake, take care of her bottom
against the reefs ; we may have a freight of price to carry
home in it.'

So presently, having returned to the Will-o'-the-Wisp,
and satisfied the eager demands of those on board, we
very soon cast off our moorings, and the trade wind
blowing steadily, we set our forestay sail and mainsail

and began to run down the channel towards the launch.
The way being well buoyed, and all hands working very
smartly, and keeping a bright look-out, there was no difficulty, and little danger in making the run, and in less
than an hour from the time I had left the launch, the
schooner glided into the fork of deep water between the
two tails of the reef, and then forging near the edge of
the weathermost bank we furled our canvas, and the
anchor plunged down, twelve fathoms to the bottom,
sinking well into the soft sand, which here formed good
holding-ground.

---

## CHAPTER XVI.

### HOW THE DWARF TURNS TRAITOR, AND OF HIS FATE.

THE launch lay at about a cable's length distance, and
Captain Jem hailed me to shove off the shallop again,
and bring a couple of hand-leads, and some strong lines
for the use of the divers, with one block of the pig-iron
which we had for ballast, and a good stout rope attached
to it.    As we pushed off with these articles on board, we
saw the naked, dusky forms of both the Mosquito Indians,
poising themselves with their clenched hands above their
heads upon the gunwale of the launch, when, after swinging and swaying their bodies for a moment or two, they
sprang into the air together, and dived head-foremost
down.    By this time, so great was the eagerness, that
half of the men were stripped as well as the Indians, and
no sooner had the latter disappeared, than near a dozen
stalwart fellows leaped overboard and dived after them.
But our countrymen were none of them skilful enough in
the art to descend through five fathoms of water and yet
keep their eyes keenly open and their wits well about
them ; and as the shallop rubbed sides with the launch,
their black, sleek heads and red, strained faces, began to
appear puffing and blowing, like so many grampuses, all
round the boats, and crying out that the water was too
deep for them.    One man alone, a slender, muscular

young fellow, a Frenchman, who had been used, when a boy, as he told us, to dive from a pier, at Brest, for sous, alone brought up in his clutch a mass of slushy seaweed, grasped from the stump of one of the masts.

The Indians were, however, yet under water, and we were getting uneasy about them, when we saw their dark forms shooting between us and the foundered ship, and presently they stuck their black heads, for all the world like seals, above the surface, holding up their empty hands in token of their fruitless plunge. They had descended through one of the hatchways into the hold, and groped about there as they best could in the dim light, but except sheets of rotten canvas and masses of rusted iron, they found nothing. Upon this, Bedloe was immediately appealed to, as to the position of the precious coffers, and he declared that they lay very deep indeed, almost at the keel of the vessel, in the stern, having probably been stowed under the great cabin. He had not been down himself, he said, as an asthma hindered him from diving, but both of his Indians had crept through the deck at the after hatchway, and he fully believed their report.

We now prepared to institute a fuller search, and with that view, making fast the great block of ballast-iron to the rope, we hove it overboard. The ponderous lump of metal fell upon the high quarter deck, and crashed through the rotten wood, into the cabin beneath, starting whole shoals of flat-fish and eels, which glided and wriggled away, and sending up to the surface a boiling volume of thickened and turbid water, with little chips of wood, and ends of rope, which, thanks to pitch and tar, had remained unsaturated with moisture. We waited for a short time until the sea had cleared, and then Blue Peter and his comrades fastened the two hand-leads round their waists, leaving the other extremities of the lines attached to them in our hands, and then going gently over the side of the boat, grasped the downward leading rope and slid along it, just as though it had been a back-stay, until they disappeared beneath the shipwrecked vessel's decks, we, of course letting out the lead-lines as the divers proceeded. A moment of great anxiety followed, and I observed that the dwarf instead of having his eyes fixed, like most of us, upon the water, was looking about him very nervously, fidgetting upon his seat, and moving and rubbing his fingers, and biting his lips, as people do who fear detection of misdeeds. Presently, the Indians again ascended to the surface, and again empty handed. There were nothing like chests or coffers they said—only casks, which being quite rotten, they had broken into and found them full of flour, hard caked with the wet. There were also some old fashioned carbines, a great grindstone, a quantity of rotten cables and hawsers, a small brass cannon, and a great unnameable mass of mouldering material, which stirred when it was trodden upon, and blackened the water, so that, after a few moments, the Indians could see no more.

At this information, there were many threatening scowls cast upon the Manxman, but he bore them firmly enough.

'Well, Paul Bedloe,' says the Captain, 'what say you to this ?'

'I presume your divers are not so expert as mine— that is what I say,' answered the little man, coolly enough.

At this Blue Peter fired up.

'I say—dere are no coffers or treasure at all dere !' exclaimed the Indian : 'and Massa Captain Jem here believe Blue Peter, who never told him a lie—oh, never, not at all.'

'Yes, Blue Peter, I do believe you,' replied Captain Jem ; 'and if the prisoner here be dealing falsely with us, on his own head be the peril.'

This was the first time that the Captain had called Bedloe the 'prisoner,' and the little man started at the phrase, very perceptibly, but he only said—

'I tell you what my Indians told me ; and one of them brought up an ingot of silver to prove that his words were true.'

I was, meanwhile, musing whether I should not try a dive myself. I remembered that I had been tolerably expert at the exercise, when a boy, and so, stripping and buckling a hand-lead to my loins, as I had seen the Indians do to aid their descent, I plunged overboard into the tepid sea, and grasping the rope, found that I descended rapidly and easily, and that the water was so transparent, that I saw above me the keels of the boats, and below me the form of the cast-away ship, as clearly as though I gazed upon them through the gloaming of a Scottish summer's evening. It was a curious sensation, that of clinging to the rope in the mid sea, with the water like a mass of thick green air, wavering and gurgling about me, and the indistinctly-seen forms of fishes gliding hither and thither, like little opaque phantoms,—and as strange was the feeling when I placed my foot, as though my body had no weight, upon the slimy deck, and felt the feathery sea-weed rise upwards at the pressure, and cling and wave about my legs. All this, of course, passed in a moment, and in the next I had descended through the after-hatchway, and steadying myself with my feet upon the lump of pig-iron, I had time to cast a hurried, but observant glance around me. A considerable portion of the deck had been torn away, or broken up, by the fall of the pig-iron, and down the aperture came a dull greenish light, showing the dim outline of great ribs of wood, and masses of timber-work, bulged and broken, with fragments of the rock projecting, here and there, through the crushed and splintered masses. Around me lay piled up rotting casks, and the fragments of bulkheads, and the smouldering remains of furniture. I saw the holes where doors had led from cabin to cabin, sea-weed came waving through them. Shell-fish clung in clusters to what had been the rudder-case, and to rusty iron-work, which as I moved, upon the rotting wood and hemp, hurt my feet. Sprawling along the wreck, and rousing slimy fish from their lurking-places, I made my way to where I saw the sheen of glimmering metal, and presently I clutched what was the brass box of a compass. Then throwing off my leaden sinker, I burst my way out of a quarter-gallery window, and rose rapidly to the surface, almost spent for want of air,--holding the compass above my head. It was a minute after I had breathed, before the loud ringing in my ears enabled me to hear the shouts of my comrades. They had seen the glimmer of the metal as I rose, and very naturally took the brass for gold; but they were soon undeceived, and after I had been hauled on board, and had time to examine my prize, I undeceived them still further, for I saw a name and a date upon the implement.

'So, comrades,' I exclaimed, 'the little man is playing us false. The Santa Fè must have been lost before the year 1507, and upon this compass case is written, " Ericson. Amsterdam, 1645."'

At this, there was a loud shout of wrath, and the seamen turned in fury to the dwarf; but he preserved a wonderful boldness,—all the nervous agitation was gone, and though he was pale, neither hand nor lip quivered.

'This is not the wreck of the Santa Fè,' thundered Captain Jem, 'and we were dolts to take it for such. Timber must have mouldered away in half the time this vile dwarf would have us believe that the ship beneath us had lain under water. But take care,' and the captain turned to Bedloe and shook him soundly,—'take care how you trifle with us, or, as you seem so fond of this wreck, by God, you shall lay your stunted bones in it.'

Paul Bedloe seemed prepared for this burst, for he said very calmly—'I have told you what I know, and if you are deceived, it is because I was beguiled myself. The Indians spoke falsely.'

'And the ingot—the silver ingot!' shouted half a dozen of the men.

'That I saw with my own eyes brought up from the water,' replied Bedloe; 'and he who recovered it said that there was much more where that came from.'

I looked hard into the dwarf's eyes. He bore my gaze for a minute steadily enough, and then tried to **turn away.**

' You have lied in your throat !' I cried—' you have lied, and you know you have lied. There are two wrecks on the shoal.'

' There may be a dozen for all I know,' said the little man very stubbornly ; ' you may drown me if you will, but that will not put you nearer the treasures of the Santa Fè.'

Captain Jem paused and looked round upon the men, as though he were collecting their thoughts. Just then, the boatswain hailed from the schooner that the weather was getting very ugly to the southward. We all looked up, and saw an ominous black cloud lying looming upon the sea, its upper edges gilded with a lurid glow, as though edged with red-hot iron. The regular trade wind, too, had ceased to blow, except in faint sickly puffs, and the schooner began to rise and sink upon great swelling undulations from the southward, so that loose ropes and blocks shook and rattled, and the gaffs of the foresail and mainsail swung to and fro with a creaking, wheezing sound. It was clear that something unpleasant was brewing.

' Fasten a spare oar to the line,' says the captain, pointing to the rope which descended to the wreck, ' we may as well buoy the place.' His directions were obeyed.

' Now, pull for the schooner. Lash that man's arms there with a bit of spun-yarn ; he has brought it upon himself.' And in a minute we were safe on board, and the dwarf, who made no resistance, was thrust well pinioned into the cabin.

' We have no time to trifle,' said the captain ; and so we all thought, precious moments had been lost, without the symptoms of the weather having been attended to.

' We were looking for the gold,' said the captain.

' And we were looking at you,' replied the boatswain. In ten minutes the anchor was up, the boats hoisted in, the sails set double reefed, and the schooner beating to the southward against heavy puffs of wind and a great tumbling swell. Our object was to weather either of the branches or horns of the shoal, then we could either scud

or lie to, having plenty of sea-room.  What we feared
was, that the force of the squalls would strike us before
we got clear of the fork in which we were embayed.
Meantime the sky was growing every moment of a more
lurid colour, as though the arch of heaven had been a great
vault of brazen metal, and the surf was breaking in awful
surges upon the reefs.

'Captain,' says Bristol Tom, who was at the tiller,
'we shall not weather the point; the wind heads her
every moment.'    And as he spoke, the sails flapped like
thunder, and a great swell lifted the schooner and flung
her bodily back a dozen fathoms.    One of the men from
the forecastle cried at the same time that the wind was
coming, for that the sea was breaking white about a
league away.

'We must run back through the shoal,' says I.

The captain paused a moment.  'There is no other
hope,' quoth he.  'Fetch the dwarf on deck;' and
immediately Bedloe made his appearance, and gazed
anxiously at the weather.  Captain Jem went below.

'You offered to pilot us already,' I said, 'and you
know the shoal well.  I have seen your chart of it.  You
must bring us through now.'

Captain Jem at this moment returned on deck, carrying
two large pistols.

'If the schooner as much as scrapes a ridge of sand,'
says he, and he pressed the muzzle of one of the pistols
so hard upon the dwarf's forehead, that when he took it
away there was a round blue ring left above the eyebrow;
'if the schooner as much as taps one oyster upon the
coral, you cease to live!'

'That is no news,' answered the dwarf, with the old
shrug of the shoulders; 'if the schooner strikes we all of
us cease to live.  Pooh, pooh, man! bullying avails not
now.  We are all of us more near being drowned than I
am of being shot.  Put up your pistols.'

I declare I positively began to admire the dwarf.  His
cool courage was heroic.  Captain Jem turned all manners
of colours, whistled, grinned, then tried to appear stern;

and at last stuck the pistol into the waistband of his trousers, looking rather sheepish than otherwise. Then there was a pause, which the dwarf broke by saying in the old jeering tone—

'Well, captain, do you want a pilot?'

'Do you undertake to run the schooner through these shoals into the open sea to the northward?' I replied.

'Why, I told you from the first I would run you into the open sea,' says the imperturbable Mr. Bedloe.

'Take charge of the schooner, then,' quoth the captain.

'Unloose my arms,' answered Bedloe. 'I ought to have as good a chance as the others.'

The captain hesitated.

'Wounds, man!' cried the dwarf; 'I give you my word of honour I am not going to take the schooner from you.'

The cool impudence of the fellow was amusing; and so, stepping forward, I cut the rope-yarns which bound him.

'Now, then,' quoth he to Bristol Tom and the captain, both of whom stood by the tiller, 'look sharp for the pilot's orders.'

The Manxman stepped to the weather-beam, looked earnestly to windward and then aloft; after which he walked back whistling. The schooner was labouring heavily upon the swells, and the sky getting wilder and wilder.

All at once, the man at the mast-head shouted—'A sail!'

We were all of us startled at the news.

'Not the Spanish frigate, Johnson?' said I.

'No, no,' returned the seaman. 'It is a sort of boat—a big canoe. I can only see her when she lifts on the sea; but she carries a high mast forward, with a small mizen astern, and she is edging in for the side of the shoals. By God, sir, she is among them!'

I was standing by the dwarf as we heard this. H

leaped upon the bulwarks, clambered a few feet into the
rigging, and then dropped upon the deck, exclaiming :—
' The Piragua !'

' What !' says the captain, ' your Piragua with the
Indians and the Welshman ?'

' That and no other,' answered Bedloe. ' You see,
gentlemen, I have told you no lies.'

' The canoe is running for the lee of the large rock,
where the dwarf lived,' cries the man in the rigging.

' Then, by the Lord, they are more in love with
coral reefs and sand-banks than I am !' replied Captain
Jem.

' I don't know that they bean't right, captain,' cries
the boatswain.  ' That rock is big enough to make a good
shelter under its lee ; and there's a little cove there, if
they can make it, where the small canoe was, where an
undecked craft will be much snugger in such weather as
this than out in the open sea.'

I was of the same opinion as the boatswain, and so I
could see was Bedloe.  All this time we continued head
to sea, thrashing away at the great surges, and just holding our own.

' Pilot !' cried the captain, ' why do you not run through
the channel at once, without waiting for the strength of
the squall ?'

' Because, captain,' answered the little man, very
promptly—' because the wind comes in puffs, with lulls
between ; and neither I nor any other man can take a
ship through these banks unless he has her in full
command.'

This was so reasonable that there was no more to be
said, and we waited impatiently for the decisive minute.
At length it came.  A heavy dank breath of air increased
gradually but surely, until the schooner careened over
heavily before it.  The horizon to windward was becoming
more and more obscured, the waves broke into white
crests round us, and Bedloe signed to put the helm up
and keep the schooner away.  As the head of the ship
fell off, and the sheets of the two great sails tore and

struggled as they were being eased off, the pilot cried to Captain Jem that he would run the schooner close past the rock where his tent was, for that the most direct channel lay by it. Captain Jem told him that the ship was now under his charge; and at the same time emphatically slapped the stock of the pistol in his belt, as a hint that the charge was a responsible one.

In less than five minutes, we were running fast among the breakers. The squall was now blowing fiercely, with pelting rain, which mingled with the flying brine, torn up from the foaming tops of the breakers. The sea ran strange and broken in the channels of the reefs, jumping and tumbling about, furrowed and rent by the fury of the wind, and the cross sweeps of the great surges, which the lines of reef flung into different directions, and often caused to sweep round and round in great seething cauldrons of foam. Through this howling waste of waters the schooner flew like a meteor, plunging along the white tops of the seas, diverging now to one side, now to another, as the skilful eye of the pilot directed; all her motions kept thoroughly in hand, and leaving reef after reef, each avoided by a dexterous jerk of the helm, lying foaming behind.

We were now in the thick of the shoal. Ahead of us, and on the starboard bow, the rock which had been the dwarf's habitation, rose blackly out of the water. I saw by the course that we were steering that we would shave it closely, and I sprang into the fore-rigging to keep a sharp look out. As I did so, I saw the mast of the 'Piragua' rocking beyond the coral ledge—the canoe being evidently well sheltered in the lee of the rock. The squall now grew heavier and heavier, and on we drove in the thick of it, the sea flashing and hissing around us. We were close upon the reef. I could have touched the coral with an oar, as the receding wave poured down its jagged ledges, when all at once Bedloe shouted with a voice, which, though shrill, was as clear as a trumpet—

'Starboard—hard a starboard!'

I started round at the sound; and just at that moment,

N 2

as the schooner's bow sheered to port, I saw the form of
Bedloe, one instant poised upon the bulwark, and the
next projected by a desperate leap into the air, and
plunging amid the silvery tumult of the surges; into
which, however, the dusky form had not yet vanished,
when Captain Jem's pistols flashed and exploded with
two rapid reports.   Instinctively I turned ahead.   The
pestilent dwarf had by his last order sought to wreck the
ship.   Before us lay a barrier of coral, over which the sea
poured, as a mighty river flashes over a weir.

'Port—hard a port—for the love of life—port!' I
roared.

It was just in time; the schooner surged round from
the reef, struggling and plunging in the tempest, and
then shooting along the rock.   We saw the piragua
tossing on the broken water, and one of the naked crew
in the act of leaping overboard with a line, no doubt to
the aid of the dwarf, whose head, as he swam skilfully and
strongly, favoured by the eddy, rose every minute upon
the tops of the uneven and broken surges.

A hoarse shout of rage burst, in one inarticulate cry,
from every one on board the schooner, but we had our
own lives to look after.   Fortunately, we were now in the
channel which I had been in the act of buoying, when we
discovered the dwarf's retreat.   My marks I could not,
of course, discern ; but I well knew the general lie of the
reefs, and keeping my station in the weather-fore-rigging,
I mustered all my coolness to con the ship.   We had a
dozen of hair-breadth escapes as we flew along.   Very often
the squall blew with such fury that the whole surface of
the sea, deep and shallow, was of the same whiteness.
Then a temporary lull would enable me to see the whereabouts of the ledges and banks, which I had already
surveyed, so that I was enabled to shout my directions to
Captain Jem with something like confidence.   But after
all, it was terrible guess-work.   A sharp eye to watch, a
skilful hand to work the ship, a steady heart to keep that
eye bright and that hand firm, were what we needed, and
that happily we possessed, so that after near half an hour,

during which we stood with hands clenched and teeth set, no man daring to draw a full breath, we shot out from the bosom of shoals, and knew from the heavy rolling of the swells that we were in deep water, and in the open sea.

Lucky for us, it was not until then that the full fury of the squall came roaring down. The sky grew well nigh as mirk as midnight, and the tempest hurtled through the air like the sweep of chariots and mighty squadrons in the clouds.

'In with all! furl and brail—furl and brail!' shouted Captain Jem.

Happily, sail is easily taken off a fore-and-aft-rigged vessel. The struggling and flapping sheets of canvas were rapidly secured, the gaffs were lowered down upon deck, and the schooner was speedily running under bare poles dead to leeward. The squall, meanwhile, increased until it became almost a hurricane: the great waves were beaten down flat by the sheer force of the wind. We rushed along, the tempest whistling and howling in the rigging in the centre of a roaring bed of foam, which the wind caught up and drove through the air in clouds which almost blinded us. Presently, a blue flash of forked lightning tore through the blackness of the sky, accompanied by a fearful roar of thunder, and then flash followed flash, and peal succeeded peal, until, what with the tumult of wind and sea, the lashing of the rain, mingling with the brine, and the incessant bellowing of the thunder, it was no easy matter to give or to hear orders. As the rain poured down heavier and heavier, the fury of the wind abated. Presently there were lulls, and the sea began to rise and heave around. At length there fell upon us such a deluge of rain, that had the hatches been off, I am confident that in half an hour the ship would have foundered. The rain continued for some ten minutes, and then the great clouds broke up, and rolled hither and thither, showing streaks of blue sky, and cracks, as it were, through which the sunlight came slanting down athwart the gloom, tinging long strips of angry foaming water with its red fire. This was the break-up of the tornado, which had not lasted, in its strength, more than ten minutes, and, in an hour, we were under single-reefed sails, beating up against a heavy sea for the shoals again.

We had now leisure to converse upon the conduct of Bedloe, which appeared to many of us to be strange and mad, but I saw a consistency and a purpose in it all through. The great error the dwarf had made was in coming on board of our ship ; but I admired the cool candour with which he had disarmed our suspicions by telling us so much of what was true of his story, as soon as he imagined that I held the clue to the secret. Furthermore, I did not doubt that, had it not been for the appearance of the piragua in the nick of time, he would have carried us clear of the banks, but knowing that she was in the lee of the rock, and being well acquainted with the eddies of the reef, he had determined, by one bold push, to drown us and save himself. Opinions differed as to whether the piragua would not have been driven from her shelter in the full force of the hurricane, but there was only one sentiment as to the punishment which Bedloe deserved, and which, if ever he fell into our hands, we fully determined that he would receive. Meantime we were gradually working up to the shoal, and an hour before sunset we saw the long line of breakers, dotted here and there with dusky beads of rock, stretching out amid the blue rolling seas. You may be sure that many an eye was strained to make out the piragua. I got into the main-top with the best glass in the ship, and although it was difficult to make out anything with exactness, by reason of the violent motion of the schooner, yet I was pretty well convinced that the canoe was not under the lee of the ' Dwarf's Rock,' as we called it ; and, furthermore, that the crew had not landed there, for the canvas of the tent was torn, and streaming in tattered ribbons into the air.

It was just before sundown that we learned the fate of the dwarf and his comrades. A great wave rising between us and the broad red disc of the sun as he set amid a streak of hazy vapour, we observed a black object tossing on the very crest of the sea. We trimmed the schooner's course for this dim speck, and after losing and regaining sight of it many times, at length made out that it was a boat or canoe, waterlogged and abandoned. The sun was now beneath the horizon—the speeding twilight of the tropics was waning fast away. The stars were already glimmering, and the leaden-coloured sea, with its great dusky opaque waves, rolled blackly and hoarsely around us; when the schooner, plunging into a trough, swept within a couple of fathoms of the wreck. It was that of a large piragua, bottom upwards, part of her bows torn away, where she had crashed down upon a reef. As we went plunging by, a surge from our bows splashed over the piragua, and, rolling her round, as she wallowed log-like in the water, we all recognised the drowned corpse of Paul Bedloe lashed to the stump of the mast, his nerveless legs and arms jerking about with the wash of the water, his blue eyes open and staring, like the eyes of a fish, and his light hair now floating out when the sea rose above him, and anon, when it subsided, settling down and clinging round his white dead face. With the next heave of the sea the canoe turned over as it lay when we first saw it, and then drifted away down into the gathering darkness of the night.

----

## CHAPTER XVII.

OF THEIR UNSUCCESSFUL SEARCH FOR THE SUNKEN TREASURE—
WEARYING AT LENGTH OF THE UNDERTAKING, THEY PURSUE
THEIR COURSE—THE LEGEND OF 'NELL'S BEACON,' OR THE
'CORPUS SANT.'

FOR three weeks and better did the ' Will-o'-the-Wisp ' lie off and on by the shoals. For three weeks the launch and shallop were day by day employed searching and dragging the reefs, but we found no treasure-wreck. The remains of the ship to which Bedloe had conducted

us were thoroughly searched, indeed the deck was altogether torn up, and some trifling amount of Dutch coin,
with two good iron guns, and the small brass cannon
were recovered, but we gained no richer prize.  Day
after day, even when the glare of the sun was at its
fiercest, might our boats be seen floating along the channels of the reef, two men at either bow, leaning over the
gunwale, so that their eyes were removed only an inch or
so from the water: but, save coral and sand, they saw
nought besides.  Still I felt certain that the treasure lay
upon the reefs, and we had many disputes as to the possibility of the dwarf having managed, by flinging certain
fragments of rock, which we found upon the eastern
edge of the shoal, and each of which was the nucleus of
immense masses of clustering sea-weed, to hide the precious deposit from strange eyes.  We all agreed that
little or nothing of the ship could possibly be remaining ;
but, as it was likely that the treasure was shipped in
strong boxes either of iron, or secured with that metal,
it was quite possible that these lay in crevices of the
rocks, their great weight mooring them, and that the dwarf
employed his leisure time before our arrival in covering them with the sea-weed grown stones of which I
spoke.  But all these opinions were but idle wind.  We
knew not the truth.  Some of the elder seamen would
have it that the whole was the work of the devil ; that the
dwarf was a demon who haunted those lonely shelves to
disturb and perplex poor mariners ; and in the evening,
when we sat upon deck smoking and drinking in the
grateful twilight, many a dismal tale was rehearsed of
phantoms of the sea, and particularly of the unearthly
creatures whom many of the crew believed to dwell upon
islands as yet unvisited by mariners, and who try to scare
away the human intruders upon their domains.

However, we at length got heartily tired of our sojourn
amid the reefs, and the more so as we began to fear that
we might miss the rich ship from Carthagena.  A council
was therefore held, at which we all agreed that we had
wasted too much time already, seeking for the dwarf's

treasure, and that the sooner the ship's head was turned to the southward the better. Accordingly, the next sunrise saw the boats hoisted up, our anchor safely catted at our bows, and the schooner running gaily upon her original course., We had rough weather and heavy seas ere we made the Samballas islands, to which we first intended to repair, and one stormy night I saw, for the first time, the appearance of that strange light which is sometimes seen on board ships at sea, and which the Spanish and Portuguese seamen know as the ' corpus,' or ' corpus sant,' and which our sailors sometimes call ' Nell's Beacon.' The Spanish word seems to me to be clearly a corruption of ' corpus sanctum '—the holy body —they tracing the light, which I believe to be nothing else than a mere harmless wandering meteor, to some religious or sacred origin. The night that the corpus sant appeared on board the Will-o'-the-Wisp was stormy and unsettled, the sky being piled with gloomy clouds, and the wind strong and gusty. I was sitting by the steersman, when, looking aloft, I saw something like a greenish-blue glare flickering along the weather end of the main cross-trees, just as if some one at a distance had been flashing a dark lantern through the rigging. I was rubbing my eyes, doubtful whether I had seen aright, when all at once the pale glimmer appeared, as it were, to become concentrated on one spot at the very end of the cross-trees, where it gleamed with a dim yet steady light, like a star.

The boatswain had the helm, and I pointed it out to him.

' Nell's Beacon,' quoth he; ' I know it well. When it burns high up in the rigging, then it is a good omen, and a sign of fair weather; but when it descends upon deck and moves to and fro then it is time for all who see it to bethink themselves of their sins.'

Meanwhile the other men of the watch having also observed the light, began to congratulate themselves thereupon, only expressing fears that it would descend to the deck, for which cause they watched it very anxiously.

Determined, however, to examine the thing minutely, I
climbed up into the rigging, and although the boatswain
tried to dissuade me, I got upon the cross-trees, and
gazed upon the meteor as closely as I would do at the
flame of a candle. The meteor surrounded the end of
the spar upon which it appeared, gleaming with a sort of
pale glow, which was not flame, but rather like the light
produced by flame, sometimes having a very ghastly
blue colour, like the blaze of burning spirits, and anon
turning of a greenish tint. Although the wind blew
strong, the corpus sant did not waver or flicker like a
flame, and I passed my hand through and through it,
without feeling inconvenience. During the time I
remained aloft, the meteor was becoming more and more
dim, and soon after I had descended to the deck it disappeared. The remainder of the watch we passed discoursing upon this phenomenon. Some of the sailors
said it was a sort of sea glow-worm, and others that it
was a jelly which shone; but neither of these opinions is
correct. Upon asking what the Spanish and Portuguese
sailors said of it, one Thomas Lomax, who had been twice
a prisoner in a ship of the former nation, told us that
the tradition of the Spaniards was to this effect:—

A Spanish bark once set sail from Cadiz, bound for
Sicily. They had very calm weather, and they feared at
last that their water would run short. All the crew,
therefore, made vows to St. Antonio, and promised to
place a silver candlestick upon his shrine if he would
send them a prosperous breeze. The captain of the ship
alone refused to join in their prayers, saying that St.
Antonio could no more send them a wind than a pig
could see it, and vowing that at all events if it were not
so, the saint was a shabby fellow not to give poor sailors
a breeze without their having to rob their wives and
families to pay him for it. But day after day passed
by, and the sails still hung in unwinking folds from the
lateen yards, and the reflection of the ship could be seen
in the sea as in a mirror. One evening, after a very hot
day, the air felt even closer than usual, and the captain

told the men that he must reduce still further their allowance of water. That night, therefore, they redoubled their supplications to the saint, and the captain who, by-the-by, was a Frenchman, redoubled his abuse of him, swearing that St. Antonio could not muster as much wind as would blow out a candle, far less urge on a ship. The words had hardly been spoken when a great light shone upon the vessel, and, running to the stern, they all saw St. Antonio, with a halo round his head, coming walking upon the water towards them. At this they all fell upon their knees, and even the French captain grew pale, and his legs almost failed him. Meantime the saint walked upon the sea up to the stern, and placing his hand upon the taffrail of the ship, said—

'This to confound thy unbelief, thou contemner of holy men and things !'

At the same giving the ship what appeared to be a slight push, but which flung her forward as if she had been a stone hurled from a sling. The saint having performed this feat, instantly vanished, and at the same moment a fearful storm, the like of which was never seen by man, suddenly arising, drove on the ship with the same rapidity as that which the hand of the saint had imparted to her. Meantime all the crew were on their knees praying to the Virgin to intercede for them with St. Antonio, and expecting nothing less than instant death. But the ship continued to drive with unearthly rapidity, although without injury, and beginning to take courage, they observed, on looking about, a bright light burning upon that part of the taffrail which the saint had touched with his hand. For three days and three nights the miraculous storm lasted. The ship flew through the water quicker than birds cleave the air, and the supernatural nature of the tempest was made still more evident by the fact that it was not general over the sea, but that within half a cable's length from the ship the ocean and the air were either perfectly at rest, or a pleasant breeze was blowing, and vessels were sailing with a fair wind in the opposite direction to that in which the saint-cursed ship was driven. Still, however, the mariners did not cease to importune St. Antonio for pardon, and the captain was loudest in his prayers, and most lavish in his vows. At length, at midnight on the third night, the light, which had never ceased to burn, suddenly moved from its place, and flitting to the mast, began to ascend it. As the meteor rose into the air, the fury of the storm lulled. The mariners, seeing this, fell upon their knees and put up loud thanksgivings. The light continued to rise until it glittered upon the highest point of the rigging, to wit, the end of the great lateen yard, where having remained steady for some time, it gave a sudden bright flash, and then soared into the air, until the gazers could distinguish it no longer amid the stars. The wind then fell as suddenly as it had risen, and the strained ship again floated tranquilly upon unbroken water. When the day dawned, the crew saw land barely a league a-head of them, and a fishing-boat coming off soon after, they learned that they were off Cape Epiphane in the island of Cyprus, having traversed, in an incredibly short space of time, almost the whole length of the Mediterranean sea. A pleasant breeze, however, soon sprang up from the east, and having obtained what water and stores they needed, they turned the ship's head westward, and arrived without accident at their port in Sicily, where great honours were paid to the shrine of St. Antonio. From that time to this, say the mariners of Spain, the light which the touch of a holy body—a corpus sanctum—created, has never been extinguished, but floats over the ocean, appearing now as a warning of approaching death, anon as a harbinger of hope to mariners.

This was the Spanish tale of the Corpus Sant, and I now asked for the English legend of ' Nell's Beacon.'

' Why,' quoth the boatswain, ' I never heard it told ; but often I have heard it sung both afloat and ashore, in the taverns at Limehouse or Portsmouth Point, and aboard many a ship in many a sea.' Thereupon, all the watch desiring to hear the song, the boatswain, in a very coarse gruff voice, chanted the following stanzas, which, rude as they are, I put down just as I heard them :—

### The Legend of ' Nell's Beacon.'

There are stormy seas do roll,
    Which the boldest well may dread,
When the east wind whistles snell
    On the cliffs of Beachy Head.
By that coast, tempest beaten,
    On the sea-weed clustered stones,
Stout-hearted sailors many,
    Have laid their weary bones.

From the sandy shores of Eastbourne,
    Nigh the rocks whereof I sing,
Sailed a brave and lusty seaman,
    And his name was Richard King.
He was captain of a trading sloop,
    Which voyaged unto the Seine,
And 'twas Beachy Head he always made
    When he returned again.

For there, from eve to dawning,
    A beacon always shone
During the time, whate'er it was,
    That Richard King was gone.
From the window of a cottage
    That beam came, ever bright,
For there sat Nelly, Richard's wife,
    And trimmed the lamp all night.

She trimmed it, for she knew
    That her husband dear would gaze,
When the white cliffs loomed a-head,
    For those love-enkindled rays;
And when he saw them flicker,
    Through the darkness of the night,
He would straightways cry right cheerily
    ' There's Nelly's Beacon Light.'

But, ah ! these long night watches,
    They paled poor Nelly's cheek ;
Her eye was bright and fevered,
    But her step grew slow and weak.
Her husband bent above her,
    And she looked up in his face—
' I'm wearing fast away,' quoth she;
    ' I go unto my place.

But you are bound to sea, dear,
    To the stormy Spanish shore;
Look, Richard, look upon your Nell,
    You ne'er may see her more!
But watch when you return, dear,
    You will know that I am dead,
If no light shines out to greet you
    From the top of Beachy Head.

' Yet death shall never part us,
    For, if it lawful be,
My soul shall fly to you, dear,
    Athwart the roaring sea;
But not a ghastly sheeted corpse
    Shall I appal your sight,
You will see an airy Beacon,
    And my soul will be the Light.'

The storm roared loud at midnight,
    With sleet, and wind, and rain;
The struggling ship tossed wildly
    On the rocky coast of Spain:
When suddenly the captain cried—
    ' Oh God, my wife is dead!'
Upon the topmast gleamed a light—
    The Light of Beachy Head!

\*    \*    \*    \*    \*

Two score of years went slowly by,
    And again the storm-blast blew,
Old Richard King, with long grey hair,
    Spake cheerily to the crew.
' Oh look aloft, my gallant boys,
    There's hope within our sight,
A kindly spirit watches us—
    There's Nelly's Beacon Light!'

But as he spoke, the Beacon
    Came floating through the air,
The captain knew the sign—he knelt
    In thanksgiving and prayer.
The tempest swept him from the deck,
    But as he sunk like lead,
Above his forehead shone the light
    Which gleamed from Beachy Head!

And still in time of tempest
Does Nelly's Beacon burn,
Sometimes it shines aloft to cheer,
Sometimes alow to warn ;
But it reads us all this lesson—
True love is never dead,
The symbol shines on every sea
That shone from Beachy Head !

## CHAPTER XVIII.

### A KNAVE OF THE CREW PLAYING WITH COGGED DICE IS KEEL-HAULED.

FOUR days after leaving the reefs, we saw land ahead, and presently were running in amid the clusters of the Samballas Isles. On every side of us, these rich islands flung, as it were, their masses of foliage into the sea ; bushes clothing the rocks where such existed, and at other points thick mangrove woods, the stems of the trees often covered with oysters, growing far into the water. These forests appeared to swarm with birds and beasts. We heard the loud screams of thousands of unknown fowls resounding from the woods ; and often, as we skirted the shore, watching places where the trees did not grow thick, we descried troops of monkeys going chattering along, or herds of peccary and deer, breaking through the bushes. Sea-birds also abounded. Great clouds of plovers flew, wheeling and circling along the shore, and the white sandy beaches and the sea were dotted with turtles basking in the sun, or lazily sleeping on the top of the smooth water. The Samballas Islands are thinly inhabited by scattered tribes of Indians, who subsist by hunting and fishing, and are very willing to aid as guides or pilots to the English and French privateers who put in here ; so that the first canoe which we saw made directly towards us, and the two Indians who guided it came on board very readily, and were treated with brandy and wine, much to their satisfaction. From them we learned that several privateers had been lately

in these islands, to careen and provision ; and that the
Spaniards from Porto Bello and Carthagena, had sent a
fleet of armadilloes, as they are called, being small vessels
of war, which had swept all the channels between the
islands, and had captured one privateer, a tartan of four
guns, commanded by Captain Coxon, having surprised
her in a creek where she was careening.  We questioned
these Indians respecting the galleon which the Spanish
prisoner at Jamaica had told us of.  They know that
many rich ships sailed annually from Carthagena to Old
Spain, but could tell no particulars, conjecturing, however, that if any vessel with a freight of price were now
fitting for sea, she would sail after the return of the
armadilloes to Carthagena, judging that they would have,
for the present, cleared the coast.  This information,
which jumped with our own ideas, made us very anxious
to take in what provisions we stood in want of, and be
off to the westward ; and the same afternoon the friendly
Indians piloted the schooner into a very snug bay, where
we lay with trees all round us, except at one point where
an opening in the woods conducted to a noble savannah,
whither we often went to hunt.  While we lay here, all
hands were fully occupied.  Upon the beach, near the
schooner, we erected a place for preparing boucan, which
we preferred to regularly salted meat : and of which
Nicky Hamstring, who had a natural turn for cooking in
all its branches, was appointed superintendent.  Then
the Mosquito men went daily in their canoe, and struck
turtle and manatee.  Hunting parties, whereof I generally
made one, explored the woods and brought good store of
peccary and deer down to the boucan.  We shot also the
tender young monkies, who often made my heart sore by
their screaming and moaning when they felt the lead,
and by the pitiful way in which, when they came by a
broken bone, they would handle the useless limb, and
grin and weep with the pain.  Besides these, we made
food of the guanas or yellow lizards, who live amid the
branches, and love to bask in the sun upon the topmost
boughs, and also of a species of red land-crab, which our

men call soldiers, from their colour, and which run
nimbly about, generally at the roots of trees, hiding
themselves quickly in holes, and burrowing like rabbits.
The Indians who conducted our schooner into the bay,
lived with others not far off, in smoky huts, which were
surrounded by patches of cleared land, wherein they grew
good store of yams and plantains, which they sold very
willingly for hatchets, saws, and such like implements,
with powder and lead. Meantime, while a great part of
the crew were thus busy on shore, Captain Jem, with
the hands who remained on board the schooner, was occupied in changing her appearance as much as possible ;
for we knew that the Spaniards have no lack of spies
either in Jamaica or the other English islands, and we
misdoubted that an account of the schooner had been
sent to Cuba, and from thence to the Main. We, therefore, repainted the ship, making a great yellow streak
from stem to stern, with false ports, and also made a
shift to alter, to the eye at least, the trim of the ship,
by placing false bulwarks towards the stern, which
heightenng her from the foremast all the way aft—the
painted streak being made to correspond with the
new bulwarks—caused the schooner to have a clumsy
look, as though she were down by the head, in consequence of carrying an ill-stowed cargo. We also
changed the set of the masts, by putting heavy strains
upon the rigging ; and lastly, we patched the sails,
although they were new and good, with old canvas ; con-
ducting our operations with such good effect, that the
crew swore to a man, that had they been away for a
week, they would never have recognised the schooner for
the ' Will-o'-the-Wisp.'

Being at length in readiness for our cruise, we towed
the ship out of the little bay, and commenced beating to
windward through the islands, passing the isle called Las
Sound, where the Buccaneers have a legend, that the
heart of Sir Francis Drake lies buried in four caskets, of
lead, of iron, of silver and of gold. I see no reason,
however, for believing that his heart was not in his body

o

when that was committed to the deep in the bay of Porto
Bello, amid the thunder of artillery, and the crash of the
martial music, in which the great admiral so much
delighted.  As we worked up against strong westerly
breezes, we met with several fleets of large canoes, laden
with sugar, hogs, yams, and corn, running before the
trades; but as we were now approaching Carthagena, we
thought it most prudent to let these piraguas pass by
unmolested, hoisting Spanish colours, and making as
though we were a friendly trader.  So in due time, we
left the westernmost of the Samballas keys to the leeward, and stood off to the north-west, designing to make
a long stretch out to sea, so as to prevent any intelli
gence of our whereabouts being conveyed along the main
land to Carthagena.

Towards the afternoon of the day on which we cleared
the Samballas, I having the charge of the deck, could not
help noticing the miserable plight of one Simon Radley,
a young sailor, who was a very quiet well-behaved fellow,
and a favourite on board.  When we left Jamaica, he had
been very well dressed in seaman fashion : but now, he
was clothed merely in rags, without a shirt, and his
shoes were only bits of canvas swathed round his feet,
and very coarsely sewn together.  Besides all this, the
poor fellow looked almost broken-hearted, and went about
his work very sadly,

' Simon Radley,' quoth I ' how came you in this plight?
Have you lost all your clothes?  Surely if you have,
your comrades will lend you some, and you can make it
up to them with the first of your prize-money.'

Well, at first the fellow would answer never a word.
At length he muttered that he had been unlucky, very
unlucky, but that it was nobody's fault but his own, and
that he would be better off soon.  I insisted, however,
on knowing what he had done with his clothes, upon
which, after a great deal of stammering and hesitation,
he plucked up his heart, and said broadly, that I had no
business with his clothes, and that, if he chose to wear a
clout, or paint himself and go half naked like the savages,

it was nothing to me, or to any one else, so long as he did his duty manfully. Just as he was speaking, up came the boatswain, John Clink.

'Simon Radley,' says the old fellow, 'you speak like a fool. It concerns us all, to see our comrades so bestowed as that they shall have the best chance of keeping their health, and not turning sick upon our hands. Now, I know where your clothes are, well. I have had my eye on you for some days past. Your clothes are in George Bell's chest, with a good quantity of the clothes of the other men as well.'

'Hush, hush,' says Radley, 'there is honour in these things. If they are in George Bell's chest, it is because they belong to him.'

'But how?' cries I. 'Have you sold the clothes, Simon?'

'Sold them—no,' says Clink. 'He has lost them, or been cheated of them, at dice, with that fellow Bell, who is a sneaking vagabond, and always skulking out of the way, whenever he is wanted.'

I remembered now that I had very often seen Bell playing dice with others of the crew, but had taken no particular notice, such games being very common among privateersmen.

'And so you have had bad luck, Simon?' rejoined I.

'Bad luck,' interrupted Clink: 'yes, and most of those have bad luck who play with George Bell.'

The conversation continuing, we gradually drew from Radley, that he had played with Bell for all the ready money which he possessed on leaving Jamaica, and lost it; that then he had played for a good set of mathematical instruments, and lost them; that then he had played for all his clothes, and lost them; and, although for some time his shipmates had supplied him, that he had lost in succession every article of cothing so given to him, in the same way; and that, finally, he had played for and lost his chances of prize-money during the whole cruize. All this the poor fellow told with great reluctance, seeming to consider such disclosures as a breach of honour; but

o 2

on John Clink saying that, in his belief, Bell had been a
common sharper in London, and had bubbled poor Radley out of his property. Simon grew very indignant, and
swore that, if it were so, he would have Bell's blood.
However, we pacified him, and made him understand
that before making any charge, we must have better
proof. George Bell at this time being below, and in his
hammock, I called up a number of the crew in succession,
all of whom said that they had played with Bell, and that
they had never won anything ; that if, now and then, a
cast of the dice was in their favour, yet that they always
rose the losers. Some of these men had had their suspicions of Bell's play, but as they had never compared notes,
they were not aware, until I questioned them, how very
similar all their cases were. They knew, indeed, that
Simon Radley had been stripped, but they were loath to
accuse a shipmate of foul play.

'Why, then,' quoth John Clink, 'that fellow, Bell,
must own about half the property in the ship, if your
tales be all true. This must be looked into.'

'With whose dice do you play ?' says I : and they all
answered, that generally it was with Bell's for that several
men who had brought dice on board had lost them, they
knew not how, but Bell had several sets. This information increased our suspicions very much, and desiring all
hands to keep the matter to themselves, and by no means
to give a hint to Bell that he was suspected, I informed
Captain Jem of the whole affair.

'The snivelling, cur-hearted miscreant!' quoth honest
Captain Jem, his plump red cheeks glowing with indignation. 'I never saw anything good in that fellow since he
came on board. He is a pitiful skulk, and never stirs
out of his hammock except when he is driven. It was he
who counselled us to strike to the Spanish frigate, but if
we find him out in his roguish tricks his back shall so
smart for it, as shall cause him to think that his spine be
stuffed full of pepper instead of marrow.'

So it was determined that Bell should be closely
watched, and the dice which he was so fond of using, ex-

amined at the first convenient opportunity. Nor had we
long to wait for its occurrence. In a little more than an
hour, the suspected culprit came on deck, not thinking
any harm, and going to the cook-house returned with a
portion of boucanned pork, off which he made a very good
dinner, with the help of a clasp-knife, and then having
washed down the meat with several hearty draughts of
brandy, he accosted my old friend Le Picard, and asked
him whether he would shake a wrist with him. Now
Picard had been also below and asleep, when the investi-
gation into Mr. Bell's character had been going on, and
the men having kept their own counsel, Le Picard had
no idea of what was in the wind. So presently, they sat
down and began to play upon the combings, or ledge of
the hatchway, Bell having produced the dice and dice-
boxes. I watched the suspected sharper very closely
when the game was going on, and noted his general sly
down-cast look, and the small way which he opened his
eye-lids, always peering about him with suspicious blinking eyes. Then, again, I observed his hand, which,
although dirty and tarry enough, was not the hand of a
man who had been all his life accustomed to handle ropes
and marlin-spikes. Meanwhile, quite a circle of spectators gathered round the players, a circumstance not
usual, as the stakes were trifling, but which Le Picard
took no notice of. Bell, on the other hand, looked often
about him, and seemed puzzled at the interest which so
many of the crew took in the matter. However, he said
nothing, but played on, so far as I could see very fairly,
and the luck went from one to the other, as is usual in
the game. At last, Le Picard grew impatient.

'Come,' quoth he '*Allons, mon camerade, jouons plus
fortément.* Let us play for a better stake.'

'I am agreeable,' replied the other, softly.

'*C'est bien, alors.* Let it be a double doubloon; I have
not many left.'

The Frenchman pulled out the piece of gold, and placed
it on the ledge of the hatchway. Bell, after some searching, real or pretended, plucked another piece from his

pocket, holding, as I observed, the dice all the while in his hand.

Captain Jem, who stood by me, did not fail to observe this as well as I, and whispered to me that the fellow by this manœuvre might well have changed the ivory. I nodded.

'A thunderstorm, or a single flash?' says Bell, meaning, shall we decide the game by one cast, or in a great many.

'Oh, one flash; short and sweet!' quoth the French man. Both of them rattled the dice and flung them forth.

'Trays,' called out Le Picard.

'Sixes,' exclaimed Bell; 'the money is mine,' and he grasped the gold greedily.

'I will hold you doubles or quits,' cried Le Picard, in true gambling spirit.

'Well, if you want your revenge, I suppose I must not say no,' answered the other, in a quiet unobtrusive tone.

The dice were again thrown, and this time the Frenchman had quatres, and Bell, as before, sixes. Muttering a great oath, poor Picard fished up the stakes from the bottom of his pocket, and was handing them to the winner, when Captain Jem cried in a loud voice, 'Stop.'

Both players looked up in surprise.

'Bell,' said the captain, sternly, 'hand me over that dice.'

'Why, captain,' quoth the other, in a cringing tone, getting suddenly very pale, and looking quickly all about him; 'why, captain, there has been no foul play, I hope? We are gentlemen adventurers on board this ship.'

And, with that, his hand stole slily towards his pocket, as if to deposit there his winnings. Observing this motion, however, I grasped his wrist and defeated his intention, the dice falling from his fingers. At the same time, Captain Jem caught him by the collar of his doublet, crying out—

'Why, thou booby, thine own words condemn thee; who spoke of foul play but yourself? I only asked you for the dice, and you straightway think you are accused of cheating.'

At this Bell looked sheepish enough, but presently recovering himself, began to bully and curse, swearing that he was a gentleman and a man of honour, and requesting to know by what right his dice had been taken from him.

'Come here, Simon Radley,' says Captain Jem, and Simon stood forth, shaking his clenched fist at Bell.

'Have you not lost every farthing you possessed, as well as your clothes and your chances for the cruise, to this man?' says the boatswain.

Simon replied that it was so, and was entering into particulars, when Bell burst out with a great affectation of scorn and indignation—

'A pretty fellow,' quoth he, 'to game with a gentleman, and then, when fortune is adverse, to go and prate of your losses, and charge your adversary with foul play! Go to, man! had I lost, I never would have accused you of cheating. But you throw no dice with me again.'

'No, that you may depend upon,' answered Radley.

'Stay,' cried Captain Jem, 'we are going but rashly to work. Let all the men here who have diced with George Bell hold up their hands.'

Thereupon, more than two-thirds of the crew made the sign.

'Good,' replied the captain; 'now, let those who have lost money, or aught else to him, hold up their hands.'

Nearly the same number of hands were immediately displayed. Bell grew yellow in the face, and glared about him with fierce spite.

'Good again,' continued the captain; 'Mr. Bell, I must congratulate you; fortune has been very kind to you—very kind indeed. Now, let those who have won money or aught else of George Bell, hold up their hands.'

Two hands were raised, and their owners being interrogated, it appeared that they had gained, one of them, not more than a couple of groats, and the other merely a small rusty pistol, which had burst the first and only time

he had fired it, and against which he had staked, being
incited by Bell, a good perspective glass.

'So, then, gentlemen and comrades,' pursued Captain
Jem, 'the case stands thus : here are a score of you have
played with this man ; and, although each man of that
score ought to have had as good a chance of winning as
Bell, yet the fellow has beaten you all, one after another ;
and the only winnings from him have been contemptible
matters not worthy speaking of.'

The crew here uttered a loud murmur of acquiescence,
and some of them began to threaten Bell with their fists.
Still he tried to put a good face on the matter, although
his tongue faltered as he spoke.

'You are mistaken, gentlemen,' he cried, 'indeed you
are ; I will take my Bible oath that I played fair ; nay, if
you do not believe me, I am willing to give up all my
winnings, and surely that ought to satisfy everybody.
But I assure you, comrades, if I were to be hanged this
minute, I would still say that you had no wrong from me. I
am incapable of cheating, gentlemen ! I do not understand
how to cog dice, upon my soul ; indeed, indeed I do not.'

'That fellow's tongue would hang him if there were but
one rope in the world,' says the boatswain ; 'he was the
first to talk of foul play, and now he is the first to talk of
cogged dice !'

'We will soon settle that matter,' says the captain, 'and
that by splitting open the ivory.'

'Oh, certainly, certainly, I agree to that,' says Bell ;
'here are my dice, sir,' and he whipped out several cubes
from his pocket.

'No, no,' interrupted I, 'never mind these ; we will
try the dice with which you won the two doubloons e'en
now.' And one of the men having fetched a hammer, I
placed the morsel of ivory upon the ledge of the hatchway. Upon seeing this, Bell went down plump upon his
knees, and raised a dismal howl.

'Ah, you can be penitent enough now, chicken-heart !'
says Captain Jem ; whilst I, having splintered the dice
with a blow, we discovered a small bent piece of lead, very

neatly inserted in one of the specks of the deuce side of
the cube, not, however, drilled perpendicularly into the
ivory, but artificially deposited in a sort of burrowing
hole, running along just under the surface of that side of
the square. It was evident, that to prepare a dice in this
fashion required a hand very skilful and well accustomed
to the work. The men crowded round to see it, uttering
furious menaces against the convicted sharper, who never
moved from his knees, but continued to supplicate most
piteously for mercy.

'Mercy!' exclaimed Captain Jem; 'mercy, forsooth.
Thou art one of the first privateersmen I ever heard of
cheating his comrades, and thou shalt smart for it, or I
no longer command this schooner.'

'Do not flog me—for mercy's sake, do not flog me!'
the fellow bawled; 'I cannot bear flogging—it will kill
me—it will be murder if you flog me. I was flogged
once, and the doctor said it all but killed me;' and so,
crying and howling, the pitiful creature cast him down
upon the deck, and bemoaned himself in the most abject
misery of spirit.

'Flogged before,' said the boatswain. 'Ay, I warrant
thee. Aboard what ship?'

'Aboard no ship at all,' roared the culprit. 'On shore.
Oh dear!—oh, dear!'

'On shore,' answered the boatswain. 'At the cart's
tail I presume?'

'Yes, yes,' cried Bell; 'but I give you my word of
honour, sir—my sacred word of honour, that I was not
guilty then. It was another man.'

'Not guilty then,' says Nicky Hamstring. 'No; no
more than you are now, I dare affirm.'

The miserable devil gave no answer, but made as
though he would catch the legs of the men about him,
and cling to them. In all my life I never saw such a
pitiful hound.

'Keel-haul the fellow,' says one of the men, 'and see
whether the brine won't wash the roguery out of him.'
And the others joined in the cry: 'Yes, yes, keel-haul him.'

At this the culprit sat up upon the deck and looked earnestly in the faces of the men through his tears. I do not think he understood what keel-hauling meant.

'Anything,' says he, whining like a hungry cat; 'any-thing sooner than flogging.'

'Very good,' says Captain Jem. 'Be it so. Truly, on second thoughts, it would be degrading hemp to put it to any other use about such a scoundrel, except hanging him.'

Meantime, half a dozen of the men, in great glee at the anticipated ducking, went about the preparations without loss of time.

The punishment of keel-hauling, I premise, that we borrowed from the Dutch. Its name describes its nature. The prisoner is fastened to a rope led under the vessel's keel, and hauled beneath her bottom, as often as his guilt seems to require. It is evident that this is a punishment the severity of which depends greatly upon the size of the ship, and the frequency with which the process is repeated. To be hauled under the keel of a great ship of war is a very different thing from being hauled under the keel of a small sloop; but in order to give the punish-ment its requisite severity on board small craft, the cul-prit is often hauled all along the keel, being let over the bows, and taken up at the stern ; a process by which he is sure to be at least half drowned and half scraped to death by the rough barnacles and jagged shell fish which generally encase a ship's bottom. In the present case it was determined, however, that Bell should undergo the easier mode of punishment, and be hauled from bul-wark to bulwark, but the dose was to be administered twice, giving him a breathing-time between. Accordingly, by the help of a sounding lead, first a thin line and after-wards a stout cord were conducted under the ship's keel, Mr. Bell watching the process with great anxiety.

'What—what are you going to do with me?' at length he cried, beginning to comprehend the nature of his punishment. 'You do not mean to drag me under the ship?'

'You have hit it my hearty,' says the boatswain ; 'hit it to a tee. Yes ; we will give you an opportunity of inspecting the run of the schooner, and if you fail to observe all its beauties the first time, don't break your heart, you will have another chance immediately after.'

At this the cowardly animal began to howl and blubber again.

'You will drown me, you will; it's murder. There were sharks about the ship all yesterday. I will never come up alive! Have mercy on me! I have a wife and family in England. I would rather be flogged than put overboard. I would rather be flogged, indeed I would.'

At this moment Captain Jem came up.

'Rather be flogged, would he? A minute ago he sang another tune. Why, you discontented thief,' roared the captain, 'you would not be pleased even although we were to hang you. Come, men, bear a hand, and have him overboard in a trice.'

Immediately, half a dozen stout fellows flung themselves upon the miserable culprit. He roared, swore, and prayed, all in a breath, kicked out with his legs and arms, and sought to bite and scratch like a wild cat. But he was speedily mastered, his arms pinioned securely, his ankles tied together, and the rope which ran under the keel made fast under his armpits. He was then lifted and carried to the larboard bulwarks, half a dozen men holding the end of the rope, which passed beneath the keel and came up on the starboard side, while two or three hands had charge of the continuation of the line, so as to steady his descent in the first dive, and to pull him back by in the second.

All this time the vagabond never ceased to abuse and swear at us, seeing that cries for mercy availed not. Captain Jem gave the word—

'Heave and pull,' and instantly Mr. Bell went with a splash into the sea, struggling for a moment on the surface, and then, as the men on the starboard side hauled the rope, disappearing in the water.

'Rattle him round,' says the captain. 'He must not drown for all he is such a villain.' The men ran across the deck with the rope; there was a surge and a jerk, when the poor devil struck the projecting keel, but he was instantly dragged beneath it, and the next moment he made his appearance on the larboard side, struggling, panting and coughing up the water, his face all blue and bleeding from having been scraped along the bottom, and his clothes torn by the jagged shells of the barnacles.

'O, Lord!' he gasped; 'murder—it is—murder;' and then the coughing well-nigh choked him.

'Down with him again,' cried the captain. The end of the rope which had been before used as a guy was promptly manned, and Bell again disappeared beneath the water, was again rudely jerked against the keel, and then hauled up the side of the ship, and cast upon deck all bleeding and insensible, with his hands blue and cramped, and his limbs quite limp and motionless. By Captain Jem's direction he was held up by the legs, when presently he vomited up a great quantity of sea water, and then began to stir and moan, with great fits of coughing. His hands and legs were then released, and he managed to sit up on deck, leaning against the mast, and looking as if he had just wakened out of a dream.

'Let this be a warning to you, Mr. Bell,' said the captain, 'how you play dice in future. I presume you will only stay in this ship until you have a chance of going on board another. None of your own property, however you came by it, will be taken away, but all that you cheated your comrades of must be restored.'

Accordingly, Bell's chests were opened, a general distribution took place, and that evening Simon Radley appeared in his former attire. As for the sharper himself, we afterwards learned that he had been a well-known rogue in London, and after having been twice flogged at the cart's tail, had been tried for ring-dropping, and transported to the plantations of Virginia, from which he managed to escape, and after divers adventures in the West Indies—whereof the greater part were more complimentary to his ingenuity than to his honesty—he had shipped on board our schooner at Jamaica, as the reader has seen.

## CHAPTER XIX.

**WE CRUISE OFF CARTHAGENA AWAITING THE GALLEON, AND I FALL INTO THE HANDS OF THE SPANIARDS.**

IN three days after leaving the Samballas Islands, we had beat so far to the norwest, that we counted upon being rather to windward of Carthagena, and from nine to twelve leagues distance from the coast. The west winds blow here with very little intermission, the land-breeze being very slight when it does come, which is but seldom. It was necessary now to determine exactly upon our mode of proceeding, and this was the plan we adopted. The prize which we expected was a private Patache, or treasure-ship, which, not waiting the convoy of the great fleet which sails once in every three years from the West Indies for Spain, intended, as we were informed by Mr. Pratt's prisoner, to risk the chances of the homeward passage unprotected. Now, it was clear, that the first thing which we had to do, was to ascertain whether the Patache, or galleon, was still in Carthagena, and if so, when she would probably come out. Our next care would be to keep to sea, and watch the coast and the harbour, so as, if possible, to prevent the galleon putting off unknown to us; while, at the same time, we managed so as to prevent any alarm being excited upon the coast. With this view, we would, of course, run in tolerably close with the land at nights, keeping further in the offing during the day, and showing as little sail as possible. But our first business, as I have said, was clearly to ascertain that the mouse was actually in the hole; and that we might be sure, we determined to venture well in towards the harbour that very night, and, if possible, capture some small coasting craft or fisherman, who could give us the information which we required. Accordingly, we turned the schooner's head to the south-ward, and ran along with a pleasant breeze abeam. By sunset we saw the land; and so correct was our reckoning, and so skilful our pilots, that John Clink and Captain Jem, who knew the coast well, pronounced the hummock, on which we were gazing, to be a high hill just behind the city of Carthagena, on which there stands a cathedral, which boasts of a very rich shrine, dedicated to the Holy Virgin, and of which more hereafter. Carthagena itself is principally built upon a small sandy island in a bay. The city lies upon the seaward side of the island, which is connected, by a long wooden bridge, with the suburbs or faubourgs along the main coast, the strait being, as may be supposed, a mere belt of shallow water. Well, by ten o'clock, we saw the lights of Carthagena quite plainly ahead of us; and afraid of venturing too near, we hove to, and kept a good look out around us. But the sea was as shipless, as though it heaved round a desolate island. The breeze was light and fitful, and we lay tossing on the long swell, our bows plunging deeply, and our gaffs and sails creaking and surging in perfect solitude. One by one the lights on shore disappeared, as the citizens went to bed, quite unwitting who was watching the gleam from their casements; and, presently, the dusky line of the shore was unbroken even by the twinkling of a single lantern. All at once, however, we saw a bright glow begin to shine forth from the top of the hill which I have mentioned. At first, we thought it a fire breaking out in a large and lofty house; but, presently, I discerned that it was the cathedral of *Nuestra a Senora de Papa*, lighted up for some night service. It was very brave to trace the outline of the great arched windows, all shining, as it were, with different-coloured fire, by reason of the stained glass, covered with the figures of martyrs, and angels, and saints; but when I was intently gazing at this glorious sight, John Clink, the boatswain, suggested that we might well run in closer. 'For,' quoth he, 'all the people of the town will be at their devotions, this place being the very Loretto of the West Indies.' The boatswain's advice was followed, and we edged in with the land, until we could hear the sound of the surf very distinctly, and made out furthermore—the stars shining out somewhat—that there were several large ships and many smaller craft in the bay. Not daring to approach these too closely in the schooner, the shallop was got out with little noise, and I was appointed to go in her to reconnoitre. I made the men muffle their oars with canvas, and we agreed that the schooner should show two lights, one above the other, for a space of thirty seconds, every ten minutes, until we returned. I also took a dark-lantern in the boat, and we pulled silently away from the schooner towards the land. Presently the white glimmer of the surf could be seen plainly, close ahead of us; and so we pulled leisurely along the outer edge, making for that part of the bay where the shipping lie, somewhat to the westward of the town. We paused on our oars now and then, and listened very attentively for sounds of alarm. But none came. There was a holy calm abroad upon the night, and the stars shone down through the stirless air. The coast seemed like a dark cloud lying on the water, except where, at its highest ridge, the festival tapers gleamed from out the great cathedral. We sat as men spell-bound, gazing on the beauty of it. Presently, it appeared as though great folding doors had been flung open, a burst of light, like a glory, streamed forth from what was a vision of pillars and arches, and great gleaming aisles; and falling on the broad steps leading to the portals, streamed over a dusky crowd of worshippers, men and women, kneeling with almost prostrate forms upon the marble ledges; and at the same instant, the mighty swell of a great organ, and the deep peal of a thousand mingled voices, rose solemnly up, overflowing, as it were, the very atmosphere, and mingling with the dim surf-music, as though both sea and land would join their tones in that great harmony. So, rude sailors as we were, we could not but listen, and in our hearts, adore. It was a Latin chant the people sung. Sometimes it fell so low, that we could hear but a faint and distant hum. Anon it rose, and pealed, and rung so gloriously out, that I could discern the very syllables of that mighty chorus, of 'Jubilate, Jubilate, Jubilate. Amen.'

At length the organ ceased, and there was silence
'Very well sung,' said Simon Radley, who pulled the
stroke-oar, ' and a very good psalm.'

Our solemn moods seldom lasted long. Howbeit, I
was sunk in musing. The grave and solemn season of a
tranquil night invokes like thoughts. I looked at our
muffled oars, and thought how, darkling, we skulked
upon the water, watching for our prey; and, as I mused,
I could not help hearing, as it were, in my ears, the echo
of a hollow sing-song voice, the utterance of that good
man, but somewhat wearisome preacher, the Rev.
Michael Wylieson, of Kirk Leslie, in Fife, who loved to
take for his text the verse which speaks of a certain
coming, as like unto the coming of a thief in the night.
But all this lasted only for a minute; I started up,
crying—

' Pull, my men, pull—we've come to seek a rich
galleon, and not to list the droning of chests full of
whistles.'

And so we stole cautiously on, until there rose, cutting
the starry skies ahead of us, the tall masts of several
ships of price. Which of these was the patache? We
gazed and whispered, and while we whispered, there
suddenly rose, as it seemed from the water, not a score
fathoms ahead of us, a loud voice singing, in the Spanish
language, and presently we discovered a small dark object,
like a canoe, very low in the water, with the form of one
man on board. As we gazed, the figure moved and turned ;
then appearing to observe the boat, the man stopped
in his song, and bursting into a laugh, so that one could
discern he was a negro, called out to us in bad
Spanish,—

' You may as good go home to your hammocks, the
pisarcros (that is a kind of fish) will not bite till the tide
turn, or the moon rises.'

' All is well, he suspects nothing,' I whispered; ' let us
make sure of him.' And so, as my comrades bent to
their oars, I replied with a sort of imitation of the song
which the fisherman, for such he was, had been singing,

and at which he laughed again in his peculiar manner.
But his mirth did not last long. Just as the shallop
came with somewhat of a rude surge against the canoe, a
couple of muscular hands grasped the poor negro by neck
and arm, while I said in Spanish, —

'Not a cry—not a sound—if you value your life.'

Immediately the poor man was pulled—all trembling
and gasping in his bewilderment—into our boat, where
he sat in the bottom, his white teeth chattering, and his
eyes gleaming and rolling, while he sputtered out broken
prayers in mingled Spanish and Latin.

'Now,' said I, still speaking the former language,
'answer truly what is asked of you, and you shall come
to no harm; but if you try to deal falsely by us, your
blood be on your own head.'

At this the poor fellow gasped out, that he would do
anything, if we would spare his life. I then questioned
him concerning the galleon, or treasure-ship, and he
answered very readily that she was in the harbour, being
one of the vessels before us; that her freight was well
nigh aboard, and that she would sail in two days at
farthest. This was good news, and we hugged ourselves
on our luck.

'Then they are not afraid of French or English adventurers in these seas?' I said.

'Surely not,' answered the negro. 'For a fleet of
armadilloes hath swept, as they think, the pirates clear
away. So they conclude to set out on the voyage to Old
Spain without more ado.'

Having said this much, the negro appeared to bethink
himself—and bursting into great lamentations—besought
us never to reveal that we had heard aught from him ;
'otherwise,' quoth he, 'there is no death so cruel my
master would not put me to.'

But we bade him to be of good cheer, seeing that now
his masters were altogether changed, and he was in the
service of brave privateersmen, instead of skulking
Spaniards; but that, indeed, if he proved a gallant trust-
worthy fellow, and would give us all the information he

P

could, he was no man's slave but his own master.
On this he plucked up a little, and said that if it would
be a satisfaction to us, we could row close up to the
galleon, and view her, as the Spaniards, being in
fancied security, kept but slack watch ; and, indeed, the
greater part of the crew had gone to the cathedral on the
hill, to a great High Mass. This was just what we
wanted, but first there was a small job to be done.
Whispering to Radley, we grasped the gunwale of the
canoe, and by a vigorous push, surged the light shell-like
thing fairly bottom upwards.

The negro looked on in consternation. 'Why do you
do that?' he said, at length.

'Look you, Pedro,' for such was his name : 'Look
you, Pedro,' says I, 'suppose both you and your boat
disappear—what will your master think to-morrow morning? a cockle-shell made of bark like that will not sink,
therefore you could not have foundered. A hurricane
has not carried you out to sea, because neither has there
been, nor is there likely to be, any hurricane—ergo, both
boat and man have been somehow spirited away. Such
being the case, there must be enemies—pirates you cal-
them—on the coast; and there being pirates on the
coast, it would be mighty rash for the good galleon to
sail. But then, Pedro, when your worthy master sees
the canoe bottom-upward, tumbled by the surf upon the
beach, the case will be different. An accident has happened,' he will say, " My poor Pedro, so faithful a slave,
and so profitable a fisherman, hath somehow, in his zeal
to catch pisareros, doubtless, overbalanced himself, and
capsized this light canoe. Woe is me, Pedro sleeps
among sea-weed." But Pedro sleeping among sea-weed
will not prevent the anchors of the galleon from being
lifted to her bows—you see.'

At this the poor fellow, understanding the device,
looked up pitifully in my face—

'I have a wife,' quoth he, 'and she will also think——'
Here his voice failed him, and the honest creature began
to whimper.

'Come—come,' I broke in : 'you may go back to your
wife, Quashy, if you like, after we have the galleon, but
till then you are one of us.' I think the negro had sense
to see, that whining would not make his case any the
better, for he dried up his eyes, and pointing ahead, told
us, that the ship riding nearest the shore was the galleon.

Slowly and cautiously we rowed, describing a great
circle round to seaward, so as to keep out of the way of
the outermost ships. Their lights fell in long rays across
the water, and we could hear the voices of the men
aboard as they talked. Once we were hailed, and I
ordered Pedro to reply—saying we were fishermen returning from catching pisareros, to have them ready for
the early market—but no one offered to interrupt us,
until the shallop floated in the shadow of the great carved
quarter galleries of the galleon. The ship appeared well
nigh deserted. The lap of the water against her sides,
and the cheep of the rudder, as it moved a little way to
and fro in the calm, were all the sounds about her. Had
there been but a slight puff of wind from the shore we
might have cut her cable, boarded her, and fairly carried
her away; but in a calm such an enterprise was out of
the question. So, we were preparing to push off, well
satisfied with our reconnoitring, when a light suddenly
fell upon the carved figure of a saint, which formed one
of the stern ornaments, and at the same time I could
hear, though faintly, men's voices in conversation. It
would appear that some one had entered the great cabin
with a light, and one of the windows being open, adver-
tised us of the circumstance. All at once it occurred to
me that, if I heard somewhat of the conversation, it was
just possible that I might pick up some information as to
the exact time the ship would sail, and the exact track
she would follow; or perhaps the vision of a rope left
carelessly dangling from the quarter into the water, had
something to do with the notion. Catching the cord, I
found it firmly attached above, and so, communicating in
a whisper to the crew of the shallop my intention, I

swung myself up, and presently gained footing amid the great masses of carved work, being wreaths and coronals of flowers, and graven figures and symbols of war and peace, with which the Spaniards overload the sterns of their ships, going to great cost for little utility ; and then a slight further exertion brought me into a gallery running round the great cabin, and fenced in with a sort of massive and curiously wrought and fretted railing. Then, crouching down, I crept to the window from whence came the voices and the light. There was a carved saint very handy, close by the casement, and favoured by his wooden holiness, I looked securely into the cabin. It was very brave in its devices and ornaments, and spacious in size. The ceiling was gilded until it glittered again in the light of the great silver lamp which swung above the table, and draperies and hangings of silk, all embroidered and passamented with gold lace, depended both from starboard and larboard, showing strangely beside the great ponderous breeches, and the strong tackle of two cannons, which you might see peeping from amid the silken bravery. The mizen-mast passed through this great cabin, and it was incrusted as it were with small weapons—pistols and daggers, most richly mounted and hilted—while below was a great beauffet, all set out with glimmering crystal and plate—flagons and vases of burnished silver, and curiously-shaped goblets of sparkling glass. But, although I had never seen such splendour on board ship, or indeed, for that matter, anywhere else, I gazed with the greatest interest on the two men who occupied this floating palace ; they sat on either side of the table, with a great crystal bottle, almost full of wine, and two long-stemmed glasses, before them. One was rather old and fat, with dark garments and grey grizzled hair. He had little pig-like eyes, and a sly greasy-looking face, and was altogether not pleasant to look on. But his companion was a handsome gaillard, as you might see in a summer's day, and most bravely dressed. He had a very bronzed face, with jet-black moustaches, which were curled, and oiled, and crisped ; and hair flowing about

his shoulders in such dainty fashion as I warrant you
cost the barber many an hour's labour ; his eye was
bright and flashing ; his nose and mouth well cut ; and,
altogether, his head would have been a fortune for a
painter to copy, only there was a leer about the eye, and
a curl about the lip, which gave the lie to whoso would
say, ' Here be a gentle cavalier.'  Round his neck he
wore great masses of lace, among which precious stones
glittered ; his cloak was of the richest velvet ; and the
arm which he stretched out to hold the drinking glass,
showed a hand daintily gloved and sparkling with rings.
On the table before him lay a rapier, sheathed and ornamented with ribbons, and beside it was a great straw
hat, or sombrero, looped up with floss of gold and
silk.

' I would I were to see Madrid as soon as you,' said
the young cavalier ; ' there is a balcony I would fain be
under but now with a mandoline,' and, so saying, he set
himself to hum, making as though he were playing an
instrument.

' Truly, Don José,' answered the other, with a grating
voice, ' there are balconies enough in Carthagena, rivals
enough to be fought with, and husbands enough to be
deceived.'

' Pshaw,' said Don José, ' colonial conquests give a
man as little credit as trouble.  I warrant you, you would
have me—as successful a gallant as any at the court, be
the second who he may,' and here my gentleman curled
his moustaches, and leant back with an air of mighty
complacency,—' you would have me waste time and in-
cense on the female savages of this pestilent corner of the
world.'

' Well,' answered the old man, ' you ought to have
bridled your valour, and not have drawn upon a gentleman in waiting in the precincts of the Escurial.  You
have no one to blame for your banishment but yourself.
Zounds, for one, court-bred as you are, and a most learned
doctor in that grave science of etiquette which rules the
king who rules the double empire of Old and New

Spain,—you showed yourself a singular pattern of discre·
tion.'

'Who could help it, most grave and tricksy Senor
Davosa?' said the other; 'what blood of Old Castile
would not have boiled over to hear an upstart, who knows
not the name of his grandfather, dispute precedence with
me—an Hidalgo of fifteen pure and unblemished descents?
By my faith—if I had any—were the guards not all the
quicker, the mushroom would speedily have been cropped
from the earth, and that, by this very piece of steel,' and
the speaker touched his rapier.

'Well,' answered the other, 'I hope such are not
the terms of the memorial I am to carry home for
you; if they be, I am likely to have but a bootless
errand.'

'Fear nothing, man; fear nothing,' cried Don José;
'I know what belongs to a memorial—I know how to
tickle the ears of a king. The parchment but sets forth
in words that would move the mainmast of this floating-
box, which you merchants and seafaring people call ship,
my frenzied groupings and stumblings in this outer
darkness, where no sun of royalty shines to cheer or
warm my forlorn spirit. There are excellent phrases,
man, excellent phrases in the thing; until I invented
them I never thought I had been so ill used. When I
read my own composition it affected me to tears—to tears,
Davosa—as I hope it will the king. And now, when
do you sail? Be speedy, my good dove, be speedy, and
bring me back an olive branch as a sign that the waters
are abated.

'We count to weigh anchor to-morrow evening,' replied the old merchant. 'The freight was long of coming,
the mules here being but slow-footed, otherwise we should
scarce have tarried so long. Every day brings more and
more risk of these accursed pirates, French and English.
who so often mar our best ventures.'

'What! fearful, after the last pair of candlesticks you
have bestowed on yonder lady, in her house upon the
hill?'

'Blaspheme not holy things,' interposed the older man.

'Oh, I cry thee pardon, good Gull,' replied the other; 'I forgot me you had as big a swallow as the rest. Ah, yes, to be sure, Our Lady of the Hill! Verily, a valorous and a venturesome dame. It was a brave device of señors the canons, that last miracle; a most surpassing feat, truly. Here is a blessed image of the blessed Virgin, dressed out as never was doll before; petticoats of cloth of gold, I warrant me, and stiff, absolutely stiff, with diamonds, pearls, rubies, and what not. Well! here comes an English man-of-war into these seas—the "Oxford," I think, they call her. Bah! how these barbarous names stick in a gentleman's throat; and so, by misadventure, this man-of-war, this heretical "Ox—Ox—Oxford," taking fire, no doubt by reason of sparks from—from purgatory, to say the very least of it—this man-of-war blowing up, what say señors the canons? Down rush they from the shrine, all through the city, clamouring, "A miracle! A miracle!" Straightway the most greasy and gullible mob throng to the sanctuary—and what see they there? The Virgin, the doll, that is, in its place behind the altar, but all bemudded, all bedraggled, her gay clothes drenched with salt water, the gold embroidery torn away in flakes, the diamonds, and pearls, and rubies, all dropped and gone from stomacher and skirt; in fact, a very mutilated memorial of her yesterday's glory. Great ejaculations of surprise and consternation! Mighty invocations to every saint in and out of the calendar! Evidently, a most dread secret, a most mighty mystery—a matter of holy wonder to the faithful!'

'Don José! Don José!' interrupted the old man, who had listened very impatiently to this tirade; 'the tongue is an unruly member. Take heed what you utter. The holy office hath ears which hear afar, and hands which smite afar. Who knows who may be even now listening to you? For my part I would not breathe to myself what you have spoken aloud, even were I alone in a boat fivescore miles from land.'

'Good Señor Davosa, it is no more your vocation to
be fearless, than it is mine to be cowardly,' replied the
brisk gallant. 'The cobwebs of the holy office were
spun to catch blue bottles, man, not hornets. But I must
tell you the story out. It is true, man, true, every word
of it, as the bills of lading you send with this galleon.
The people, then, wondered and worshipped, but could
make nothing of the matter. Not so the canons. By the
soul of the Cid, but they are dexterous fellows, the holy
canons, and they caught the clue to the secret in brief time.'
"See you, my brethren," said the head of the black cas-
socked brigands, "see you here. An heretical, a very
heretical and damnable ship, called the 'Oxford,' hath
been clean destroyed by fire, kindled no one knows how.
Immediately after, coming to say our early prayers, what
find we ? This sacred effigy bedraggled and besmirched,
as you see. How came this so ? My brethren, the
thing shall be clear unto you. The burning of the 'Oxford' is a very apparent and notable miracle. It was
Our Lady's hand held the torch. In the darkness of
the night, when no eye saw it, she left her shrine.
Many a league hath she walked over land and sea ; as,
indeed, the state of her garments may well make clear
unto you all. Doubtless she hath scaled great mountains, and crested great waves, going with speed, so as
to return by daylight to this her temple. The proof is
very clear. The 'Oxford' hath perished ; Our Lady
hath spoiled her clothes ; therefore hath Our Lady clean
destroyed the 'Oxford.'" And so, "Ave Maria Puris-
sima," shout the crowd, grovelling in their credulity.
But the best—the very cream of the joke is behind—
good Davosa, as thou shalt hear. "Good brethren and
faithful," quoth the chief canon again, "it seemeth clear
unto me, that after such a miracle wrought in our favour,
the least we can do—I mean you can do—is to restore
the gold, and the diamonds, and the pearls, and the
rubies, thus spoiled and lost by our good Lady. And
look ye, it may well be that you shall thus be clear
gainers ; for if our Lady had not destroyed the 'Ox-

ford,' mayhap the 'Oxford' would have destroyed
Carthagena, and thus would you have been all clean
ruined and undone." So, "Gloria in Excelsis," again
shouted the poor fleeced mob; and the image is to have
new jewels, and the canons to have the old ones, as well
they deserved them for their ingenuity.'

And so saying, Don José drank off a full glass of
wine, and leaned back, laughing lustily. His comrade
arose—

'That I have listened thus long to you, Don José,' he
said, 'you owe to personal courtesy, not to any sym-
pathy with your heathenish spirit, so full of unbelief and
mockery. Have you any further commands?'

'No: none—none,' answered the cavalier, still laughing. 'But thou knowest, Davosa, that in your heart,
man—at the bottom of that cold deep well you call a
heart—you are laughing with me in very cordial merriment.

The old man rose up. 'If you have no further commands,' he was beginning, when Don José, who had got
upon his feet, and was assuming his rapier and sombrero,
while he repeated—'No—none at all,' suddenly stopped,
and said, laughingly—

'Hold—yes, one. You have heard of Don Octavio y
St. Jago—every duenna in Madrid knows him to her
cost. Well, he and I are close friends; I have writ to
him. The letter is in the packet you hold; but one
material circumstance I have forgotten. It is an old
paction between us, that each should inform the other
of all his love passages, so that, as it were, we should
mutually act as spurs to each other's gallantry, and so
keep up our reputation.'

The merchant at this shrugged up his shoulders.
'But,' quoth he, 'I thought you deemed the ladies on
this side the great ocean no better than savages.'

'Well, well, my good Davosa, and, if I did, know you
not that there may be, for once in a way, a certain
savour and tastiness about savagedom which speaks to
the palate? Look you, the man palled with nectarines

and peaches may well pluck a bramble as he loiters in the field. And so, pray find means to inform my friend that there dwelleth in Carthagena a very ripe, and not altogether untempting bramble, having the shape of a very innocent-hearted and simple-souled damsel, who having rejected one or more of my courtesies, put me in the mind to tame and humble her completely ; that unto this end I have gained over her mother, who is a widow and also a fool, believing very firmly in the saints, and a great number of other phenomena, myself among the number ; and that—that—in fact I shall impart to him the conclusion of the tale when we meet at Madrid.'

The old man drily promised to observe the message, and then both drunk to the success of the voyage.

' To-morrow evening, then, you turn your faces eastward ?' said the cavalier.

' If there be but a breath to clear us of the land, I trust we may say our vepsers at sea,' replied the merchant.

' And if there be but that same breeze,' I whispered to myself, ' you may chance say your matins aboard the Will-o'-the-Wisp.'

Then as the couple walked towards the cabin-stairs, I lowered myself into the shallop in safety, whispering to my comrades the good news I had overheard. They could scarce refrain from shouting, but caution overmastering joy, we pulled swiftly away. To some degree, however, our good fortune had made us bold, and instead of rowing out straight to sea, we made for the principal cluster of ships, as they lay in the line of our progress towards the schooner. We had passed several, when we suddenly heard the dash of several oars, vigorously pulled, close aheap.

' Santa Maria !' cried the negro, springing up, for he was terribly frightened at being found with us, ' Santa Maria—the guard-boat !'

And, true enough, just round the bows of a large tartan came a great launch, impelled by six oarsmen, and

with a glitter of arms and lanterns shining out of her.
Well, we had hardly time to gasp, when, with a great
clamour at our sudden appearance, and all her crew
starting up from their oars, the Spanish boat ran right
into the starboard quarter of the shallop, hitting us a
blow, which well nigh swamped the light craft; the
Spaniards roaring out to curse our stupidity in not having got out of the way. For all this, we might have got
clear off, they taking us, in the dark and confusion, for
one of their own boats, had not Simon Radley shouted
out involuntarily a great oath, cursing them for clumsy
Spanish thieves, that knew not where they rowed. At
this, a Spaniard aboard, who, it seems, knew the sound
of our language, cried out—' Los Ingleses—los Ingleses!'
and straightway our enemies, yelling and screeching like
madmen, jumped up with intent to board us. Half-a-
dozen pistol shots went off in a minute, as I shouted to
my small crew to pull for their lives, and the boat started
forward, scraping past the oars of the launch. Just then
we gave a loud hurrah, as Englishmen love to do, to
show their mettle. The bowman of the Spanish boat
made a desperate leap, alighting with a surge on the
stern of our shallop. Even while he was in the air, I
started up to grapple with him. Our arms grasped each
other's doublets. I felt his hot breath on my cheek.
We stood erect but for a moment, twining, as it were,
around each other's limbs, and then both of us, linked
with brawny muscles together, fell splash into the sea,
amid a great shout, which mingled in my ears with the
rushing and gurgling of the water, into which we
plunged. For a brief space I thought we must be
drowned together, so desperate was the clutch with
which we clung round each other's throats; but rising
in a minute to the surface, I found myself amid the
blades of the Spanish oars, and, so clinging to them, I
fought with my foeman, seeking to cast off his grip. At
the same time I looked about for the shallop, but she
was not to be seen, having evidently got off clear. And
so, when the Spaniards grasped me to haul me into their

boat, I fought and struggled desperately, that the shallop might have the greater start, in case they pursued her. At length, however, being mastered, I was dragged into the guard-boat, just as, half an hour before, the negro was dragged aboard the shallop, and cast violently down on my face in the stern sheets, while my hands were fastened behind me. This done, one of my captors gave me a kick, and told me to sit up, which I did, in the centre of a circle of ferocious-looking sailors and soldiers, who all began to question me at once, with the most savage oaths and curses ; to all of which I replied never a word, but shook my head, as though quite ignorant of the language. So presently, the officer in command, thinking, no doubt, that it might be so, ordered silence, and then saying that it was useless to chase the small boat in the dark, and that the prisoner must be taken ashore, and given up to the alcaide, bade his men stretch to their oars, which they did ; and, presently, passing close by the galleon, my old friend Davosa called out to know what was the matter. The officer who steered answered, that they had come upon an English boat lurking in the harbour, and had captured one of her crew, and that he suspected there were more of the rogues not far off. Then presently, coming to a quay or jetty, they forced me up the slippery steps, and being guarded by two soldiers, each with a drawn sword they marched me away.

---

## CHAPTER XX.

### I AM TRIED AND TORTURED BY THE SPANIARDS.

My heart was sad enough and heavy enough, I warrant the reader, as I turned my back upon the sea, and toiled through the dry hot sand of the beach, followed by a group of the boat's crew. There was no one stirring in the town, only we heard the echo of songs, and the jingle of glasses, from taverns or posadas, where drunken sailors were carousing. Presently we passed through several very narrow streets, not savoury by any means; for rotting garbage lay thick and foul around, and overhead the far-projecting eaves, almost meeting each other, seemed to have been built so as to keep the stenches the better in. Once I heard the twangle of a guitar, or some such instrument. This was as we passed a house, nearly hidden in orange and other trees, and situated in a retired corner of an open space amid gardens; and, looking for the musician, I saw beneath a balcony the slender form of a young man, of just such a size and shape as my gay cavalier Don José—that is to say, so well as I could judge in the light of the newly-risen moon. But I had other fish to fry than to attend to his love-making; for, to tell the truth, I felt by no means certain that I would not be hanged for a spy. All the stories of Spanish cruelty I had ever heard—and they were not a few—came up into my head; and I think, when I called to mind the tortures they ofttimes put their prisoners to, in order to make them reveal what they knew of their comrades' designs, I felt a greater sinking of heart than even the idea of the halter gave me. But, notwithstanding, my good Scots blood was but for a minute chilled; and then it rushed with fiery force through all my veins, and involuntarily I raised my voice, and made oath by all I worshipped, and all I loved, that they might wrench my limbs out of me ere they got a word to their purpose.

'What does the rogue say?' inquired the lieutenant, for such he was who walked behind. My sentinels answered that I spoke somewhat in an outlandish gibberish they could not understand; and presently, seizing me by each shoulder, they turned down a great arched gateway, beneath a long straggling house, with pillars in the front, and a flag over the roof. Here were sentries, who challenged our party and received the countersign, and then we entered a large bare room on the ground floor, which was dimly lighted by but one lantern, placed at a desk, where a soldier, whom I judged to be a sergeant, was writing. Along the sides of this room ran a slanting

ledge of wooden boards, on which hard bed full a score of
soldiers lay sleeping in their *ponchos,* or loose cloaks.

'What springald have we here?' said the sergeant,
rising from his writing, and flinging the full light of the
lantern, which did not cause any very great illumination,
over me, as I stood, somewhat pale, I daresay, and all
dripping from my bath. But just at that moment the
lieutenant, who was my captor, entering, the sergeant
saluted after military fashion, and despatching one of his
men, the officer on duty presently walked in, having his
uniform doublet unbuttoned, and a silk napkin tied round
his head, as though he had been roused from an after-
supper's nap.

The officers made each other very ceremonious bows,
and then he of the sea delivered me formally up to he of
the land, as a person unable or unwilling to give any
account of myself, and captured from a strange boat in
the harbour, one of the crew of which, at all event, spoke
English. The word made quite a sensation in the guard-
room. The half-waking soldiers rolled off their benches,
and came scowling and muttering about—the sergeant,
bestirring himself, went to his desk, and from a clash of
iron there I concluded, and justly, that he was selecting
his heaviest pair of handcuffs—and the officer with the
napkin round his head, who did not appear altogether
sober, crossed himself very religiously, and, cursing me
for a damnable heretic, ordered the men back, telling
them that they would see me much better when I came
to be hanged. He then demanded whether I understood
any Spanish ? to which interrogatory, as I had previously
determined, I replied that I did a little; and then, to
their great astonishment, I asked very fiercely whether
Great Britain and Spain were at war, that an English
mariner was to be dragged out of his boat while giving
offence to none, forcibly bound, and taken to a Spanish
watch-house.

'*Madre de Dios*—here's a goodly crowing,' cried the
officer of the watch ; 'why, thou pernicious heretic and
contemner of saints, thou buccaneering and piratical

rogue, for such I see thee with half an eye, what business hast thou or any of thy pestilent countrymen to sail these seas, which belong to His Most Catholic Majesty, the seas of the Spanish Indies? I tell thee thou shalt be hanged, were it for nothing else but rousing me from a comfortable doze; therefore, bethink thee of thy sins, and that the more speedily, inasmuch as their catalogue is, doubtless, long, and thy time as surely short.'

Having made this speech, the gentleman staggered slightly, and then, recovering himself, looked round as if to say, 'Who suspects that I have taken too much to drink? if there be any, let him stand forth and say so;' then, shaking his head very gravely, he observed that the world was getting wickeder every day, and added that he was much concerned thereat. Here the sea lieutenant, as fearing a scandal, broke in, and suggested that I should be at once taken before the alcaide; but the sergeant, assuring him that that was out of the question, inasmuch as his honour was then supping with his reverence, the chief canon, and that, above all things, his honour disliked to be disturbed at meal times—the captain of the guard interposed, and, swearing that he respected the peculiarity of the alcaide, it being, indeed, one in which he confessed himself a sharer, ordered the sergeant to lock me carefully up until the morning, and to give me the dirtiest cell and the heaviest irons, in honour of the Catholic religion. Then, addressing me again, he said that I might make myself easy, for he saw the gallows in my face; and so, taking the arm of the naval lieutenant, he swaggered out. The sergeant then approached, holding the irons; these consisted simply of two rings for the wrists, connected by a chain about six inches long. There was no use in resisting; so the cold, greasy-feeling metal speedily enclasped my wrists, each ring locking with a smart snap.

'How came it that your comrades deserted you, friend?' quoth the sergeant, in rather an amicable tone.

'I will tell you nothing about my comrades,' I replied;

'I do not want to be uncourteous, but you shall hear nothing from me on that score.'

'Hum!' said the sergeant, 'that is but a bad tone to take. We shall see about that to-morrow. However, the thing is your own business, not mine; so come along, and if you are used to lying hard, you can sleep upon it.'

I followed my jailer, who really was not an uncivil man, through several long passages, with great doors, studded like the doors of tolbooths, with iron nails. The lantern cast a dim fickle glare in these hot airless passages, and the cockroaches went whirring along, dashing their horny bodies and buzzing wings against the glass covering the light, and in our faces.

'Here is your quarters, my Buccaneer,' said the sergeant, stopping at a door nail-studded like the rest, and marked No. 15. 'There are worse rooms in the place, so you have to thank me for this. Your countrymen are not always so civil when we fall into their clutches.'

I hastened to assure him that he was quite mistaken in that matter, but he cut me short, and, unlocking the door, made a sign for me to enter, saying that there was a chair on which I could sleep if I had a mind. Then he locked the heavy door behind me with a great clang and crash, and shot two or three bolts, after which I heard his footsteps die away as he walked back to the guard-room. The cell or dungeon in which I was confined was a narrow, bare room; the floor paved with flagstones and very filthy. This I ascertained by the first step I took. I felt the walls; they were composed of large roughly hewn stones, very strong and dungeon-like. Up in one corner, close to the roof, and almost ten feet from the floor, was a small window, barred with iron. Through this a ray of bluish-tinted moonlight streamed down, and showed me the chair which the sergeant spoke of. I dragged it into a corner, and sitting down with a heavy heart, I began, for the first time since I was taken, to meditate on my situation. I had never before sat a prisoner in a jail, and the gyves felt sad and **strange upon** my wrists. How silent, and dismal, and hot, the place was! what a change from the breezy deck and the clattering voices aboard the 'Will-o'-the-Wisp.' I listened and listened until I almost thought I could distinguish the deep hoarse tones of Stout Jem and Nicky Hamstring's cheering laugh. Was I ever to see them again? I had my doubts of it. For the present, at all events, our enterprise was balked. The Spaniards would doubtless send out a squadron of their armadillos. The schooner would be forced to leave the coast, and when or where, even supposing I was to get scot free out of the hands of my present jailers, I could meet her again, was but a discouraging question to put to myself. To-morrow I was to appear before the alcaide, and perhaps his court was but a stage on the way to the gallows. To be strung up and choked at the end of a rope—faugh! why did I not die upon a bloody deck, amid the thunder of our guns, and with the anthem of my comrades' cheers ringing through my brain? Or, why was I not to take up my rest like my father before me in the sea, which was my home, swept over by a stifling wave in some wild mid-watch, or calmly sinking with the sinking ship? These were not pleasant subjects to ponder on, but they would flow into my head as water drains into a leaky vessel. I tried hard, but vainly, to keep them out. I tried to sing a jolly sea song I had often heard my comrades chant most lustily:

" Aloof! and aloof! and steady I steer,
'Tis a boat to our wish,
And she slides like a fish,
When cheerily stemm'd and when you row clear!
She now has her trim,
Away let her swim.
Mackerels are swift i' the shine of the moon!
And herrings in gales when they wind us,
But timing our oars, so smoothly we run,
That we leave them in shoals behind us—
Then cry one and all!
Amain! for Whitehall!
The Diegos we'll board to rummage their hold,
And drawing our steel, they must draw out their gold."

The first verse of this song, called ' Sir Francis Drake's Triumph,' I got through. In the first line of the second my voice choked as though there were churchyard dust in my throat. I got up and walked to and fro in the cell. Through the window I could see the little square patch of blue sky, dotted as full of stars as the door behind me was full of nail-heads. Through the opening there floated the rich smell of flowers and herbs wetted with the cooling dews of the night. There was a garden, belonging, probably, to the alcaide, or governor, behind my prison. I tried, why, I know not, perhaps my nervous restlessness impelled me, to clamber up and look out, but my fettered hands forbade. So, at length, thinking it wisest to attempt to compose myself to sleep, I flung me down on the bench, and though the chill of my wet clothes sent shudderings through me, I at length fell off into a disturbed doze, dreaming confused and frightful visions, which every now and then woke me up with a great start.

In the morning I had some bread, stock-fish, and water for breakfast, and was thereafter conducted before his worship the alcaide. The chamber which was his court was a barely-furnished room, with a dais, or raised step, on which was placed a long table. Behind it stood a comfortable leather chair—the throne of justice. On one side of the table there was a desk all strewed with papers, where sat the clerk. There was no bar for the accused, who simply stood in the centre of the floor. surrounded by his guards or jailers, while a few benches round the walls furnished accommodation for the spectators. When I entered, the alcaide seemed just to have taken his seat. He was a burly, morose man ; his swarthy face all torn and seamed by the smallpox, and a blue scar rising up from one of his black bristling eyebrows. He had great gold earrings, and his thick brown fingers were gemmed with rings. The clerk, who sat near, next attracted my notice. He was an old little man, and all his lean weasen face was one pucker of wrinkles, out of which gleamed two greenish eyes, spark-

ling like those of the ferret, as the creature fixes its long
front teeth in the jugular artery of its prey. As I gazed
upon the aspect of my judge, and his counsellor and
assistant, I felt my hopes of life and liberty oozing out
of me at every pore. Two more ill-looking gentlemen
you might not find in a long day's search. The court
was tolerably well filled with spectators, for the news of
an English pirate, as they called me, captured in the
harbour, had spread like wildfire, and I found myself the
centre of a thick mass of swarthy faces, and black gleaming eyes, and long curling jet-black moustaches. The
officer of the boat which had captured me, was placed,
out of compliment to his quality, upon a chair near the
judge, and close by him sat the military gentleman who
had been so certain of my being hanged when delivered
to him over-night. This man had very bloodshot eyes,
and a fierce look; indeed, he seemed made of the same
kidney as the alcaide, to whom he frequently whispered,
in a hoarse, husky voice. The sergeant or the soldiers
I did not see at all. My jailers were mere ordinary
turnkey-looking fellows, not rougher or more brutal than
most of their class. Just before the proceedings com
menced, who should enter but my old acquaintance, for
such I considered him, Don José! He made his way
through the crowd very cavalierly, and ascending the
dais. was welcomed by the dignitaries there, with whom
he seemed tolerably well acquainted, and presently had a
chair brought him, and talked and laughed gaily, until
the alcaide hemming loudly, and settling himself in his
seat, the old ferret-eyed clerk took up his pen, and the
court was formally opened.

'Bring up the prisoner!' said my judge, and I was
moved forward nearly to the table.

The clerk peered at me with his green eyes.

'I think the fellow is like one of the gang of that
notorious thief and murderer, called Morgan. If so, the
proceedings need not last long; the individual called
Morgan, and all his band, being already many times condemned for murder, sacrilege, treason, and robbery com-

Q 2

mitted by them on the high seas, in the islands, on the main, and elsewhere.'

It was the clerk who spoke thus, in a thin squeak, like the cheeping of rusty iron.

'I said, when I saw him last night,' added the army officer, 'that there was gallows written in the heretic's face.'

'Strong corroborative testimony that!'—said Don José, with a sneer, which he seemed not to think it worth the trouble to conceal. 'Worthy alcaide, do you not think the case all but proved against the prisoner? My most astute friend, Lopez'—here he bowed to the clerk, who glanced back at him with wrathful eye,—'and my warlike friend, Guzman'—here he indicated the scowling officer—'seem inclined to save everybody, but the hangman, any trouble in the matter.'

The alcaide, whose perceptions appeared none of the quickest, looked from one to the other of the speakers, with a grim smile, and then asked whether I could talk Spanish; I answered I could; and so the examination began. I told very truly my name and country; I said I was a mariner on board a schooner, sailing under British colours. I added, that I had been seized by an armed boat, and dragged out of my own; that the assault had been made upon me and my boat, that there was no law or justice for it, and that the Spaniards well **knew.**

Now, although I took this tone, I was very well aware that it would serve me nothing. For, although England and Spain were at peace, yet so were never Englishmen or Spaniards to the south of the line; whichever fell into the other's hands smarted for it; and that all of us knew right well, and I had made up my mind accordingly.

'Friend,' quoth the spiteful clerk, 'do not choke yourself with big words, insomuch as we shall presently save you the trouble by means of a gallows, which ever standeth in the court-yard, with a convenient rope.'

'I knew by his face it is what he would come to,' replied Guzman.

'Truly, friend,' said Don José, addressing him, 'you have a very pretty knack at the telling of fortunes—much serving to encourage and support your fellow-creatures at a pinch.'

'Silence!' proclaimed the alcaide, 'the course of justice must not be interrupted.' The little clerk made a bow, and Don José laughed outright.

'Why did you enter in your boat the harbour of Carthagena?' the judge demanded.

I said, that not recognising his authority to ask I should not answer the question.

'Take down,' said the alcaide, 'that he denies the authority of the king of Spain in this, his new empire.'

The clerk obeyed, with a sort of joyful chuckle.

'On what voyage were you bound?' I was next asked. I remained mute.

'We shall make him find his tongue presently,' grinned the clerk; 'even though we should squeeze it out of his thumbs.'

I guessed the meaning of this hint, but still held my peace.

'Where was your ship when you came into the harbour?—speak, sir!' thundered the alcaide, 'or it will be the worse for you.'

But I answered very quietly, but firmly, that these were matters on which he could not expect me to give him any satisfaction. At this the little ferret-eyed man grinned and rubbed his hands, after which he took down my answer, very formally.

'Dost thou know—thou heretical rogue—that the very shadow of the gallows is upon thee!' cried the alcaide. 'If thou valuest thy life, at the rate of a brass marvedi, make a clean breast of it. Confess—speak the designs of the pirates, thy comrades, and it may be that we will have pity on thy youth; and instead of cutting short thy days, send thee to labour for some lengthened space in the mines of Darien.'

There was a pause after this alternative had been offered to me. Then I collected my thoughts and spoke thus :—

' I am in your power, and I can make no resistance to
your will, but I pray the judge to consider whether he, a
Spanish gentleman, being in the hands of his enemies,
would feel that he did right in betraying staunch comrades for the sake of his own life.   As to your threats, I
fear them but little ; I am of a race having stout hearts
and tough sinews, and I tell you, Spaniards, that if I
come to evil in your hands, there will be those left
behind me, who will dearly wreak my death on all men
of your nation, whom the fortune of war may fling into
their hands.   I speak this not in idle braggadocio ; I am
young, and it is hard for me to leave this world, in whom
are many I love well ; but I will not save my life by
turning a traitor from fear.   There have been Spaniards
ere now in my power, and I let them go.   They had not
even to ask their lives—they were granted freely.   We
English and Scotch mariners love not to spill defenceless
blood—we rather fight with swords and pikes than with
halters.   But if you be bent upon my death, I warn you
again, that many a Spanish throat will bleed for it, ere
the bark in which I was a mariner see Jamaica
again.'

I spoke this with a warm energy, which surprised myself, and a better flow of words than I thought I could
muster in Spanish.   Don José struck his hand upon the
table as I finished, and cried vehemently out—

' Well said, by the soul of a Cid ! Pedro-y-Monte, you
must not hang this spark.   It will do you no good, man.
The youth hath a spirit, and bears himself boldly.   Pedro,
you must let the fellow go.   What, man ! he will not
take Carthagena from you ; I will insure that, although
my warlike friend Guzman may not feel himself justified
in saying so much, on behalf of his own valour.'

The officer so alluded to, turned rapidly from red to
white, and white to red.   He mumbled and grumbled to
himself, and then forced out somewhat about its being
known ; that he, a simple soldier, could not compete in
word-sallies and figures of speech with so renowned a
courtier as Don José.   He was interrupted by the alcaide,

who said that it was ever his pleasure to honour so honourable and great a gentleman as Don José; but here was a matter in which he but spoke the written words of the law, and these words said that the doom of pirates was death.

'Yes, I grant thee,' exclaimed my unexpected advocate; ' but is the youth a pirate? You go too fast, good Master Alcaide. Justice is blind; but you see more than there is to behold!'

The alcaide, who evidently wished to keep well with Don José, and who as evidently wished to string me up, began to get very red in the face, and to mutter half-suppressed words of passion. Just then, the ferret-eyed man whispered him at one ear, while Captain Guzman possessed himself of the other. After listening for a few seconds, the judge seemed to decide what he should do; accordingly, he hemmed twice, and began in a loud pompous style—

' The court,' he said, ' hath been in an unseemly manner interrupted by a noble person now present. Such irregularities cannot in any way be permitted, even to the highest of the land; and it is therefore craved that the noble person in question do refrain henceforth from interrupting the course of justice.'

Don José, at this laughed scornfully, and flung himself back in his chair, which he balanced upon the hinder legs, twisting and twirling his moustache at the same time, with the air of a man who deems his company vastly beneath him, and curling his lip as he did when relating the miracle of Our Lady of the Hill blowing up the ' Oxford ' man-of-war.

The wrinkled man next took up the speech. Peering with the bitterest glances out of the corner of his blinking eyes at Don José, he squeaked out, that those suffering banishment for offences committed against the law, were not the most proper supporters of the authority of his Majesty.'

The hidalgo answered, by removing his sombrero, and bowing, with a wonderful air of mock gravity and con

descension, to his reprover. Then the examination recommenced :

'Did you not arrive with your comrades off this peaceful coast in an armed ship, your intent being to kill,
sink, burn, and destroy ?' the alcaide next demanded, with
ruffled brow, and a savage eagerness in his speech.

I remained mute. 'Silence gives consent,' said the
clerk. Don José shrugged his shoulders, and leisurely
used a golden pick-tooth. The clerk wrote down something, probably an entry, that I had confessed that such
were our intentions.

'Were you not taken in the act of playing the spy
in the harbour of Cathagena ?' roared the alcaide again.

I still remained mute. What need was there of speech ?
The alcaide and the clerk consulted together ; then the
former made a sign to one of the turnkeys, who stood by
me. The man nodded and withdrew. This motion did
not escape Don José, who forthwith rose up, and said
very briskly—

'Señor Monté, beware you do not somewhat tran-
scend your commission. I have not lost my interest at
the court of Castile. That youth may be a pirate, but
you have in noways proved it. Besides he hath borne
himself both modestly and manfully. I am of a house
which hath ever protected the weak against the strong ;
and I swear, by your Lady of the Hill, that if the youth
come to wrong, you and your underlings shall answer
and abide the consequence !'

At this, there was a loud and threatening murmur
among the spectators ; and the turnkeys, thinking that
Don José might attempt a rescue single-handed, griped
me tightly. As for the alcaide, his grim and disfigured
features grew white, and worked and grinned with spite,
while the little wrinkled man, shaking with rage, whispered tremulously to his superior. In a minute the
alcaide burst out. He started off his seat, and with his
fists clenched, and the shaggy hairs of his moustache
bristling for very passion, he roared out—

'A pretty thing—a pretty thing! that I am thus

crossed and insulted in my own court; that my warnings
and reproofs are set at naught, and I am threatened on
the very judgment-seat! Caramba! Let those who do
so look to it. Who dare come between me and—

'And your prey, kite!' said Don José, with the old
bitter sneer gleaming on his face.

The alcaide foamed at the mouth, and bellowed rather
than spoke.

'The pirate—the pirate shall die the the death! I say
it! Here prevail no traitors' counsels!'

'Whoso says I am a traitor,' cried Don José, 'lies in
his foul throat, and I will push the words back into his
lungs with my sword!' So saying, he advanced upon the
judge.

'Guards—guards!' screamed out the clerk. 'Turn
out the guards! Where are the soldiers? Treason!
The life of the alcaide is in danger!'

At the same time, the mob in the court, who had
hitherto remained passive, burst into loud execrations,
and clenched fists and gleaming knives were shaken at
Don José. The latter drew himself up with that majestic
motion and gesture, which your high-bred Spaniard knows
how to assume, and curling his thin lip, and flashing his
black eyes upon the roaring crowd, stood, unmoved as a
stone statue in the aisle of a minster.

Meantime, the alcaide entirely threw off all appearance
of a judge's impartiality.

'Townsmen!' he shouted, 'are we to be insulted, spit
on, and because, forsooth, our contemner is a noble of
Castile?—are we to cower as meek as flogged hounds
before his highness? I say the fellow before us is a
pirate. He is, at all events, an Englishman, which means
the same thing. He is a heretic and a buccaneer-spy,
and he shall strap for it. Holy Mother! shall we turn
loose the rogue to prey upon our vitals? I hate him
—I hate his race! They have spoiled great ventures
of precious merchandise; they have captured ships I
equipped; they have harried treasures I amassed; they
pillage and harass our lawful trade; they intrude them-

selves on our coasts, and in our seas ; they have burnt
Panama; they have taken Nicaragua; they have taken
Santa Maria; they have taken Gibraltar in Venezuela;
they have raged and thirsted for our blood ; they are the
enemies of our faith, and of our nation ; and so may my
right hand wither, may my right arm wither from socket
to wrist, but those of the murthering pirates who come
within my grasp, shall go thieving no more! Said I well,
townsmen—said I well ?'

This furious tirade was answered by a great shout
from the people, who crowded round me, cursing and
flashing their broad-bladed knives in my face.    One
fellow raised his arm to strike; I saw the swell of the
moving muscles, and the glitter of the poised knife, when
Don José, with one bound leaped from the dais, and
scattering the crowd, as a charge of horse scatters broken
infantry, he dashed up the arm raised to stab, and drawing his rapier, the mob fell back from him, while he
shouted in tones which rung like trumpet-notes—

'Hounds that you are!—would you murder in cold
blood an unarmed and manacled man ?'

There was dead silence for near a minute.  'Alcaide
of Carthagena,' continued my defender, 'look well to
yourself—what I have done, was that the ends of justice
might be served, and I will answer for my acts.    I can
do no more—I leave this man in your hands—you shall
be answerable for your treatment of him.    Make way
there, and permit me to go forth.'

Again the mob yielded a passage.  'He speaks like a
king,' said one fellow.  'Truly, he hath the bearing of
an emperor,' murmured another.    And so, still holding
his unsheathed rapier in his hand, his features being calm
and composed, save that there was on his forehead a
slight flush, and a hot sparkle gleaming in his eye, he
passed through the yielding crowd, who instinctively fell
back before him—walking with the port of a conqueror,
who enters a fallen city—this man—a banished libertine
—but still a grandee in whose veins ran the haughty
blood of Old Castile !

As Don José disappeared, I felt that it was all over with me. His advocacy failing, I stood in a position much worse than before. I was the cause that a friendship, or at least an intimacy, had turned to a bitter enmity, and that the alcaide had been publicly insulted on the judgment-seat. Therefore, I tried to compose my mind, so as to withdraw it from things of the world, which already began to seem like matters in which others might have an interest, but which possessed none for me —like things, indeed, which were but dreamings, wherein, to him who stands upon the last step of life, is nought, save only deceitfulness and vanity. I was roused from this fit of musing by the harsh voice of the alcaide, who, having now recovered his composure, thought proper, perhaps, to smooth down somewhat of his last oration.

'Despite,' quoth he, 'despite the ill-advised attempt of a noble person, now gone forth, to bar the proceedings of this court, the prisoner may depend upon it he shall receive just judgment at our hands.'

The clerk grinned to himself, and bowed to his master, who called upon him to read a decree of the court which it seems had just been written. It was to this effect :—

'The accused, a Scots mariner, by name Leonard Lindsay, a buccaneer, or pirate of the sort called Brethren of the Coast, unlawfully in arms against his Most Christian Majesty, having refused to answer certain interrogatories put to him in open court, it is decreed that his examination be continued in private.'

By the hum which arose, and the broken words I could catch uttered around me, when this decree was read, I was presently aware of its real meaning. It signified interrogatory by torture. I clenched my teeth, and made a great effort to show no sign—not even by the tremor of a finger—of flinching. The turnkeys touched me on the shoulder, and I walked mechanically out between them. We passed through divers corridors, I taking but little notice, however, where we went, until we arrived in a bare chamber ; here there was a heavy table of plain wood and one or two benches, but most part of the room was occupied with some machines or apparatus, the nature of which I guessed, but the forms whereof were concealed by a coarse linen cloth flung over them. This cloth was stained with patches of blood. Beside the table stood two men; one of them, a thin, mean-looking personage, poorly dressed in a worn doublet, with a cold passionless face and stony eyes. The other was portly and pleasant-looking, and seeing me advance, eyed me from head to foot, saying at the same time, 'Hum! a goodly patient.'

'*El medico*,' whispered one of my conductors. He had no cause to tell me of the profession of the doctor's companion. Close behind me came the alcaide, his clerk, and the ruffianly captain. The naval gentleman was not there, and on the ferret-eyed man asking for him, an attendant said that senor, the lieutenant, had been sent for in haste from the harbour. Our group was now ranged in a circle, I being opposite to the alcaide, the executioner standing on one side of me, and the doctor on the other. The clerk carried an open book for writing in, and a turnkey beside him held the ink-bottle.

'Accused,' said the alcaide, 'do you still refuse to reply to the questions put to you in open court, and which shall shall now be rehearsed by the clerk?'

I said I would not put him to the trouble of reading them—I would tell nothing.

'Take off his handcuffs,' said the magistrate. They were removed. The executioner looked inquiringly at his patron.

'I am not a cruel man,' said the latter, drawling out his words, as though longer to enjoy my suspense and horror. 'I would not wrench thy handsome limbs so as to spoil their symmetry. No, no; gentle means at first, Mr. Provost-Marshal—a squeeze or so on the nerve of the thumb, no stout-hearted Buccaneer can complain of.'

Instantly the provost-marshal, as though he had anticipated this commencement, whipped from his pocket a little instrument of iron. It was a thumb-screw, a 'thumbikin.' as my countrymen called it, and long was it remembered with curses in many a strath, and on many a hill side, in my native land. For the dragoons of James Graham, of Claverhouse, were wont to carry them in their pouches or haversacks; and, many a long year after I had left the Spanish Indies, when I talked to old Scotchmen about my adventures there, and told them of the alcaide and the provost-marshal of Carthagena, they would reply, 'Ay, ay, we know somewhat of such torments. Even here, in Scotland, many a joint was wrenched, and many a bone splintered, of the men who in the old troublous days stood staunchly up under the blue banner, and bore faithful testimony for a broken covenant and a persecuted kirk.'

But I must hasten with the tale of my own trials.

'Do your duty, provost-marshal,' said the alcaide, gloating on the accursed iron machine; 'but let us have all things in moderation—one thumb at a time; the prisoner cannot say that we have no bowels.'

Fortunately for me, as it turned out afterwards, the executioner stood upon my left. He laid hold of the hand nearest to him with cold, clammy-feeling fingers, which touched my flesh, to my thinking, like small twining snakes or worms, and with great dexterity slipped the iron apparatus upon my thumb, turning at the same time a screw, so as to make it press tight. The next twist I knew would produce torture.

'Accused,' began the alcaide again, 'if you choose to tell us what you know of your comrades' designs we will, even although your obstinacy hath been great, proceed no further in this business; if not, in the name of the law and the king I ordain the provost-marshal to proceed.'

I said not a word, but drew a long breath, and nerved myself, trying to fix and resolutely wind up my mind and body to endure. There was a pause for a minute, and then the alcaide nodded. The provost-marshal stepped forward, grasped my wrist with his left hand, and then, at the same time looking steadily into my eyes, twisted the screw round with a rapid wrench, and instantly a pang, a throb of pain horribly keen, cut, as it were with a knife,

from the thumb up the arm to the shoulder-blade. I felt
a hot flush come out upon my face, and then, the first
agonizing jerk over, a horrible tingling began, pricking
the limb as though myriads of red-hot needles had been
thrust into it.

'Do you still refuse to answer the question?' said the
alcaide. I bowed. He nodded, as before, and round
again went the screw. This time the agony was fearful.
I ground my teeth, my knees shook, and I felt the cold
sweat start out in beads among the roots of my hair.
The involuntary desire to scream was almost overmastering, but I curbed it with a mighty effort, swallowing
down, as it were, the anguish, by violent efforts of the
muscles of the throat. All this time the group who
surrounded me preserved silence. There was a grim
smile upon the face of the alcaide, but the ferret eyes of
his clerk were gleaming with excitement, and his features
were twisting with very pleasure. The doctor and the
provost-marshal behaved like two men engaged in a per-
fectly-indifferent matter.

Again the alcaide questioned me, again I made the
same reply, and again the provost-marshal wrenched
round the screw. This time, amid the slight squeak of
the revolving iron, all heard the crackle of the bone; the
skin too, had given way beneath metallic pressure, and a
gush of black bruised blood spurted over the iron and the
thin fingers of the provost-marshal, and then dropped in
thick plashy globules upon the floor. Almost at the same
instant a mist came up before my eyes, and hid the fierce
faces which surrounded me. I tottered, and leant upon
the surgeon, and a cold feeling of sickness almost unto
death gripped my very being, and seemed to stop the
fountains of life. It was the very depth of that suffering
which drew from me the only low shuddering moan I
uttered. But hardly had the sound escaped than there
was a tramp of footsteps rushing into the room, and a
loud voice which cried—

'Señor the alcaide is wanted upon the beach; a
schooner with English colours set, which hath been

hovering in the offing all the morning, is standing in for
the harbour, as though she would carry the galleon even
under the very guns of the batteries.'

And in an instant, as though to roar a chorus to the
words of the messenger, the heavy reports of great guns
shook the ill-fitting casements of the chamber; and a
great and confused jangle of many bells, and the echoes
of a shouting crowd, came floating together upon the air.
I started up—the mist cleared from before me—even the
sense of pain and sickness left me, and looking with exult-
ation on the pale and scared faces of my tormentors, I
shouted, 'Huzza! for the bold Brethren of the Coast!
Courage, comrades! courage, and the day is our own!'

'Send the fellow back to his cell,' said the alcaide, very
hurriedly. 'Captain Guzman, turn out your guard.
We will finish with him when we have finished with his
comrades in the harbour. Perhaps there will be more to
deal with presently.'

'The more the merrier,' said the ferret-eyed clerk, and
they shuffled hastily out together. Meantime, the provost-marshal unscrewed his thumbikin with as much
coolness as he had adjusted it. My hand was all bloody
and swollen. The doctor looked at it, felt the thumb with
his fingers, and then said, 'My good fellow, your comrades came to your aid just in time; another wrench and
that hand would be of small use to you for the rest of
your life.'

The provost-marshal, who was wiping the blood from
his instrument, smiled meaningly. 'Why, good doctor,'
quoth he, 'considering what is like enough to be the
extent of the youngster's life, I do not see the great hard-
ship of disabling him.'

The doctor shrugged his shoulders, and walked out.
The only turnkey who remained clapped his hand on my
shoulder, and I followed him, binding up my lacerated
hand with a kerchief. I was presently conducted to the
same cell as that which I had already occupied; but,
to my great astonishment, instead of shutting me in and
leaving me to my meditations, the man first cast a rapid

glance up and down the corridor, and then closing the door upon both of us, caught me by the collar of the doublet, and whispered : —

'You have a good friend. Keep up your heart, and you may yet have a chance for your life.'

The blessed words fell upon my ears like rain on parched herbage.

'Who—who is it ?  Of whom do you speak ?'  I cried, eagerly.

'Of one who gave a shining doubloon to tell you so much ; and he bade me add, too, that you should hold yourself in readiness for a quick journey.'

'But, tell me,' I interrupted—when we heard the voice of the provost-marshal without, calling, 'Lazarillo, Lazarillo, what keeps you ?'  The turnkey made but one bound of it to the door, locked the cell with a clash, and hurried away, leaving me with an aching hand, but a palpitating and a very grateful heart.  All was not yet over with me.  I had still a right to the rays of the sun.  The black grave, which in my mind I had seen for the last hour continually yawning before me, was gone.  Most blessed of the moods of the heart, Hope, slid again into my being, and sent the hot blood dancing madly through my veins.  I paced up and down the cell wildly.  I tried to leap at the barred window.  The pain of my lacerated flesh I remembered no more ; and clenching both fists, I vowed that, once without these walls, it was only a dead body which the Spaniards would bring back.  The roar of the conflict in the harbour, which still continued, worked me up to the highest pitch of excitement.  I sought to distinguish, in fancy, between the guns of our enemies and those of my friends ; and every time I heard the sharp ring of the smaller metal, which I concluded was fired from aboard the schooner, I broke out in rhapsodies, calling upon the ball to fly truly home to its mark, and to hit that pestilent alcaide or his ferret-eyed clerk.  At length I began to cool down, and get somewhat ashamed of my fervour.  Besides, the noise of cannonading abated—the reports of the guns coming fainter and

fainter, as if the fight were being carried on more to seaward. From this I judged that the schooner had been
beaten off. Indeed, I could expect no other termination
of the attack, which, when I came to think of it in sober
earnest, appeared to me to be little short of madness, and
I wondered how Stout Jem had come to attempt it.
From these matters I began to think more reasonably of
my own situation. I little doubted but that my unknown
friend was no other than Don José, who appeared to my
mind to be as singular a mixture of base and generous
qualities as a man could be composed of. But how was he
to help me? Was the mode of escape to be by force or
escalade? To cut the window-bars would require a file,
and to mount to them a ladder. Then, my left hand was
in a bad condition for either working or clambering, and
even should I succeed in making my way into the city,
whither was I to go next? I had no place of refuge, but
the woods, and without arms or ammunition, little hope
of aught but a lingering death there, either by starvation
or wild Indians. Indeed, the more I mused, the more
gloomy after all my prospects seemed.

The excitement at the first notion of escape thus
passed away. My wounded hand, although not altogether
disabled, was very stiff and painful, and I had not even
the means of washing away the clotted blood. So, sitting, in no merry mood, pondering, upon my bench, the
slow hot hours crept by. The sunlight came in a fiery
stream where the blue moonbeam had lain the night
before. The buzz of insects and the rustling of rich
foliage, waved by the fresh sea-breeze, sounded cheerily
from without, and sometimes a puff, stronger than common, would find its way into the hot cell, and play
round my cheeks and nostrils, bringing with it the cool,
fresh savour of the ocean.

It might have been about one o'clock, when the
friendly turnkey unlocked the door and entered, carrying with him a very fair dinner of meat and roasted
plantains, to which was added a small measure of generous Spanish wine. I entreated him, all in a breath, to

R

give me more information touching my projected escape,
and also as respected the fate of the schooner. In regard
to the latter affair, the man said, he believed that the
attack had only been a sort of a feint, or bravado, and
that, after some cannonading, a boat with a white flag had
put off from the schooner, which had thereupon ceased
firing; but the Spaniards not being willing to come to
any truce with pirates and sea-robbers, as they called us,
had continued to fire upon the boat, and a ball breaking
the oars on one side, and very narrowly missing the
boat herself, those in her pulled round and back to the
schooner. A small squadron of armadilloes then got
under weigh, and the schooner had nothing else for it
than to stand out to sea, the armadilloes following her,
and both exchanging long shots at each other. This I
afterwards understood to be a very fair account of the enterprise, which was indeed undertaken only in the hope of
wresting me out of the Spaniards' hands. But I had
other friends at work, as the reader will see. The turnkey, who was, or rather pretended to be, in some agitation at the thought of the work which he had been
bribed to undertake, now told me that about two o'clock,
at the hour when most of the inhabitants of Carthagena
are in use to take their siesta, or day-sleep he would be
with me again.

'You may be thankful,' quoth he, 'that you were not
taken as prisoner to the fort, where, indeed, there would
be little chance of escape, let you have what friends you
might; but this is not a regular prison, being only a
sort of guardhouse, attached to the alcaide's mansion, for
the convenience of keeping accused persons for examination. Therefore, once out of your cell, and furnished
with the pass-word, you will have little ado in making
your flight to the woods, where you must shift for yourself—he who has paid me to peril my place in the matter
having no refuge to offer you.'

The reader may be sure that I exhausted myself in
compliments and thanks to my benefactor, whom the
jailer obstinately refused to name, but about whom there

was in my mind no doubt whatever. Neither was I in any great surprise, when I came attentively to consider the state of matters, at the mode in which the affair was to be arranged, and the easy compliance for some trifling bribe of the jailer. I called to mind how often I had been told that, in almost all Spanish prisons in the Indies, the jailers and magistrates were just as great rogues as the thieves they dealt with. Nay, I had no doubt but that the alcaide himself would have taken a bribe to let me go, as readily as the turnkey, only he would have been very like to break his engagement, and hang me after all; thus gratifying himself in both ways. As it was, I considered that my chances were very good. The turnkey did not at all seem to apprehend any interruption from his comrades. 'We live in very good intelligence,' quoth he; 'and none of us cares to spoil the other's game. There is but one man I dread, and he, I hope, is out of the way. Curses on that sharp-eyed clerk of the alcaide's, he takes a pleasure in marring the best-laid schemes.'

But I swore within myself, that were I interrupted by this official, he would have small chance of ever looking out of his ferret-eyes again. I think the jailer understood what was passing in my mind, although I spoke not, for he smiled meaningly, as he said, peering into my face, with a curious expression on his own—

'And this clerk is but a weak slip of a man after all. I warrant you a stout fellow would smash his brittle bones as easily as I would so many pipe-stems. However, that is no business of mine. In half an hour, Señor the Buccaneer, all will be ready.'

## CHAPTER XXI.

### HOW I ESCAPE FROM THE SPANISH GUARDHOUSE—AM CHASED BY BLOOD-HOUNDS IN THE WOODS, AND HOW AT LENGTH I FIND A STRANGE ASYLUM.

THE clock, from a neighbouring church, struck two. My cell-door opened gently, and the turnkey appeared, carrying in his hand a tolerable-sized bundle, which I eagerly asisted him to undo. It contained a good suit, such as is commonly worn by Spanish sailors, with stout leggings fitted for scrambling in the woods, and a broad-brimmed and steeple-crowned felt hat. The doublet was tied round my waist with a broad silk sash, and into this I stuck a gleaming knife, similar to that carried by almost all Spaniards. But when the turnkey produced, from under his doublet, a short-barrelled carabine, or musquetoon—a *trabucco*, as he called it—with a fair supply of shot and slugs, I burst out into exclamations of gratitude.

'Long live Don José!' I cried. 'I fear not the woods now; there is life and food within this hollow iron.'

'Look you,' said the turnkey, 'here be the words of the nobleman who hath sent these. "Tell," quoth he, "tell the Scots mariner, that as he bore himself before the alcaide like one whose word and good faith were dear to him, that I supply him with these weapons, upon his solemn promise that he will use them only to procure himself food, and that he will not turn them against any Spaniard, excepting only strictly in the way of self-defence."'

You may be assured that this reasonable pledge I gave with the utmost readiness, and poising my musquetoon, and trying how it fitted to my shoulder, I cried, gaily—

'Come—come! Despatch—despatch! good master jailer; your friends will be rousing themselves from their siesta. Faith, man, were you as near the gallows as I am every moment I linger here, you would pant to hear the free rustle of the branches above you.'

All the while that the turnkey was helping me on with my new costume, I kept thinking of where I should bend my steps as soon as I got clear of Carthagena. It was very likely, I thought, that the schooner would keep hovering upon the coast, still waiting for the galleon, the sailing of which would no doubt be delayed by what had happened. I considered, moreover, that the Will-

ɔ'-the-Wisp would be most likely to ply to the eastward, so as to keep the weather-gauge of the port she
was watching, and that it was quite possible that she
might approach near enough the shore for me to make a
signal, by kindling a fire, or by any other means which
might seem available, in order to attract her notice. So
I determined, as soon as I could get fairly free of the
town, to turn to the eastward and to descend again upon
the coast some eight or ten miles from Carthagena.

'Now,' quoth the turnkey, 'you will easily perceive
that I am not to be seen in this business. Your escape
must appear to have been effected by yourself, and it
will be the more easy, inasmuch as the lock on this door
has seen much service, and is not difficult to wrench off;
especially when a man is provided with such a weapon as
this,' and he handed to me a strong iron chisel, or rather
short crow-bar.

'Listen,' he continued; 'I will again lock you up.
Let five minutes elapse, then wrench open the door;
take the two first turnings to your left, the next turning
to your right, the next to your left again, and you are
opposite the street. A sentry stands there. If he be
asleep, as is not unlikely, good and well. If he be awake
and challenge, reply, "Guarda Costa,"—that is the
countersign. You must then shift for yourself. Farewell, Señor Buccaneer, and if ever you meet Don José
fail not to tell him I behaved honestly by you, and earned
his doubloons well. You will not forget "Guarda Costa."
Adieu.'

The door closed on him; I waited in silence and with
a beating heart. It was a long five minutes which
elapsed; but at its expiration, as nearly as I could judge,
I inserted the short crowbar between the staple which
held the bolt, and the lintel of the door. The wood was
crumbling and rotten, and the iron eaten with long
gathering rust. Gradually, as I applied my strength,
the mouldy timber gave way beneath the pressure, and
the metal creaked and crackled. I could have burst it
off with one effort of my muscles, but I feared to make a

noise ; and so, gradually working the point of the crow-bar further and further into the wreck of the dilapidated fastenings, I increased the strain, until at length, with one long, steady and vehement wrench, I tore the staples from the yielding wood. The metal fell with a clash upon the floor ; the door, which opened inwardly, swung back ; and I saw—the ferret eyes and the twitching visage of the alcaide's clerk, staring and grinning through the opening.

I started back as though a demon had looked me in the face. The small wrinkled and puckered features worked and twisted, and the eyes gleamed so as to resemble nothing earthly. Then I saw the hand of the clerk creep stealthily towards the bosom of his mean doublet, without doubt to pluck therefrom a weapon : his lips moved, and the first syllables of a cry of alarm had passed them, when I sprang forward, and the grasp of my fingers round his meagre throat smothered the words. All this took place in an instant. I dragged the wretch inside the cell ; struck to the door with a blow of my foot, and clutching both his thin wrists in my left hand, gripped his throat with my right, until the skin got blue, and the eyes protruded all glaring and bloodshot. I thought for a moment to strangle him as we stood, but as I felt the weak struggles of the hapless creature, who writhed like a child in my grasp, my heart softened. I released my hold upon his throat.

'Were you strong and I weak,' I whispered to him, 'there would be little pity shown. You are athirst for my blood, but Providence has willed that you shall not be gratified. As I grant you mercy now, show mercy to others.'

The clerk tried to speak, but only husky murmurs passed his lips.

'Lie there,' I continued, 'until your friends come to your rescue.'

With that I flung the man upon the floor, so as partially to stun him, and then, with the aid of some ratline stuff, which sailors go seldom without, and which

was in the pocket of my old doublet, I both bound and
gagged him, not very completely, it is true, but sufficiently, as I believed, to prevent any alarm being given
until I had got a good start. It was pitiful to see the
impotent spite with which the manacled creature writhed
upon the ground, gibbering with his speechless mouth,
and flashing his green eyes as though he could have shot
blistering venom out of them upon me. But I had little
time to bestow upon the spectacle: with a quick step and
a beating heart I fled along the corridors. During my
scuffle with the clerk, the turnkey's directions had never
ceased to ring in my ears. The two first turnings to the
left, the next to the right, the next to the left again.
The silent passages echoed to my footste, s with a hollow,
ominous sound. There were many nail-studded doors,
similar to that of my own cell, on either side. As I
made the last turning, I had a glimpse, in the distance,
of the guard-room into which I had been at first conducted, and then, looking straight ahead, I saw before
me the narrow street, with its deep, dusty ruts, scorching, as it were, in the hot sun. The passage terminated
in a great gateway, with pillars and a portico, and on the
left side of the door stood a sentry-box, painted white.
Pausing for a moment to assume all possible coolness, I
walked steadily out humming the butt-end of a Spanish
sea-song, which the mariners of that nation sing when
leaving the anchor to the bows.

Just as I passed the porch I glanced at the sentry.
He was a young man; his features bronzed almost black
with the sun, and wearing silver earrings, glittering
among t his long greasy curls. The fellow was sitting
leaning against his sentry-box; his musket, with his
bayonet fixed, flung carelessly across his knee. As I
strode by, he half opened his sleepy eyes, and muttered
mechanically as though speaking in a dream.

'Guarda Costa,' I said, carelessly. The man muttered
something again, and his chin fell upon his breast. Like
a phantom I glided up the hot and silent street. Not a
soul was to be seen. The cloth of outside blinds and the

gay draperies hanging from balconies, rustled in the cooling wind, while those thin slices of wood, forming what are called in the Indies, 'jalousies,' clattered with a merry rattle. Dogs lay listlessly stretched out in shady corners; bullocks, harnessed to clumsy carts, lay chewing the cud between the shafts, and two or three mendicants, as I judged them from their rags and filth, were stretched beneath gateways and under pillars, where the breeze came freshest. But the spell of sleep was everywhere. Midnight in New Spain might bring the time of gallant assignation and joyous revel, but the drowsy afternoon shone upon a city steeped in sleep, even as though one of the mighty charms which I used to read of in idle chronicles of old fancies, were abroad over the dreaming people, one of those charms of glamour and gramarye of the days when Michael Scott split the Eildon hills in three, and Thomas of Erceldoune was courted of the faery queen!

'So, blessings on that good old Spanish custom, the siesta,' I cried to myself, as I sped along the deserted thoroughfare. Carthagena is not large, neither is it fortified towards the land side. Very little time had therefore elapsed until I found myself fairly beyond the city, and running along a rough road, with great plenty of trees and bushes on either side, and patches of fields, wherein grew the broad brown-leaved tobacco plant, and here and there a hut, with a yam garden about it, or the country house of a Carthagena merchant, with prim terraces and avenues of limes, and fountains sparkling among the leaves. These I ran past as speedily as possible; but there was no appearance of aught stirring about them more than in the city. The siesta was everywhere, ay, even in the great woods, which at length I reached; the birds sitting motionless upon the branches, and the beasts of the earth hiding in dens and holes from the fervid noontide heat. The road which I had followed gradually disappeared, splitting as it were into many little tracks made by hunters or other wanderers in the woods. Around me there soon rose rocks and steep hills, and the tangled underwood and the long grass

made walking difficult. However, I was in too great
spirits to feel much weariness. Every step I took was
almost as a year added to my life. So, at last, when I
saw that I had really plunged fairly into the wilderness,
I forced my way amid the rank vegetation, tearing
through brake and thicket, and singing and shouting
lustily in the fulness of my heart. The sun was my
compass, and by him I steered eastwardly.

'Ho! ho! Stout Jem,' I cried to myself, ' mayhap, we
are but now laying the same course ; the gay schooner
out upon the tilting sea, and he that loves her well amid
the shady woods and green savannahs of the main. So
we shall meet again, comrades—we shall meet again!'

In this merry mood I traversed several miles before I
thought of refreshment or of rest. It was just as my
limbs began to ache and my breath to come short, as I
breasted a steep hill, that I came to a fair fountain
gurgling from a rift in a low mossy rock. It was not an
unknown well of the wilderness, for human hands had
placed a doubled leaf, through which, as through a spout,
the living water ran from the runnel, and tinkled out
into a natural basin beneath.

So here I sat me down and wiped the perspiration
from my brow. It was a lonely spot, and I wondered
whose hands had plucked the leaf and laid it in its place.
From the basin I speak of, the water ran amid rustling
reeds, and great floating leaves, and gaudy flowers, until
it spread itself out into a shallow pool, half covered with
greasy scum, but elsewhere as clear as the air above it.
In the centre of the pool sat a little bird of the diver
species, with the glossy neck and the bright beady eyes
which I love in water-fowl. He took little notice of me,
and I sat and watched him as he glided to and fro amid
the floating leaves and twigs which had fallen from the
trees. While thus occupied, I heard once or twice the
distant bay as of a dog.

'Ho!' thought I, 'the siesta is over, and Señors the
dogs are the first astir.'

My eye fell upon the water-fowl again. It seemed

disquieted, and swam quickly to and fro, making a soft quackle, and jerking its little head, as its kind do when listening. The bay of the dog was heard again—it seemed to have come nearer—and, directly, the water-bird, half swimming and half flying, beating the surface with its wings as it went, took refuge in the thickest of the sedges and disappeared. This little incident roused me. I started up and hearkened. Again, the deep hollow echo of the hound's bay struck my ears. It was very different from the yelping of a woodman's cur; and the dogs of the Indians do not bark. Immediately a thought flashed upon me—a ghastly—appalling thought: the Spaniards were upon my track with bloodhounds! Almost instinctively I started up and fled, stumbling as I went. I had a horror of these fiends of dogs, trained to hunt men; and, as I flew along, I thought every moment that I heard the savage creatures panting close behind me. After about ten minutes' quick running, I stopped, quite spent, to breathe, and, listening for a moment, a faint sound of hallooing, and a burst of baying, loud and long, came floating on the wind. I turned and fled again, straining every nerve mechanically, although I knew but too well that, fleet as was my foot, every time it touched the ground it left the mark which guided the avengers. I, therefore, tried to leap and double, and even got up into a tree and swung myself along by means of the interlacing branches. But this was slow work, I dropped to the ground, and ran again. All this time the voice of the dog was sounding nearer and nearer behind me, and I wondered how my pursuers could keep up with him, at the rate he was evidently running. Nevertheless, I loosened the knife in my girdle and prepared for the struggle. As I did so, I thought of my blunderbuss. Heaven! I had left it behind in my first alarm at the well. The token would have told the Spaniards that their four-footed guide was as sure as it appeared swift. The baying of the accursed hound came close and closer. Oh! how I envied the birds as they rose with a rustle and a scream from the foliage, and soared away in the air, which leaves no track to tell of who has cleft it. Covered with sweat and dust, and reeling with fatigue, I ran almost at random. Twice I disturbed glistening snakes, which coiled their spiral folds and flashed their black eyes at me, and then glided away like slimy painted ropes pulled by some unseen hand amongst the herbage. But at that instant the bite of the labarri, or the hollow tooth of the rattlesnake, had hardly more horror for me than the gripe of the crunching jaws which were fast following on my track. By this time, the thunder of the hound's voice was so close that I involuntarily turned at every step to see him make his appearance. The final moment came at last. Crashing with a great rustle through a bed of yielding bushes, sprang a huge, tawny dog, black and foaming at the muzzle. The creature ran, cat-like, with his belly close to the ground, his big, muscular limbs, showing as supple and slamp as a tiger's, and his broad deep chest, and great hanging ears, all speckled white with flakes of foam. I looked for his master, but saw none ; and, gazing more closely, observed a leash round the creature's neck, and a broken leathern thong trailing beside him. This at once explained the rapidity with which he had overtaken me—the animal having broken away from those who led him, and it also sent a cheery flush of hope, dancing through my brain. Oh, how I cursed my heedlessness in leaving the carabine by the well! A handful of slugs would have stopped the blood-hound for ever, and my pursuers deprived of their guide, could seek me but at random through the woods. Could I manage him with the knife ?—that was the ques- tion. I had no long time to debate it. I must either slay or be slain—there was no choice. I stopped, faced round, tore off my doublet, and wrapped it, in thick and heavy folds, round my left arm—shielding my wounded hand in addition, by grasping with it the inside of my strong and stiff felt hat. Then clutching my knife in my right, I knelt on one knee, and waited for the onset of the blood-hound.

I had, indeed, hardly assumed my position of defence

when he was on me. True to the instinct of his kind, he lifted neither eyes nor nose from the ground—running, truly and steadily, by the scent, until he was scarcely a couple of fathoms from me. Then, indeed, he flung up his nostrils in the air, and suddenly seeing me, uttered a loud splitting yell, champing at the same time the foam in a hot shower from his jaws, and then, with a great scrambling bound, furious and open-mouthed, pounced upon me, driving his teeth into the folds of the doublet, which I held before me as a shield, and dashing me, by the very force of his spring, over and over amid the grass, scrambling and tearing the skin from my shoulders, with his huge horny paws, and furiously shaking and riving the stuff of the doublet which, luckily for me, was both thick and strong. For a moment or two, I had no opportunity of using the knife, I could not see where to hit. There was before me but a vision of great foaming, tearing jaws, and flashing eyes, and struggling limbs— sometimes above me—sometimes beneath, as we rolled over and over in the scuffle. But at length, I had a chance ; the broad muscular chest of the noble creature was left, for a moment, unsheltered by his fore-legs, and in a second I had driven the keen strong knife, through and through his lungs, the handle smiting the dog's breast with a hollow blow. There was an immediate convulsion of the animal's limbs. Letting go his hold of my doublet, he flung his muzzle into the air, and with a sound between a cough and a yell, threw up a hot sputtering shower of blood. Quick as thought, my reeking knife was withdrawn, and again and again plunged in up to the very hilt—the muscles of the creature's body—a moment before, all strained and tense as iron bands— gradually collapsed—the fierce eyes turned, so that the yellowish whites shone, with a grim glare into mine, and it required but a slight effort to shake off the quivering and bleeding creature, which as I rose trembling and panting from the fray—fell heavily from my limbs, and lay gasping in its blood among the grass. Truly, it was a noble dog, as large and more powerful than the mightiest stag-hound, but its deep chest had uttered its last bay, its giant limbs had run their last race. The life passed out of the quivering flesh, as I stood and gazed at it. Then flinging over my shoulders my doublet, all torn, and stained with blood and froth, I addressed myself again to flight—thankful and joyous for my deliverance. 'Three good thrusts of this trusty steel,' said I to myself, sheathing my knife, 'and the utmost spite of the Spaniard has been baffled.' I was reckoning without my host. Hardly had the words escaped my lips, when, again, the accursed bay of a blood-hound came floating in the wind. I paused and listened with clenched teeth. For an instant, I hoped that it might be but the dying growl of the animal killed. But, no, he lay stark, and the foam was already cooling upon his jaw. Again and again, came the ominous sound—I could not be mistaken. My pursuers had started with at least a brace of dogs—and they were still following fast and hot upon my footsteps. A shuddering chill passed all over me, and I felt sick at heart—then I roused myself. 'Perhaps,' I argued, 'the blood of the dead hound will confuse the scent of the living one. I have heard of such things.' But afterwards I learned that the Spaniards, seeing the body from a distance, had not allowed their four-footed guide to approach it closely, but that leading him in a circle round the carcase, the animal had again struck upon my scent—closer and fresher than ever. Thus it was, that as I forced my way through the thickets of bushes, and long rustling grass—I ever heard behind me the hollow boom of that accursed creature, as he gave loud tongue, and the distant hallooing as the Spaniards answered him with shouts and execrations. Summoning my resources, I tried, as I ran, to call to mind the legends of men chased with blood hounds—of which I had heard in my childhood, and the means whereby they had baffled their pursuers. For many such tales are told on winter nights by Scottish hearths—of the bold moss-troopers of Teviot and Annan, and the wild northern caterans beyond the Highland line. But my memory seemed to have forsaken me. I could

remember none of the devices which I had so often
admired—although it is possible that were I keeping a
calm mid-watch at sea, heaps of such stories would have
flocked unsummoned into my brain. So I did naught
save press instinctively forward—having little idea of the
direction I was pursuing, and indeed seeking only for the
open glades and avenues of the forest, through which I
could make the better speed. But hope began again
rapidly to leave me. The waves roar not after a scudding
bark, with more unceasing tumult, than there arose
behind me the clamour of my pursuers. I winded and
doubled—I ran north—then turned on my heel and
speeded in the opposite direction; but still, as a cock-
boat follows a ship to which she is made fast, through all
her tackings and veerings—so did my pursuers tread
steadily in my track. I began to grow desperate. Again,
I drew my knife from its sheath, and stopping, and leaning,
panting, against a great tree, I made up my mind to rest
there—recover what strength I could, and sell my life as
dearly as might be. At that moment, I heard a low
continuous sound—a deep hollow boom echoing faintly in
the wood. I listened intently, and then started up,
almost with the vigour with which I had began my flight.
I could not be deceived—what I heard was the roar of a
waterfall, and the sound in an instant brought, as it were,
a vision before my eyes. It was the vision of an old,
iron-clasped book, which we had at home at Kirkleslie.
Its cover was thick parchment, its leaves were brown with
age, and the letters were strange and quaint. This book
my father had prized next to the Bible, and those which
treated of holy things, and often was it in his hands, both
out at sea and by the cosy ingle-nook in the stormy winter
time. It was, indeed, an ancient chronicle of the ' Life
and Death of King Robert the Bruce,' and at the same
instant of time as I remembered it—one sentence in
particular loomed, as it were, before me, until I could
almost fancy I saw the very strange old letters quivering
in the sunshine. This was the sentence :—

" And now the Kynge being sore pressed by the Blood-houndis of ye iraytour Lorne, ye whyche had followed him even from ye up gettynge of ye sun, and beyinge come unto ane small rivere, did straighte enter therynne, and in such mannerre pursue his flyghte, so that ye libing waterres washynge clean alwaye ye scente of his footsteppes, the blood-houndis were ut faulte, and ye traytour Lorne was baffled for that tymme. Thus did ye Kynge escape ane great dangere."

'Fool as I was,' I exclaimed, 'not to have thought of the Bruce and Macdougall of Lorne before!' With new life and vigour, I pressed forward in the direction of the waterfall. The noise came every instant louder and louder upon my ear; and in a short space, I had burst my way down a steep bank, and to the edge of a deep pool, or cauldron, into which a large rivulet came thundering and foaming down, through a deep chasm in the rocks above. I had little time to admire the loveliness of the cataract; but rushing to the outlet of the pool, I saw that the stream went dancing down a pebbly bed, intersected here and there with low veins and ledges of rocks, like weirs, over which the bright water flashed and foamed right merrily. So, with a cry of joy, I bounded into the stream, and began rapidly to splash my way downwards, running with almost frantic haste, sometimes slipping and stumbling over the smooth slimy stones, sometimes floundering into a deepish pool, scaring the fish, which flew gleaming away, like wedges of burnished metal, to seek shelter under the ledges of rock, or amongst the twisted roots of trees upon the bank, among which the water frothed and gurgled.

'My great and fervent benison be upon water,' I cried to myself. 'It hath ever been my home, and now is it my refuge and my safety. Thanks, thanks, good secret-keeping stream! Amid the merry music of thy murmur, thou wilt never prate the whereabouts of the poor flying mariner. Rush speedily on with me, fair and living waters, sweeping my track fast downwards to the sea!'

With such-like rhapsodies, I relieved the fulness of my heart, as I followed the stream, splashing down in its

very centre. Sometimes when a small waterfall interrupted its course, I had to scramble ashore and make a
brief circuit, but I soon took to the water again. In
about ten minutes after I had first entered the river, the
bay of the bloodhound ceased to be heard ; but I distinguished the sound of a clearly-blown horn or trumpet,
and the report of one or two guns, as though one party
were making signals to another. Still I pressed on, but
more cautiously—watching the banks very narrowly, and
at the places where the stream flowed silently, pausing to
listen with all my ears. There was no alarm, and I
began to grow very confident, when all at once it
occurred to me, as I glanced at the point of the horizon
to which the sun was now hastening, that I must be
rapidly returning either to Carthagena, or to some point
very near it, upon the coast, where, undoubtedly, this
rivulet emptied itself into the sea. This consideration at
once arrested my footsteps ; and creeping among the
roots of a tree, beneath an overhanging bank, I began to
muse upon what was best to be done. I did not doubt
but that my pursuers had fairly lost my traces, and that
it would be a hard matter for them again to find the
scent. Indeed I considered that I might very safely
leave the water, and pursue my original westward route
amongst the woods ; but then I was unarmed, excepting
my knife, and without even the means of lighting a fire
how was I to live among the forests and the wildernesses
which stretched backward from the coast ? As I mused,
a thought struck me. When first captured by the
Spaniards, I had several double doubloons, and a few
pieces of eight about me. This money I had been
careful to preserve, and possessed it still, save one of the
doubloons, which I had given to my jailer, as he bade me
adieu. Why, then, thought I, should I not return to
Carthagena as soon as the night falls, and endeavour to
purchase fairly what I want ? I speak Spanish sufficiently
well. I am dressed like a Spanish sailor. Why should I
not, by a circuitous path, reach the seaward part of the
city, and making believe that I have landed from a vessel

the bay, purchase what arms and ammunition I require, not forgetting some food, and so leaving the town again in the darkness, pursue my way westward? The more I thought of this scheme, the more feasible did it appear. To be sure, there was a risk of being taken, and perhaps hung; but if I plunged unarmed into the woods, I had at least the certainty of dying a lingering death by starvation, or of being murdered by the savages. Therefore, without much ado, I decided upon braving the immediate danger, and purchasing what I wanted in the town, from which I had so recently fled. With this design, I began again to wade slowly down the river, thinking to myself that if any one noticed the wet state of my garments, I might easily account for it, by saying that I had but just now landed in a small boat through the surf. My progress was of course but slow; and several huts being built upon the banks of the stream, I was obliged now and then to leave the water and take circuits round about, keeping as much as possible in the shadow of the woods. I met, however, with no interruption; and so, in about the space of an hour and a half or thereby, I heard the sound of the surf. On gaining the coast I found it to consist of considerable sand-hills, with many small bays, and lines of breakers extending several cable-lengths from the shore. The weather being moderate, however, the surf was not violent. My first act was to creep to the top of one of the highest sand-hills, and look anxiously to seaward. There were the sails of one or two fishing-boats, and as many coasting craft of small burden in sight, but nothing like our schooner; so I descended and began to move to the eastward. Before I had taken many steps, however, I recollected that Carthagena was fortified at its seaward extremities, and I asked myself whether I could safely attempt to pass through the line of defences. The countersign I knew, but it might have been changed since my escape, or perhaps it only applied to the guard of the alcaide's house. While I was thus debating the matter with myself, I suddenly saw floating in the shallow water near the mouth of the small river a

s

small boat or canoe, bottom upward, and, running hastily towards her, found her to be no other than the negro fisherman's canoe, which we had upset the night of our unfortunate reconnoitring expedition. I straightway determined to turn this piece of luck to account, and, instead of proceeding by land, to paddle round and disembark in any quiet corner of the bay. On righting the canoe, I found she was but little damaged, and the paddles having been secured by pieces of spun yarn, as is usual in the boats of fishermen, were both ready for use. Therefore, without more ado, I got into the boat and pulled her off to sea. There were not less than three bars formed by the sea at the mouth of the stream, and the breakers burst white upon them all. However, by watching my time, and carefully attending to the run of the seas, I got over the inner two very easily. On the outward bank the surf broke heavier, and once or twice I expected to have had to swim for it. However, I had better luck, the canoe was very lively, and danced like a cork on the broken seas, so that at length I fairly made the smooth swell, with a boat, however, half full of water. After baling her out I began slowly to paddle eastward, the boat being impelled by the dying powers of the sea breeze, and presently, just as the sun was dipping, I opened the bay of Carthagena, and seeing an old slimy wooden jetty, only used apparently by a few fishermen, I made for it. Truly, says that brave man, (and also as brave a penman,) whom afterwards I well knew, William Dampier, 'Carthagena is a fair city open to the sea.' The level beams of the setting sun glowed upon the heaving water, and upon the great Spanish ships, lying like piled castles, with high forecastles and carved and galleried poops, slowly rocking to the solemn moving seas; and shorewards, upon the bright line of gaily-painted houses, with verandahs and balconies all fluttering with tinted draperies; and the pinnacles of churches and convents, from whence the evening bells came pealing out into the rich glowing air. One or two small fishing-craft were slowly making for the beach, and a canoe or two would now and then glide between the shipping and the shore ; but to my great comfort no one seemed to pay the slightest attention to my humble self. Therefore, I made fast the canoe to the jetty whereof I spoke, and which was all hung with nets put there to dry, and walked, the more boldly as it was now grey dusk, into the city, looking for some shop or store where I might be served with the articles which I needed. The traders and merchants were now beginning to close their warehouses, and so it behoved me quickly to find a suitable shop. The streets in which I wandered being very narrow and high, were all but dark ; lights gleamed out of the houses, shadowy figures moved upon balconies, and grave men with long cloaks stood by doorways, talking in their sonorous tongue, and smoking great pipes of tobacco. Still no one took notice of me, and I was the more assured, inasmuch as I saw around me many seamen dressed as I was myself, one or two of whom hailed me ' comrade,' and would have taken me to be treated at the Posada. I moved, however, with a quick stealthy step, keeping my eyes warily abroad, and at length, in a small street or lane, found a low-roofed shop, or rather stall, quite open to the thoroughfare, in which, in the middle of a collection of fire-arms, and steel weapons of many kinds, sat an old, hook-nosed, grey-headed man, with a very dirty face and great iron spectacles, drinking a bowl of savoury cocoa, and at the same time dictating to a little lad, dressed in a thread-bare fashion, some bills of charges which the boy was writing in a great greasy account-book, by the light of a single candle, which flared and flickered in the open shop. The old merchant I concluded to be a Jew, and judged that so long as I paid a good price for what I wanted, I would be asked no questions which it might be inconvenient to answer. I, therefore, entered the shop, and was about to speak, when the Jew, who had not perceived me, suddenly raised his voice, and, addressing some one whom I had not seen by reason of a pillar which supported the roof of the shop, said—

s 2

'Not a pistole—not a maravedi! Father of Abraham! I think it is a robber thou art. Here be your last bills of exchange, for which I advanced thee money, returned dishonoured by the goldsmith at Cadiz. Go thy ways—go thy ways ; thou shalt have no gold here!'

Upon this discouraging address, a man in military attire rose grumbling from a chest upon which he had been sitting, and at the same time making as though he would draw his weapon on the merchant. But the latter seemed little to heed this motion.

'Take thy lantern, Moses,' he said to the boy, 'and light out this honourable cavalier, who hath found at last that impertinent importunity doth not always unbutton a man's pouches.'

The lad stepped with his light towards the spot where I stood, and the would-be borrower following him, still muttering and threatening the Jew with all sorts of vengeance as an unbelieving hound, who would trample on the holy Cross—the latter cried out, 'Hold up thy lamp, Moses, and give the cavalier light enough to swear by.'

The boy waved his lantern with a grin, and the light flashing on the soldier, I recognised in an instant the flushed and gross features of the Captain Guzman, noways improved in expression by the little scene in which he had no doubt been an actor. The recognition was, unfortunately, mutual, for just as I recoiled back into the shadow so as to allow him to pass, he roared out—

'Holy mother! the English dog of a pirate, who escaped to-day, after half-throttling the alcaide's clerk !' And with these words, he pounced upon me; but I was prepared, and striking him a blow in the face, which, I hope, showed him every star in heaven, and a few additional ones besides, dancing before his eyes, I closed on him, and hurled him back into the shop, upsetting the Jew boy with a crash over a pile of casks and bales, and immediately extinguishing the light. Having paid this last attention to my friend, who was so sure that I would come to the gallows with all speed, I took to my heels incontinently, running at random. But Guzman, although overthrown, was not stunned, and continued to bawl out clamorously, to catch, or shoot, or stab the English pirate. The alarm was very quickly taken up, and the whole street was in a commotion. However, as every one was running about in the dusk, which already approached to darkness, as well as myself, and as I shouted to secure the English cutthroat as lustily as ever a Spaniard of them all, I was more inclined to laugh than to be much alarmed at my mischance, when a pestilent fellow, who had run out of a house in his shirt-sleeves, grasped me by the arm, and earnestly besought me to tell him where the heretic was. I replied that I had seen the rascal running down a certain lane, to which I pointed, when the man, turning short round upon me, and having most likely a good ear for his own language, asked me, very abruptly, from what part of Spain I came. For all reply, I made an effort, shook him clean off, and darted away. But the fellow was as nimble as I was; he was at my heels in a trice, shouting at the same time at the top of his voice, and pointing me out to others as we ran. We had a hard race of it. Half-a-dozen times I was grappled by willing hands, but my impetus in running enabled me again and again to burst away, while, to distract attention, I shouted and pointed ahead just as did my pursuers. All this, the reader must conceive, passed with breathless rapidity. It was a confused scene—narrow, gloomy streets, all sparkling with lights as people rushed to doors and balconies, and echoing to the clamour of voices and the tramp of footsteps, as the shouting crowd ran wildly, jostling and tripping each other, and many of them swearing that the English pirates had returned to the attack, and that there was nothing but pillage and murder for Carthagena. Howbeit, in the midst of all this confusion, I could not but be sensible that the man in the shirt-sleeves and his original comrades had not lost sight of me for an instant. Therefore I put forth my utmost speed; plunged from street to street and lane to

lane, fearing every moment that I would run into what
the French call a *cul-de-sac*; and, indeed, at length, as I
emerged from a confused cluster of narrow, winding
streets into a more open way lined with high walls, along
which I ran, almost spent with toil, and panting for
breath, I heard a great shout of triumph behind me, as
though I was at length trapped, and looking narrowly
ahead, I saw a high wall with iron trell's-work at the
top, and over which ran the branches of trees, barring all
passage. I was close to the obstacle before I saw it in
the dusk, and at the same instant I became sensible of a
small wicket-door, which, before I had time to think,
opened, and the forms of two ladies, dressed in black,
veiled and hooded, with lace and silk capes, stood
before me.

Hardly knowing what I did, I flung myself on my
knees upon the ground. They started back, and the
younger, as I judged, uttered a slight scream.

'Ladies,' I gasped out, 'I am an unfortunate Scots
sailor; your countrymen pursue me to kill me. Gentle
ladies, save my life!'

Just as I said this the footsteps of the Spaniards echoed
between the high walls.

'Where is the English rascal?' they cried; 'he shall
die the death!'

After a single whispered word, hastily passed between
them, one of the ladies bent towards me, started back,
came forwards again, and said in my ear, in a timid, fluttering voice:

'Rise, young man; and pass in.'

I sprang up and rushed through the wicket, which
the ladies closed again from the outside; then, couching
breathlessly by the door, I listened. In a moment I heard
the gruff voices of my pursuers, evidently asking the
ladies whether they had seen me. What answer was returned I could only guess at, from hearing the disappointed exclamations and the retiring footsteps of the
Spaniards. Then I fell upon my knees, and called God
to bless the kind hearts which had saved a flying man

from his deadly foes. I was in a garden. The high wall seemed to shut out the clamour of my pursuers, which had, however, doubtless, died away, as the search seemed to be unsuccessful. Around me were rich trees and shrubs, and gaudy flowers. Fresh from the tumult of a street scuffle, how peaceful a spot it seemed! The fire-flies shot amid the bushes like sparks from anvils. The hum of the wings of night insects sounded like the low breathing of Nature sleeping. The cooling dews fell balm-like upon my hot, wet forehead. I sank back, leaning against the wall, exhausted and utterly worn by the excitement, the pain, and the great fatigue of the day. I felt, even before I had been ten minutes couched amid the sweet smelling and clustering shrubs, a sweet lethargy come over me, and stretching my overwrought limbs among the herbage, I fairly fell into a deep, calm sleep.

## CHAPTER XXII.

I WAS wakened by some one flashing a lantern in my face, and hastily starting to my feet, for I feared that I might have been discovered, I found myself standing beside a personage well-stricken in years, of grave but pleasant aspect, and soberly clad, as one of those old decent serving men, who become, as it were, members of the family on whom they attend.

'Fear for nothing, young man,' said the servitor, seeing, I suppose, the momentary flurry and tremor in which I was; 'you are in a very secure asylum. My good mistress, whom heaven preserve! is known for her charity, and the Virgin directed the steps which led you here to-night.'

This discourse, you may be sure, was very pleasant to me; and while I was blessing my stars for my good luck, the old man, who was sufficiently garrulous, went on praising his mistress and the Virgin alternately, so that it became difficult to determine which he held in the greatest respect.

'Not a lady is there, either in Old Spain or in New—the saints be blessed for it! who hath even a tithe of my mistress's virtues. So was it indeed with her father before her, and so will it be with her daughter after her; for I have well-known all three—albeit my young mistress is not yet turned of seventeen. Notwithstanding, however, she is already a most dainty and brave lady ; her equal not being to be found in any city or colony in the Main, for which I bless the saints, and particularly Saint Gieronimo, who is indeed my mistress's patron saint, and would be mine also, were it not that I would not venture to intrude upon his holy notice my poor concerns, his attention being no doubt, fully taken up with those of my betters.'

Running on in this random way, the old man led me, while he talked, through the garden towards the house. It was his lady's pleasure, he said, that I should eat a good supper, repose me in a good bed, and that I should to-morrow be introduced to herself and her daughter, they having, however, as I learned much to my surprise, already been made acquainted with some portions of my story, and longing to know the rest. As we spoke thus, we entered a wing of a handsome mansion, pillared and porticoed all round, and having a flat roof, whereon were set pots and tubs containing delicate flowering shrubs. We traversed divers passages, through which the fresh night air freely penetrated, and I could not but admire the delicate carving of the polished wood which formed the wainscoting of the walls. At length we entered a pleasant chamber, where was a bed, and a table well laid out for supper. You may imagine that I played a very good knife and fork, and the old steward or intendant, or whatever he was, bore me company with rare good will. After supper, we drank some of the most delicious wine to which I ever put my lips ; and then, in answer to my earnest entreaties, my companion informed me of the name and quality of my preservers and hosts.

'You are not to suppose, Master Mariner,' quoth he, ' that you are in the mansion of a grandee of Spain. Because, for many generations, the family of the late Bartholomew Moranté were merchants, having great possessions both in Old and New Spain, at Alicant, upon the Mediterranean Sea, and on this side the ocean, at Havanna in Cuba, and here at Carthagena. Now, the wealth of Señor Bartholomew, my late master, who is with the saints, was so exceeding, that the king would have made him a noble, but to this dignity Señor Bartholomew did not in any way aspire. The first part of his life was very fortunate; not a galley, not a caravel sent he out, but it returned to him with the venture increased manyfold. But as he waxed old, the saints, doubtless having a mind to try his faith, it was so ordered that he experienced many crosses and losses, in such wise indeed that he left Alicant, not having any longer the means to keep up the brave state he had formerly supported, and came hither, and settled in this house at Carthagena. But his ill-fortune—praise to the saints, who, doubtless, took great interest in my late master, seeing that they were pleased thus to afflict him!—his ill-fortune, I say, following him, he was obliged to send away his agents at the Havanna, and at length, his greatest bark, richly freighted, being taken at sea, and all on board of her killed or sold into slavery, by a French devil incarnate, whom they call Mountbars, and whom may heaven, in its mercy, cause to be eternally tormented—my good master took to his bed, and we weeping all around him, and blessing the saints, who, without doubt, had thus broken his heart, in order that they might take him to themselves, the worthy Bartholomew Moranté departed this life to enter into a better world where are neither spoilers nor stealers, nor doth there happen any manner of trouble or cross. His widow, whom still I serve, dwells here in this house, and places great confidence in me, looking up, although I say it, to my advice and counsels; for I am old in the world, and have seen much appertaining to domestic service, and am also much enlightened in visions by the holy saints, who are pleased to make my hours of sleep as profitable to my good patroness as my times of waking.'

From this rambling discourse of the old gentleman, I
saw plainly of what kidney he was—to wit, a very honest-
hearted simpleton, who loved his mistress dearly, while
she, if her steward spoke sooth, was probably as simple-
minded as himself.    But, desiring to know somewhat of
the young lady, the serving-man broke out into raptures
concerning her innocence and her beauty.

'Her name,' quoth he, 'thanks to the saints! is Joseffa
—Joseffa Moranté—a rare brave name for a rare brave
damsel.    But she will change it sometime, mayhap.
Nay, very soon—if all go right, and the saints will it.'

So saying, the old fellow began to smirk and nod, and
look as wise and as sly as he could, and then fell to chuckling to himself.

'The rarest match,' he presently commenced again.
'Her mother, having as I said great confidence in me,
consulted with me on the matter.    "Martin y Vesdras,"
says she to me, "Joseffa is marriageable; and here hath
come a suitor well-favoured and marvellously well-recom-
mended, and a nobleman to boot.    Thou wilt do well,
Martin, to see him; nay, hold converse with him, and
report to me your opinion."

'But I, having no opinions save what the saints send
me, went straight to bed and dreamed upon the matter.
Never had I a more encouraging vision.    Good Master
Mariner, as I am a true man, St. Gieronimo himself appeared at the foot of the bed, holding a wedding ring,
which he seemed to throw towards me with a very
pleasant smile, and so when I woke I actually found the
symbol upon the coverlid.'

'Truly,' says I, 'Martin, this was but little short of a
miracle.'

'Master Mariner,' quoth the simpleton, 'I rejoice to
hear you say so.    So indeed think I, and so thinks my
mistress, only——'

'What,' cries I, 'does any one refuse to believe the
token?'

'Ay, verily,' answered the old steward, 'even Mistress
Joseffa herself, who is in noways inclined, at the present

time at least, to this wedding, and so she contends, half
in mirth half in pretty pettishness—the saints guard her!
—that the ring is not a marriage ring, but truly only one
of the brass curtain rings which she sayeth dropped upon
my nose in the night, and gave me my dream. "Look
you, Martin," says she, "the ring is plain, just like the
other curtain rings."

' "But look you again, Mistress Joseffa," says I. " all
wedding rings are plain, just like this ring."

' But she, sir, in noways put down by my argument,
answers, "Truly, but wedding rings are also gold, and
this is brass, Master Martin." '

' Well,' says I, ' how did you answer that consideration? Methought, it pushed you home.'

' Answer it,' cried he, ' I hope I know better than to
dispute obstinately with the daughter of my good mistress. No, Master Mariner, I held my peace, as became
me, being but a servant; yet I do, nevertheless, steadfastly believe the vision, and I hope that the saints will
inspire the sweet Joseffa with kinder thoughts to her
suitor, who is truly a goodly man and an honest, and
what is better than both, favoured of St. Gieronimo.'

Then I, making inquiries of the steward as to the
young lady's features and carriage, he answered that to-
morrow my own eyes would inform me better than his
tongue, which could in no way do justice to such a theme
as the great virtues and loveliness of his charming young
mistress, whose single fault was that she laughed at the
wedding ring of St. Gieronimo. Soon after this, our conversation broke off, the steward telling me he would be
with me betimes in the morning. I lay long awake that
night, conjuring up visions of Joseffa; at length, as sleep
was coming over me, I heard, or dreamed I heard, the
low tinkle of a guitar, and a manly voice, as of a sere-
nader, singing to it beneath an outside balcony.

' The favoured suitor,' I murmured, half asleep; and
forthwith began to dream that I was his rival, and that
Saint Gieronimo appeared again to explain that he meant
the wedding ring with a view to my coming, and that

Martin's interpretation of the vision was quite erroneous.

The morning came, and I was ushered into the presence of my most kind benefactors. They sat—the elder lady on a couch, the younger on a footstool at her feet —in a great lofty withdrawing-chamber, the walls and ceiling rarely carved, the floor of sweet-smelling wood, highly polished, and almost as slippery as ice, and the whole apartment darkened by blinds of a peculiar construction, which excluded the heat, but allowed the fresh breeze to pass in freely. As I advanced, the Señora Moranté held out her jewelled hand, which I kissed very respectfully. She was a tall, stately-looking dame, dressed in morning-robes, and her hair, which was beginning to turn grey, covered with festoons of black lace, gracefully arranged, and falling down upon her shoulders. But my eyes were, as the reader may guess, fixed with a far more delighted gaze upon Joseffa. She was, indeed, a beauty of the true Spanish mould. Her form vibrated, as it were, with a graceful suppleness which made her every movement a charm to see. Her oval face—lighted by eyes which alternately flashed and melted—was beaming, sometimes with the joyous rapture of gaily flushing spirits, sometimes, as it were, shaded by a grave expression of pretty coquettish modesty and bashfulness. Her lips were full and pouting, and every moment there came a merry smile upon them, with a sudden arching of her dark eye-brows, which quite enabled me to understand the sportive nature which laughed at poor Martin, with his ring of St. Gieronimo. She bowed slightly as I advanced, and then, flirting and twirling and shaking a fan made of gaily-coloured feathers before her face, stole rapid glances at me; all the while pouting her lips, and sometimes looking down to the ground, and then starting up, and whispering and laughing softly in her mother's ear, or unto herself, playing all the while with one hand among her long black hair—her white fingers glancing nimbly amid the glossy clustering locks.

The señora received me with a sort of goodnatured

dignity, and bade me sit on a low seat hard by. She then began to inspect me, as I thought, as curiously as though I had been some sort of strange animal, muttering to herself, and sometimes whispering her daughter; to my no small embarrassment; all at once, she said—

'Young man, I fear me you are a heretic?'

I replied softly that I was of the religion of my fathers.

'But you are a pirate,' she commenced again; 'and you put our people to death very cruelly, and you pillage our ships. See, what being a heretic leads you to. Perhaps it was very weak in me t⟩ save you, and I know not what father Anselmo will say when next I go to confession.'

I answered that, far away in Scotland I had a mother, who I was sure would do for any poor hunted Spaniard what she had done for me, and that, though we did not worship in the same fashion, yet that never would my mother forget in her prayers the kind heart that had saved her son.'

I spoke this very earnestly, for I felt what I said deeply, and kneeling down, I took the señora's hand again, and kissed it. She paused a little time, and then asked, what made my countrymen and the French so vengeful against the Spaniards. Now, this was an argument which I had no will to enter into—seeing that such a debate could but breed angry feelings on both sides; and so I endeavoured to turn the matter off by saying, that it was the two nations, and not individuals, who made war—on account of the heritage of the new world.

'But, señor, said Joseffa, and all my nerves tingled as I heard her voice, 'you are of a very cruel and vindictive nation; for when my poor father's great bark, the Trinidada, was taken, all the sailors were struck down and murdered upon the deck.'

To this I answered, that I understood that the Trinidada had been captured by Louis Montbars, a Frenchman; that I had myself been prisoner in the hands of that captain; and that it was only by a dangerous flight that I escaped being sold into slavery by him in the isle of Tortugas.

This revelation all at once seemed to alter the position in which I stood in the favour of the ladies, who, up to that time, although they had, as I understood, received a good report—but from whence I could not guess—of my conduct before the alcaide—were yet partly prepossessed against me, as a heretic and a pirate of that class which had brought so much desolation on their house. So, presently, they desired to hear somewhat of my adventures, which I told them very faithfully—the narration occupying the greatest portion of the day. While I sat speaking, my eyes often encountered the dark orbs of Joseffa fixed on mine. Then would we both drop our glances to the ground, and my voice, despite myself, would falter, and a red blush would spring over the bright olive cheeks of the young Spanish lady, and her feather-fan would flutter more violently than before.

That day I dined with my hosts. In the cool of the evening I walked with them in the garden; but at the board, and beneath the orange-trees, I saw but one face and one form. In my sleep the star-like eyes of Joseffa haunted me; her voice rang unceasingly in my brain. When I ventured to take her hand, mine trembled as though I were a palsied old man—when she left me, the salt of existence seemed to have lost its savour. I went and came musing. I took no pleasure in aught save what related to her. In short, I had fallen certain fathoms deep in love.

And, verily, it was not wonderful. I lived in a state of existence so new, that it seemed to me, then, and seems to me still, a Dreamland—a long, sweet unreal vision. Consider what I was—a rude mariner, ever brought up in the coarse company of rough and unpolished men, with hands fit to swing a lead-line, or tie a reef-point; with a voice good for hailing the fore-top in a gale of wind; but with neither hands nor voice trained for the soft requirements of a lady's bower.

I laugh, with a melancholy mirth, now, when I think of what my uncouthness must have been. Here was I a rough and round sailor—a fellow who had been kicked about in Scotch brigs, and buccaneering small craft all my days—to whose tongue the lingo of the forecastle came as my mother-speech ; who had hardly slept but in a swinging hammock—ate but of lobscouse and sea-pie— sang but roaring sea-ballads, or thought but of storms and calms, and ships and rigs, with now and then a waking dream of old boyish days, of the Royal Thistle and the Balwearic Burn, or mayhap the memory of an ancient Scots legend, or a warm gush of feeling when I pondered on my old mother, by the ingle-nook in the fisher's cottage, near Kirkleslie Pier. Such was I then, such my very nature, body and soul, and yet now did I find myself the lover of a gentle Spanish lady, walking with her through garden bowers, communing with her under shady verandahs, talking of things I hardly dreamt of even as lurking in the bottom of my soul. And she neither jeered at my port, nor flouted my rough speech. She loved to hear of my country, and when I told her our gallant tales of the Bruce, of how he was crowned King of Scotland, crowned not in an abbey, by no holy hand of priest, and without the ancient symbol of the sovereignty of the realm, but in a wilderness, with a circlet of gold hastily wrought out, and by the hands of a famous heroine, dear to the heart and memory of a Scot, for ever—the Countess of Marr—when, I say, I told such tales, Josefa would hang, as it were, upon my lips, and then saying that Spain also had its great heroes and mighty men of old, would draw her fingers strongly across the thrilling strings of her guitar, and with flash- ing eye and widened nostril, sing the glorious ballads of her nation, of the battles between the Spanish chivalry and the Paynim Moors, of the conquest of Alhama, and the life and death of Diaz de Bivar, the peerless Cid.

And so flew weeks away. I know not to this day how the Señora Morante observed not what was passing in our minds. She had taken me into great favour, and consulted me much upon family matters, and upon her design to cross the ocean and return to Alicant; and often she hinted mysteriously at the noble husband her

daughter would espouse after her return to Spain. This
suitor I knew to be in Carthagena, I knew he ofttimes
visited the house. Yet, upon these occasions, the mother
managed somehow adroitly to receive him when I was not
by. From Josefia I could learn but this, that the gallant
favoured by her mother was not loved by her ; that she
received him but to humour the fancies of her parent,
who was but a weak, though good kind of woman ; and
finally, she said to me, in low tones, for her eyes were
looking closely into mine, and her breath was warm upon
my cheek,

' Do not regard him—Leonard, my own sailor, I will
marry only you."

But a week before these sweet words were spoken, we
had (the custom is of Scotland) broken together a crooked
coin. Joseffa wore one half of it attached by a braid
round her neck and next to her heart, and I wore the
other.

So, as I have said, weeks flew by ; sometimes I thought
sadly of my comrades, and wondered upon what seas the
gallant Will-o'-the-Wisp was sailing ; but these were
only passing moments. My life was a long sweet dream,
checkered only by such considerations as I have mentioned, and by doubtings and misgivings touching the
strange suitor who persecuted Joseffa with his importu-
nities.

' Tell me but his name,' I would say ; ' bring me but
face to face with him ; I ask no more.'

But she would reply, ' Be tranquil, Leonard ! You
have my heart. My mother loves me well, and it pleases
her to nurse herself in fancies which can never turn
to reality. Before you arrived here, a ship sailed hence to
Spain ; she must be now upon the ocean again, with her
bows hitherward. When that ship sails a second time, I
trust well that my mother's eyes will be opened, and that
what is now passing will be remembered but as an idle
cloud, which hath come and gone.'

But I was not satisfied. And so I applied very earnestly to Martin, professing to consult him as to a vision

with which the saints had blessed me, touching the wedding favoured of St. Gieronimo. All I could obtain from the old man was, that the cavalier, for certain private reasons, wished that his visits should be kept secret until the nuptials had actually been arranged.

Now, all this appeared to me a most strange and needless complication of a simple matter, and, calling to mind certain words of Josefia, I could not help wondering whether the cavalier held the same language to the mother as to the daughter. The allusions to the persecution which Josefia was undoubtedly undergoing, out of deference to her mother's foibles and prejudices, coming probably to an end when a certain vessel sailed for Spain, would seem to imply that in that vessel would also sail her tormentor; and, pondering upon this circumstance, a thought suddenly flashed upon me, which made me certain I had caught a clue to the mystery. As all this came up into my mind, my brow flushed and my blood boiled.

' Come what may of it,' I swore, ' the next time that this man crosses the threshold, 'tis I who will receive him.' I bided my time warily and well. I watched; I lay in wait; not a motion of the old steward or of the señora but I followed; and the next day I had my will. I knew the mysterious suitor was in the house. I knew that the señora had gone to summon her daughter, who, I also knew, would be long of coming. Therefore, gathering up body and soul for the interview, as I had done once before for the torture, I burst hurriedly into the withdrawing room, and saw there, dangling his bonnet and playing with his sword-knot, the man I had expected to see—Don José!

Making a great effort, I composed myself, and stood firm, looking at him, but not daring to allow my tongue to utter a sound. On his side, Don José showed not the slightest emotion, only a dark shadow seemed for a moment to pass over his face, but it went almost as soon as it had come; and then, stepping up to me, he said, in such a frank, open fashion, that I could hardly believe my ears:

T

'Hey, my old friend, the Scots Mariner! I am heartily glad to see thee again. I knew that thou hadst found refuge in this very hospitable mansion. And so, friend, thou hast doubled both upon blood-hound and alcaide. It was very well done, man. I gave thee a good character to the Señora Moranté, and I hope it hath availed thee. But indeed the ladies lately told me, that thou wert still here, behaving thyself most reasonably, for a pirate and a heretic—nay, that, in sooth, thou wert getting to be quite a favourite. A rare time for thee, Friend Buccaneer. How wilt thou like sea-fare and sea-company, after such an interlude?'

'Don José,' said I, speaking in a low and tremulous voice, for very passion; ' it were best that you leave this house.'

'Truly, friend,' replied the cavalier—' you are the least hospitable person within it. What may be the meaning, I pray, of a recommendation, which, in thy mouth, I find somewhat singular?'

'Don José,' I replied, ' you have saved my life. It is now in your hands again. I am a rough, untutored mariner, not skilled in your courtly ironical phrase,—I say again, you must leave this house, or I will drive you from it—you may return with officers and alguazils, but at any rate, you will not return in the character which now you falsely pretend to.'

'My good man,' said Don José, still playing with his sword-knot, and, as he spoke, flinging himself on a sofa, and dangling his legs gracefully—' My good man, have you ever, in the course of your buccaneering, come across a cut on the forehead from a well wielded piece of steel? Because if so, at certain seasons, the brain may still feel the smart. You ought to purge and bleed—my good pirate,—purge and bleed.'

I was likely to lose my senses in reality at this cool effrontery, and so, going up close to the Spanish nobleman, I said—

'Remember, Don Ottavio y St. Jago, who is known to every duenna at the Court of Madrid—remember, your mutual bargain, and the message which you sent your friend by the mouth of Señor Davosa, a merchant, who has doubtless by this time sailed for Old Spain, on board of the galleon.'

Don José started to his feet, as though a cannon-shot had been fired close to his ear. His tawny features were flushed with a sudden redness, and as he jumped up erect upon the floor, he drew his rapier, as though an armed enemy had leaped suddenly upon him. As for me, I thought it just as well to be run through where I stood, as to be dragged again to prison—again tortured and finally hanged. So I remained motionless, gazing upon him. He paused for a moment, with his arm upraised, as though to strike, and then suddenly lowering his weapon, he said—' Have you nought wherewith to defend yourself?' I replied, that I was unarmed, as he saw, but that I was not afraid of dying, that he had already given me life, and that now he might himself revoke his gift. He seemed to pause again, to take inward counsel. His face, from being flushed, grew suddenly pale, and his features worked, and his lips quivered. At last he spoke—

"Eavesdropper!' he cried, ' you were lurking in your boat, beneath the cabin galleries of the galleon.'

I answered, composedly, that I was no eavesdropper, but an adventurer who sought, as is common in war-time, to obtain information as to the designs of his enemy. He laughed scornfully, and then turning on his heel, sheathed his rapier with a clash. In an instant, however, he swung round again, with his fierce eyes all aflame.

' Ha!' he exclaimed, ' I see it—a rival. By all the gods, a rival! A successful rival! Good!—a jest worth telling. The blood of Old Castile against a tar barrel—and the tar the favoured fluid of the twain.'

As he spoke thus—his hand again clutched the hilt of his rapier, but he withdrew it, with a loud angry ' Pshaw!'—and strode, fuming, up and down the room. Then he paused, came close to me, and said—

' Most grateful mariner—most worthy pirate—a goodly

return have you made to the man who gave you liberty
and life. Why! thou heartless knave! were it not for
me, you would long ago have swung a hundred-weight of
carrion from a gallows, and now this—this is the gratitude thou showest.'

'Yes, Don José,' I said, vehemently, 'it is. To
save a gentleman from committing a base action, is to
make the worthiest recompence for a favour he has con-
ferred.'

The Spaniard looked at me from head to foot, raised his
eyebrows, and gave a slight whistle.

'Truly, a pirate of a most moral breed—he reproves
incontinence, he rebukes sin. Most righteous of Buccaneers, thou hast mistaken thy trade. Turn priest, man.
Ha! I daresay you heard me tell the story of the diamond and pearls on the Virgin's petticoat? Behold a
career for thee. Get thee to the Cathedral on the Hill.
To rob gaping Spaniards in a church is more profitable
and more safe than to plunder fighting Spaniards on the
sea. Turn priest, man. I warrant thee the rarest hand
at the confessional.'

'Don José,' I answered, 'promise me, on your honour,
to give up the wicked purpose with which you visit this
house. You may then betray me to my enemies, and I
swear to you, that not a word of what accidentally I overheard shall pass my lips.'

He turned impetuously to me. 'You know me not,
mariner,' he cried, vehemently. 'Your life is safe for me.
We Spaniards are not all of us alguazils!—human bloodhounds! Go! You have crossed my path, and chance
has given you the advantage. But you have spoken well
and acted well. I do not blame you—I think well of
you. Once I would myself have done what you have
done; nay, perhaps so would I still. But, caramba!
Why put myself in a heat about such a trifle. Win her
and wear her, man! The stakes are yours.'

Don José took two or three turns from one end of the
apartment to the other, I still remaining motionless where
I had first addressed him; then suddenly stopping, he

said, 'If ever in future years you visit Madrid, seek me out, and I will be your friend.'

. Just then, the Señora Morantè entered. 'Don José,' she said, 'I have looked everywhere for Joseffa, but——

Here she observed me, and suddenly became silent. Don José went up to her, and took her hand.

'Señora,' he said, 'you will think me fickle, but I have become convinced, that in Josefa's hand, should I be fortunate enough to secure it, I should find no heart. The saints would prosper no such union, señora. What I say I have full warrant for believing. Señora, adieu! Here is your persecuted Scotch mariner. Make much of him—he is a leal man and true. I told you that I thought so, now I know it. Adieu, señora. Adieu, my flower of pirates. May Heaven prosper thee! Be moral —and a Buccaneer!'

And so saying, with a reverence the most graceful and profound, Don José stepped gaily from the room. Oh, heart of man, what strange wild tunes thou playest— what discords mingling with and marring thy harmonies —what harmonies mingling with and attuning thy discords! Courteous and rude, paltry and noble, magnanimous and base. A man can be all these in an hour, in a breath, the grandest and the foulest thing in nature!

Now, that I have told at length the strange chances which brought Don José and I face to face so often, and in such curious relations to each other at Carthagena, I would fain pass quickly over the story of my after stay in that city. The history leads to but a sad ending. Often and often, since I left the Spanish main, in rough dark middle watches, as well as in soft and balmy nights, when my ship stole through a waveless and shining sea, have I flown in fancy back to those bright days of hope and love—often have I meditated and pondered, until the very image of Josefa has seemed to waver in the air and smile upon me, until the well-remembered tones of her voice have sounded audibly in mine ear amid the dash of waves, or the rustle of the swelling canvas. Sometimes crouching alone in the rocking top, with straining ropes

and surging sails around me, I have peopled that airy
platform with the household of the old merchant's
dwelling at Carthagena.  The señora Moranté has pleaded
with me, urging me that I should abandon my heresies
and become a true son of the ancient church—the prating
Martin has told his visions of angels and of saints, and
Joseffa—Joseffa, who wore the token of our love upon
her heaving heart, has looked up with her dark eyes and
her smiling lips into my face.

Vain phantoms all ! the stately señora, the garrulous
old steward, Joseffa herself—the sea entombs them all !
The crooked coin I gave my love lies deep with her in
caves which no line hath ever plumbed.  The ocean is the
most inscrutable of sepulchres.  I know not, and no man
knows, the place of their resting.  The breeze was fair,
and the sea smooth, which bore from Carthagena the ship
in which they embarked to return to Spain.  She was
a stately merchantman, and as she left the port cannon
thundered and church bells clashed from echoing steeples.
Then spreading her fair white wings to the wind, and
towering in her pride over the fleet of small craft which
joyously, with shout and blessing, convoyed her out to
sea—the good ship disappeared, holding her steady course
for home.  Since that day, no man has seen her or aught
of her.  No token of the ill-starred craft has been driven
on any coast, or picked up on any sea ; no bottle or flask,
carrying a despairing message from dying to living men,
has floated to any human hand.  The fierce fire may have
seized on her—the starting of a plank may have brought
on the fatal leak.  A sudden tornado may have crushed
her under the howling waters.  Beaten and belaboured
by a long-blowing gale, she may at length have succumbed
to the force of roaring winds and seas.  God only knows
her fate.  She never came to land.  She joined that
mighty navy which rests, manned by bleaching bones, far
down beneath those good keepers of secrets—the waves
and swells of the ocean ; those waves on which gallant
fleets and living men ride buoyantly, joyously, all unwitting and unthinking that, mayhap, a mile below the

keel, rise the topmasts of what was once a merrily bounding ship, now peeping forth amid the green branches and slowly waving boughs of those great forests which learned men say grow at the bottom of the sea.

Sleep well, Joseffa, in your mystic entombment! It was a long tryste which we gave each other. When we parted we agreed to meet again in Spain, and there, being married, you would have sailed with me to see that Scotland of which we so often spoke. Man proposes—God disposes. It was not to be so. Although years had gone by, and I knew well that the ship which bore you had perished, still I kept the tryste at Alicant. I stood upon the sea-stretching quay upon the day and the hour we had covenanted. I kept the tryste as though it were a duty of my faith; it was soothing to my spirit to do so: but not even a shadowy phantom of my beloved flitted to my side. There were loud voices and busy throngs around. It is in the silence and the dusk of evening and of dawn that best we seem to see each other. And even these moments, what are they?—Times of musing, idle phantasy. People laugh at them and at me, and, perhaps, with reason. Who, indeed, would believe, seeing the grizzled locks and weather-beaten visage and horny hands of the man who is now captain of the Scotch brig 'Royal Thistle,' why so called we know well—that he, that jolly yarn-telling mariner—that tough old tangled lump of sea-weed—can yet remember the day when the flush of loving blood was hot within him? Who will credit that that pair of oozy, blinking eyes can yet see, as it were, looking into them bright and loving human orbs, long ago turned into pearls beneath the deep waters; and, finally, who will conceive that that square-built, stout-paunched veteran of the ocean was once a slim youth, with flowing love-locks, whom the voice of beauty thrilled, whose tears, the well-remembered tones of that voice will still provoke to flow?

I have here shot a-head in my story, and anticipated other things. Were I, however, to have persevered in narrating, point by point, the adventures of my Buccaneer

life, I should, perhaps, have left the tale of my early love
but half told. I have, therefore, thought it better at
once to make an end with that sad history. In a few
words—Joseffa and I were betrothed, and her mother
blessed us. Marriage then was impossible, for further
claims against the father were every day arising, and
when all were finally adjusted, the mother and daughter
would be nearly as poor as myself. At length, all such
matters being settled, they sailed for Spain, as I have
narrated. Long before that time, however, I had quitted
Carthagena, after solemnly engaging to meet my betrothed in three years at the city of her family, at Alicant.

During that time I trusted well to amass treasures.
The days whereof I write were those in which a single
lucky capture made a fortune—in which one daring
assault upon a Spanish battery might send the conqueror
rolling home upon ingots of Indian gold. God forgive
us if we were thieves and robbers of the sea ; such we did
not account ourselves. The Spaniards loudly swore that
no European banner but their own should stream upon
the trade-winds of the tropic—that no Europeans but
themselves should traffic with those golden regions of the
west. Upon this quarrel we fought, and—to the death.
I never drew trigger upon a Spanish ship, that I did not
deem myself as helping to unshackle the fettered enterprise of Protestant Europe. Why should we not, as well
as its first discoverers, share in the spoils of the new
world ? The Spaniards held but inconsiderable portions
of the soil—islands lay desert, great stretches of continent were tenanted only by handfuls of savages ; but the
Spaniard would keep all to himself. We did not admit
the claim, and hence arose the Buccaneers. I said, that
these adventurers oft-times made a great fortune in a day.
In many cases, these masses of wealth were no sooner
won than they were lost. A week in Jamaica was quite
sufficient to dissipate the spoils of the luckiest cruize.
What brave sabres won, cogged dice lost ; what gallant
but foolish men amassed, at peril of their lives, infamous

women squandered on brazen orgies. Little indeed of the wealth wrested by Englishmen from the Spaniards turned to happiness and content in the captor's grasp. Well was it said, by an ancient Buccaneer, that gold ill-won by Spaniards, and ill-spent by Englishmen, enriched the latter no more than the former; that in the end the spoil slipped from the hands which grasped, as well as from those which held it; and that after all the fighting —all the suffering of these long wars—the yellow metal, for as much as it benefited either party, might well have been left in the mines by the Spaniards, or flung into the sea by the English.

Still, as I have said, there were great exceptions to the general rule, and of these I trusted to prove one. There fore, when last we saw each other—when last I felt Joseffa's form clasped to mine, I whispered in her ear, that I well trusted in three years at Alicant, to come to her, not a poor-hearted fugitive, but a well-endowed lover. And thus we parted. When I write these latter words I doubt not but that I have penned all necessary to be said, to picture the scene by those who take interest in such passages. We parted, and we never met again!

Interest had been made with the captain of a small coasting craft, a good fellow, and a friend of Martin's, bound eastward to the Pearl Fishery, to take me along with him. Once at sea again, I trusted speedily to find means to transfer me to a deck above which floated the battle-banner of England. The Pearl fisherman sailed to join the fleet by night. Nearly four months had by that time elapsed, since I was captured in Carthagena harbour. Don José had obtained a reversal of his sentence of banishment, and had sailed for Spain. Concerning the alcaide and his clerk, I heard nothing; but Captain Guzman I saw as, in the gathering darkness of the evening, I hurried to the beach—lurking, like a troubled spirit, round the shop of the Jew money-lender.

Joseffa had wept upon my neck—her mother had blessed me—Martin had told me of a special vision, in which St. Gieronimo had appeared and promised to watch over me!

'God bless them all!' I had not thought shame to weep in saying it.

Another half-hour and the ocean was again beneath my feet.

'Hurrah, for a new cruize! Hurrah, for new shipmates! Hurrah, for the riches of the ocean! Hurrah, for the pearl banks of the Rio de la Hacha!'

## CHAPTER XXIII.

### HOW WE SAIL TO JOIN THE PEARL FLEET, AND THE NEGRO DIVER'S STORY.

THE night I sailed from Carthagena was as starry and still as that in which I entered the bay. Negro fishermen, in canoes, again sung rude ditties as they shot their lines for pisareros—the rigging of stately merchantmen again cut with many dark and interlaced lines the sparkling sky—and again, and for the last time, I heard the bells of the rich Monastery of the Hill come pealing over the music of the surf.

The night-breeze was very faint and feeble, so 'Out sweeps' was the word; and presently all the crew, myself among the rest, were tugging at our great heavy oars, and slowly urging the small bark out to sea. We were not alone upon the water—close to us, another vessel of our own rig and size, and bound upon the same voyage, was making head in the same way—the blades of her long oars sparkling in the sea, and both crews singing and shouting cheerily to each other. Every year there sails from Carthagena to the pearl banks of the Rio de la Hacha, about a dozen or a dozen and a half small vessels, called the Pearl Fleet. The greater part of the squadron had already gone, with a man-of-war to guard them. We were laggards, but Garbo, so the captain of our bark was named, trusted in a few days to join his comrades upon the banks. The Pearl Fleet is composed of small ships generally used for coasting. When I describe our craft, called the Pintado, the reader will have a good notion of all. She was, then, a two-masted vessel, of about thirty tons burthen, very shallow, and of great beam. Her mould was beautifully designed, sharp and wedge-like at the bows, with her sides towards the gunwale gently curved, as it were, like the lips of a bell, so that let her lie over before a smart gale, as much as she would, it was next to impossible to capsize her. She was but partially decked, towards the stem and stern, having an open space amidships, which was used when fishing for heaping the oysters in. Her crew consisted of four Spanish seamen, the captain, and two negro divers, of whom more anon. Thus there were eight of us in all, and we lived stowed away as we could best manage it, in the two little choky cabins, forward and aft, there being no distinction made between captain and crew. My up-bringing was not, as you may guess, much calculated to make me squeamish about where I lived and where I lay, but I confess, that the sweltering holes, all greasy and foul, with their brown swarms of cockroaches, and every now and then their stray centipedes, in which the Spanish sailors ate their garlic-smelling messes, and in which they flung themselves down often in their wet frowzy steaming clothes to sleep—I say these cabins were so horribly choky and miserable that, day and night, I kept upon deck, although, from the sharpness of the bark's model forward, and the quickness of her pitch, she was very wet. Indeed, when it blew stronger than common, we shipped so much water, that we had to cover the open waist with a species of grating on which tarpaulings were stretched tightly, otherwise we would speedily have filled and gone down. The bark carried two tall, slim masts, raking very much aft, and supporting a couple of large lug or square sails, over which two broad, but low topsails, could be hoisted. Round her decks, at stem and stern, was a low iron rail, but no bulwark, so that the washing of the sea over us, in a breeze, was almost incessant.

Garbo, the captain, was a good fellow, and a prime

seaman, and he only on board knew that I was an
Englishman, and what my real intentions were. The
rest of the crew were told that I was a mariner of the
Low Countries, who had also served in Spanish ships at
home. They were a wild-looking set of fellows, with
short trousers, not reaching much below the knee, broad
leathern belts, in which were stuck formidable knives, and
round their heads they wore yellow silk kerchiefs, over
which they clapped broad straw hats during the heat of
the day. All of them carried crucifixes of a black wood
ornamented with gold, and if they did not pray much to
the saints, at least they swore sufficiently by them. The
two negroes took no part in the management of the ship,
except it might be now and then lending a hand to their
shipmates when a rope required an extra strain. One of
them was very tall and gaunt, the other was short and
stout. The latter, who was called by some common
Spanish name, which I forget, was, or pretended to be, a
Christian. He had a crucifix slung round his neck by a
bit of rope yarn, and gabbled away about the saints like
the European part of the crew. Further, he was quite
'Hail fellow, well met,' with the Spaniards. He played
a sort of wooden drum, and sung strange uncouth songs
of his country to them, and sometimes he would mimic
the manners and voice of some one of the Spaniards very
skilfully, and to the great delight of the rest. In fact,
he was a fat, little, good-natured, hearty soul, with a grin
almost always upon his black mug, and, except when he
was asleep, his chattering tongue never lay still. He
would go gambolling about the deck like an overgrown
monkey, whooping, and grinning, and singing, so that not
a soul on board but he would set at last to laughing as
loudly as himself. His comrade was a man of a very different sort, and him I would describe particularly. He
was the blackest negro I ever saw, not having anything
of the brown copper colour which some of that people
and the Indians show. On the contrary, his skin was of
a most sooty black hue, without the least redness of tinge.
I have seen many big and strong men, but a **vaster,** a

more gaunt, yet sinewy form, than that of this black, saw
I never. He was more than six feet high; his great
spreading shoulders were lumps of bone and hardened
muscle, and his huge chest rose and fell so slowly, that he
seemed to breathe but half as often as other men on
board. His limbs were immensely gaunt and spare, and
nothing but his great splay feet, which covered more
than two streaks of the deck, could support the pile of
bone and sinew which they bore erect. The face of the
diver was most ill-favoured and lowering. It was a broad,
flat visage, like the face of a grim and grisly idol. Just
under the low, wrinkled forehead, two little pig eyes
winked forth, half hidden by the patches of eyebrow
which scowled in hairy folds above them. The corners of
the fat blubber lips were drawn down with a most sour
and evil expression, and all round them, and on the chin,
were ragged sprouts of beard, like flakes of black wool
stuck upon the grisly visage. Such was the tall diver,
who was called by his African name of Wooroo. His
speech was broken Spanish, which he did not speak half
so well as his countryman, the short negro. But, in
truth, he seldom spoke at all, being generally squatted on
his hams in some remote corner of the vessel, where he
would pass hours muttering to himself. He wore a pair
of tattered old breeches, and upon his naked chest, fastened round his neck, there lay a sort of amulet, or
charm, made of feathers, stuck through a ball of hard
baked clay, crammed into a rude wooden case full of
uncouth carvings. He was a worshipper of Ob, and this
was his fetish.

'Look at that hangdog thief Wooroo,' said Garbo to
me the second afternoon we were at sea. 'That fellow
has just two good qualities. He is the best diver who
ever went into the sea, and he is tractable to me who am
his owner. I took him from the mines among the mountains, and the animal, after his sort, is grateful. For, in
truth, I believe that he is amphibious in his nature, and
that the water is as necessary for him that he may live,
as is land, and, perhaps, a little more so.' In answer to

my further inquiries, the captain said that he was a slave,
brought from the Guinea coast. where of late a great
many negroes had been delivered up bound by tribes
hostile to them, and sold to Spaniards, Englishmen,
Frenchmen, and others, who employed them in those sorts
of work in the Indies, which white men cannot perform
and live. Soon after this, imagining, from the sombre
and brooding look of this savage, that he could if he
pleased tell us some story of his nation and of his captivity which would be worth hearing, I communicated my
thought to Garbo. The captain laughed. 'What can
the savage have to say,' quoth he, 'but that some other
savage fetched him a blow on the head with a war-club,
or battle-axe, and then sold him to some Spanish trader
for a cup of strong waters? But you shall be gratified :
that is, if the monster chooses to unloose his tongue.'

That night, the captain keeping the first watch, the
weather being clear, and we and our consort sliding slowly
over the long swells of the sea, the captain called the
negro aft to where we sat upon the deck. The savage
came with his usual slouching gait and scowling visage.

'Wooroo,' quoth the captain, 'we want to hear something about you; where you were born, and how you
came hither.'

The gigantic African only stared.

'Come, now,' says Captain Garbo, 'tell us your story,
Wooroo—tell us about what you were in Africa, and
what you did there.'

The black at last opened his blubber lips, and replied,
in broken Spanish, which I may render into English thus :
'What am me to you? What you want hear about me
for?'

'Never mind that, Wooroo,' says the captain, 'if we
have a fancy to hear you speak. I will give you brandy,
man.'

The eyes of the negro glistened, and Captain Garbo
winking at me, went on : 'You shall be drunk, Wooroo ;
drunker than you ever were before, Caramba! so drunk
that you can't lie flat even without holding on by the mast.'

It was pitiful to see how the brute-man shook himself with pleasure, and how his features worked.

'You make me very drunk — dead drunk?' he grunted.

'As dead as though you were smothered in a brandy cask, you two-legged hog,' returned the captain; 'and what's more, you shall have a draught to wet your whistle, and set your tongue loose at once.' So saying, the Spaniard disappeared down the narrow hatch, and presently emerged, bearing a large leathern bottle, with three drinking mugs, one of which he filled with hot, strong brandy; the savage tossed it off and held out the vessel for more.

'No, no,' said Garbo; 'you shall not get drunk until we have the story out of you. Come, heave a-head!—heave a-head!'

The black at this began to speak. First, he discoursed in a monotonous tone, all the while eyeing the brandy, and evidently thinking of it. But presently, as he proceeded, he warmed over the tale, and spoke with emphasis, and often in a loud, fast tone, making violent gesticulations with his black, brawny arms, until, at length, as his excitement increased, he would, every now and then, burst from the broken Spanish, in which he, no doubt, found it difficult to clothe his thoughts, into his own tongue, a strange, husky sputtering, rising, as it were, from his very stomach; but being promptly admonished on these occasions that we were not savages, and understood not the gabble of his coast, he would stop, ask for a little brandy, and having drunk it, resume again his narrative in such Spanish as he could speak. I will try to give in English some imitation of his words; only the reader must remember that they seemed doubly strange to me, hearing them, as I did, in the harsh, deep tones of the savage, and marking his glistening teeth, and white, staring eyeballs, and clenched fists wildly waved around while he spoke. Somewhat in this fashion ran his tale.

## The Story of the Negro Diver.

'I come from across the sea, and I am a slave. I dive
into the water, and I bring up shell-fish, with white
stones, which Spaniards worship. I am a great diver,
and I can kill sharks with the sharp knife I carry in my
hand. I was born in a wood, near a river. I curse them
who carried me away. I make fetish to curse them. I
ask the big Spirit that lives in fever mists to torment
them. They are not alive, but bad wishes follow dead
men to where they go. I helped to kill them, but still
they carried me away across the sea, and I am here!

'I was born in a wood near a river. The trees grew in
the water, and the slime of the water was oily at their
roots. At night a hot mist came—very damp. Sometimes no moon, no stars, shine through that mist. It is
the breath of the spirit of that land, and it kills strangers
who come from afar. In the woods it was very dark, the
branches kept the sun out; but near the river were huts,
and round them corn grew and maize, for there the
trees were burnt with fire, and the sun came hot—hot.
My father was a warrior, and could slay his foes. He
was strong, and had a great fetish. His war-club was
heavy, and his bow was long, and his arrows hit the mark.
My mother toiled, she reaped and baked, she thatched
the hut, she paddled the canoe, she was strong. If she
grew tired, my father lifted his war-club and then she
worked on. In the hut was a broad bed of leaves, also
calabashes to drink from, spears and clubs, and tools of
iron. Also knives and an axe, which white men made.
Also a god of palm-wood, with a necklace of wild beasts'
teeth. One hour from the hut, the brown river met the
sea: there was a bay there, and many huts. Where the
river met the sea were rocks: canoes could go from the
salt-water to the fresh, but not ships, because of the rocks,
on which were white waves, very fierce and high. In a
big hut near the sea, the king lived, with all his wives
and slaves. He was a great king, and made war upon
other kings. My father went to these wars, but I stayed

in the hut at home. When I was yet little, I learned to
dive and to swim, and to paddle a canoe. I loved the
water better than the woods. I loved the brown river,
and the sea which tossed and heaved. If the waves
filled the canoe, it was nothing to me; I laughed and
swam. If a great root of a tree in the brown slimy
river upset the canoe, it was nothing to me; I laughed
and swam. I did not fear the shark out in the blue
water; I could dive under him when he turned upon his
back to swallow me, and his teeth glistened in white
rows. I did not fear the muddy crocodile in the river,
and in the silent creeks, black and deep, which he loves:
his back is hard, but his belly is soft, and I could drive a
knife into him, so that he would lash his scaly tail and
die. I tell you I could swim on the water like birds
which live there, and I could dive like the fishes which
are beneath. My father could swim and he could dive,
but I could swim further and dive deeper. My father
called me the "Long-breathed," and when ships came to
where the river joins the sea, I dived down from them,
and the mariners gave me cloth and nails. Then I was
happy; I had enough to eat, and oil to anoint me and
make my limbs supple and strong, and a fetish which
was very good.

'Soon came a great ship to where the river met the sea,
and the men of our nation and the king went on board
to trade. We had oil to give them, and the teeth of
great beasts, and the dust of gold all glittering, which
merchants brought from where the sun rises. But the
captain said to the king, I not want palm-oil, nor teeth,
nor gold. I want men, I want slaves, and I will buy
them; not palm-oil, nor teeth, nor gold. When the
king heard this, he went to war, and the warriors of my
nation went with him. There was a battle, likewise
many huts burnt, but the captain gave the king guns,
and he returned with many slaves, men and women—for
bows and arrows are not so good to fight with as guns,
which shoot thunder. Then the slaves were sent on
board the great ship, and the captain gave us strong

U

drink, and we were drunk and happy, and we said we
would go to war and bring more slaves.

'So afterwards this was our trade. I likewise went to
war—I likewise made slaves. We went many days from
the sea, to where there were other nations. We had
guns, and they had but bows and arrows, likewise lances,
and clubs of wood which fire had hardened. Therefore,
many were killed, and many were slaves, and we kept
them until ships came, and then sold them, and they
were taken away over the sea ; but we were rich and
powerful, and had plenty of strong drink, which we
loved ; though many died of it.'

'As you will, Wooroo,' says Captain Garbo, interrupting him, 'if you only get enough of it.'

'Give some now,' answered the negro. He drank off
a small mugful, and went on, with more and more anima-
tion, as follows :—

'Once a ship came, and she waited for slaves outside
the rocks, where the sea burst white. Then I had a hut
and a wife, and slaves of my own, and lived near where
the king lived, and he knew that I was a warrior, and
exceeding skilful in the water. One night the sky was
black—black—and the sea moaned like a slave that
moans for his country and his wife, and there were
sounds amid the branches of the big trees ; also birds
sang strangely, and the frogs croaked very loud from the
marsh where they lived. Therefore, I knew that a great
wind was coming to the land, from far off in the sea :
and when I lay in my hut upon blankets, and listened, the
storm blew loud, and I heard the great noise of the waves.
In the morning, the sun was red in the sky, and I looked
and saw the ship that was waiting for slaves, and she
was tossed upon the waves, and the white men were
waving their arms to us, who stood upon the shore.
Not far from the ship were great rocks, and we knew
that if she struck upon such rocks, she would break, and
the white men would be drowned. But for a long time
she was safe, because heavy anchors and strong ropes
held her in her place : but the wind was great, and the

ropes broke : then the white men cried with a loud shout, and the ship struck upon the rocks and was broken, and the white men drowned. In the night, the wind went to sleep and the stars shone, and on the morrow the sun was hot and bright upon the sea. So, soon we went to the broken ship; there were great treasures there of iron and cloth, and powder, which we dried, and casks of strong drink. There was more iron and cloth, and strong drink, than we could get for many slaves, won at many battles. Therefore we were glad that the rope broke, and the white men were drowned, because we had all. After this, many ships came, but great winds did not come, and we went to war, and my father was killed; but for all the slaves we brought, we did not get so much cloth, and iron, and powder, and strong drink, as we got when the ship was broken, and the white men drowned. At this the king was angry—I was angry : all the warriors of my nation were angry—and when a great ship came again, the king went into the wood to an Obi man that lived there, and asked him that he would make a fetish, so that a wind would arise out of the sea, and break the ship, that we might have all. The Obi man was good. He answered in these words— "I will make a fetish and give it to Wooroo. Great ropes hold the ship, but sharp knives can cut great ropes. Then a small wind will break the ship upon the rock. The white men fire at canoe, if canoe go near the ropes; but Wooroo a great diver—Wooroo a great swimmer— Wooroo has a sharp knife—Wooroo can dive deep down below the sea, and cut the ropes."

'Then the king told me what the Obi man said, and I was glad, and sharpened my knife, and waited for a wind. The men of my nation knew it too, and we were glad, and said that the Obi man was wise. At last a wind came strong over the sea, and rattled the boughs of the forest, and the waves were white on the rocks. Then I went into the sea to swim and dive and cut the ropes. The surf was wild, but I am a great swimmer, and the surf could not drown me; and so I swam away out from the coast. I swam long. When I sank down into the valley between the waves, I could only see water—not land, nor the ship. Thus I passed to windward of the ship. If they saw my head, they thought it was a piece of wood, or a bird, or the head of some creature that lives in the sea. At length I was near the ship, and I saw the great rope from her bows going down into the water. I looked what way the rope went—it was under me. I drew my knife—I took a long breath—I dived. Down many fathoms I saw the rope; it stretched dimly out in the green sea. I clutched it; it shook—it trembled. Sometimes it slackened—sometimes it jerked out like an iron bar. I clung to it. The sea heaved and twisted me round and round it; but the knife was very sharp—my arm was very strong. The knife was half through the rope, when there came a jerk through all its strands, and it was torn asunder. One part was wrested out of my grasp, the other sank slowly into the sea. I rose up to the surface. I was almost spent; I swam faintly; I rested on the rolling sea. Then from the top of a wave I looked at the ship; she was already near the rock, and her side was to the waves. Men were in the rigging and among the ropes; they strived to loose the sails, but they had no time. The ship struck—the waves went over her—the masts fell—the crew were drowned! As I swam to land, I heard the people of my nation—how they shouted and were glad! That ship fared like the others—she broke, and we had the spoil. The powder, the cloth, the iron, and all things which we valued. Only three white men were saved, and we made them slaves. We sent them up the dark river, and into the dark woods far from the sea. They cried, and were in despair. They were sold to another nation, and we had the riches and rejoiced.'

'You infernal villain!' cried Garbo. 'The fellow talks of wrecking ships and drowning men by his devilish treachery, as if the tale were of building churches and saying masses.'

'I say truth,' replied the negro. 'Give me more strong

drink.' The captain shrugged his shoulders, and refilled the savage's cup. The barbarian, whose eyes now began to gleam like a wild cat's, broke out into a hoarse, guttural laugh, so savage and strange, that the watch on the forecastle called out to know what the noise was.

'It is only Wooroo singing,' answered the captain. 'Go on, Wooroo.' The negro, who was now getting excited by his story and the drink, needed no spurring.

'Ha! ha!' he began, with that horrid laugh again. 'Two ships come after. Two times I sharpened my knife; two times I went into the sea; two times I cut the great rope, and the ships struck the rocks and were broken. Some of the white men were drowned. Those who were not, we sold, and they were taken away, many days' journey to the rising sun, and there will be until they die, as I am, slaves.

'But we were wealthy and great. The king was powerful. He had more carabines, more iron, and more cloth than any king before. Strong drink ran amongst us like water in a river. We drank, we yelled, we whooped, we flung brands from the fire among the huts, and they were burned. Evil demons lived in those casks, and when we drank the fiery drinks, they entered in unto us and made us mad, and no man knew his brother. We fought among the burning houses, and the charred rafters were wet with blood. At length there came a ship to which we had already given slaves. We went aboard. I was on board with the king. We went into the great cabin, and they gave us more strong drink. They heard of four ships having been broken on the rocks hard by, and they asked us how it was. We said that a wind came up out of the sea, and that the ships were broken. They then asked us where the white men were, and we said that they were all drowned in the sea. On that they gave us more strong drink, and fires began to flash before our eyes. It was sweet drink, sweeter than ever we had tasted, and we drank greedily. The white men encouraged us, but they did not drink themselves, and they talked of the ships that were broken. But we were getting mad, and we knew no more what we did. So the white men said that, if the king's people were cunning, many more ships would be broken, and the king's people would be rich. Then we fell into the snare, because we were mad with the strong drink, and we yelled out, and danced, and told the white men that they were but fools, and I drew out my knife, and I said: "Look here. This knife cut the great ropes that went down to the bottom of the sea, and the ships were broken. I cut the great ropes. I have a strong fetish. I am a great diver and a great swimmer." After this I remember nothing, but that I was asleep, and that I awoke. It was in a dark place, very hot, and I could scarcely breathe. On my arms and legs were mighty chains. I called out, and a voice answered me in the darkness. It was the voice of the king, and he said, "I am chained, I know not where." We shouted, and screamed, and clanked our chains, and then when we lay still, we felt the prison we were in move with a regular motion, and we knew that we were in a ship upon the sea. So, white men came with lanterns, and they told us we were slaves. We roared and howled at them, and spit upon them, but our chains would not allow us to rise and kill them. Therefore they laughed, and asked me if I would swim and dive and cut the great rope that held the ship to the bottom of the sea, so that the king's people might be rich. First, we trusted in our fetishes, but they did not help us ; and the king said : "Once go ashore, and me catch the Obi man, and send the tum-tum drum through the wood, and the people come, and me burn the Obi man for a sacrifice ; me burn him with fire, and torment him till he die." But we did not go ashore—we were slaves. Then other slaves come, men and women, and lay down in the dark with us. The white men were there with whips and sticks, and they tormented us, until we lay so that we were one great lump of human flesh. All through the ship, oh ! there was the heat, and the stench, and the sweat, and the roarings ! There was no light but from two little hatchways with gratings, and square bits of light came down there; but I was far from them, and the air I breathed was more foul than the mist fever that comes up out of the swamp with the smell of the rotten mud.'

The poor devil told this part of his strange tale with a visible shudder. He went on.

'The ship sailed away, and there were waves very rough, and the slaves lay sick, rolling over each other, roaring and fighting to get near the hatchways. But white men, with iron bars, struck them, and drove them back. The white men struggled backwards and forwards, and beat and slashed the slaves with iron bars and knives. They carried lanterns at first, but the fire went out in the bad air and the stench. The place was only as high as half a man; there were hundreds and hundreds driven into it. The smoke of our bodies rose out of the hatchways. We struggled and tore each other with hands and teeth, because of the agony of sickness and smothering. We coughed, and gasped, and panted, and dashed ourselves here and there in our chains. Soon many died. The white men dragged out the corpses and took them away. In our struggles, we kicked the dying beneath our feet. Sometimes they clasped our legs, and tried to scratch or bite. The corpses were cold and soft beneath us, and all around was slime, and dirt, and air that was rotten, and one stench of corruption and of death.

'In half a moon, more than half of the slaves were dead and thrown overboard. The king was yet alive; when he came on board, he was oily and fat, but now his bones were sticking out like knots and splinters, and he was covered with sores, as a leopard with spots. We lived on the flour of cassava and water. White men came down with great baskets of it mixed, and we plunged in our hands and drew out lumps of leaven, and ate. We did not now fight or struggle, but lay and tried to sleep; we had more room, and five or six died every day, because the stench had brought the fever spirit, and he sailed with us in the dark hold. Then, one night when the white moon was coming down the hatchway, the captain of the ship approached, and turned his lantern upon us as we lay—the king and me—where they had first chained us down. Then he began to ask where were the white men who were carried off after the ships broke, to be slaves. But he stopped and said to two sailors who were with him, "Take off their chains and bring them on the deck; it is better to speak there in the moonlight, than in this stench." Our chains were taken off—we climbed the ladder—we passed the hatchway—and we stood upon the deck. The moon shone, as it shone above my hut—above the dark woods—above the dark river—above my country; the breeze was sweet to taste, as palm wine after bitter water. The white men slept upon the deck—the ship went steady before the night wind which came over the sea. It was good. The captain asked us again where the white men were slaves, and we told him a moon and two moons and three moons from where the dark river joined the sea. Then we said, that if he carried us back the white men would be found, and he would have them, and we would go ashore and we would make war and bring him many slaves and never cut the great ropes again. The captain spoke to the two white men who were with him, and very soon they took us down below, but they did not chain us again; many other slaves were also unchained, for all were very quiet; and when the white men struck them, or cut their flesh with their knives, they only groaned or cursed in their throats. I lay awake all that night, and the god that stood in my father's hut, with the necklace of wild beasts' teeth, gave me thoughts in my heart. I said to myself, we are slaves, but we may be masters; only one watches at the hatchway—at night the wind is small and the sea is smooth—the white men sleep in the moonlight—we may arise and kill them, and have the ship and its riches. I thought these things long to myself, and before the dawn I wakened the king and told him, and we conversed in whispers; the next day we told others, who were the stoutest men left, and who could speak the language of our nation. Thus we agreed, and we searched for billets of wood and spikes of iron, and bits of chains or fetters, to arm ourselves. The night came again, and the moon shone again through the hatchway. The wind was small and the sea smooth, and on deck the white men slept in the moonshine. Then every man adored his fetish, and called upon his god that he believed in, to help. I gave the sign, which was a shout of war, such as we raised when we rushed upon a sleeping village of our enemies to capture slaves. Then we all rushed at the hatchway—we tossed aside the grating of heavy wood and iron, as though it had been of the wattled hurdles which we planted round our fields. We were free. We shouted—we climbed—we leaped—we swarmed out in the moonshine. The white man who stood armed by the hatchway had only time to fire his carabine among us. Then a score of sticks, and iron chains, with handcuffs swung to them, split asunder his head. In a moment he was overboard and sunk in the sea. The white men were conquered. Some were asleep in hammocks, some on the deck. With great shouts and screams we rushed at them. We tore them from their beds. We dashed them on the deck. We slashed them with the knives we found. We hove them overboard. And the sharks which followed us from Africa, and were fat with the flesh of our fellows, swallowed the white men also. Therefore we were the masters of the ship, and it seemed a good slave; for when all the white men were dead and gone, it sailed on, and the small wind blew, and the sea was smooth, just as before. I looked then for the king, but he was dead. The one shot which the white man fired struck him—the ball drove the fetish of feathers, which was upon his breast, into his heart. He was dead, and the sharks had him also.

'Then all my countrymen called out, and said that I was king in his place, and that we must go back to Africa, to the deep forests and the dark rivers, to their huts, and their wives, and their slaves, to where the panther leaped and the crocodile swam, and the large bats hung in clusters from the trees. So they led me to the helm, and they said, "Steer us home." There were clouds.

then over the moon, and the night was dark. I said,
"Wait until the morning, and I will steer you home."
The morning came, the clouds passed away, the sun rose,
and the wind came fast over the sea. They said again,
"Steer us home." But I looked around. I looked far
and near. There was no land, only water. As in the
desert there is only sand; so round us there was only
water. It was the same on the right hand and on the
left. There was the sky and the sea, and that was all.
How could I steer them home? But if I said I could
not steer them home, they would kill me; therefore I
took the tiller in my hand. I stayed by it all day.
Those who were the masters of the ship and of me,
danced and sung about the deck. Sometimes they asked
when we would be at home. I said, soon. They thought
that I could conduct the ship to land. They would not
let me leave the tiller. They brought food there. I slept
there. I was afraid to move. I did not know the road
home. Days came and turned into nights, and nights into
days again. The sun rose out of the sea, sometimes on
the right hand, sometimes on the left; sometimes before
us, sometimes behind us. We were wandering upon the
sea; a moon passed over us, and they said to me, "We
are not yet at home; there is no land, only water. Take
us home, or we will kill you, as you made us kill the
white men." Then I was sorry that we killed the white
men. The night after, the wind grew loud, and the
waves beat over the ship. I did not know what to do.
The sails were left as the white men had spread them.
The ship was tossed. She moaned, and groaned, and
plunged deep into the waves. The sails made strange
noises, the masts reeled and bent as trees in a hurricane.
Then one by one they broke, and fell into the sea. The
foam flew over us all night. A great load of masts, and
ropes, and sails lay upon the decks, and from the decks
they reached down into the sea. These we cut asunder
with hatchets, for they were pulling the ship down into the
depths; and when the morning came, the wind had gone
away, and the ship lay quite still. She had no masts,

and no sails; and as a man without legs cannot walk, so a ship without rigging cannot move upon the ocean.

'And still all on board cried, "Take us home." Then I said to them, "We cannot go home, there are no sails; we must die here upon the sea." Then for the first time I left the helm. I knew one thing that none else there knew—I knew where there was the strong drink.'

'Ay, that I'll be bound you did!' said Captain Garbo.

I watched, and when none saw, when it was dark, I took a great vessel of strong drink, and also bread and meat, and went down with them into the deep places of the ship. I went near the keel. I sat in darkness, with beams around me, and ropes, and the rotten water that flowed slowly in from the sea—and which moved with regular tides, backwards and forwards, because of the ship rolling on the waves. That water had the smell of the thick mud in the creeks among the woods, after the rains, when the mists arise. It washed and gurgled over the slimy wood, and also the rusty chains and nails which lay at the bottom of the ship. There I ate and drank, and no one saw me. I heard them howling up above, for they knew not where I was; but they knew they were to die upon the sea. I stayed there drinking and sleeping. The strong drink was good, it made me drunk; it made me as if I was back again where the dark river joins the sea. When the jug was dry I went for more. It was night, and a great wind was blowing over the waves, and the ship rose up and sank down, like the first ship that went upon the rocks and was broken. The people were running on the deck—they were in fear; they said the sea was coming up over the ship. I did not care; I knew where the strong drink was. I got another jug, greater than the first, I also got some bread. As I passed in the dark, I heard a man say to a woman, "In two days there will be no food left." I did not care; I went with the strong drink into the secret place of the ship. There I lay among the ropes and beams, and the stinking water which gurgled among them, as the waves beat hard on the outside. It was like a cave in the

woods : it was like the den of the wild beasts. I burrowed
in it like the crocodile in his abiding place, among the
weeds and the thick herbage which grows by the creek.
There I ate, there I drank—oh, much—much. The
strong drink was like fire in me, and like light to me ; it
showed me my hut, where the river joins the sea ; it
showed me sun, and moon, and stars, and the sky over
the woods and the sea; it showed me the deep waters
where I paddled my canoe, and where I swam, and where
I dived. I shouted and sang war-songs, and those above
thought that the spirits of their enemies were exulting
and were singing. When the jug was empty I went on
deck. Many days had come and gone away into the past.
The deck was full of people ; they lay upon the planks,
they groaned and cried, they were starving, and they
yelled out for water, and for cassava, and millet, and maize,
and rice. I went to the secret place where were the
strong drinks. Lo ! there were no more ! Others found
out the place, and took the drinks. I searched everywhere, but there was nothing—not a drop—not a crumb.
There was no more food, no more drink—now we must
die. I sat upon the deck, so did all ; no man or woman
spoke : sometimes one moaned—that was all. It was
the same in the sunlight and the moonlight—when the
air did not move and when the wind was strong. I
looked upon the sky, it was always blue, there were no
clouds from dawn-time to sun-setting : there was no rain
to cool our lips; our tongues swelled and our throats
were dry—as dry as the hole which the scorpion burrows
in the hot sand. The people died one by one. When
they died they lay upon the deck where they fell ; they
rotted there amongst us, but we did not move to throw
them to the sharks. At last there were ten men and
women dead, to one man or woman living ; then we spoke
and we talked who would die next. One said he would,
and another, that he would. When we die we fly back
to Africa, and we said one to the other, "If you die first,
you say we are coming : you say we are flying in the air
behind you to Africa, to the dark woods and the dark

river." Then I sent messages to my father, who was killed in war, and to the king; I sent them by a young man who was very weak, and whose eyes were glazed. He lay close by me. I watched him well. His breath came longer and longer—then it ceased, as a branch you move ceases gradually to swing—and the jaw dropped down. I said, "Ha! my messenger has departed; I am glad." That night there were but five left. I was the strongest of the five, but I could not rise from my seat amid the corpses. The breeze came fresh in the night; clouds came with it, and out of the clouds rain fell. We held up our mouths and we were refreshed. So, by means of the sweet rain, four out of the five lived until the grey light came out and showed fogs hanging on the water. The wind was small, and the sea smooth; and as the sun climbed out of the ocean, the fogs rose up and melted away, and we all gave a faint shout together, for not half an hour from us, a great ship, with many sails, glided like a bird upon the sea. As we looked, a canoe, with white men, came from the great ship, paddling fast towards us, and soon the white men leaped up among the corpses on the deck. They gave a great cry of horror when they saw all the planks covered with bodies, some sitting, some lying, some piled up upon each other in heaps—where fathers and sons, and brothers and sisters, and husbands and wives, had died together—and they were about to go back hastily into their canoe, but we all cried as with one voice for water. Then they turned and beheld us, and after some talking, they lifted us up and put us into the canoe, and rowed us to their ship. So was it that we became slaves again. Then they spread forth all sail, and our old ship, with its cargo of corpses, was left drifting about on the sea.

'We had good food and good water; we grew stout again, lusty, and strong. A moon passed away, and then we saw land, and a city of the white men. The city was called Porto Bello. We were sold there. My master took me up far into great mountains, where there was gold. The gold was down in the earth. The slaves dug

holes in the sides of the steep hills. We crawled
into these holes. We dug and hammered in dark places
under ground, and white men with whips lashed us if
we stopped to rest. But I longed and panted again for
rivers and the sea. I grew weak, and my arms were
soft and thin, and a spirit whispered to me, and I put
earth and clay into my mouth, and swallowed them.
Other slaves did the same, and slowly they died, and
flew back to Africa. I wanted to die, and I ate much clay.
I was very sick and weak, but they flogged me with
whips, until I crawled into the holes, digging and hollow-
ing under the earth for gold. At last—'

'At last,' said Captain Garbo, 'you have got so far
with your story, that I may finish it for you. Being on
a visit to see some of the gold mines of Darien, the overseer
of one of them told me that he was losing almost all his
negroes of the disease or superstition peculiar, I believe,
to those Africans and called ' dirt-eating.' He pointed
out to Wooroo there, as one of them who was dying the
fastest, and on my speaking to him, he told me what he
has several times repeated, that he was a great swimmer
and a diver. So such being the case, and being then, as
now, much engaged in the pearl fishery, I bought the fellow
for a trifle, took him down to the coast, and I am bound
to say that a better hand under water never plunged over
a boat. As soon as he was afloat, he recovered his health
and spirits fast; and now, I suppose, there are not two
men, white or black, in the fleet, that the fellow could
not grasp in either of his hands, and smash their heads
together.'

As soon as his master had interrupted him, and bade
him cease speaking, Wooroo lost all the look of intelligence and excitement which had gleamed in his eyes. He
sat like a brainless statue of black wood. He had
performed his task, and at length he held out both hands
towards the spirit-flask, and only muttered—

'Give me the wages you said—make me much
drunk.'

Captain Garbo, without a word, filled a large measure

with brandy, and handed it to the savage, who rose with it, and walked to a corner in the deep-waist of the ship. Passing there an hour after, I saw the brute lying insensibly drunk, with the empty measure still grasped in his hand.

---

## CHAPTER XXIV.

### MY ADVENTURES AMONG THE PEARL FISHERS, AND MY ESCAPE FROM THE FLEET.

ALL this time we were beating gaily up to windward in company with our consort, both boats proceeding at much the same rate, and frequently hailing each other and sailing nearly alongside. On the third day from that of our departure, we saw upon our right, towering in great blue masses out of the sea, the high land of Santa Martha. Mariners say that it is higher than the Peak of Teneriffe, and that when the weather is very clear, there is a certain circuit of the Caribbean sea, not far from hence, where, from the tops of a lofty vessel, you may see at once the distant ridges of Hispaniola, the Blue Mountains of Jamaica, and the Peak of Santa Martha upon the main land. The next day, the coast line being far distant, and being cloven, as it were, by the great river De la Hacha, which here comes into the sea, we saw riding at anchor, in-shore from us, a squadron of small ships. We being still well at sea, the water beneath was of a deep blue ; but where the Pearl Fleet, for such they were, lay, the hue of the sea was a light green. It was as glorious an afternoon as ever shone under the tropics, as bowling cheerily before the sea-breeze, we ran down for our sister ships, they lying at their anchors above the great bank of pearls. There were fourteen or fifteen barks similar to our own, and at some distance was a stately frigate, which protected them, lying-to.

'That is the convoy of the Pearl Fleet,' said Garbo ;

'we must first speak her, and she will allot our station on the bank.'

And, in fact, as he talked, the great maintop-sail of the Spanish ship was filled, and her bows, falling off from the wind and pointing to us, she moved slowly out to meet us. As she drew near, I could not help thinking that she was the same vessel which had chased the 'Will-o'-the-Wisp.' At any rate, she had the same richly-carved bows, full of figures of angels and saints, and the same goodly fabric of rigging towering up against the blue sky. Presently, she hove-to again, our small sails being becalmed under her lee, and Captain Garbo, with two of his men, went aboard her in the small canoe which the bark carried. As for myself, I did not care to trust my neck on board a Spanish man-of-war. Indeed, I kept as much out of sight as I very well could, pretending to be busy about a thousand little matters on board the bark. I noted, however, that the Spaniard bore twelve great guns upon either side, besides double batteries upon forecastle and poop. Her high decks swarmed with men, who scrambled over into her chains and out at her port-holes, and chatted with the Spanish part of the bark's crew, and mocked and gibed at Wooroo as he sat upon his hams on the deck, taking no more notice of what was said to him than the mast. Presently the captain returned with a card in his hand, whereon was inscribed the station of the bark upon the bank. Each boat had its own appointed place; and the frigate was there not only to protect the fleet against Buccaneers, but to enforce the rules which the Spanish government, to whom the fishery belongs, lays down to be observed by the barks which prosecute it. The pearl bank extends for a great many miles in length and one in breadth, there being a deep channel about three or four leagues broad between its inmost edge and the land. Our position was towards the eastern extremity of the bank, and so we beat up towards it, passing many of the anchored boats, who hailed us cheerily, and asked what news from Carthagena. As we sailed along, we saw the divers, all of them either Indian or negroes, standing often upon the edge of the boats, poising their bodies for a moment, and then plunging head-foremost down into the sea. Some of the fleet were more deeply laden than others, that depending upon the number of the oysters which chanced to lie scattered under each boat. As soon as the cargo is made up, the pearl fisherman weighs, hoists his lug sails, and runs in for the shore; but if the frigate fires two guns, one close after the other, he must lie-to, until a boat from the big ship comes and gives him leave to proceed. Although the rule, however, is, that each boat fishes and sails for itself, without attending to its neighbours, yet the convoy always tries as far as possible to arrange matters, so that the fleet may sail in a body to the shore, the frigate attending them to windward. If it be suspected that there are Buccaneers upon the coast, the ordinary rule is indeed altogether suspended, and no boat is permitted to weigh anchor until the commodore fire a gun, and hoist a blue flag at his foretop-gallant-mast head, when the whole squadron run gaily together for the Ranchiera, as the pearl village is called, upon the banks of the Rio de la Hacha. When we joined the fleet no danger was, however, suspected, and by the time that we had taken our station, and let the anchor splash from the bows, about half the barks, which were deepest in the water, had weighed; and hoisting their brown patched sails, scudded away before the last of the sea-breeze. As soon as it became dark each boat hoisted a lantern to its mast-head; the frigate showing two, one above the other, in the fore-top-gallant rigging. The night was calm and still. Every now and then we would hear the faint sound of songs, coming over the water from distant barks; and, as hour after hour passed away, it was marked by the clang of the great ship's bell. Meantime, on board our bark, we were busy preparing for to-morrow's fishing. The waist was cleared out, and the decks fore and aft lumbered with the coils of rope and old canvas, flung aside to make room for the expected overflow of oysters. Then the baskets to be used in lifting them from the bottom of the

X

sea, strong cages of thick wire, all rusty and bent, were prepared; the tackle was rigged, and lines were affixed to heavy pieces of lead, furnished with handles for the divers to grasp, so as to sink the quicker to the bottom. These preparations over, we cooked and ate our suppers and turned in, leaving but one hand on deck for an anchor watch, as sailors call it.

'Now,' thought I, as, according to my custom, instead of crawling into the little cabins, which were not much better than the hold of the ship which had carried Wooroo from Guinea, I laid myself down on deck, well muffled up in old sails, to keep the heavy dews away—'Now,' thought I, 'I have heard of kings and queens who slept on beds whereof the curtains were heavy with pearls, all glittering in their lustre above them, but here am I now, and here be a fleet of us poor sea-tossed mariners sleeping upon a bed with more pearls beneath and around us than there are in the treasuries and the thrones, and on the royal bed-curtains to boot, of London, or Paris, or Madrid.' I know not whether the kings and queens whereof I have spoken slept the better for the pearls above them; I know I slept well with pearls below me, being indeed favoured, perhaps by St. Gieronimo, with a vision in which I saw the 'Will-o'-the Wisp' suddenly appear in the midst of the Pearl Fleet and engage the Spanish frigate, Stout Jem himself fighting in single combat with the captain, and at length, by one stout thrust, pinning him to his own mainmast; when, just as I was about to spring forward to haul down the golden flag of Spain from the man-of-war's topmast, a loud voice, coming from real flesh and blood lungs, smote my ear, and, starting up, I saw Captain Garbo and the rest scrambling through the hatchways in their shirts, while the anchor watch was shouting lustily that there was a strange vessel rowing with sweeps through the fleet, and that he had even heard the muttering of the voices on board of her. At this, I confess very willingly, my heart made a leap into my mouth. Was my dream a true vision—was Stout Jem, indeed, so near? We all held our peace and listened, but we heard nothing. It was now quite dark. The night had got cloudy, and there were neither stars nor moon. The air, too, was quite still, and the tap-tap of the water against the ridges of overlapping planks on the clinker-built side of the boat, as she rocked slowly on the swell, was the only sound we could distinguish. The lights of the other barks were gleaming on the dark ocean, and the two lanterns of the frigate swayed slowly from side to side, as though they were meteors playing among the stars.

'Tush, Pedro,' said Captain Garbo, 'you fell asleep, man, and dreamed you saw a ghost. You deserve to be dipped alongside, just to waken you.'

But at that moment we all started, for suddenly there came over the water a loud crash, as of two ships meeting, followed all at once by a crackling volley of musketry, which glanced bright through the darkness, gleaming in fiery streaks over the black oily-looking water, and then, mingling with the reports of the fire-arms, a great hearty cheer, such as Englishmen give when they leap upon the decks of an enemy. By the flashes we saw that one of the largest and heaviest laden of the pearl barks had been laid aboard by a very long low-built boat with three raking masts, like those of the vessels which the French call *chasse-marées*, and moved by a number of great sweeps, which extended from her sides like the long legs of some huge insect of the sea.

'The Pirates! the Buccaneers!' screamed all our crew together, and they rushed to haul down our lantern, so that we might the better escape in the darkness. In the meantime, there was a great crashing and scuffling, with heavy plunges in the water, as though men had leaped or been thrown overboard, and then, in the course of a moment, there was again silence, and the light of the captured vessel, for such no doubt she was, disappeared. But on board of the rest of the fleet there sprang up, as you may conceive, the strangest uproar. Instead of hauling down their lights, as we had done, in less than a minute the sea was all a-fire with the infinity of lanterns

and torches which they waved and flashed from rigging
and deck, while such a clamour of shouts, blowing of
trumpets and conch shells, beating of drums, and firing of
muskets and pistols, I never heard.    It appeared, indeed,
as if the pearl fishers imagined that they would drive
away their enemy by making a noise and hallooing ; all
this, however, was done, Captain Garbo said, to alarm
the convoy ; but, truly, they must have kept sleepy
watch aboard of her, if they did not hear the tumult
of the first attack.    But in the meantime the great
ship was aroused—a flash of red flame gleamed from out
her sides, showing for a moment boats full of men surging in the water beneath, and her sails falling in great
white patches from her yards, as she prepared to give
chace to the enemy.    But these broad sails were useless ;
not a reef point rattled against the canvas in the great
stillness of the night ; but we heard the dash of oars and
distant shouts as the boats of the frigate pulled away
from her among the fleet.    Meantime, the din on board
the different barks subsided, but we could see the crews
as they ran to-and-fro upon the decks, still carrying
torches and lanterns, while every minute or two the frigate fired a great gun, for what purpose I know not,
only that it seems as if Spaniards, like Frenchmen, seldom think they are doing anything if they be not making
a noise.    But where, meanwhile, was the Buccaneer row-
boat, or galley ?    I strained my eyes through the darkness in the direction in which I had seen her.    Could she
be an Englishman, I thought to myself, and, if so, would
it be possible for me to board her ?    A light canoe floated
alongside our bark, on which my eye fell as these ideas
rose up in my mind.    But, when I reflected a minute, I
saw how mad would be any attempt to make my way in
the darkness, and amid pursuing boats, to the vessel,
even although she might be, what I had no certain means
of knowing her—a friend.

    While I was pondering thus, Captain Garbo accosted
me in a whisper—

    ' This is but a mad freak of your countrymen,' he said,

' for such I judge them to be. They could not expect to
carry off the bark from the middle of a fleet, and without
a breath of wind either.'

Just as he spoke, a jagged flash of lightning, which
dazzled me, tore right across the sky to the westward,
and the loud crackling thunder had not ceased to explode
above us, when a heavy puff of wind, bearing broad plash-
ing rain-drops before it, struck our bark, and made her
swing round to her anchor like a weathercock.

' A squall,' I cried out, ' and the privateer knew it was
coming. It was that made them so bold.'

Just then a whole row of lanterns was run up to the
gaff of the great ship.

' See,' said Garbo—' a squall indeed. That is the
signal for the recal of all her boats.'

There was nothing which appeared to me very ominous
in the look of the night. I only expected a pretty sharp
outburst of wind and rain with thunder and lightning.
And so, indeed, it proved, for in less than five minutes
from the first flash, a strong gusty wind, driving before it
a pelting rain, was whitening the sea around us, and hissing and whistling through the few ropes which formed
our rigging, while the bark herself tore and plunged at
her anchor, as if she would have wrenched it out from its
hold amid the oysters. In a moment the flaming torches,
shown from so many of the fleet, were blown out or
quenched; but the great ship, burning a bright light in
her main rigging, we saw her all lurid and blue in the
glare, leaning heavily over to the blast, her slanting
yards dotted with the seamen, who were taking in sail as
fast as they had spread it forth. In a few minutes again
all around was darkness, except where the glimmer of a
lantern, tossing and tumbling as though a giant were
flinging it from hand to hand, showed where one of the
Pearl Fleet was jerking and straining at her anchor. The
strength of the squall was not alarming, but it tore up
the sea upon these shallow banks into quick cross-running
and angry waves, and the rain was driven in our faces so
sharply that the drops struck like hailstones.

'The only thing I fear,' said Garbo to me, as we stood holding on by the foremast, 'is for the frigate's boats. There will be no great damage to anything else.'

Just as he spoke, a man beside us shouted, 'A boat! a boat!' and looking forth ahead, we saw, clearly relieved against the whiteness of a breaking sea, one of the frigate's barges coming tossing down upon us, while, almost at the same instant, a couple of dark sails shot, as it were, like dusky shadows into the faintly lighted circle around us, illuminated by the half-dozen lamps which, in imitation of the rest of the fleet, we had fixed to different parts of the rigging, and then in a moment, as the vessel which bore the canvas rose upon the crest of a sea, we all recognised the long, low galley which had laid the pearl boat aboard. She was flying along close hauled to the wind, the white foam beating in showers over her long dusky form, and sometimes over the two patches of sails which she carried. The boat of the frigate lay right athwart her track. There were two loud shouts from those in the boat and those in the sailing galley, then, in an instant, a straggling volley of musketry was shot by the former. The flashes illuminated the sea, showing the sharp and carved prow, ending in a serpent's head, of the adventurous craft, and the grim faces of a cluster of men, who waved their hands and shook axes and cutlasses at the Spanish boat. Then there was a sudden order, in English, on board the galley, 'Port! Hard a-port! and give them the stem.' The bows an instant fell off from the wind, lifted on a sea, and crushed down upon the doomed boat, driving her under water like an eggshell, while, with a loud hearty hurrah, the Buccaneer swept past us, not three fathoms from our bowsprit, and, in a moment, disappeared in the night.

'A sail, close to astern,' was at the moment sung out from the other extremity of our craft.

'Never mind the sail astern,' shouted Garbo. 'Here —ropes, oars, anything—there is a boat swamped ahead, and as he spoke, there appeared the wreck of the man

of-war's pinnace, with some of the men clinging to it,
and others striking out amid the sea, and shouting lustily
to us for help. A dozen of lines were flung to them at
once, while the fat negro leaped overboard, calling to the
struggling mariners to fear nothing. Wooroo never
moved an inch during the whole affair, except to shake his
woolly head when a heavier shower of spray than ordinary fell upon him. The Spaniards, who could most of
them swim well, soon scrambled up our low sides, none
the worse of their ducking. Not a man was missing,
thanks to the aid of our little pearl diver, who had made
directly for the wreck of the boat, and very dexterously
lashed a couple of ropes round the only two of the crew
who, either by being stunned in the collision, or from the
bewilderment and suddenness of the whole affair, were
clinging for life to the shattered boat, without having in
the least the power of helping themselves. Such a scene
of outcry, and swearing, and hubbub of all sorts, as the
Spanish man-of-war's men made when they got aboard, I
never saw. They ran from end to end of the craft, shouting
out, in the darkness, after the vessel which had run them
down ; roaring, by all the saints, that they would be re-
venged upon her, and that when the frigate caught her,
they would not leave a French or English throat uncut on
board. As for me, I deemed it politic to chime in with
these declarations—to the great amusement of Captain
Garbo, who was a very good fellow, and kept my secret
like wax. When we had a little settled down—the squall
having also fallen, and the sea getting smoother fast—the
captain called for the man who had reported the sail
astern, and asked him what like she was ?

'Truly,' said the mariner, ' I can tell you not only
what like she was, but what she really was—the vessel
being no other than the bark which the Buccaneer laid
aboard, and which no doubt she captured, for both ships
were lying the same course—one passing ahead and the
other astern of us.'

' Ay,' said the officer of the man-of-war, shivering in
his cold wet clothes, ' it was the ship the scoundrels

wanted, and there is no denying but they have carried
her off very cleverly.'

I was of the same opinion myself, and I could not but
admire the judgment of the Buccaneers in rowing into the
centre of the sleeping squadron, just before the outbreak
of the squall, and then swooping off with their prey,
in the midst of the confusion which it created.    The
weather soon cleared up.    By midnight the stars were
twinkling forth, and the frigate having worked up near
us, we hailed that the crew of the pinnace were safe, and
presently another boat coming on board, carried them to
their own ship.    With the earliest peep of the dawn I
was at the mast-head of our bark.    The fleet, with the
exception of the one spirited away, were riding at their
stations.    The boats which had, yesterday evening, gone
into the river with their cargoes, were again standing out
for the bank.    The frigate lay to windward—rising and
falling on the froth-laced seas, with her main-topsail flat
to the mast—but elsewhere the ocean was sailless.    The
Buccaneer and her prize, one of the largest and quickest
vessels of the fleet, had disappeared.

That morning, we began our proper business of collecting pearls, the method of which I will briefly describe.
First, the fat negro went in the canoe to several points
round about the vessel, diving into the water at each, and
thus finding where the shell-fish lay thickest.    This having been ascertained, he placed a small buoy upon the
spot, and the bark was warped up to it.    The iron-basket,
which I have mentioned, was then let down to the bottom
of the sea, the depth of which was hereabouts nearly five
fathoms, or almost thirty feet.    Then Wooroo and his
comrade prepared for their day's work, by stuffing their
ears full of the down of the cotton-tree, without which,
or some similar precaution, divers frequently become
deaf.    They anointed their limbs, too, with some sort of
vegetable oil, and then taking the sinkers of lead, which I
have spoken of, in their hands, they poised their bodies,
standing upon the gunwale of the ship, and keeping time,
as it were, to her roll, flinging back their arms and

shoulders, and breathing deeply, so as to puff out their broad chests with air. Wooroo, while so standing, looked like a great black image of Strength. At length they leaped simultaneously, making but one splash, and as the water settled over them, we could see their black forms wavering and quivering, as it seemed, owing to the motion of the sea, and then presently clinging to the projections of rock, all tufted over with green sea-weed— in the rifts of which the oysters lay thick. As soon, however, as they began to tear up the latter from their beds, the water became so much mudded that we could not remark the process. In the meantime, we hauled up both sinkers, which the divers had let go on reaching the bottom, and placed them on the gunwale, all ready for the next plunge. The little man came up to the surface first—puffing and blowing. There was a sort of broad-stepped ladder, with three or four rounds, which was let down into the water, and upon one of which he sat to rest, basking himself in the hot sun. Wooroo did not appear at the surface, until I began to think that he would never come up at all—and said as much to Garbo.

' Drowned,' said the good-tempered Spaniard; ' that's not the fate he was born to. Caramba! that fellow's lungs will hold as much air as the biggest bellows that ever were puffed.' And accordingly, after an unconscionable space of time, the negro rose, and clung to the ladder, his features appearing only a little swollen, and his vast chest heaving a little faster, as the consequences of his plunge. As soon as the basket was reported filled, it was drawn up and emptied into the deep waist, and then let down again. In the course of the day, another negro and an Indian, both expert divers, arrived from the shore to help us, there being generally four divers to each boat. Two cages were then let down together, and by nightfall, the bark had half her cargo on board.

In consequence, however, of the bold attack of the pirate, or Buccaneer, the captain of the frigate determined that all the pearl fishermen should proceed together to the shore, and from thence back to the banks, sailing

in a squadron; and as the greater number of the boats
had their full cargoes on board, we all weighed anchor in
company, stealing in slowly for the shore, upon a smooth
sea glistening in the starlight. It was a fair spectacle
that small squadron, with their white sails just sleeping
in the light breeze, and with the great frigate, her huge
lanterns shining over her poop like sea-beacons, and now
and then belching forth a sheet of red spouting fire, as an
admonition to any of the faster boats, which might appear
to be inclined to take the lead of the rest, not to break
the order of sailing. As we glided along, the crews of
the barks often sang in chorus, the music being re-
echoed and reflected as it were between the many sails
spread out, until it appeared as if hundreds of choristers
were joining in the burden. About midnight we crossed
the bar of the Rio de la Hacha, the frigate remaining
outside, and presently anchored near the shore, in a
shallow bay, where the water was brackish. The land
hereabouts is low and sandy, with abundance of thin-
stemmed, narrow-leaved herbage, and few trees. The
town is a mere assemblage of huts, kept up for the
purpose of the pearl fishery, and inhabited by the Indians,
being principally old men, women, and children, who
open the oysters, under the constant superintendence of
watchful Spanish overseers, who are there to keep a sharp
eye upon the pearls. Notwithstanding all their care,
however, they are very often cheated, and the most
valuable pearls hidden and conveyed away. I had often
opportunities while on board the fleet, and ashore in the
ranchiera, or village, of seeing the process of opening the
oysters. These were brought from on board the barks in
flat-bottomed barges to the shore, whence they are
carried in baskets, upon the heads of the Indians, to a
sort of store-pit, or receptacle, into which they are flung.
Close to this deposit are ranged a great many narrow
tables, each of them consisting only of two rough planks
set upon trestles, and shaded overhead by a roof of
withered grass heaped upon hurdles. All along the
tables, on one side, are ranged great lines of the Indian

slaves opening the oysters, while upon the other side of the tables, stand the Spanish overseers, there being one overseer to every dozen or so of openers. When an Indian finds pearls, either of the large or the seed sort, he shouts out, and his superintendent immediately goes up to him, and takes charge of the precious substances, which he is bound in turn to give to the chief superintendent, who registers their size and value in an account book.

The slaves are principally fed upon the meat of the oysters, which they prepare in a particular way, passing a string through a great number of oysters in the manner of threading beads or decorations, and then hanging the festoons thus made up to dry. They likewise live upon manatee and the flesh of wild cattle, the ranchiera being amply provided with hunters, whose business it is to supply such stores. The slaves work from sunrise to sunset, with about three hours intermission when the heat is the fiercest. They are a poor, dogged, sullen-looking sort of people, with long straight black hair and big cheek-bones. It is miserable to see them at their work, crouching under the whips of the overseers, not daring to whisper to each other nor to cease for a moment, but, bending down their heads over the board, and, when they find a pearl, calling out in a low whining tone to the overseer, who presently relieves them of it. I have often, having found occasion to be sometimes on shore during the day, sat upon a little sandy hillock, sheltered from the sun by a sort of umbrella made of plaited grass, many of which the Spaniards use, and gazed upon the scene. To seaward was the surf thundering white upon the bar, and almost on the horizon the pearl barks, like black specks, guarded by the big ship, as a little hamlet is by a castle. On one side the river came shining down, amid a waste of sand-banks and knolls, spreading out and slackening in its speed, as it began to feel the near influence of the sea. On its banks vast flocks of birds disported. The flamingos stood in red rows, drawn up like soldiers. Great cranes waded in the shallow water, like men on

stilts. Ducks of many sorts flew by in long lines or in
the shape of wedges, with a brave old drake to lead the
fleet; while small water birds, which dive, floated upon
the brownish river, sometimes tipping down to the bottom
with a saucy jerk of their spruce little tails, and then
coming up with a flutter and a quackle. By the margin,
fixed to posts and stakes, lay a fleet of canoes, and the
flat-bottomed boats which carried the oysters ashore;
and here and there, lurking among the sand-hills with his
gun, you might descry a Spanish sportsman, creeping
along the shore to get a good shot at widgeon or teal.
Upon the landward side there stretched out in the hot
sun a wavy, sand-heaped shore, feathered here and there
with a palm, bending in the sea-breeze. The village,
which was two or three straggling streets of huts, built of
wood and wattled branches, with some roofs scattered
here and there of tarred canvas, which sailors call tar-
paulin, supported upon stakes, boats' masts, oars, and
what not, lay, as it were, roasting brown in the fierce
glare of the sun. A few black and stark-naked children
played in the sand before the doors, and a Spaniard or
two, with their white linen jackets, and broad straw hats,
and red sashes tied round their middles, and everlasting
pipes of tobacco in their hands, would be sitting in the
shade, outside the long low hut which was the posada of
the place, drinking draughts of wine from gourds or cups
made of cocoa-shells mounted with silver, and playing
cards or dice for shining dollars. At one end of the
village was a rude sort of fort, built of unhewn stone,
piled up and supported by a framework of stakes; it had
no cannon, but was loopholed for musketry, and was set
all round with sentry-boxes, in which Spanish soldiers
dozed away the greater part of the day and night. Above
the ramparts or palisades, which were not more than
twelve feet high, and planted upon the roof of an inner
house, rose a flag-staff bearing the broad red and yellow
banner of Spain. In this fort, or stockade, lived the
governor of the fishery, the chief superintendent, and
the captain of the convoy, when he was ashore. All the

pearls which were found were conveyed thither twice a-day, and overseers were continually passing and re-passing from the great gate down to the opening tables, which stood in divers ranks all round the central pit into which the oysters were flung. From among those tables, half covered by their thin roofs of grass and hurdles, and lined by the dusky rows of working slaves, continually came the sharp crack of the whip, followed by a loud howl from some poor wretch detected whispering to his neighbour, or pausing a moment in his toil. Now and then an Indian would run hurriedly away from the tables towards the village, that man having found and delivered up a pearl above a certain weight, which entitled him to a holiday until the next morning; while, again, perhaps a poor brown devil would be walked off between a couple of the soldiers who attended at the tables, and taken to the fort, there to be flogged to an inch of his life for some offence given to the overseer of the board.

Such, then, is a true picture of the pearl ranchiera, on the banks of the Rio de la Hacha. Meanwhile, days, and weeks, and at last months, slipped away, and I found myself no nearer my design of getting on board an English ship than when I left Carthagena. I went off every day in the pearl bark, and many an anxious look I cast to windward for a sail. One or two I saw, but at a great distance, and they did not seem inclined to come nearer. Indeed, the frigate being put upon its mettle by the recent attack, the governor of the fishery having, as I heard, rated the captain soundly for not keeping a better look out—the frigate, I say, was very vigilant, generally keeping to windward of the fleet; and when we remained all night at our anchors, burning blue lights and other fireworks constantly, and having all her heavy boats, with their crews armed to the teeth, rowing guard through and around the squadron, from sun-down to sun-rise, like most vigilant watchmen. Thus I did not think it probable that any privateer, excepting, indeed, a ship of great size, would dare to attack a fleet so guarded. So I considered myself almost as much a prisoner as when in the house of the Señora Moranté at Carthagena, and with as little prospect of speedy release. I panted for the sound of my countrymen's voices again, and often and often did I start from my sleep, dreaming I heard Stout Jem's hearty talk, or Nicky Hamstring's cheery laugh. Thus I got downhearted and mopish enough, and often thought of purchasing from Captain Garbo, for I was not —thanks to my friends at Carthagena—penniless, the canoe belonging to the bark, and taking my chance in her to run down before the trades to the Samballas. Indeed, the unpleasantness of my situation increased day by day. Although I spoke Spanish reasonably well, and put great restraint upon my speech, so as never to drop a hint or a word which might betray my secret, I saw that I was suspected, and two or three times I thought it best to retreat as rapidly as I could from the lowering brows and fishing questions which the crews of the other barks, and sometimes the soldiers on shore, received me with. At length, one evening, when, much against my own will, I had accompanied Captain Garbo to the posada, so many hints were dropped about ' spies,' and ' sailing under false colours,' and so many interrogatories were put to me, touching the Spanish ships in which I had sailed, and the ports from which they set forth, that I made up my mind to take the very first opportunity of leaving my present comrades. Captain Garbo, who being a good deal heated by wine, must needs defend me with great warmth, and tell many lies in his zeal, each lie being, as is generally the case, quite inconsistent with the other, made the matter worse instead of better ; and half-a-dozen times, just as the talk was turning upon something else, he would start up, and flourishing a knife in his pot-valiancy, would threaten that any man who said I was not a good comrade and a good fellow, should brook the stab. Now, among the company was one man to whom I took a special dislike, because he encouraged Garbo with all his might to defend me, at the same time dropping hints that I stood in need of the utmost eloquence which my protector could exert, and all the time slily laughing in his sleeve at both of us. This man was a squat, broad-shouldered little fellow, with a greasy, threadbare doublet, and a cunning-looking weasen face, lighted up by two bright winking eyes. He never seemed to me to sit a moment in the same position, but was always shifting about and fidgeting, and speaking here and there, to almost every one at once. This man, whom the rest called Señor Peralta, was, they told me, a merchant who came hither every year at the pearl season to purchase pearls of the chief officer of the fishery. He had a large half-decked piragua of his own, and was accounted by the Spaniards as a very adventurous and clever fellow; and being liberal with his money, and always ready to treat the commoner sort of men, as well as to sing merry songs, and crack merry jokes over his liquor, this Señor Peralta was quite a great personage in the ranchiera. The evening of which I am talking, I often observed his eyes fixed with an intent look upon me, and once or twice, as I judged, he made a sign with his hands, but what he meant I could not for the life of me divine. Next day, some accident—what it was I forget—prevented Captain Garbo taking his bark out to the bank, and so having nothing to do, I went wandering, low-hearted enough, among the sand-banks and knolls of grass down by the sea. At length, seeing a comfortable shade formed by some thick bushes, which kept off the sun, but let the sea-breeze whistle through, I sat me down, and began to think upon my project of obtaining a canoe, and chancing the run to the Samballas. While I was thus musing, I suddenly started to hear a voice near me singing softly; and I started again, and a thrill of pleasure went through my veins, when I recognised the words of the song for English. Almost afraid that I was dreaming, and fearing to awake, I listened while the musician, who appeared to lie concealed among the bushes behind me, sang with a clear, lusty voice these verses, which I remembered to have heard in the play-houses in London :—

'Sir Drake, whom well the world's end knew,
  Which thou did compass round,
And whom both poles of heaven once saw,
  Which north and south do bound.

' The starres alone would make thee knowre,
  If men were silent here ;
The sun himselfe cannot forget
  His fellow-travellere ! '

The song being ended, I turned hastily round, exclaiming aloud—'A countryman—a friend!' And at the
same time the bushes being rustled aside, out of them
popped the grinning face of Señor Peralta! I staggered
back with wonder, while the pearl-merchant called out,
in good English—

'Truly a young bird, and to be caught with the veriest
chaff! Why, man, thou art a pretty dissembler indeed,
when thou canst not hear the butt-end of an old ballad
of our country, without leaping and bellowing like a
moon-calf. I can tell thee, that had I been as unwary, I
should have danced from the end of a halter aboard
yonder frigate, long ago !'

By this time, I was recovered from my surprise, and
running up to Peralta, assisted him to scramble out of
the bushes, beseeching him at the same time to explain
to me this mystery, and tell me what he was. Before
answering one word, however, he led me quite away from
the cover of the bushes, down to the seaside. ' Where I
was hidden,' he said, ' another can hide—the open beach
keeps safer counsel.' Then sitting down upon a great
stone—the surf almost coming up to our feet—

'I suspected you for an Englishman,' quoth he, ' the
first day I saw you. And last night I took the liberty
of making myself quite sure. I don't think you liked
the process. But I am an old hand in these matters,
and he must understand his business well, who makes me
believe falsely that what he seems he is. Now, just tell
me candidly how you came here, and perhaps I may help
you to what I am pretty sure you want, and that is a
means of getting quit of our friends in the ranchiera
yonder.'

I acknowledged that he had divined my thoughts, as
well as he had penetrated my disguise ; and so, in a few
words, imparted to him some outline of my story. He
heard me out very attentively ; and then says he—

'If I were you, I would go to Jamaica, and claim my
property.'

'What property ?' I said, in amazement.

'Why,' quoth he, 'have you not heard of the fate of
the Carthagena galleon ?  She was taken two days' sail
from the coast by a privateer schooner, which I understand to be no other than yours—the Will-o'-the-Wisp.
It was the richest prize that hath been captured in these
seas for many a year.  The privateer sailed with her into
Port Royal, in Jamaica ; and as you say that the captain is
a staunch-hearted fellow ; and as Mr. Pratt, whom I know
to be a very honest gentleman, is concerned in the matter,
I do not doubt but that your share of the adventure, to
which you are fully entitled, and which must be very
considerable, will be duly accounted for to you.'

This was great news indeed.  I only lamented that I
had not been on board in the action, but the pearl merchant, who, it seems, had got his information from those
who had spoken with the mariners of the galleon, after
they landed on the main coast, being sent back in their
boats by the privateers—my pearl merchant, I say, told
me that the Spaniards having been boarded in the night,
and when they were in no posture of defence, had made
next to no resistance, and that the galleon had been very
easily secured.  Of course, this intelligence made me
doubly anxious to make my way to Jamaica, or to any
port where I could regain my comrades, and I eagerly
asked my new friend whether he could not put me in the
way of getting thither.

'Why,' says he, 'if I could not, I shouldn't have made
myself known to you at all, but the truth is, that I need
your services as a seaman.  I have got a very large
decked piragua—you may see her masts as she lies there
in the river—in which I have, as I may say, sailed the
whole Caribbean Sea.  This trip, however, I have been

Y

unfortunate, having lost a very good fellow—a negro—
my prime seaman, who died about a month ago of the
small-pox. I have but two men slaves of my own left
with me, and I was thinking where I could get a good
fourth hand, who knew somewhat about the sea, when
fortune sends you to my aid.'

I protested my willingness to serve him, and we had a
long discourse together. He told me that he was an
Englishman by birth, but that his father was a Spaniard
and his mother a Frenchwoman. Thus, he said, he had
learned from his earliest youth, a smattering of all the
three languages, and having lived long in London, Paris
and Cadiz, in after years, pursuing his craft of a jeweller
and goldsmith, he had very little difficulty, when need
was, in passing himself off for a native either of England,
France, or Spain. For some years back he had been, he
told me, sailing about the West Indies, trafficking in precious stones and gold. He had no fixed place of abode.

'Sometimes,' quoth he, 'I kneel very piously at mass,
and make the sign of the cross, in the great cathedral at
Havannah—and then I am as grave a Spaniard as the Cid.
Again, I shall sing and dance at a merry-making in
Tortuga—and, there, credit me, I bear a heart as light
and as French as ever did the good king of Yvetot.
Anon, I shall drink and shout with our good friends,
Archemboe, Davis, and the rest at Port Royal, and not a
bully of them all but shall swear I am as bluff a Briton
as jolly King Hal!'

I then intimated my hopes, that his trade so ven
turously conducted was a profitable one.

'As for that,' quoth he, 'what with my poor efforts in
the New World, and the exertions of my good correspondents at divers courts in Europe, I thank the stars
that there is more than one imperial regalia the wearer
of which oweth me more, perchance, than he will ever
pay. But I am not exacting. When a sensible man
deals with kings, if he does not get money, he can always
have money's worth.'

This speech the pearl merchant, or jeweller, delivered

with abundance of nods and winks and shrugs, as though
there were many meanings in it, out of which I was welcome to take my own. Then he whispered—

'If you would have gold cheap, know the miners. If
you would have pearls cheap, make much of the divers.
Deal at the fountain—go to the well-head—the well-head,
my son!'

At this he laughed very complacently, and I thought
it best to laugh too, although for my life I could not
fathom the meaning of the riddling words which the man
spoke, and which he accompanied with so many expressive
shrugs of the shoulders and grotesque leers, that I was
as much puzzled by what I saw, as by what I heard.
All at once, however, he broke off, and said, plainly
enough—

'Now we know each other sufficiently for the present.
My time for remaining in this oystery part of the world
will be over in two or three days, and I presume that you
will have no objections to ship in my piragua, and take
the chances of the sea to Port Royal?'

Of course I engaged to be ready at a moment's warning, and we were about to part, when he said suddenly—

'I have little to do this evening, and I suppose you
have less. Come and sup with me. Any one will show
you the hut of Peralta, the poor pearl merchant. Come
at ten.' These words he spoke with one of his habitual
leers and shrugs. I promised very readily, and then
Señor Peralta walked away demurely, counting his beads.

I lost no time in communicating to Captain Garbo
that I had now an opportunity of shortly getting a passage to one of the English islands. He was very desirous
to know how I had managed it; but upon that head I
would give him no satisfaction.

'Well,' quoth he at last, 'so be it, Señor Lindsay; but
I say, the first time you and your comrades take a Spanish
bark, be lenient to my countrymen; be as merciful as
you can to their goods and chattels for the sake of old
Manuel Garbo, the pearl fisher.'

At ten o'clock exactly I took my way over the sandy

beach to Peralta's hut, which stood a little apart from the other buildings, towards the landward extremity of the ranchiera. As I plodded along, sometimes tripping over mounds of oysters; sometimes stopping to look to seaward, where all the lights of the pearl squadron glimmered as the fleet sailed towards the shore, I suddenly heard a loud outcry, in which I could distinguish the yells of an Indian, and the gruff voices of Spaniards high in oath, and who, I conjectured, from the clash of arms, were soldiers. In a minute or two I saw faintly a dusky group of people, whites and Indians, some of them carrying lanterns, which gleamed on drawn swords and bayonets. The men bearing them disappeared through the principal gate of the fort, and then the Indians, who were left outside, raised the most pitiable cries and howls, until they were threatened by the sentries, and told they would be fired upon if they did not disperse. As I was somewhat late, I did not stop to inquire into the cause of the tumult, but I judged that it was probably occasioned by the arrest of an Indian who had committed some crime; perhaps, as was very common, stolen or secreted a valuable pearl. However, I did not think much of the matter, and soon arrived at Peralta's hut. It was a large house as compared with most of its neighbours, fenced all around with walls formed of double lines of strong tough stakes, the space between them being filled up with stones gathered apparently from the sea beach. On knocking, I was admitted by Peralta himself, who led the way into a small room, with walls roughly built of wood and stone, through which the starlight was shining at many cracks and crevices, and mingling with the smoky glimmer of a great brass lamp. The place contained but the most ordinary sort of furniture—a hammock hung in a corner, an oiled bag for holding clothes, a table, and two or three small chairs, or rather large stools. The table, however, was laid out for supper, and showed a capital repast of fish, flesh, and fowl, while a couple of flasks, with slim necks, and all cob-webbed and begrimed, as though they had long lain deep in a well-stocked cellar, made a curious contrast to the cracked crockery and wooden platters, and hacked and broken knives and forks which lay beside them.

'You see,' quoth Peralta, 'that, though I may have dealings with kings, I don't by any means live in a palace. There are idle vanities and substantial vanities, my friend. Diamonds and pearls, laces and gildings, brocades and velvets, are of the former class; but good meats to eat, and good wines to drink, are of the latter. Now you see I am an admirer of the substantial vanities. I love to feed upon the daintiest morsel, though it be picked up with a broken one-pronged fork, and I love to drink the choicest vintage of Rhine or Rhone, without at all caring whether I put my lips to a golden cup which Benvenuto hath wrought, or to a calabash which Quako hath scooped before supper.'

So saying, the pearl merchant started the cork from one of the flasks, and I tasted certainly the most delicious draught which ever tingled on my palate.

'Ha!' quoth my entertainer, as I held out the empty cup to be refilled, 'you find that better than even the the most skilful compound of rye brandy and bilge water. *C'est bien alors*—you have a palate, which I grieve to say many gentlemen of your kind and profession possess not, preferring the hot strong drinks of Jamaica, and Tortugas taverns, even, to such adorable nectar as this. Why, man, hold out thy glass again, the grand Louis himself cannot fish up a choicer flask from the most sacred crypt beneath the marble pavements of Versailles.'

Talking in this way—relating to me strange anecdotes touching great generals and statesmen, and even kings, with whom my host, to believe his words, had held familiar converse, and the moral of all these stories being, that the generals and statesmen and kings in question were as stupid, and as easily to be gulled and laughed at, as mere ordinary mortals—the supper and one of the wine flasks were soon despatched. Then, placing the fragments in a corner, Peralta produced a sort of purse or bag of filigree workmanship, in bright silver, and which seemed to be the only thing of price in his dwelling—always excepting the meats and wines— and taking from it some tobacco of most delicate savour, we began to smoke and discuss the second bottle, which was of a different kind from the first, the wine being of a deep rich red tinge, and coming, as he told me, from Dijon, in Burgundy.

While we sat thus, my entertainer took almost all the conversation to himself. He spoke of things new and strange to me : of the crown jewels of mighty potentates pledged to rich Hebrews dwelling in the filthy back lanes of the cities of Europe—in the Jewry of London, the Judenstrasse of Frankfort, and the Ghetto of Rome.

'And your brave Christian goes past, stopping his nose for the savours of fish fried in oil, and elbowing and jostling the hook-nosed, shabby old men who make way, with many a ' Give you good e'en, my lord ;' and ' Faugh !' says he, ' these stinking unbelievers ; why be they not packed bodily off to their holy city again' — and so passes he by, to kneel, and cringe, and kiss the king's hand ; while all the time—ha ! ha ! ha !—that very king is thinking and pondering in his small mind how best he can squeeze the next subsidy out of his faithful cities and towns, and so release the brightest jewel in the regalia, now held in pawn by old Isaac, or old Jacob, or old Abraham, the very dirtiest, raggedest, yellowest-skinned and hookedest-nosed of the whole brotherhood—ha ! ha ! ha !'

The pearl merchant said this with so much gusto, and laughed with so much glee, that I began to think he must be one of the fraternity himself. He seemed to divine my thoughts, for, as if I had spoken them, he, as it were, replied—

'No, no, no ! Señor Buccaneer, although I have much traffic with the seed of Abraham, I am none of their kindred ; were I such, I would be wiser than to come here to live in a sty on this scorching coast, driving hard bargains for sick oysters.'

My entertainer then went on with his stories of
European courts, and I was listening with open mouth,
as he told, with many a quip and many a sneer, how,
under the guidance of one Chiffinch, he had one night
passed up the back stairs at Whitehall to hold a secret interview with Louise de Querailles, since Duchess of Portsmouth, touching certain jewels which it was convenient
to raise money upon until there should come a remittance
from the court of Versailles, through Monseigneur
Barillon, the ambassador of Louis; when all at once
there came a loud rap, accompanied by a shrill whistle, at
the door.  Peralta started quickly up, but without appearing at all discomposed, and opening the door with speed, a
handsome fellow, a mulatto, dressed like a sailor, bounded
in, exclaiming at the same moment, in a loud whisper:

' Juan and Blanco are both detected!'

Then seeing me, he stopped as suddenly as though he
had been shot.  But Peralta speedily reassured him.

' Go on, man; go on.  He who standeth there is my
friend ; he is one of us.  Go on.  Have they confessed ?'

' All,' replied the mulatto.  ' They first told the truth,
and then a great deal more than the truth, in hopes the
better to save their necks.  I squeezed in with them
into the fort, and heard it all.  The soldiers are coming.
I heard the order given.'

Peralta stood still for a moment, and then said hurriedly,
' Doth it blow ?'

The mulatto replied, that there was a light air only,
from the eastward.

' With the tide two hours on the ebb.  That will do
well.  Disco is on board the piragua ?'

The mulatto nodded eagerly.  Peralta turned to me—
' I suppose,' quoth he, ' you have no objection to make a
start of it this very hour ?'

' None, none,' I replied ; wondering with my whole soul
at the meaning of this strange scene.

' Follow me, then, and do as I do,' replied Peralta.
He swallowed his last cup of wine, and smiled when he
saw me copying his example to the letter.  Then, blow-

ing the lamp out, we all three sallied forth into the
night, walking quickly but cautiously amongst the
scattered huts. I knew that it was no time for questions, so put none, though I was almost bursting with
curiosity. In a minute or two we heard the measured
tramp of soldiers advancing, and presently the clash of
their arms and the gleam of their lamps burst forth
together as they marched round the corner of a small
street, followed by a great many Indians. There was a
hollow place close by where we stood, with ridges of
oyster shells on either side. Into this Peralta sank
suddenly, flinging himself flat upon the ground, while the
mulatto and I followed his example. In a minute the
soldiers marched by, with their attendant rout of Indians
gabbling and chattering very eagerly.

'Now,' quoth Peralta, 'for the beach, and make as
little noise as you can in running.'

With these words off he set, going over the ground
much faster than to look at him I should have thought
possible. However, the mulatto and I kept close behind
him, meeting nobody, although we heard a distant tumult
of voices in the ranchiera, and the tramp of people running hither and thither. There were half a dozen skiffs
and canoes moored to as many stakes rising from a small
slippery jetty, and sheering backwards and forwards as
the current of the ebbing tide ran swiftly beneath them.
Into the outermost of these skiffs Peralta leaped as
nimbly and steadily as if he had been a waterman at
Whitehall Stairs, we following closely upon his heels ;
but just as we had, as by instinct, sat down to the oars,
Peralta cried out to us to hold, and then stepping back
upon the jetty, very coolly cast loose the painters of the
whole of the remainder of the boats from their fastenings, and gathering the ends of the ropes together, as a
coachman does his reins, he shuffled back again into the
stern sheets, casting off our moorings as he passed by,
and then, with a low chuckle to himself, we pushed off
and rowed into the stream, the squadron of boats following in our wake.

'Pull away, my good fellows,' Peralta then said, taking an oar out of one of the skiffs behind us, 'I will steer you.' Our course was down the stream, and we swept along very rapidly, while, looking back, we could see, by the lights which came dancing all down the beach from the houses, that the Spaniards were in hard pursuit. In a minute more a cluster of these lanterns shone upon the jetty, and instantly their bearers raised a clamour and shouting that all the boats were gone. Señor Peralta only laughed to himself.

'Well,' he muttered in a moment or two, 'it is a shabby way to leave old friends, but needs must when the devil or an angry Spaniard drives.'

All this time we were shooting swiftly down the river, the broad surface of which, gleaming in the starlight, now began to heave and undulate, as the swells of the sea, rolling over the bar, affected it. As we pulled, Peralta, taking advantage of a great shout faintly heard from the shore, hailed, 'Disco! Disco, ahoy!'

A long shrill whistle was the reply, and, looking round, we saw the low dusky form of the piragua, with her two high raking masts, and, pausing on our oars, we heard the rush of the tide against her sharp bows.

'Disco is all awake,' said Peralta, and in a moment more we were alongside and tumbling into the piragua, which, notwithstanding her very considerable size, was so light as to rock violently as, one by one, we leaped over her gunwale.

Disco himself, a Musquito Indian, as I judged him, appeared to have been just aroused by the clamour on shore, and he asked eagerly what the matter was.

'The matter,' said Peralta, 'is, that we must get to sea as soon as we can. Thank God the breeze comes fresher—that puff quite ruffled the water. Jenipa,' this was to the mulatto, 'jump forward and cut the cable— no time for weighing. Disco, get a sweep or an oar out on the larboard bows to cant her head round. Lindsay, bear a hand, my man, and get the canvas upon her, or some of our friends ashore will be swimming down upon us with their knives in their teeth.'

The coolness of Peralta was capital to see. Just as Jenipa's knife went with a cheep through the strands of the hemp, Disco's oar dashed into the water, and the stream catching the larboard bows of the piragua, she swung round with her head towards the shore we had just left, while Peralta, who worked as though he had been afloat all his life, flung loose the foresail from the long supple bamboo yard, and then both of us clapping on to the haulyards with all our might, the light canvas, all dripping with the night dew, rose steadily to the top of the mast, and then catching the faint puff of the sea breeze, which has but little power when it blows in the night-time, the sail swelled gracefully out, while Peralta, with the sheet in his hand, leaped aft, catching hold of the tiller, and calling to us all to get the mainsail upon the piragua. We were, as the reader may guess, in no humour for trifling, and accordingly the big lugsail was very soon hoisted by rapid jerks, up the mast, and when, after having made fast the haulyards, and trimmed the sheet aft, I paused a moment and looked round, I was quite bewildered. The breeze was hardly sufficient to keep the wide sails sleeping. I heard no loud rushing gurgle, such as a vessel makes travelling fast through the water ; yet the lights upon shore were flying by us as though we were borne on horseback towards the sea—the great white flakes and stripes of froth which had floated into the river from the bar, glanced past, showing like light veins and streaks in dark marble—while the skiffs which Peralta had cut loose were almost out of sight astern.

I uttered an exclamation of wonder, at which Peralta laughed pleasantly.

'Your Will-o'-the-Wisp may be fast, Señor Buccaneer,' he said, 'but no craft that ever came off the stocks of European ship-builders will sail with the boats which the Indians—savages we call them—can scoop with rude tools out of a single glorious tree. Do we not move like an apparition—a sea spirit ? Let the Spaniards chase us in their clumsy wooden boxes, the piragua will earn her right to her name though all the navy of Old and New Spain were flashing in her wake. I call her the "Ghost;" does not she glide like one fleeting to the sepulchre at the first glimpse of the light of the morning?'

I looked at Peralta, beginning to suspect that the sudden flurry, coming after the humming wine, caused him to vapour a little—but, if it were so, he very soon came to himself.

'Hark!' said Disco, 'the surf on the bar.'

'And see,' added Jenipa, 'the lights of the Pearl Fleet close to in the offing.'

'Forward, and look out, both of you,' cried Peralta, sharply. 'Keep your eyes open on either bow.'

Meantime I crouched down by the steersman on the weather-quarter. The lofty lights of the frigate were much further to sea than the squadron she guarded. Indeed, the great ship cared not for approaching too closely the many banks and spits of sand, which run out from the bar, and over which most of the smaller barks could float very well. The leading ships, however, appeared to be as close to the bar on one side as we were on the other.

'Now,' said Peralta, 'grant that the stupidity of those fellows on shore will keep them from making any signal to their comrades out at sea.' But the words were hardly out of his mouth, when the water and the sky were lit up with a mighty flash, and the loud report of a great gun—a small battery of which was planted before the fort—came rolling down the river; and immediately afterwards a straggling volley of small arms rattled all along the bank, as though the soldiers were dispersed and running down towards the sea. By this time, the white water on the bar was close ahead.

'Starboard—starboard. Keep her a little away, master, the channel is on the lee-bow,' cried Disco. The course of the piragua was altered accordingly, and glancing ahead, I saw the streak of dark water, leading to the open sea; at the same time that the fleet of pearl fishers answered the alarm from ashore, by kindling torches, waving lanterns, and shouting and blowing horns, just as they had done the night that the privateer had swooped down in the centre of them, and carried off one of the very best in his clutch. At this moment, we having drawn clear of the sand hills on shore, the breeze freshened, sweeping down the coast, heavy with the dew of the night air. The light sails swelled stiffly out, the sheets tautened, the thin supple masts swayed and creaked, and the few ropes which stayed them upon the weather-side stretched out as rigid as iron-bars. And yet the piragua flew by every swell which rolled in from the offing—not plunging into the great green seas, and flashing the foam sparklingly up into the air, but moving rather like a bird, which, with spreading and far-stretched pinion, just glances over the sea, rather flying than swimming—borne more by the winds than the waves. Truly, I had never sailed in so wonderfully-fashioned a craft—so thin and slight was her construction, that she appeared, as it were, to yield, and bend, and quiver in the seas—but ever on, gaily and lightsomely, she went, sliding, as it were, without noise and without shock, leaping with a quick, buoyant, bounding motion, right over and over the swells, which now, as the water shoaled upon the bar, began to roll by us, white with milky foam. Verily, Peralta did well when he likened his piragua to a noise-less gliding ghost.

While I was still wrapped in amazement at the per-formances of the canoe, she was flying across the bar in the very midst of the fleet of pearl fishers. The whole thing passed over me like a vision—a dream of flashing foaming water, plunging and dripping ships, with their canvas flapping, and their booms, and yards, and ropes, creaking and moaning, and rattling together—of fierce, eager faces, and hurrying, dusky forms, running on the decks, leaping into the riggings, flashing their torches and lanterns; shouting, yelling, and hailing the piragua and Peralta to lie to, and put about—and some of them flourishing glimmering knives and firing pistols in the air

All this, I say, appeared to pass by me like a vision, or a dream—and it only lasted for a few brief moments—for the piragua, which was steered in a fashion which made me look upon Peralta as a sailor rather than a merchant, flew through the panic-struck squadron, who could no more catch her, than they could the shadow of her tall sails upon the water. Once, and once only, a heavy hook or grapnel, attached to a stout line, was flung by a lusty arm, and lighted in the piragua's fore-rigging, but even before the rope had tightened, Disco leaped to the spot, his knife flashed, the severed hemp fell back into the sea, and the useless iron tumbled down into the bottom of the canoe. The next moment we were fairly at sea, with the whole of the squadron, save one or two loiterers, behind us. Just then the frigate, who was a couple of miles or so in the offing, fired a heavy cannon, and showed a number of lights, by which we saw swarms of men, rushing from the high carved bulwarks into the rigging, as if they designed to make sail in all haste.

'Ho! ho! ho!' laughed Peralta. 'Here comes the elephant chasing the weasel, and the elephant thinks that the best way to begin the race is to roar a little.'

And, indeed, any attempt of the big ship to follow us would have been just about as hopeless a chase as that to which Peralta had likened it. So, after firing a few more guns, whether with shot in them or not we neither knew nor cared, she stood cautiously in for the bar of the river, sending her boats before her, as we conjectured, to learn the cause of all the uproar. Meantime we had struck a light, keeping the lantern, however, well masked, and then setting the head of the boat about nor-nor-west, that being as near the wind as we could lie, and at the same time make good way through the water, we trimmed the sails neatly, and cried, 'Northward Ho! for Jamaica.'

For about an hour, during which time little was spoken, Peralta held the helm. He then called us all round him, and apportioned the watches in the ordinary seaman fashion—I being placed with Disco, and he taking his turn of duty with Jenipa. This settled, we tossed up whose watch should begin first, and it falling to the turn of Disco and myself, Peralta gave me the helm, instructing me, as I was not well acquainted with the management of piraguas, to call him if the wind freshened so much as to seem to demand the taking in of a reef. Then creeping beneath the half-deck, which extended from the bows to abaft the foremast, he coiled himself up along with Jenipa, and the pair went very quietly to sleep. During our watch, which was tranquil, I tried to obtain some information from the Indian touching the habits and pursuits of his master, and also relating to the causes of our very sudden departure. But the fellow, although he would talk glibly enough upon the weather, or the piragua, or the manner of our escape, was as close as wax as regarded everything else. Indeed, he reminded me very truly that I ought to know more about the reason of our departure than he, having come from the shore, while he had been sleeping on board the piragua. At that I told him what I had heard from Jenipa, about Juan and Blanco having been detected and taken to the fort, where they had confessed not only the truth, but, as I had heard, more than the truth. The Mosquitto man merely shrugged his shoulders, and said he could make nothing of it, although I saw very well, by the intelligent look of the fellow's face, as the binnacle lamp shone upon his bronzed features, that he understood much more of the matter than he chose to confess. Finding I could make nothing of the Indian, I set myself to consider the whole affair, and putting Peralta's hints about the way to get pearls cheap, in connexion with what I had actually witnessed and heard, I was not long in arriving at the conclusion, that, in all probability, for every pearl which the merchant bought of the captain of the fishery, he obtained another, and at a very considerably cheaper rate, by dealing quietly with the openers themselves, to which class I concluded that Juan and Blanco must belong. This solution of the riddle seemed the more probable, when I remembered much that I had heard touching the great number of pearls supposed to be

secreted by the Indians, in spite of the utmost vigilance
of the Spaniards. Jamaica sloops had, I knew, ere now
gone to hover near the Rio de la Hacha, having their
agents and correspondents, in various disguises, lurking
upon the coast, and of course keeping up communication
with the Indian divers and openers; but the adroitness
and courage shown by Peralta in living as a Spaniard
openly amongst Spaniards, and supporting the character
of a regular pearl merchant, communicating with the
captain of the fishery, while in reality he was driving the
best part of his trade by underhand dealing with the
Indians, conducted, no doubt, at great and constant risk
of detection and death; all this inspired me with no
small respect for the abilities and the nerve of the owner
of the piragua. Then I thought with what cool general-
ship he had conducted the retreat, not losing a moment
by delay, yet taking his measures with as great composure
and deliberation as if he were departing upon a pleasure
cruise. Afterwards, I began to wonder that I had not
observed him, when leaving the hut, take with him the
amount of pearls which I felt sure that he must have
amassed; but a few minutes' reflection convinced me,
from the perfect unconcern with which he had walked
out of the hut, not caring to pick up any one article of
those strewn about, that all the valuables which he possessed on shore, he carried constantly concealed about
his person. Indeed, in the matter of such costly toys as
pearls, or precious stones, a man's own garments formed
by far the safest depository to be found in the ranchiera.

While brooding over these things, the night passed
silently away. With the grey dawn, Peralta relieved me,
and we crept in our turn under the half-deck, and slept
until the sun rose high into the unclouded heaven, and
the piragua was staggering along under reefed canvas,
bending over to the whistling trade-wind, and leaping
from sea to sea, like a hunted stag. During the day,
little of note occurred. Peralta avoided taking me
further into his confidence, and I had tact enough to see
that I ought to refrain from seeming to intrude upon his

mystery. As I watched him, however, I often saw him
bite his thin lips, and wrinkle his forehead, and clench
his hand, as if distressing thoughts haunted him; and at
last he broke out, addressing nobody in particular, but
speaking moodily to himself—

'Those poor fellows!' he cried, 'those poor fellows
Juan and Blanco—I would give every pearl the venture
hath brought that they were safe and sound in this
piragua. The Spaniards will hang them; nay, indeed, it
may have been already done, and their bodies are swinging in this same sea-breeze!'

Here Jenipa interposed very respectfully, and said that
no effort we could have possibly made would have sufficed
to rescue the Indians, and that we had nothing to
reproach ourselves with on that score.

' No, no,' said Peralta. 'We could not have got them
out of trouble; but we have been the cause that they fell
into it.'

He pondered for a minute. Then putting his hand
into his bosom, he drew it forth, the hollow of the palm
filled with small pearls, all glistening in the sun, like
beads of frozen milk. Then he poured the precious
morsels from one hand to the other, the pearls pattering
and rattling like chips of shivered glass and pebbles, and
began again to speak, like a man who talks in his sleep.

' Ay,' he cried, 'and you will sparkle in the coronets of
nobles, or mayhap you will rise and fall on the white
bosom of some peerless beauty across the western sea.
Little will she think how her braveries have been won.
Little will she think that the gems of her adornment are
but as coagulated drops of human blood. Red, red, you
ought to be, and not of that lying virgin whiteness—red,
red, you ought to be, as the guilt of him who hath
purveyed you, and the blood of the hapless men who, ere
now, are doubtless but as lumps of brown carrion—only
good to feed the vultures and the crows!'

At this, I observed Jenipa and Disco exchange curious
glances with each other; but Peralta, after musing for a
short space further, put the pearls back into their hiding-

place, and resumed, to a certain degree, his usual manner.

'I doubt not,' he said to me, presently, 'but that your acuteness hath taught you much of what last night you burned to know. The two poor savages, of whom I spoke, were indeed my agents among their brethren; and, thanks to their ingenuity and courage, many a rare pearl hath come to my wallet, instead of the poke of their Spanish task-masters. But all is over now. While I remained on shore, I risked the danger borne by my confederates. Had it been within the power of man to have saved them, I would have perilled limbs and life to bring them off, but it fell out otherwise. What is writ, is writ. Adieu, poor Juan and Blanco, and may you find the next world a better one than this.'

Having pronounced this curious sort of funeral oration, Peralta straightway resumed his former demeanour, and I never heard him allude to the subject again. Meantime, we bounded merrily across the ocean, masts bending, canvas swelling, and sheet and haulyard cracking and straining; the blue heaven, with not a cloud to fleck it, all a blaze of azure light and glory above, and the crystal sea foaming, and tumbling, and gambolling beneath the swift piragua, as, with dripping prow and polished sides, she tore away upon her headlong course. My spirits, long drooping under captivity, now came flushing back, sending the young hot blood tingling through my veins. I leaped and danced about the piragua for very cheery-heartedness—Peralta smiling slily at my antics—and sometimes lifting up my voice, I sang an echoing chorus to the music of wind and wave! 'A day or two,' I thought, 'and I shall see, sleeping in the smooth water landward of the Palisades, my gallant schooner, which I love, and hear ringing from beneath her snow-white awning the cheery voices of my old comrades, of Stout Jem, the true-hearted, and Nicky Hamstring, the merry-minded!'

Alas! not so fast, Leonard Lindsay—not so fast! There are perils and sufferings for you, by sea and land, ere you step upon English ground again!

## CHAPTER XXV.

THE PIRAGUA IS PICKED UP BY A GREAT PRIVATEER, AND I FIND
MYSELF AMONG NEW SHIPMATES.

WE were within a day's sail of Jamaica.    At the setting
of the sun we had seen, even from our low vessel, the
distant outline of the Blue Mountains.    Peralta had the
middle watch.    I roused up about an hour and a half
before sunrise, and found the piragua heaving upon
smooth, oily swells, all unruffled even by a puff of wind.
There was a great dank mist around us, packing upon the
water as thick as smoke from a man-of-war's broadside,
and the very air seemed loaded with chill damp.    I
walked up and down the small fore deck of the piragua,
trying, in my thin garments, to keep myself warm, and
whistling for a breeze to blow away to leeward the filthy
fog, which seemed, as it were, to enclose us round, and to
cling and settle in its densest volume about the piragua.
Standing at the bows, I could not see the stern, and as
for the heads of the sails they were lost in the thick
opaque air.    It was curious to gaze out upon the water
as the black looking undulations of the sea rolled under
us, the mist seeming to rise and fall with them, and
sometimes boiling and eddying from the motion of the
waves, although not a breath of wind strayed over the
ocean.    I might have been upon duty about half an hour,
when I almost leaped from the deck with amazement to
hear suddenly, coming from whence I knew not, but
ringing shrilly through the thick air, a loud cry or scream,
like that uttered by a man in mortal anguish.

'Disco,' I shouted, 'did you hear that ?    What was
that cry ?'

But the Indian, instead of answering me, stood dumb
and trembling, as though struck with terror.    Instantly
the cry was repeated, and even louder and more vehemently than before.

'It is a spirit,' said the Indian.    'It is some bad spirit
of the fog.    It will come to us and kill us.'

But I heeded not the superstition of the ignorant creature, and made but one bound to where Peralta lay sound asleep, clutching and shaking him to arouse him, and telling him in the same breath that there was either a ship or a boat close aboard of us in the fog. The pearl merchant and Jenipa were upon their legs in a moment, and for the space of about ten minutes we listened with all our ears, but heard no sound, other than the flapping of our sails and the creaking of the yards, as they rubbed and swayed against the masts. It was odd that, although both Disco and myself heard the cry so distinctly repeated, we neither of us could tell the direction from which it appeared to come. Perhaps the fog affected sounds passing through it. At all events, although we got out the oars, we knew not in which way to row, so as to put as much sea as possible between a ship which might very likely be an enemy, and which would certainly be more than a match for the light piragua and her crew of four. All this while the dawn was gradually brightening through the mist; the fog, which before was of a pitchy darkness, becoming gradually of a pale grey hue, and then lifting and opening here and there, so as to show lanes, as it were, and patches of clear air, which, in the next moment, would be again filled up by rolling masses of the vapour. However, the mist was evidently thinning as the sun approached to the horizon, and we watched warily to catch the first glimpse of our unknown neighbour. Presently, the fog began to change its cold white hue for a tinge or blush of warm and golden light, which appeared, as it were, to penetrate and pervade the vapour, and by which we knew that the sun had risen ; while, at the same time, our glimpses into the ever-shifting lanes and clear spaces continually being formed by the motion of the seething wreaths and masses of vapour, becoming every moment longer and clearer— Peralta, who was standing upon the starboard gunwale of the piragua, suddenly exclaimed, in a low, earnest tone : There ! look there !'

We all turned round at once, and saw, not thirty

fathoms from us, the dusky broadside and towering rigging of a ship. She was gracefully rocking upon the long seas, the mist all curling round her, and floating, as it appeared, in blurring patches and masses among her extended sails, so that the masts and all the fabric of spars and canvas which they bore were half lost in the bewildering vapour. We had no time, however, to make any very minute examination of the stranger. She saw us as soon as we saw her, and half a dozen men, clustering into the main rigging, shouted out, in French and English, that we should pull the piragua alongside. I looked at Peralta. He slightly shrugged his shoulders. ' If there were but a bladder full of wind,' he said.

' Ho ! the piragua ahoy !' was now again hailed from the strange ship—' come alongside, d'ye hear, or it will be the worse for you.'

This threat had hardly been uttered, when, as if to back it, a cannon was fired from the maindeck, and we heard the ball, with a loud whistling hiss, pass above our masts. But the discharge of that gun had an effect which seemed almost miraculous upon the fog, clearing away, and, as it were, condensing and annihilating, by the shock of the explosion the vapour all around—so that we saw, very plainly, a goodly ship of three masts, carrying at least twelve cannons upon a side, with top-sails and top-gallant-sails spread, but the yards braced clumsily, the canvas ill set, and much of the rigging in a loose and disorderly condition—the jib indeed hanging in great festoons down from the bowsprit—so that when the ship plunged by the head, the canvas dipped into the sea, from which it would presently arise, the water pouring from the belly of the sail as from a tub. On board this disorderly-looking craft there seemed to be a great swarm of men, who suddenly clustered upon the bulwarks and in the rigging to gaze at us, and one of whom, a varlet with long unkempt hair and torn and dirty linen doublet, suddenly screamed out—

' Why, comrades, never believe your eyes—if it be not Old Rumbold of Port Royal in Jamaica, and Heaven

knows how many places besides. What cheer, Old
Rumbold?—Hast been a privateering in a bark canoe—
or chaffering with and cheating the honest Indians of the
Main?'

Peralta seemed in no way put out by this recognition,
for he immediately took off his hat very gallantly, and
called out that he was heartily glad to meet with so many
friends and gallant gentlemen adventurers on the high
seas. Upon which the men on board the ship cheered
lustily, and shouted to Peralta or Rumbold that he was
an honest fellow, and that he must come aboard, with all
his people, and that we should have a jovial cruise
together. I watched the pearl-merchant, and saw that he
was in reality much concerned at this unexpected stoppage
of our voyage.

'Had it not been for that cursed fog,' he whispered,
'this would not have happened. But these fellows are
savages if their temper be crossed. We must e'en row
with the tide and humour them.'

Accordingly the piragua was speedily floating alongside
the great ship, and, following Rumbold, as I may now
call him, I clambered up the high sides. But what a
sight did the deck present to me—a sailor hitherto
accustomed to orderly vessels. Strewn everywhere about
were great heaps of luggage and ship stores—trunks and
mails mingled with coils of rope, and masses of sails—
buckets, boat anchors, flags, handspikes, and what not—
while, tumbled hither and thither in this chaos, sprawled
more than a score of drunken seamen, some of them fast
asleep and snoring, with empty bottles and glasses still
grasped in their hands—others, still sitting up, babbling
and singing, in maudlin fashion, over their liquor—or
disputing fiercely with thickened speech and blood-shot
eyes. The relics of a feast lay scattered over the decks,
slippery with the wine and liquors spilt upon them.
There were broken glasses and empty flasks, the smashed
fragments of tobacco-pipes, divers dice-boxes, and packs
of greasy cards. But the principal object on which my
attention dwelt was the form of a stalwart, big-limbed

sailor, who lay with his head resting on the knee of a man who was tending a hurt upon his temples. Looking more closely, I saw that the wounded man had received a desperate slash with a knife, which had laid open the side of his forehead and part of the cheek, narrowly missing the eye. From this gash the blood was pouring fast, while the surgeon, for such he was, who tended the wounded man, cleaned the ghastly cut, from time to time, with sponges dipped in hot water, while he prepared his instruments to sew it up. The patient was insensible, breathing hard and loud, and having his glazed eyes open, and gleaming with a wild, vacant stare. As I gazed, I immediately comprehended that it was the cry uttered by this man, as he was wounded, which had alarmed us in the piragua, and looking towards the bows, I saw a fellow, with his doublet-sleeve all bloody, being marched off in custody by a group of his comrades—all high in oath at the cowardly hound of a Portuguese, (as they called him,) who had used his knife instead of his fists in a quarrel among friends.

Meantime, Rumbold seemed to be heartily welcomed by the more sober part of the crew, with the captain, as I judged him, at their head. This captain was a long gaunt man, with a slouching gait, and lank black hair falling straight down upon his shoulders. He had such a squint that it was, as I afterwards knew, a common saying in the ship about Le Chiffon Rouge—for such he, being a Frenchman, was called—that no one could tell at any moment whether he was looking forward or aft, up to the vane on the mast-head, or down into the hold. This ill-favoured personage—for besides his squinting eye he had an ugly hare lip, showing tusks which would not have been out of place in the jaw of a boar,—this ill-favoured personage, I say, protested loudly that his good friend Rumbold must positively sail out the cruize with them—that he would not be denied—and that the hills of Jamaica being in sight, for the mist had rapidly cleared away with the rising of the sun, the two Indians could very well carry home the piragua, while hammocks would be slung aboard for the worthy pearl merchant and his friend—meaning me. The captain was well seconded in these propositions by the chief mate, who was an Englishman, a coarse, fat personage, with bristling red hair, a ferocious expression, and a loud harsh voice. He was called Jerry, and I soon found that he was the real commander of the ship; Le Chiflon Rouge yielding to his judgment in all cases of emergency, and the pair keeping very close together. Now, for my own part, I was much puzzled to know the reason of this welcome, which was so much warmer than we wished for. If the ship was a friendly one, why did not she go her way and leave us to go ours, instead of detaining us prisoners; for that was what the affair actually came to, on board. I saw that Rumbold's countenance was clouded, and that, although he put a good face on the matter, he would have freely given a round sum for a start of a league or so in the piragua. But wishing was useless. The Indians, who continued in the canoe, were, to their great astonishment, ordered to run for Port Royal, and to take word that Mr. Rumbold had joined the good ship, 'Saucy Susan,' for a short run down by the Mosquitto coast, and that she might be expected in Jamaica in a few weeks. By this time the morning trade-wind was beginning to blow, and the piragua speedily crept away, wafted by its first faint fannings. Then Jerry suddenly began to bestir himself—

'Here,' he shouted, 'here men, clear away the decks, fore and aft. You, boatswain, get the yards braced, and put all things aloft ship-shape and Bristol fashion. What! d——n my eyes, is the ship to be always in this cursed mess? Here, you two boatswain's mates, come and kick these drunken hogs. Overboard with barrel and bucket. Draw water, will you, and souse these fellows who are littering the deck, soundly. Curse and confound me, but a parcel of wild Indians would have more decency aboard ship! Doctor, how is that fellow's skull? We shall serve out the thief who cut him, presently. Come, men, look alive there, or by all the devils

dancing in hell, I'll make you feel the flat of my cutlass !'

At this energetic speech there was a general bustle on
deck.  About half of the drunken fellows staggered to
their feet, and began to tumble about, half asleep, lurch-
ing and pitching against each other, owing to the roll of
the ship.

' Quick, will you there !'  Jerry roared ;  ' get the
buckets full, and baptise these brandy kegs ;' pointing to
the drunkards, who were still sleeping.  In a minute a
dozen pails were over the ship's sides, and immediately,
amid shouts of jeering and laughter, copious floods of the
cooling brine were dashed over the heads and bodies of
the snorers, who started up all bewildered, shouting and
spluttering, half-choked, and swearing at such scurvy
treatment.  However, in a few minutes a wonderful
transformation was effected—the decks were cleared—
those of the crew who had not sufficiently slept off their
debauch to be able to resume their duty, were tumbled
down the hatches to their hammocks—the yards were
braced properly for the course which we were lying—a
steady-looking old seaman was at the wheel, and the
' Saucy Susan' began to move slowly upon her course,
rising heavily to the seas, and butting at them with her
great broad bows as they came rolling past.

Meantime, I kept alongside of Rumbold—to whom the
captain was explaining, with great gravity, that having
last night taken a small Spanish sloop, aboard which
there was very excellent wine, the greater part of the
crew had been drunk all night, a thing, he admitted, not
very seamanlike : ' But what then—what could he do ?
*Messieurs les aventuriers* would have their way.'  Presently,
however, stepping forward to confer with Jerry, who was
certainly bringing the ship into hand again, in the style of
a man who knows his business, Rumbold whispered to me :

' I know something of this ship.  She is manned by
the worst set of rogues who sail from Jamaica.  There
may be some honest men aboard, but both the Frenchman
and Jerry, his mate, are as great rascals as ever rode colt

foaled of an acorn, and I doubt it not but that a crew of
their choosing will be found to match bravely.'

I inquired what he thought were the reasons which induced them to detain us on board?

' Why, as to that,' says he, ' I doubt not but that some
of the rogues have a shrewd guess where I come from,
and that I have pearls of price about me. I hardly think
they would rob me openly and divide the booty in the
face of day, but there are dozens of these cursed jail
birds who would think no more of drawing a knife across
a man's weasand while he slept, if that would help them
to filch a brass-farthing's worth, than I would of smoking
a whiff of tobacco.'

Then Rumbold asked whether I recognised the young
fellow who first hailed him by name? and presently
pointed him out, laughing and talking to Jerry. ' I know
the rascal well,' said the pearl merchant. ' He hath
nimble wits and nimble fingers. I warrant 'twas he first
tipped Jerry and the captain the wink in this matter. If
it be so, depend upon it that the three intend to keep the
thing snug to themselves, and share the plunder—that is,
if they can get it.'

Our converse was broken up by the captain and mate
walking aft together. The vessel was by this time put
into proper trim, and standing on her course, with sails
very well set, and swelling gaily in the breeze. The
mate looked to windward. ' I think the weather will
hold steady,' he said. Immediately, the captain shouted
out to the boatswain to call all hands, and, presently, in
answer to that shrill, sharp whistle, which penetrates
down to the very keel of a ship, the crew tumbled upon
deck, most of them being by this time sober enough, and
trooped aft to the break of the poop, upon which Le Chiffon Rouge and Jerry stood. The ship was then hove to,
with her broad maintop-sail laid to the mast, and Le
Chiffon Rouge taking off his three-cornered hat, as it was
the custom of the captain of a privateer to do when he
addressed the whole crew, began to speak in a smooth,
plausible fashion, to this effect—

' Last night, gentlemen, as you well know, the "Saucy
Susan" captured a Spanish sloop, out of which we took
what we wanted, and then dismissed her. You cannot
complain, any of you, that you had not as much of the
good wine which we found aboard the sloop, as you could
swill, with plenty of time and space to drink it in. But,
gentlemen, here hath an ugly accident turned out in your
revelry, and which it behoves me to inquire into. One of
our honourable company hath drawn his knife, and
wounded a comrade, in his cups, and that, by all the
rules of privateers-men, must be punished. It is not
that I much care about a kick on the shins, or a box on
the ears, given or taken when the wine cup is full, and
the dice-box rattling—but cold steel, comrades, we must
keep for the Spaniards, and not get into the habit of po-
lishing our knives against each other's ribs.'

The crew applauded this address, which seemed reasonable enough; but Rumbold whispered to me, that he
would lay his life upon it that either Le Chiffon Rouge,
or Jerry, had some cause of spite against the Portuguese;
otherwise, said he, the whole ship's company might hack
the flesh off each other's bones without interference.

' Now then,' continued the scowling captain, ' some of
you fetch Vasco, of Lisbon, hither, and Doctor, do you
bring up Shambling Ned.' So, in a few minutes, the
Portuguese, with his hands tied behind him, was hurried
along the deck, and the wounded man came out of the
cabin, leaning upon the surgeon, and looking very pale,
his blood still clotted in jelly-looking masses among his
long hair. Vasco, in spite of his great name, seemed to
me to be as hang-dog looking a rascal as ever I saw, with
a low flat forehead, and only one eye. He was a lithe,
slightly made young fellow, with a thin, ragged beard and
drooping moustache. When he was confronted with the
captain and Jerry, the latter cast a look upon him so full
of hate and spite, that I soon perceived that Rumbold
was in the right in his conjecture. The Portuguese
never appeared to notice the wounded man at all.

' Now, then,' the captain began, ' you, Shambling Ned,

'tell us how you came by that trench upon your fore-head.'

But Shambling Ned, who was, as I have said, a stout seaman, but with a hitch in his gait, from whence he obtained his nickname, gave but a very confused account of the transaction. What between the quantity of wine which he had drunk, and the quantity of blood which he had lost, his wits appeared to be still gone a wool-gather-ing, and all that he could say was, that he had been play-ing dice for small stakes with the Portuguese, when they had a quarrel about a cast, and that blows had passed; but who had struck first he really did not know; that in the middle of the scuffle, however, when they were staggering about among their comrades and tripping over the masses of goods and stores which lay upon the deck, he suddenly saw a knife in the hand of his adver-sary, and, almost at the same instant, he had received the violent cut upon his head, from which the hot blood came pouring down; that after that he knew nothing, until he was brought to himself by the smart of the surgeon's instrument sewing up the wound.

The evidence of several of the seamen was then taken, but they all gave different accounts; some maintaining that Vasco had begun the fray, and others that Sham-bling Ned had first seized up a knife himself, so that I saw very plainly that the whole affair was the effect of a drunken squabble, in which one was probably as much to blame as another. At last, however, the young man who had recognised Rumbold, stood forth, and I saw very plainly the glance of intelligence which passed between him and Jerry.

'Now for Tommy Nixon's testimony,' said the captain; 'and I warrant that he will speak more to the purpose than these noddies there, who seem to make no more use of their eyes than if they were boiled gooseberries!'

So Nixon began to speak in a low, whining sort of tone, professing great regret for the disturbance, and particularly that Vasco, whom he said he loved as though he had been his own brother, should have so shamefully

outraged all the laws observed by gentlemen adventurers.
Still the truth was the truth; and if he must tell what
he knew, it was this, that Vasco having tried to cheat
Shambling Ned out of the piece of eight which they were
playing for, and having been reproached by the latter for
his meanness, had straightway hit Ned in the face; and
that when Ned had risen to his feet to defend himself,
the Portuguese had immediately drawn his knife and
struck the blow, swearing at the same time that he
would like to do as much for every Englishman on board
the ship.

At this, the Portuguese, who had hitherto stood, with
downcast looks, listening to all the evidence, burst out in
violent wrath, sputtering vehemently forth his broken
English, and almost screaming in his excitement—

'That a lie—a lie, a lie!' he shouted. 'A lie, Nixon
—Jerry tell you say that—you liars both!—I no wish to
stab my shipmates, but Jerry hate me, and you Jerry
friend—and you lie!'

There was a murmur among the men, for it was not
difficult to see that Jerry and Nixon had great influence
over them, and many a clenched hand was raised against
the Portuguese, who, I believe, had certainly cut open
Ned's head, not, however, with premeditation, but in
the scuffle and the heat of blood. Meantime, Nixon
turned up his eyes to heaven, and shook his uplifted
hands, as who should say, ' Patience—patience, friends, I
can afford to bear the calumny.' Not so Jerry, however. His nature was different; and so, dashing down
his hat upon the deck in his rage, with his moustaches
bristling, and his flashing eyes fixed upon the culprit, he
roared—

' Here be a pitiful hound of a Portugee for you, who
dare raise his murdering arm to stab a freeborn Englishman, and then asperse the witnesses of the cruel deed!
If he remain unpunished for it, I leave this ship, and I
would advise all them who don't take the part of the
white-livered scoundrel to do the same—that is, if they
don't want to feel his murdering knife tickling their ribs!'

'Jerry,' cried out Vasco, all at once, 'I know what you mean very well. You no care for either blow or stab, that you no get yourself. You stab Nickel, the Dutchman, in Tortugas; you shoot John Cox off St. Christopher's. You a pretty fellow to talk!'

But here Jerry interrupted him. 'Now, then,' he roared, 'what are you about there, that you don't clap a marline-spike in the fellow's jaws? I suppose he intends to bully us out of the ship!'

Instantly half-a-dozen stout fellows threw themselves upon Vasco, who still, however, contrived, before he was effectually gagged, to yell out in broken sentences—

'Jerry—I say, Jerry—you do this because I prevent you marry my countrywoman, who keep tavern at Tortugas, and tell her, you have one, two, three wife already!'

But Jerry's orders were speedily obeyed, and the Portuguese—with a stout rope passed through his mouth, keeping the jaws wide open, and made fast to the back of his head—could only grin and flash his one eye upon his successful persecutor. Jerry was now in his glory. His ugly face was all lighted up with the excitement of gratified spite; and roaring to the men, that now they would teach a cowardly Portugee to lift his hand upon his betters he proposed that, as a punishment for what he had done, Vasco should be made to run the gauntlet, from the mizenmast forward to the heel of the bowsprit and back again. This proposal was received with acclamations by the rest of the crew, most of whom were brutal fellows enough, and quite under the thumb of Jerry, who, as I have said, was really captain, though he pretended to be only second in command; and so, presently, Le Chiffon Rouge, after whispering to his mate, ordered an old pair of topgallant-sail haulyards to be cut up into lengths of about three feet each. This was soon done, and then each man was armed with a piece of the strong stiff rope, with which, of course, one could strike as with a cudgel. The culprit eyed all these preparations in sulky silence, and made no resistance, even when Jerry himself, with a devil-like leer of delight in his eyes, tore off his doublet and shirt, leaving his swarthy back bare for the blows which awaited it.

'That man,' whispered Rumbold to me, indicating Jerry, 'is as great a fool as he is a brute. These Portuguese are not the fellows to forget a scar marked upon their backs. Sooner or later, unless he have very marvellous good luck, the knife which cut open Shambling Ned's head will make itself acquainted with Mr. Jerry's inward anatomy also.' In this remark I very cordially agreed; but Jerry seemed to be under very little uneasiness on the score, for he went joking about, showing the men how to grasp the ropes, so as to lay on the most vigorous cuts. The punishment of running the gauntlet is one which its executors can make as light or as heavy as they choose; and in the present instance the culprit did not seem, judging from most of the faces around him, to have much to hope for; while those of the crew who had, perhaps, given and received over many knife-slashes themselves, to have any very great horror of the crime, stood too much in awe of Jerry to favour the culprit.

At length, all being in readiness, and the crew, to the number of fifty-five, ranged in a double line, one on the larboard and the other on the starboard side of the deck, the hands of the Portuguese were tied behind him, and his ancles hampered so as to prevent his taking but little steps. Then Jerry, whose duty it was, as mate, took the poor devil by the ear, and, giving it a wrench, the Portuguese shuffled on until he stood before the first man in the line.

'Now, Jack,' said Jerry, 'here's the mark for you; let's see what pith you have got in your muscles.'

So the seaman addressed flourished his rope cudgel aloft, and then brought it down upon the naked back of the Portuguese, with a blow which echoed over the deck, and raised a broad white-coloured bar of flesh, which started up from the shoulder almost to the loin. The sufferer staggered under the weight of the stroke, and immediately all his back, except just where the scourge fell, turned to a burning red; but he uttered no sound.

'Very well struck, Jack,' said the mate, and then dragged the prisoner forward to receive the second blow. Ten minutes passed over at least, before the Portuguese had got through one-half of his punishment, by arriving in the bows of the ship; for Jerry prolonged the torture by stopping to joke with each man before he struck, and advising him to lay it on well. The whole scene was a very brutal one, and I would gladly have left the deck if I could. There was no escape, however, and I saw the poor wretch flogged up one side of the ship and down the other, each blow given by the full strength of an un- wearied arm. When the prisoner had completed his miserable walk, he was trembling all over; great drops of sweat were running down his face, and his back, although the skin was not actually cut, was a mass of ugly-coloured swellings.

'He will faint in a minute,' said Rumbold, 'and cheat Jerry of the finishing stroke.'

But, as if the mate had been aware of his danger, he hurriedly flourished his scourge round his head, so as to give it the full swing of his brawny arm, and then brought it down upon the sufferer with a buffet which might have broken the spine of a bull, and which drove the wretch who received it flat upon the deck, where he lay stark and motionless.

'Well,' said Le Chiffon Rouge, who, being captain, had not personally interfered in the punishment, 'it is to be hoped that Monsieur Vasco hath had a lesson upon the disadvantages of drawing knives upon comrades.'

'And upon the disadvantages of making enemies of more powerful men than himself,' whispered Rumbold. 'I dare say the fellow is a rascal, but he was flogged, not for cutting open his shipmate's head, but for preventing the mate from getting a fourth wife.'

'Here, men,' roared Jerry, as he twitched up the head of the prostrate man by the hair, and then allowed it to fall with a thump upon the deck, 'slush this carrion with a bucketfull of salt water, and then tumble him down the hatchway. I warrant he don't lie on his back in his hammock for a month of Sundays.'

These orders were speedily carried into effect, and the Portuguese having been taken below, the maintopsail was filled, and the ship again stood upon her course.

In the course of the day, Jerry and Nixon came up to me together, and proposed, very civilly, that, as I was a sailor, I should join the ship for the cruise; in which case, they told me, that I should have my regular share of the prize-money as if I had been on board since they went to sea, about three months ago. Of course I had nothing for it but to agree to the proposal, although I loathed the whole set among whom I had been thus so strangely thrown. 'Oh,' thought I, 'things were different on board the " Will-o'-the-Wisp," with Stout Jem for a commander, and a hearty set of fellows under him, as honest as they were brave.' But there was no help for it, and so my name was duly enrolled in the great book of the ' Saucy Susan.'

This being done, I of course took up my quarters with the crew, while Rumbold was accommodated in the great cabin. It was truly a virtuous company in which I found myself enlisted, almost every second man of them having left England after having made it too hot to hold him. One young fellow, with a ready laugh and a quick eye, told me that he had been thrice left for execution in Newgate, and was each time saved by the interest of friends. At last he was sent to the plantations, where he was purchased by a confederate, and set at liberty directly. Another man told me, that he had broken half the jails in England, and boasted that there never was smith made a lock which he could not pick with a rusty nail. A third fellow had been a foot-pad on Blackheath, and fled the country with the Hue and Cry at his heels. There were many more who had been thieves and rogues all their lives, having, indeed, been brought up to that business in the streets of London, in which they had been, as it were, born, and then allowed to run wild like

young savages—their hands against every man, and every
man's hands against them. By one of these men I was
told, that he never knew the name of either his father or
mother. The first thing he could remember was, that he
used to fight with dogs in Lincoln's Inn Fields for garbage and bones. He slept upon bunks in the streets in
summer, and among the ashes in the glass-houses in
winter, until having amassed money by many fortunate
robberies, for, quoth he, ' my street education made me
sharp,' he got to live in White Friars, the Mint, and
places of that kind, where he cared little for either
warrants or thief-takers. ' I promise you,' quoth he,
' the Lord Chief Justice cannot take a man there unless
he come backed by a company of musketeers.' Another
of our most virtuous crew had been a highwayman, and
used to infest Gadshill, particularly after a ship had been
paid off at Chatham, and the seamen came swarming up
on the London road to expend their money in town
debauchery. Having been apprehended sleeping in an
inn on the borders of Epping Forest, where it seems he
sometimes lay in wait for Cambridge scholars journeying
past, a prosecutor was found to come forward against
him at Newgate in very curious fashion. He told me
the story himself.

' There were six of us,' quoth he, ' and they had suspicions against all, but no witnesses. The fact was, that
they knew very well that we had walked Watling Street,
and perhaps other roads also, but they could find no one
to prove it. So this was the plan the lawyers hit on.
They published a notice in the *London Gazette*, to say,
that six persons, reputed highwaymen, would be publicly
exhibited in Newgate, dressed in riding suits, and just as
they appeared on the road, so that any one who had been
recently robbed might be able to tell whether the thief
was in the clutches of the law. So the day came, and we
were made, every man of us, to don our riding gear, and
then with boot and red doublet, pistols at our belts,
and just a morsel of crape dangling from our hats, we were
paraded up and down the long galleries, while a crowd of

2 A

ladies and court gallants examined us with their glasses,
and joked and laughed and coquetted, and told us to
turn, first one way and then the other, and said, as each
passed by, "No, no, he is not the fellow who robbed me;
bring up the next, good master turnkey, and make him
turn well round, so that we may see his face to our
satisfaction." It would have been very well, however, if
all the remarks had been like these. But, one by one,
my poor companions were marked out and carried away.
"Here be the very man who eased me of my purse on
Gadshill," quoth a fat grazier of Kent, and stout Tom
Clinch was straightway taken to the hold.' "O' my life,
the rascal who stopped her ladyship's carriage on Houn-
slow, and made us all hand over watches and cash," says
a mincing carpet knight, and the fate of brave Moonlight
Dick was settled. Even thus our misdeeds came home
to us; so that in the space of an hour and a half I stood
alone, and then, the crowd of spectators beginning to
disperse, I had good hope that my lucky stars would prevail, and that I would be allowed to go forth for lack
of evidence. But alas! in the nick of time, just as the
captain of Newgate was thinking of turning me adrift
with a kick and an oath, up there trips a dainty gentlewoman, whose face I knew in an instant, for I had said
some few flattering words in praise of the brilliancy of
her eyes, and what not, to which she listened nothing
loath, while I conveyed to my own pouch a golden
locket she wore, filled with hair, which I warrant you
grew never on the bald head of her spouse, an old lawyer
of Lincoln's Inn. So she stared at me very hard, while
I twisted my features first one way and then the other,
now cocking my eye, now leering it, so that I saw she
was mightily puzzled. But just then old Diggory, the
thief-taker, fetched me a wipe over the chops; "Take
that, you mumper," says he, "and keep your ugly face
quiet till the gentlewoman decide." But it was no such
easy matter for her to pronounce; and at length quo' my
madam, as cool as an' she had been in a raree-show, and
wished to hear the lion roar. "Make him speak, good

master keeper, make him speak, and I shall know the voice." So says old Diggory, "Come, Helter-Skelter Joe, you hear what the lady says, tip us a few tongue flourishes." So I commenced grumbling and snorting through my nose, but it wouldn't do. "Stow that," says Diggory, "or we shall have the hangman in with his cat-o'-nine tails." Then I set to gabbling in a high treble, like a dame of Billingsgate whose comrades had stolen her fish,—but it was all in vain, they made me talk in my own voice at last, and quoth the bona roba as soon as she heard the patter, "Oh, good master jailer, it is the villain, indeed." So I was tried—condemned—left for execution, and I can tell you it took both money and friends to prevent my going up Holborn Hill in a cart.'

There were others of the crew, however, more reputable characters, so far as regarded actual roguery, but they were one and all a devil-may-care set, without thought or morals, and only anxious for plunder and debauchery. Several of them had been kidnapped, as they told me, from Bristol, Norwich, Newcastle, London, and other places. These were all of them youths under twenty, and two or three of them had been, they said, sold by their parents. They had all of them, however, managed, after serving for different periods, to make their escape from Virginia, and to find their way into the West Indian seas. They gave doleful accounts of their treatment in the plantations—how they had been flogged and starved, and of the great numbers who had died from fever and sun strokes. Those who had been kidnapped frequently fared worse than the convicted felons, because the former, being generally of tender years, were less able to protect themselves than the old thieves and vagabonds who were transported thither from the jails of England. The reader will easily understand that a great number of the crew of the 'Saucy Susan' were but very poor sailors, and clumsy fellows in blowing weather aloft. Indeed, it was sometimes rare sport to see the boatswain and his mates, armed with big rattans, thrashing the skulkers out of their hammocks, and chasing them up to their duty from all the secret holes and hiding-places in the ship; while Jerry would be storming and raving on the poop, and swearing that he would shoot the last man who got out on the yard in reefing topsails. Among these lubberly rogues, however, there were a handful of prime sailors, chiefly old men, who had swung in hammocks nigh half a century, and had been tossed on every sea all round the world. The great fault they had was, that not a single man of the whole lot would keep sober if he had an opportunity of getting drunk. For all that, however, Jerry was forced to depend upon these sailors, his 'Mother Carey's chickens,' as he called them, for the safe navigation of the ship; knowing very well that, if the rest of the crew were but fresh water seamen, they were as good, with cutlasses and boarding-pikes in their hands, as the most daring veterans of the sea. With these ancient mariners I chiefly consorted, we forming a company who kept somewhat aloof from the rake-helly set we lived among, and during the many calm mid-watches I kept on board the 'Saucy Susan,' I picked up many legends and tales of the sea from these old men, who had passed long lives upon the face of the waters. I have already given to the reader one story, as a sample of the kind of legends which we Buccaneers loved to listen to, and I shall here add another of the same sort, relating to a notion which was very common amongst seamen of the time of which I speak, but which has now, I believe, except with the most ignorant of the class, wholly died away. I mean, the idea that particular capes or headlands running out into the sea are haunted by evil demons, who hate ships to pass by, and who, therefore, raise tempests to beat them back, and prevent them from doubling the point, or spot of land in question. This belief, no doubt, rose from the general stormy nature of the seas off capes and out-stretching tongues of land. The two great capes of the world—the Cape of Good Hope and Cape Horn, many sailors believed to be haunted by most powerful demons, and regarded the awful gales which blew, and the fearful

seas which run thereabouts, as nothing but the work of
these Cape devils, if I may call them so, not remember-
ing that the phenomena in question are simply the effect
of geographical position and the unchanging laws of the
elements. However, I proceed to my story, merely pre-
mising that the seaman who told it, and who was an
old mariner with a white beard, did devoutly believe in
all the extravagancies which I have just mentioned, as
well as in the fantastic tale which he told. I give it in
rather better language than the narrator made use of;
his speech, indeed, being much seasoned with forecastle
expressions, not of the most delicate nature. But it is
worthy of a new chapter.

## CHAPTER XXVI.

### THE LEGEND OF THE DEMON WHO HAUNTS POINT MORANT IN JAMAICA.

OLD Josiah Ward, for such was the name of my story-
teller, recounted the legend to about a dozen of us, as we
sat in the lee of the long-boat on the deck, the breeze
blowing gently, and the 'Saucy Susan' running slowly
before it. Thus he spoke—

'Just one score of years after the great Christopher
Columbus discovered the New World, there sailed westward, across the Atlantic, a ship, or rather galley, of
strange make and fashion. She was very long, shipmates,
and floated low and deep in the water, but her prow, all
carved and fantastically wrought, rose up above her deck
curved like the neck of a swan, and ending in a great
eagle's beak. This head and beak were of iron. At the
top of both her masts, for there were two, this galley
carried broad, swallow-tailed pendants, quite black, except that there were in the centre of each an eagle's head
and beak of red colour, just like the head and beak at the
prow. The galley sailed marvellously fast, and the wind
that bore her was ever fair. Yes, shipmates, weeks and
weeks rolled on, and not a mariner on board her had need
to start sheet, or tack,—and yet tempests swept across

her path, and the crew of the galley saw Spanish caravals
founder in the great waves, not a bow-shot from their
ship, while they were speeding over water ruffled only by
a gentle breeze. And the reason was, shipmates, that
an enchanted wind filled the galley's sails, and before its
breath the natural storms of the air could not prevail.
There was always, as it were, a spot of fair wind upon the
ocean, running rapidly westward, and in the centre of
that spot, the galley swept across the waves, going with
sails and oars.

'The sailors who manned this strange bark were men
of very fair complexion, of light blue eyes and long flaxen
hair, and the language they spoke was the tongue of that
far northern land—whence, in the old days, came forth,
each in his war-galley, the fierce sea-kings—the Buccaneers of the North—shipmates, to plunder and to spoil.
These men were heathens and unbelievers—they worshipped gods, called Odin and Thor, and each had a
magic sword, the steel of which was wrought by little
demons who live under ground, and in hollow places,
which they scoop in great rocks and stones, and where
they forge such blades that no weapon, were it even
welded by the cunning makers of Damascus, could prevail against them. But the strangest thing of all, comrades, was that the captain of this ship was a woman—
a woman of great stature, and fierce and lofty aspect.
Her name was Tronda, and she was a sorceress ; she
could make the winds blow as she listed, and she had a
crystal into which those who looked could see the future.
This Tronda, mates, was a witch of great power, and she
came from one of the northern islands, near that huge
whirlpool called Lofoden, which can suck great navies
down into the abysses of the sea. She wore a sea-green
coloured tunic, with a necklace of beads made of a pebble
called adder-stone, which hath strange virtues, and her
head-gear was formed of the fur of the wild cat. Likewise she wore a very broad girdle, on which were embroidered strange words and letters in gold, and to it
was attached a pouch, in which she kept the charms and

spells with which she conjured. But her great power was over the elements, shipmates, for Tronda was a witch of Lapland—that dreary coast of snow which mariners skirt, sailing into the White Sea—and her name was known as a potent trafficker in such powers as ordinary mortals possess not, and many shipmen came to her and spoke her fair, and gave her money, and she sold them fair winds to waft them on their course. But I have heard, shipmates, that such was the nature of these unnatural breezes, that they wrecked every seventh ship which sailed before them. Six would go prosperously to their port, but the wind which the seventh had purchased, would gradually swell and wax great and mighty, until it became a hurricane, which tore sail and mast before it, and beat the ill-fated ship down into the sea.

'It was by certain rhymes, comrades, that Tronda and the other Lapland witches ruled the air, and made the storm-clouds fly as they wished. I have heard that she would stand high on a rock, or upon the poop of a ship, when the sea was calm below, and the summer air clear above. Then would she toss her arms above her head, and kneeling down, with her fair hair streaming over her shoulders, sing the magic song, which brought forth clouds upon the heavens, and unchained the wind, to rush over the howling sea. No one understood this song, but its name was *Vard lokur*—and it was in an ancient northern tongue called Lap, many words of which have power over the swart demons, and dwarfs, and elvish workers in metals, who live under the mountains of Finland and Jutland.

'Now, Tronda was a miser, and loved gold, and when mariners came to her and told her legends about a new world lying to the west, far across the ocean, and where the yellow metal and stones still more precious glistened and shone, on every mountain and on every beach, she said—"I, too, will depart and see that golden land, where there is neither frost nor cold, but diamonds bright as icicles, and pearls as white as snow." Then she embarked in her galley, and raised a magic wind, which bore her across the Atlantic, and at sunrise one bright morning, she saw before her the land of the New World. But the galley had not coasted far, when two caravals came forth and gave her chase. The Spaniards knew little with whom they had to deal; Tronda stood on the poop of her ship, and stretched her arms forth, singing her magic rhymes in Lap, and straightway a squall came rushing down from the land, and before the Spaniards could lower their sails, it broke upon the caravals, and ships and crews sunk together in the sea.

' So, the fame of Tronda, the Lapland witch, that could sell winds, was noised abroad all over the Indies. She never went ashore—but in her galley, with the eagle's beak, she cruised among the islands and along the main. The Spanish captains often went aboard the galley, and humbled themselves before the witch, and bought winds to carry them from isle to isle, and port to port, each wind being purchased with a lump of gold. When the Inquisition, which was established in Cuba, heard of this strange trafficking, they sent caravals of war to capture the sorceress, but her powers baffled all their skill. Sometimes, she stilled the air, so that all the ships lay motionless together. Then, just as the Spaniards would get out their boats to row to the Norse galley, a gentle breeze would fan her sails, and she would glide deftly away, while Tronda, who took a pleasure in tormenting her pursuers, would stand upon the poop, worshipping her strange gods, and singing her unlawful incantations. At other times, she would raise mists, in the midst of which the Spaniards would grope for days, firing guns, and ringing bells—so that, at last, the ships of war gave up the chase, and returned to the Havannah. But no one who sought Tronda to buy a wind, had ever any difficulty in boarding her galley. She received all such with fair words and courteous bearing, and gave them, in return for their gold, each a large stoup, or jar, the mouth of it sealed with wax, bearing strange figures and signs. This jar each captain took with him, and directly the anchor was lifted, Tronda would instruct him to break.

the seal, when immediately the fair breeze would fill the sails, and the ship would move gaily on her way. So, by this traffic, Tronda amassed vast riches, and every week the galley sunk lower and deeper in the water, with its increasing freight of precious stones and gold. But it was not alone fair and gentle breezes which the Lapland witch trafficked in. She sold adverse winds and awful storms to the enemies of luckless mariners. She sold calms, too, which haunted a hapless ship, chaining her, as it were, to the unruffled sea, until, drop by drop, the fresh water was drunk out, and the sailors died on the deck, or cast themselves overboard in their raving delirium of thirst. And so many a customer came to Tronda to buy prosperous winds for friends, and wrecking tempests for enemies. The smug merchant purchased a fair wind for himself, and a baffling breeze for his rival in the trade. The love-lorn maiden bought a prosperous gale for her sweetheart's ship, and the jealous dame paid gold for a tempest to wreck the bark of a faithless lover.

'Now, comrades, years moved slowly on, and the Norse galley was so deep in the water with gold and precious stones, that, had it not been for enchantment, she would have sunk outright. Then the blue-eyed and long-haired mariners entreated Tronda that she would allow them to look again upon the mountains and the Fiords of Norway, and that she would raise a westerly breeze to carry them home across the ocean. But the witch scoffed at their requests, giving them foul words, and saying that she must have more gold. The chief of the crew was a young man called Torquil, and he it was who sighed most for home, because he had left a maiden there whom he loved, and from whom he had been long parted. Therefore, after Tronda had retired to the great cabin, where she lived alone, Torquil entered it unbidden. It was quite dark, for the cabin was beneath the water, and no light came down to it from the deck, but an ancient lamp of bronze swung slowly from the beams overhead, and in this lamp burnt a flame, although there was neither wick nor oil to feed it. The witch was sitting in a great chair like a throne, and before ner were open boxes crammed with lumps of gold, which gleamed in the flicker of the bronze lamp. On the table lay the magic crystal in which the sorceress could see the future : and upon the high back of the antique chair, in which she sat, perched two ravens, grey with age, both of which uttered a low, hoarse croak as Torquil entered.

' " Mother," he said, for all who spoke to the witch so addressed her—" mother, I would go home to my own country ; I long again to see the face of my father and of my betrothed. Therefore, I bid you raise a favouring westerly gale ; for, if you do not, neither I nor one of my comrades will put hand to rope on board this galley again."

' With that the witch rose slowly to her feet. " Look you, Torquil Randa,' quoth she, " whoso in this galley disobeys my orders, the elements, which are at my beck and bidding, shall overwhelm him.'

' But Torquil stood erect, nothing daunted. " I know your powers, mother," he answered ; " but as well be sunk in the sea as wander for ever upon its surface, homeless and friendless. You heard what I have spoken ; I will not live longer away from kindred and home."

' And so saying, the bold mutineer left the cabin. Tronda followed him on deck, muttering her Lapland rhymes, and waving her arms aloft in the air. As she did so, great banks of black clouds began to rise from out the ocean, and the sea-birds flew round the masts of the galley, screaming with affright. There was a dead calm in the air, and it grew so hot that the mariners gasped for breath. The bright tropic day, shipmates, seemed to be changing into night, and the clouds got lower and lower until they appeared to rest upon the topmasts of the galley. All this time the witch was kneeling upon the poop, chanting her accursed rhymes, and Torquil was standing alone beside the mainmast, for his comrades were terrified, and slunk away from him as from a man under a curse.

'Suddenly the witch stopped, and shaded back from her eyes her long flowing hair, gazing intently at the sky. In the next moment, a flash of lightning—so bright that every one on board the galley, except the sorceress, was dazzled and blinded by the glare—tore out of the dark heavens ; struck the main topmast of the galley ; and with a crash, like that of all the artillery in the world fired off in one salvo, passed gleaming down the wood, shaking the ship as though she had been lifted a hundred feet, and then allowed to fall splash into the sea. The explosion was followed by a thick sulphurous smoke, which seemed to come steaming up out of the inmost recesses of the galley, and while the crew, blinded and almost choking in the yellow sulphurous fume, were groping about the deck, they heard the loud screaming laughter of the witch, followed by the croak of the ravens from the cabin.

' At length the smoke or mist gradually cleared away, and as it did so, and the men recovered their eyesight, they saw Tronda standing as usual on the poop, with her old aspect of haughty command. Her first words, comrades, were—

' " Fling that carrion into the sea, and take warning by the fate of Torquil Randa how you dispute the will of such as I."

' So the sailors advanced, all trembling, to the foot of the mainmast, where lay the body of the man of whom the witch spoke. He had been struck by the lightning, comrades, but there was neither scaith nor scar upon his flesh, only on the forehead a small round blue spot. So the mariners lifted up the body, and while it was yet warm plunged it over the side. It sunk feet first, and as the head disappeared, the crew thought that the dead face frowned.

' That night Tronda sat alone in her cabin, beneath the bronze lamp, as she had done when her victim entered. The crystal lay upon the table as before. All at once, the flame of the lamp flashed high up, and then sank down into the bronze, so that the cabin was almost in

darkness, and the two ravens fluttered and croaked.
Tronda lifted up her head, and her livid face became as
the face of a statue carved out of blue and grey marble,
for before her, standing as he had already done that day,
was the form of Torquil Randa, with the blue spot upon
his forehead where the lightning had struck it.

' There was silence for the space of a minute, and then
the form of Torquil spoke.

' "I am sent from the dead," it said, "to give you a
last warning."

' "Return to those who sent you," answered the witch ;
" I take no warnings."

' "I am bid to tell you," said the spirit, "that the
measure of your iniquities is nearly full."

' The witch of Lapland rose erect, and stood confronting
the apparition.

' "I have no fear of aught, either dead or living, spirit
or flesh," she replied. "Get you gone, or I will call up
the spectres of the winds, who will chase you to the
uttermost ends of the earth."

' The figure of Torquil Randa gave a sad smile, and
stretching forth its hand, touched the magic crystal,
which immediately crumbled into black dust. "The
powers which are given to me," said the spirit, "are
greater than yours."

' Tronda's frame shivered as she saw this, but she lost
no whit of countenance, and looked her terrible visitant
steadily in the face.

' "There will be given you one last opportunity," the
apparition said. "Will you repent?"

' "No!" said the witch of Lapland.

' The figure of Torquil Randa grew less and less dis-
tinct, and as it disappeared, the flame of the lamp
brightened up again, and the ravens, which had nestled
at Tronda's feet, flew back to their perches on her
chair.

' The next day, the galley meanwhile lying not far from
Cape Tiberoon, in Hispaniola, there came on board, in a
small canoe, a Spanish girl, who seemed, shipmates, to

have hardly life in her to climb up the low side of the galley. This girl was of a beauty rarely seen upon the earth, but those who looked upon the bright red spot in her white cheek, and the sickly flash of her black floating eyes, knew that there was hardly a month's life flickering in her bosom; so she went slowly into the cabin, and fell upon her knees before the witch.

'"Mother," she said, "I am dying fast, as you can see. I have a lover, my betrothed. He is coming across the ocean to bid me farewell. Oh, that I might live to see him! I have little gold, but for what I have, grant him a fair breeze, that his ship may come to land before I die, and that I may give up my spirit in his arms."

'So saying, the Spanish girl held forth a piece of gold the size of a walnut. Tronda had opened her mouth to speak, when a third woman entered the cabin. She was a tall and haughty dame, and as she observed the dying girl, a smile like that of a fiend passed over her face. Her cheeks flushed, and her eyes glanced with the fire of deadly spite. The younger girl started back at her aspect, and then sunk all trembling and sobbing upon the floor.

'Then the elder spoke thus—

'"I hate that woman. She is my rival. She has won from me the man I love. I would prevent their meeting. She is poor, but I am rich. This, for a wind which will keep back his ship, until she be no more."

'With that, shipmates, the woman laid upon the table a lump of virgin ore, as big as a cocoa-nut. The other girl said nothing, but still held out her smaller offering. Tronda stood between them musing. At last, she took the large lump, and dropped it into the great chestfull at her feet.

'"You shall have a baffling wind," she said to the jealous rival. The poor girl, who was dying, rose feebly, and passed out weeping; the crew let her down with careful hands into her canoe.

'But at the moment when Tronda had made her decision, the sudden moan of a hollow sounding wind passed through the air, and the galley rocked and laboured, as though an invisible hand had smote her. The witch remained long musing in the cabin, until, hearing the dash of oars, she rose and went on deck. The galley was deserted, the whole crew, embarked in the boats, were pulling fast for the land, while the horizon was again clouded as it had been when the witch drew lightning from the heavens. Tronda mounted upon the poop, and stretched forth her arms, to curse the faithless crew, when her eye suddenly fell upon Torquil, standing as he had stood, beneath the mainmast, when the levin bolt struck him. Then she forbore, and remained with drooping head, gazing into the sea below. But what was remarkable, was, that when the whole crew of the galley left her at once, instead of rising, she sunk still deeper in the water ; and as a heavy swell began to lift and heave around, the ship rolled and pitched with a strange sickly motion.

' Then came another portent. Tronda still stood upon the poop, when she started to hear a sudden pattering of feet, and a squeaking and scratching all around her. Immediately there poured forth from every hatchway a whole legion of rats—young ones and old—brown and grey—all of them making for the side of the vessel, and then plunging with a loud shrill squeaking into the sea, which was speedily dotted with their little heads, all swimming merrily to land. When the last had leaped overboard, the figure of Torquil Randa glided softly aft and confronted the witch.

' "Rats," quoth the figure, " leave a sinking ship." And, as he spoke, the galley appeared to float in the water more heavily and deeply than ever, while the swells rose in great rocking billows, and the moan of a coming wind hurtled over the sea. Still Tronda confronted the apparition with a lip which never quivered, and an eye which never blinked.

" My ancestors," said she, " were champions and heroes ; one of them—Eric Westra—descended into the tomb of Sigismund, the sea king, and bore from thence the bronze sepulchral lamp which burns beneath, although it was guarded by monsters and potent spells. What art thou, then, that one in whose veins runs the blood of such a hero, should tremble and quake before thee ?"

' But the apparition said—

' " I come from a power which is mightier than that of Odin and of Thor, and I am commissioned to pronounce to thee the doom thou shalt undergo as a punishment for thy wicked sorceries, even until the end of time."

' At that there rose a mighty wind, and the galley started away before it. In vain Tronda bade the elements to cease their strife—in vain she knelt upon the poop, and, with her drenched hair all streaming in the tempest, sung her magic rhymes and screamed out her most potent charms. The winds blew, and the clouds lowered, and the waves rose, unheedful of her spells, and so at last she started up from the deck, and cried in a lamentable voice—

' " Alas ! alas ! my power is gone from me, and the elements obey me no more !"

' At these words there was a flutter and a croak, and the ravens, flying from the cabin, soared up into the tempest-tossed air, wheeling round and round the rocking masts of the labouring ship.

' " And you too," said Tronda, looking up at them, " leave me !"

' The sentence, comrades, was no sooner spoken than the foul birds darted off, each his separate way, and were speedily lost in the darkness. Then the storm burst out with all its fury. Had it been a bark manned by mortals, the galley would not have lived an hour in that sea ; but enchantment kept it afloat until it had finished its destined course. For some space the Lapland witch and the figure of Torquil Randa were the only forms visible in the ship. But as the night fell, and the darkness grew intense, pale flashes of lightning showed troops of phantoms upon the deck, who worked the ropes and sails as mariners in a gale. These shapes, comrades, were the spirits of the seamen whom Tronda by her incantations had drowned. But still the witch stood erect and fearless through all this tumult of horror, lifting up her unabashed forehead to the gale, and flashing all around her wild grey eyes. The figure of Torquil stayed ever by her side.

'At length, comrades, in the thick of the roaring tornado, with all the gibbering ghosts dimly seen flitting on the deck amid the flying spray and foam, there was shouted from the prows, in a voice which boomed like the tones of a church bell, "Land."

'At this the spectre of the Norse mariner turned to Tronda, and said—

'"Now hear your doom. From this time forth you will haunt the cape on which we are driving; and there you will have power over the winds which blow. Your evil nature, which is as a mighty devil within you, will ever impel you to retard rather than to advance the course of mariners; but yet, for every moment of time a ship is hindered on her course, will you pass a year of torment, such as it is not in the breast of man to conceive. And this shall last even to the day when the sea shall give up its dead."

'In a moment after, mates, the galley was crushed into splinters, and not a vestige of her, or of her precious cargo of pearls, and jewels, and gold, were ever seen by man. But Tronda, the evil spirit of Cape Morant, still haunts that desolate beach and these stormy breakers, and sometimes in wild mid-watches, the mariner has caught a glimpse of her pale face and stony eyes, and floating locks, driving through the scud of the storm, with her arms tossed above her head, as though she were still singing the chaunt which raised wind and waves. I never spoke, comrades, with those who saw her; but I have heard tell of a sailor of Sir Francis Drake, who being, in a night of storm, clinging to the end of the bowsprit furling a split sail, beheld the ancient face of the hag, with her grey, fishy eyes, looking into his own, and who came near letting go hold of the spar in his fright, and tumbling into the boiling sea below. But he managed to make his way, all pale and shaking, on board the ship, where he told what he had witnessed ; and certain old men of the crew said it was a most evil omen, and that either the ship would be lost, or he who saw the appearance would be drowned. Now, word being passed through the ship of what had happened, it came to the ears of the stout-hearted admiral himself; and presently Sir Francis appeared out of the main cabin.

' " What is this I hear, men," says he,—" that one of you has been frightened by a demon ?"

' " It was the devil, Sir Francis !" said the sailor, by name James Gilbert.

' " And what if it were ?" quoth the admiral. " He is but a coward. If he shows his face to you again, pluck the grisly fiend by the beard. The devil fears all who do not fear him."

' But for all these bold words of the admiral, the old sailors were right. Before the ship had made Porto Bello, whither she was bound, Gilbert was flung from the lee foretop-sail yard-arm into the sea. After the first plunge, he never came to the surface, and the old sailors knew that what had happened was in consequence of his having seen the demon who haunts Point Morant.'

---

## CHAPTER XXVII.

### WHAT HAPPENS ABOARD THE 'SAUCY SUSAN'—AND THE ENDING OF HER AND HER CREW.

THREE days after we boarded the 'Saucy Susan' I was the look-out man during a dark mid-watch. The wind was fresh, the sea high, and we were plunging rapidly along ; the sails straining and surging, and the masts and rigging cracking with the pressure. I was standing on the heel of the bowsprit, with my arm round the forestay to balance myself, and occasionally ducking and stooping as I best could to avoid the cold showers of brine which our sharp bows tore up, when some one pulled my doublet, and, looking round, I saw Rumbold.

'Is there any one about?' quoth he; 'I want to speak to you privately.' But the breeze, although it blew strong, was steady, and the watch lay dozing under the lee of the long-boat between the masts.

'My mind misgives me,' says Rumbold, presently, 'that they have a design on me. That fellow Nixon watches every motion as a cat does a mouse. I know that Jerry, Le Chiffon Rouge, and he, are aware that I have pearls about me, and I go in constant dread. Did you see the three rogues to-day, how long and how earnestly they talked, and what sly glances they, every one of them, threw at me? It was ticklish work living among the Spaniards at the Rio de la Hacha, but I warrant you I feel never a bit more comfortable among my countrymen here.'

I inquired where Jerry, the Captain, and Nixon were?

Rumbold replied, that they were all three drinking in the great cabin, and that being pretty far gone, he had been able to slip out to seek me.

'Now,' quoth he, 'I don't intend that these rascals shall have my pearls, if I can keep them—and what is more, I don't intend that they shall have them, even although I may not be able to keep them—they shall go into the sea, which they came out of, first.'

I said, that surely the fellows would not murder him for his wealth.

'Well,' he answered, 'they would not murder, if they could steal without it—but if they can't, I do not suppose that a throat or so cut, would make much difference.'

Upon this I replied, heartily shaking Rumbold's hand at the same time,—

'You helped me, at my time of need, among the Spaniards. Perhaps, I can help you now—will you entrust the pearls to me?'

'My good fellow,' says Rumbold, with great eagerness, 'that is precisely the favour I came to ask of you.'

And with that, he fumbled in his bosom, and presently

drew out a sort of flat pouch, made of thin but tough leather, with straps which buckled round the body. We both looked eagerly to see that we were not observed, but not a soul could be seen stirring upon deck. A lantern, swinging from the weather-foreshrouds, cast a dusky gleam around upon the dripping bulwarks, and the wet and slippery planks—but we were alone.

'Hush!' says he, softly. 'The pearls are in this pouch—there is a good thousand pounds worth—strap the belt tightly round you, under your clothes, the first time you have an opportunity. If you deliver it up to me safely at Jamaica, a third of the profits shall be yours —if anything happens to me, I make you my legatee— keep pouch and pearls, and make the best of them.'

He had hardly made the transfer, when a shadow glided darkly between us and the lantern. We both rushed aft as far as the foremast, and pried eagerly about, but not a creature was to be seen.

'Bah!' said Rumbold, 'it was only the light, swinging with the ship as she rolls.' But my own belief was that some one had glided across the deck, and mounted the weather-forerigging. I had not time, however, to communicate my thoughts to Rumbold, when we heard loud voices, and saw a glimmering of lights aft, and immediately Jerry came forwards, walking not very steadily, although he had good sea-legs, and clinging to the rigging, when the ship made a wilder lurch than ordinary.

'Farewell—take care!' exclaimed Rumbold. 'I must not be seen here.'

So saying, he slid over to leeward, and crept aft, under the black shadow of the sails. Meantime, Jerry approached, and taking the lantern from the forerigging, grasped my shoulder, and asked me—in a thick voice and with a hiccup—whether all was well? I replied in the affirmative: upon which he steadied himself on the deck as well as he could, and began to hum over a song to himself—sometimes stopping to put the same question to me, half a dozen times over, after the manner of a drunken man—when, all at once, the ship giving a violent lee-lurch,

2 B 2

he was pitched bodily against the bulwarks, and at the
same moment a heavy marline spike fell with a crash from
the rigging, tearing up white splinters in the deck.    Had
it not been for that lucky lurch, that sharp and ponderous
iron would have cleft the mate's head.    All this happened in a moment, but the weapon had hardly struck
the deck, when Jerry bounded to his legs, and with a tremendous oath, that there was treachery somewhere, called
to me to go aloft in the weather-rigging, while he took
the lee.    The danger he had escaped seemed to have
sobered the mate at once.    I sprung into the tightened
shrouds, half bewildered at the thing, while Jerry screamed
to me, from the opposite rigging, to look sharp and take
care of a knife-thrust, for he was certain it was that
villainous Portuguee dog who had flung the marline
spike.

Up we both went into the rocking rigging.    We climbed
over the rail of the foretop at the same moment, and I
saw that Jerry held the barrel of a small pistol between
his teeth.

'The murthering rogue!' he cried.    'But he has made
his last cast—either he or I go down on that deck a dead
man!'

We both looked up to the heel of the top-gallant mast.
The white canvas was tugging and straining upon the
bending yard, and the loose lee-rigging was rattling
against the mast and sail.

'There he is—there's the thief!' Jerry roared, and we
both sprang into the topmast rigging.    Holding on by
the top-gallant yard, I discerned a black figure, like a
shadow, against the light-coloured canvas.    All at once I
saw its arm move, something bright gleamed through
the air, and Jerry shouted—

'Devil confound him—he has sent his knife into my
shoulder,' and immediately stopped, grasping the shrouds
as though he feared to fall.    Knowing now that the Portuguese had no knife, I sprang rapidly up the shrouds to
grapple with him.    Just then, a faint watery glimpse of
moonlight fell upon the ship, throwing a great shadow

upon the broad sails on the mainmast, and I saw above me, crouched upon the yard, the form of Vasco—his grim face gazing at me, and his hands clenched, as though he was determined to sell his life as dearly as he could. The next moment, we had grappled together—neither of us spoke—but the Portuguese attempted to seize my throat with his teeth; I caught him however by his hair, and wrenched his head backwards, while I sought to gripe his right wrist and so overpower him. But the creature, although he had no strength to cope with me, was as lithe and slippery as an eel, and suddenly striking me a blow between the eyes, which made abundance of lights dance before them—I felt in a moment his cold long fingers twining round my throat, and closing upon my windpipe. In the instinctive struggle for breath, I let go hold of his hair, and at the same instant, a sudden and tremendous swing through the air, as the ship rolled violently below, made me clutch the ropes about me, or I should have been flung off into the sea, like a stone from a sling. At that moment the grasp upon my throat relaxed,—and with a litheness and agility, which were like the qualities of a monkey and a snake united in one creature—the Portuguese slid, as it were, from me, upon the main-royal stay, crawling and worming himself along towards the other mast. But Jerry, who had by this time recovered the first faintness from his cut, kept his eye steadily upon the rogue, for I calling out that he was escaping to the mainmast, the mate replied—'Ay, ay, I see him:' and, then, steadily taking aim, the explosion of the pistol re-echoed loudly, from sail to sail, and the Portuguese suddenly dropping his legs from the stay, hung to it by his hands only.

'Stand from under,' shouted Jerry, 'and allow the villain to drop clear. He has stabbed me as he did Shambling Ned.'

Vasco uttered no sound, but he raised his legs again, seeking by a mighty effort to recover his position upon the rope. His feet had, indeed, touched it, when the muscles relaxed again, and he hung as before by his hands,

swinging dreadfully with the motion of the ship. All this
time, Jerry was clutching the forerigging, not having
moved since the knife of the Portuguese struck him.
The watch upon deck having been aroused by Jerry's
cries, and the report of the pistol, were running to-and-
fro with lanterns, and some of them were ascending the
rigging towards us, when Jerry roared out again—

'Stop—stop, every mother's son of you, where you
are till the fellow falls, and then stand by to pitch him
overboard.'

The Portuguese heard this, for he turned round his
head to Jerry, and I saw his white teeth, as the wretch
grinned in his agony. The mate answered this look with
a loud laugh.

'Some of you there below,' he cried, 'go into the great
cabin, bring up a flagon of wine—and we'll drink to the
murthering dog's speedy arrival in hell.'

The Portuguese now let go hold of the rope with his
right hand—and then, as if to reserve his strength, hung
for awhile with the left. I did not think that the man
would have had such endurance in him, but he was of a
light weight, and the muscles of his arms were
strong.

All this time he never uttered a sound. Jerry, too,
held his peace, and the crew below waited in silence, with
their lanterns glimmering on deck. There was something
very solemn in all this—the struggling and tossing ship—
the rigid figures of the seamen—the silence, except for
the wind and waves, and the writhing creature waving in
the air.

At length, he uttered one loud shrill cry of mortal
agony, which echoed again and again between the sails,
and immediately afterwards dropped like a stone. I
heard the heavy thump with which he crashed down
upon the deck. Descending as quickly as I could, I
found that Jerry, in spite of his wound, which was, however, only a flesh cut, was standing over the Portuguese,
who lay all doubled up where he fell.

'Up with the hound, and over the side with him to the

sharks!' said Jerry, in a low stern voice. Immediately
the poor wretch was plucked from the deck, and four
sturdy fellows bore him to the bulwarks. He gave no
sign of life; but just as they heaved him up for the fatal
swing, the lanterns being all gleaming around, I saw him,
his eyes still shut, make the sign of the cross upon his
forehead. He was, therefore, still alive.

'One!' cried Jerry.

The four executioners, who seemed to like the job well,
gave the wretch a swing.

'Two, three!' thundered the mate, and at the last word,
Vasco of Lisbon was hove a fathom from the ship's side,
into the boiling sea. As he plunged down into the brine,
every one heard for a moment, and no more, such a cry as
he uttered just before he fell from the rigging. Then his
voice was choked for ever.

I could hardly deny but that the Portuguese merited
his fate; but the flinging overboard of a living man,
without form of trial or condemnation, seemed a hasty
and cruel deed. Nevertheless, none of the crew, except
myself, appeared to be of that opinion, and most of them
said openly, that it was a very good riddance, and that
whether he had attempted the life of the mate or not, he
was better in the sea than the ship. As for Jerry, he
had his wound, which was, as I have said, a flesh cut on
the shoulder, rubbed with brandy, and seemed to think
no more about the matter.

When my watch was up, I went below in no merry
mood; and, presently, found an opportunity, while lying
in my hammock, which swung among near twoscore of
similar sleeping places, to dispose of the pearls as Rumbold had recommended. The grey light of the morning
was coming down the hatchway, and I had not yet slept,
for the end of the wretched Portuguese was still in my
head, when there was suddenly a great thumping over
head on deck, and an outcry for all hands to turn out and
go to quarters. It is curious to observe, at this summons
the sudden rousing of all the sleepers in the ship—how
in a moment, grim heads start out of the warm blankets,

and a whole legion of stalwart naked legs come down together, from a score of swinging hammocks upon the
deck. But a sailor is soon dressed; and, accordingly, two
minutes had not gone by since I lay in my hammock,
when I was at my post, staring over the weather bow, at
a small sloop, built very low, and which seemed to sail
very quickly, which was running along with us, leaning
over before the breeze, so that we could see almost the
whole of her decks, upon which about half-a-dozen of
sailors were running with sleepy scared looks, while the
steersman was calling out and gesticulating violently.
Looking forth upon the sea, I saw that a mist, almost as
thick as that in which we had stumbled upon the 'Saucy
Susan,' was just lifting from the water, and driving in
vapoury volumes before the wind. It appeared that the
mist had partially dispersed just before all hands were
roused up, and that the look-out had directly spied the
sloop, close to windward of us. If there had been less wind
and sea, our small friend would very speedily have shown
us his stern, for the sharp bows, and rounded sides of the
vessel were evidently formed for quick sailing; but the
heavy tumbling ridges of sea hove him so to leeward, that
he had no chance with a more powerful ship. Meantime,
Le Chiffon Rouge mounting into the weather-mizen
rigging, trumpet in hand, hailed to the sloop to surrender ;
and Jerry, in a breath, roared out to know if the guns
forward were all ready.

'She is a barco longo—a Spanish express boat, comrades,' he shouted ; ' and we must overhaul her despatches
before we part company.'

Still the captain of the sloop made no sign, standing
very staunchly by the steersman, and conning his ship.
Once he motioned to the latter to put the helm down, as
if he intended suddenly to luff, and go round on the other
tack ; but changing his mind, he glanced at our sails, and
continued his course. Le Chiffon Rouge again hailed the
sloop to surrender, but still without effect, and I observed
that in a temporary lull of the breeze she was beginning to
draw away from the ship. Then the bull-like voice of

Jerry thundered out along the deck—'The first gun ready there—send your cold iron aboard of him !'

Josiah Ward was the captain of the cannon by which I was stationed. His old dim eyes flashed up at the notion of a fray ; and so, stooping over the gun and sheltering the priming from the wind with his trembling hand, he glanced warily along the mass of iron as it pointed now up to the zenith, now down to the billows, according to the motion of the ship, and at length suddenly dashed the burning end of a rope, which served for a fusee, into the powder in the pan, which flashed up, while the hollow iron belched forth its flame, and started back with the explosion, the carriage cracking, and the tackles rattling through the blocks, until the discharged cannon lay near the centre of the deck, its grimed mouth yet hot and smoking. The discharge was a lucky one. The ball tore a hole in the mainsail of the sloop, and just then a gust flying heavily over the sea, the canvas was rent from top to bottom with a loud harsh shriek, and blew fluttering in rags out of the bolt-rope.

'Back the main topsail,' cried Jerry. 'The run is taken out of him.'

But just as the yard swung round, the captain of the sloop made but one leap down into his cabin, the sky-light of which was open, and directly re-appeared, carrying in his hand a small metal box or casket. He had not taken a step upon the deck, when I heard the report of a carabine from our ship, and the Spaniard leaped three feet into the air, and fell in a heap upon the deck, above his burden.

'That is the despatch box,' quoth old Ward. 'He meant to fling it into the sea, but Tommy Nixon was too sharp for him.'

Just then Le Chiffon Rouge hailed in good Spanish that if any one of the crew of the sloop dared to meddle with the box, he would hang every one of them up to the peak of their own vessel. At that the Spanish sailors hastily retired in a body to the bows of the sloop, and our stern boat being manned, was lowered dexterously into

the sea, a man standing at bow and stern to unhook
the tackles as she touched the water.  Nixon had the
command of the boat, and pulled right aboard the sloop,
the crew offering no resistance.   The first thing he did
when he got on deck was to wrench the despatch box
from the grasp of the Spanish captain, who had been shot
through the body, and was dying fast.   The poor fellow
lay in his blood upon the deck, coughing from time to
time, and sputtering the thick gore from his mouth.
Meantime, Nixon had two of the Spanish sailors brought
aft to him, and after examining them, by means of one of his
boat's crew, who spoke a little bad Spanish, he hailed that
the despatch box was all safe, and contained advices from
St. Juan, in Porto Rico, to Truxillo, under Cape Honduras, and that he would presently search the cabin for
further information.  Meantime another boat had been
got into the water, and I was ordered to form one of the
crew.   Jerry himself was in the stern-sheets, and presently we all leaped on board the Spaniard.   The first
thing the mate asked for was the despatch box.   It was a
very stout casket of lead and iron, but by means of a
heavy hammer and a marline-spike, which he brought with
him, Jerry very soon wrenched open the lid, and we, who
were crowding about him, soon saw a good packet of
letters, and despatches of different lengths, tied for the
most part carefully with silk, and bearing huge seals with
manifold devices.

Jerry straightway sat him down upon the deck, and
while the rest looked anxiously on, began with great
coolness to peruse the documents one by one.  They
seemed to be but of little interest, for as he read, his
brows darkened, and he crumpled up letter after letter,
and flung them overboard, where they were soon floating,
like so many white birds between the sloop and the ship.
At length he opened a paper, sealed with black and red
wax, which he had no sooner seen than he started up,
crying, 'Ha, this will do, even though there be no
other!'   And then stuffing the letters he had not
read back into the box, which he gave me to carry, he

asked, in a sudden fierce tone, of one of the captured Spaniards, whether there was an axe in the ship? The man shrunk back from the question.

'Why, you fool,' continued the mate, in broken Spanish, 'I am not going to chop off thy head with it; but I tell thee what, if the axe be not forthcoming speedily, I may find means of making thee a head shorter without it.'

So the weapon was duly produced.

'Now, Benjamin Mackett,' says Jerry, addressing one of the first boat's crew, 'I heard you boast the other night how speedily you could fell a tree in Virginia. Take the axe, and prove thy words on the mast of this sloop.'

At this the Spaniards, who guessed by the gestures which passed what was to be done, set up very dismal lamentations, and began to conjure us, by all the saints, to leave them the means of getting to land.

'You may get to land,' replied Jerry, 'very well under a jury-mast, but I intend that you shall be some time about it, or we shall have a score of pestilent armadilloes out swarming about our ears.'

In the meantime Mackett, who was a sturdy fellow as might be, first applied the axe to the standing rigging, and in a very short space the shrouds and stays, cut away from their fastenings at the bulwarks, collapsed, as it were, round the mast, which, being thus deprived of its supports, began to sway and work with the rolling of the ship, creaking and cracking in its step. Then Mackett, flinging aside his doublet, laid the broad bright axe to the wood with good will. The white chips glanced about the deck, and in a few moments a gash was cut so deeply into the mast that I expected to see it snap short at every roll.

'Now,' says Mackett, stopping in his work, 'which side of the sloop shall I send the mast over?'

'Over any side, with a murrain to thee, so thou makest haste,' answered Jerry.

Mackett watched the roll of the seas narrowly, and just

as the sloop lurched heavily, as a great ridge of water
heaved up under her keel, he struck the finishing blow
with such good will that the axe sunk a couple of inches
into the wood, and with a crack like a musket-shot, the
mast, with all its appurtenances of rigging and fluttering
canvas, fell crashing into the sea, smashing to dust the
light bulwarks of the sloop, and causing it to careen
heavily over as the jagged and splintered end of the
timber continued to rub and rasp against the side of the
vessel, impelled by the heaving of the swell.

'And now, Spaniards,' said Jerry, 'you may get to
Truxillo as speedily as you like, and give our compliments
to the good folks there.'

With that we all got into our boats again ; most of the
crew jeering at and flouting the disconsolate looks of the
Spaniards, as they stood like men bewildered upon the
deck of their crippled ship.   Before I went over the side,
however, I raised the head of the Spanish captain ; the
man was quite dead, and becoming stiff and cold already.

Our oars fell into the water, and the boats were
speedily hoisted up to the davits of the 'Saucy Susan.'
Then Jerry, going aft, touched his hat to Le Chiffon
Rouge very ceremoniously, and presented him with the
casket of despatches and the particular letter which he
had read, the ship all this time lying to, but gradually
drifting to leeward of the 'Barco Longo,' which now
exposed but little surface to the wind.   After a pretty
long communion between these two worthies, Le Chiffon
Rouge ordered the boatswain to call all hands, and
presently the whole crew were grouped round the mainmast.   Then the captain, taking off his hat, began to
make one of his usual speeches, a part of his duty, in
fact, which he appeared fond of, being of a long-winded
nature, and given to using fine words on such occasions.
The main points of what he now said were as follows :—

The 'Saucy Susan,' as they all knew, was bound on
a cruise to the Mosquito and Honduras coast, but,
happily, they were their own masters, and could change
their cruising ground as often as they thought fit.

Well, here were certain despatches newly captured from the 'Barco Longo,' and as one of them related to a rich Spanish ship which was shortly expected in these seas, the captain proposed that it be read aloud in English, for the benefit of Messieurs the adventurers, that, upon knowing the contents of the paper, they might determine as they thought fit.

The crew received this oration with signs of great satisfaction, and one or two cried out, 'Ay, ay, translate the Don's patter, and then we will consider.' Upon this, Le Chiffon Rouge made a sign to Rumbold, who came forward, and placed the important letter in the pearl merchant's hands. Rumbold looked at the manuscript, which was written in a fair hand, and then read out very fluently as follows ;—

'From my House at Ferrol.
Upon such a date.

'Good and trusty Manual—
'You having been absent at the mines in Darien, when, in sadness and sorrow, I returned to the main land in the long-boat of the great galleon, reft of all the treasures which the ship carried, by the hands of plundering heretics, who, for our sins, the saints permit to infest the Indian seas, I was not able personally to let you know the particulars of our misfortune, and indeed I had but small time and less heart to write the story. You are aware that in a few days after reaching Porto Bello, to which place we scudded before the wind, which was boisterous, I found a quick ship sailing unto Spain, and having taken passage in her, we were so favoured as to avoid all pirates, flebustiers, and buccaneers, and sail very prosperously across the Atlantic hither. But as touching the Carthagena galleon, that was indeed a heavy loss, and I have made it my petition to the king that he will cause representations to be sent to their majesties of England and France touching the conduct and bearing of their subjects in our Indian seas. The manner of our capture was very sudden. Two days sail from Carthagena, we beating to windward, a sail was

descried an hour before sunset, but which vanished before
the dusk closed, so that little or nothing more was thought
of the matter.   As is my wont, I retired early to rest,
the worthy captain of the galleon assuring me that all was
well, and a very good look-out kept from all parts of the
ship.   But truly, our look-out must have been maintained
with but sleepy eyes, for as I was dozing, just after
having heard midnight chime from the clock in the great
cabin, and looking half asleep half awake at the lamp as
it swung to and fro, and made strange glimmerings and
shadows upon the tapestries, I suddenly heard a tremendous outcry, and the running of feet upon the deck
above, and then, Manual, a volley of musketry, and one of
those savage ' hurrahs' which are the war-cry of the
English, followed almost on the instant by a shock which
made the great galleon tremble and surge from side to
side.   At that moment there came flying down the cabin-
stairs our friend Collado, of the Hermitage Plantation, his
face like unto grey ashes, and exclaiming that we were
ruined and undone, for that while the watch on deck
slumbered, being incited thereto by the calmness of the
weather, a pirate schooner had suddenly laid the galleon
on board, and that our good captain had fallen in the very
volley I had just heard discharged.

' But even while he was speaking the uproar on deck
was renewed.   I heard the grating and rasping as the
sides of the two vessels encountered when they rolled,
and the fierce outcries and clash of steel, and frequent
pistol and carbine shots fired while the pirates were
clambering up our lofty sides and leaping upon the deck.
They were devils, Manual.   No man could resist them.
They yelled and fought, and seemed to despise their
lives; and accordingly, in a moment, and ere I could
even put on my garments, in came the spoilers, rushing
down the cabin stairs ; a tall and strong old man, naked to
the waist, and with a handkerchief twisted round his grey
hair, leading them on, sword and pistol in hand.   Thus
were we constrained to surrender.

' Nevertheless, Manual, I must do our spoilers this

justice: they sought not to harm our persons, and were even (in their way) courteous to us their prisoners. This I say specially of the leader, who was of lofty and somewhat dignified aspect, and whom they called ' Captain Jem," and sometimes "Stout Jem." '

Here Rumbold made a pause, as if to cough, and glanced slily at me. Oh, how my heart leaped as I listened. Honest, noble Captain Jem! No prisoners but what would have mercy and courtesy at thy hands! Rumbold continued—

' This old man presently desired to speak with me privately, and, quoth he, "There was one of our crew captured by Spaniards at Carthagena; tell me truly, is he dead or alive?" At this I bethought me that there had been, indeed, an English prisoner examined at the alcaide's ; for that strange man, Don José, had informed me of the fact, and also that the Englishman behaved very boldly when put to his trial; and this I told to the pirate captain, adding, that I understood that he had made his escape into the woods, and, although he had been seen in the streets of Carthagena at night, and hotly pursued, yet that he had given all his followers the slip, and got clear off, whither none knew. At this the old man wrung my hand in a strange fashion, and whispering me, "I loved that young man as though I were his parent," added, "We make war upon you Spaniards, but we are no thieves ; therefore let each man of you take his clothes and his private stock of money, and descend speedily into the boats. The ship and cargo we claim, but not the private goods of passengers and crew."

' I give thee all these particulars, good Manual, because thou art deeply interested in all which befalls me, and so thou wilt not find them tedious. And so, presently, with sorrowful hearts we descended into our boats, and saw the galleon and the schooner trim their course for Jamaica. So far touching our disaster ; now to another matter.'

' And the matter which concerns us most, shipmates,' said Jerry. ' Go on, Mr. Rumbold.'

I give the latter part of the letter with all its details although the information involved in it came at last to nothing. Nevertheless, I think it right to recount at length the document which caused us to change our plans, and indirectly led to the loss of the ship. The letter then ran somewhat as follows .——

'And now, good Manual, our friend and correspondent, Juan Gramada, of this town, designing speedily to send forth a goodly ship, bound to Truxillo, and laden with wines, cloths, laces, and divers sorts of goods proper for the Indian markets, I have advised him that he should cause her to pause in her course at a certain barren cluster of islets to windward of the Dutch possession of Curaçoa, and considerably to the east of the usual cruising places of the pirates, who, as I learn, do not often sail to windward of the Gulf of Venezuela. These islets are called *Isles des Aves*, or Bird Islets. I have landed upon them; they are not inhabited, save by countless flocks of sea birds, and they are full of good harbours and creeks, where a ship may commodiously ride at anchor. My advice, then, to Juan Gramada, and he hath taken it, was to let his ship pause at these islands, her captain having been there once before; and that, in the mean time, you getting this letter, as I hope you will, about a week or a fortnight after the ship sails from Spain, do dispatch an agent in whom you can put trust in a good piragua, or small sailing sloop, to the Isles des Aves, bearing intelligence as to whether the seas westward be pretty clear, so as to make the run across the Gulf of Darien as safe as possible. In case of your agent bringing unfavourable or doubtful tidings, then the captain of Gramada's ship has instructions to direct the course of the vessel to any other port in New Spain, or to the Havannah, as you may think fit, where the wares can be disposed of to advantage.'

These were the chief points of the letter, the remainder being devoted to private matters not of interest to any of us. But I started again when I heard the name of the writer pronounced. It was Pedro Davosa.

When Rumbold had ceased reading, Jerry took up the word. 'Now, comrades,' quoth he, 'you have heard the news. What say ye, shall we continue our course to the south-west, or is there enough in that letter to make us haul our wind, and beat up for the Isles des Aves ? I tell you that a cargo such as the writer mentioneth is worth looking for, and it may be that we shall in the mean time light upon prey as valuable running down from the islands as we should have met upon the coast of the main.'

Upon this, Josiah Ward, being one of the oldest men on board, gave as his opinion that we ought to steer eastward for the Isles des Aves, keeping not far from the mouth of the Gulf of Venezuela, a bay which many Spanish ships were wont to enter and depart from. This seemed to settle the matter. The main-topsail was filled, and the direction of the ship altered from south-west to south-east, and then, with a hearty cheer as an opening to our new cruise, we moved away, leaving the Barco Longo, with her overthrown mast, sadly drifting on the sea.

For three days we made good progress on our new course, descrying occasionally small sails, but none we thought it worth while to pursue. In the meantime Jerry was pleased to take much notice of me, and often sounded me as to my relations to Rumbold. I deemed it right, however, to give him but evasive replies. At length he entreated me one evening to come and crush a bottle in the great cabin, where he and certain others of the choicest spirits on board, as he said, intended to drink success to the new venture of the Isles des Aves. I was in no great humour for such festivities as I knew prevailed on board the 'Saucy Susan,' but of course I could not but signify my acquiescence. So, soon after it was dark that night, and having seen that the watch on deck were sober, and that everything appeared to be going on well, I repaired to the great cabin, where I found the company assembled, and already pretty jovial.

The cabin in question was but a filthy hole, close and

2 c

stinking. with the beams so low that none could stand
upright in it, and the furniture all broken and hacked in
the drunken orgies which often took place there.   There
were arms and coils of rope, and broken boxes, and
casks half full of provisions and liquors stowed away in
corners amongst dirty bedding, and heaps of sea clothes
flung upon them, all wet as their owners had descended
from the deck.   Upon the present occasion the usual
rank smell of bilge was overpowered by the fumes of
tobacco, which all the company smoked, some of them
seated at a table covered with mugs and glasses, the
others where they best could, on casks, and boxes, and
hammocks, or lying on the floor, upon which, for the
convenience of those who had no better place, were scattered lanterns, that they might see their liquor and light
their pipes the more readily.   When I entered all the
company were singing lustily a chorus to a tune called
' Ye Buccaneers of England,' and having at length
finished the ditty, I made my way as well as I could to
Rumbold, and managed to get a seat beside him.   The
conversation then went on, Jerry's loud voice and sturdy
oaths bearing conspicuous parts in it.

' Doctor,' quoth Le Chiffon Rouge to the surgeon, a
lanky young man, more than half fuddled, but who was
discoursing learnedly to his neighbour about the practice
of phlebotomy as recommended by Galen—' is it good for
Shambling Ned, who came by the cut from Vasco's knife,
to drink raw rum.'

' Shambling Ned,' quoth the doctor, gravely, ' hath a
skull so thick, that neither steel nor spirits can very easily
reach the brain, and therefore—'

' Whoso says I have a thick skull,' retorted the patient,
starting up, to the great surprise of the doctor, who had
imagined him not there, ' lies in his teeth, and as a testimony to what I say, I fling this into them—'

With these words he dashed a pannikin of raw spirits
right into the doctor's face, who started up, gasping and
sneezing, and vowing vengeance, but was straightway
pulled down into his place again by those about him, who

comforted him by saying that brandy was not to be quarrelled with in whatever way a man came by it. Just then the highwayman, who had given me the account of his detection in Newgate, and who was seated upon a high tub, over which he dangled his legs as gracefully as he could, broke in as follows :—

'Why, stap my vitals! here be a parcel of cullies to call themselves gentlemen, forsooth, and brawl in their cups, like so many mumpers of Lincoln's Inn. Take an example by me, bullies, who am the very flower of courtesy, having been noted therefor on every heath round London. For shame, gentlemen, for shame!'

'Ho! ho! ho!' laughed the doctor; 'here be a footpad teaching us politeness, and the rules of the most courtlike society.'

'Footpad in your teeth, Master Doctor,' cried the highwayman. 'I scorn the word. A rider, sir; a rider by moonlight, for the benefit of my health and my pocket.'

'I tell you, Harris,' Jerry here broke in, his roaring voice bearing down all before it—'I tell you, Harris, he lied to you. Curse me! I know the roadstead well. I ought to, for I groped in there in as dark a night as ever lowered on this side of hell, and boarded a Spanish bark that was at anchor, and made all the fellows leap into the sea in their shirts. A rare sight, I promise you; like geese flying into a mill-pond. Those who could swim got ashore, and those who couldn't were drowned; so that in some sort they were all provided for—ha! ha! ha! send the brandy this way. Care killed a cat!'

'And so you made the dons jump into the salt water in their night-gear?' cried an old man, with a villanous looking face above a grey beard, and whose name was Cole. 'It was prettily devised; but not such good sport as I have seen in the plantations. Od rot it, man! that be the place for your true sportsman. Why, I mind me, about a dozen years since, when there comes a cargo of cheat-the-gallows birds from over the water in a ship of old Lumper's, he that hath the wharves by Rotherhithe,

and behold you, some dozen of stout fellows being drinking on board, and getting the latest news of the bona
robas down by Finsbury Pavement from old mother
Black-i'-the-face, who came over then for shoplifting in
the Poultry,—says Silas Blood, him who was killed in the
Tortugas by Francy Doubledee, says he: "How's the
scurvy aboard this time, captain?" "Scurvy!" quoth
the captain; "bad enough, I warrant thee. Here has
been some dozen rogues put aboard, just after the gaol
fever—and measly salt pork down among the bilge water
there, plays the devil with them. Scurvy, say you? they
are more like lepers than anything else." "By God!
then," says Silas—he was ever a joking man, "they ought
to be washed clean. Let's duck the lepers from the yard-
arm." Well, captain, you know, the rogues were not
worth a sixpence to anybody; not a planter would buy
such scabby dogs. So we had them up on deck, and it
was the rarest sport, man, the rarest, since eggs brought
forth chickens, to see the ragamuffins all screeching and
yelling when they were triced up to the tackling and
doused alongside, them being just all in a fever, as you
may say, out of the hot blankets. We got the bona robas
out of the fore hatch to see the game, and didn't they
shriek out for laughing, as the scurvy dogs went lick
down into the sea!"

At the conclusion of this delectable tale, the old villain
burst out a laughing, rubbing his hands, which were
shaking as though with palsy, and chuckling with his
toothless gums. It was relief to turn from him to the
highwayman, who was recounting stories of his exploits.

'"—But, good Mr. Robber, says she," so was he
continuing, as I caught his voice; '"but good Mr.
Robber," and she put her pretty face out of the coach
window, taking from it a dainty vizard all fringed with
lace of silk and gold, "leave me just one of the lockets,
and I promise thee that when thou comest to be hanged
I will send thee so gay a nosegay that all the pretty
women from Holborn Hill to the Oxford Road shall cry,

"Ay, I warrant you, he hath that from his sweetheart!"
And so I, shipmates, being the pink of gentlemen riders,
could not but assent with a low bow, saying, "Madam,
here be two miniatures, one set in gold, very massive and
rich, and the other only in very ordinary stuff; I will,
out of my admiration for you, leave you which you may
decide on;" and with that I handed her the twain. I
wish, comrades, you could have seen her holding a portrait
of an old gentleman and a young gentleman in each hand :
"Here be my husband," quoth she, "very richly set and
preciously adorned; and here be my lover, with no gold
at all around him. Master Highwayman, affection is
dearer than gold; I give thee my husband, and I keep
my lover."'

The highwayman's story was even more applauded
than old Cole's reminiscence of the plantations, and then
drinking went on very hard, Jerry, in particular, tossing
off bumper after bumper of raw brandy, and laughing and
shouting verses of loose songs, so that he might have been
heard a league off. All the thorough brute in the man's
nature was now becoming apparent. Most of the others
were bad enough in their liquor, telling such tales as I
have given specimens of, but Jerry swilled down his
draughts of fiery spirits, and, as a dog which hath so far
derogated from his natural instincts as to get drunk
might do, merely roared and yelled, and caught at the
men who sat near him by the doublets, cuffing and shaking
them, and shrieking out that that was what he loved,
and that they would all be drunk! drunk! drunk! together! Of those who kept themselves soberest, I
remarked Tommy Nixon, who, I noticed also, gradually
edging his way round to Rumbold, who sat almost silent,
his acute mind and far-extending knowledge disdaining
to clothe his thoughts in words, and cast them before
such swine.

'Master Rumbold,' said the worthy Nixon, 'do you
love oysters?'

At that question I saw very well what the man was
driving at, and watched him narrowly—'Because,' he

went on, 'men say there are delicious ones on the banks of the Rio de la Hacha! Perhaps you dived and picked up a few during your recent voyagings in that half-decked piragua, from the dangers of which we were so kind as to rescue thee.'

'Truly,' replied Rumbold, 'if by oysters you mean pearls—'

'Hush! speak lower,' said Nixon; 'thou art a sensible fellow, and being a gentleman, knowest that thy passage on board the "Saucy Susan" must be paid. As for me, I am not greedy, as all the world can testify!' and here he dropped his voice to a whisper. 'None but the captain, Jerry, and I, know aught. Let me make thy terms; it will be the better for us all.'

'Why, Tommy Nixon,' said Rumbold, 'I marvel that a man of thy discretion should go forth with a handful of salt to put upon the tail of an old sparrow like myself. Why, the pearls are all gone in the piragua, and I trust that by this time my agent in Jamaica hath them under very advantageous lock and key.'

Rumbold said this with such perfect coolness, and with so frank an air of simple candour, that I hastily passed my hand inside my doublet to feel if the leathern pouch were really there, or if I had dreamed the whole matter. No, there was the precious burden, pressed against my bosom. I looked warily at Nixon; he seemed disturbed and vexed.

''Twere better not trifle, Harry Rumbold,' he made reply; 'come, give me a ransom, and I shall let you off the rest. I can twirl Jerry round my thumb; he is only a strong animal and a good sailor, and as for Chiffon Rouge, he is captain but for our own reasons. Pay me a ransom, old Harry, and all shall go well with thee; come, only a small handful of the seed pearls. Thou hast got them cheap, thou old thief, thou knowest thou hast—come.'

'I tell you,' answered Rumbold, 'I have not a pearl in my possession. Search me an' you like. You are too clever, Tommy Nixon, and you cheated yourself when you took me aboard. Search me, man, and be satisfied.'

Nixon and Rumbold looked stedfastly into each other's eyes for the space of a minute. The former, at length, muttered, as slowly as if the words were dragged from him by some other force than that of his own will, 'That thou hast not a pearl in thy possession—that, Harry Rumbold, will be seen!'

But just at this moment, a burst of discordant singing, led on by the bellowing voice of Jerry, drowned in a moment all the clatter of conversation, and the jingling and clashing of pannikin and glass. What were the words or what was the air of the song, it would be difficult to say, seeing that every man sang according to his own peculiar liking; but Jerry's voice rose above all, hallooing this elegant stanza of a ditty common among certain of the Buccaneers—

'Haul, cheerily, jades of Jamaica,
    And trulls of Tortugas also,
The wenches have hold of the tow-rope,
    And across the salt sea we do go—
Across the salt sea we do go, boys,
    To the Sues and the Prues on the shore,
Where he hath no wife may find one,
    And he who hath one may have more.'

'Excellent, upon my reputation!' shouted the highwayman; 'Sedley could not have made better, nor Tom D'Urfey either. Well did I know both.'

'Sedley! Tom D'Urfey!—who be they?' roared the drunken mate. 'That song was made of a rare merry night, carousing in a burnt house of Maracaibo, when the place was taken under stout L'Olonnais and Michael le Basque. Here, more brandy; fill up, comrades. On your feet—your feet! He who standeth not, saving only he be dead drunk, will I cut down with my hanger. On your feet, I say, and do reason to a pledge. Here's to our next carouse on the Isles des Aves—on the wines that come from Ferrol in old Spain. Huzza!'

And the sots upon the floor, staggering to their feet,

waved lanterns and flagons, and shouted and yelled with
drunken voices—'To our next carouse in the Isles des
Aves.'

'Drink—drink, all of you—the liquor is free ; it costs
nothing,' Jerry continued, staggering as he rose from
his seat ; 'drink, I say, or I'll cram an empty bottle down
the gullet of every man that's sober.'    And, with a
drunken hiccup, he seized a lantern, and, waving it round
his head, flung it to the other end of the cabin.

The revellers shouted a furious chorus of applause.

Meantime, the watch on deck, hearing the tumult,
began to flock below, when their comrades seized them,
and, with maudlin caresses, held up to them cups of
drink, which they, nothing loath, swallowed greedily
down.    All discipline seemed over and gone, for not a
soul was left upon the deck to tend the sails, to conn, or
to steer.

'Comrades,' cried Jerry, articulating with difficulty,
'I propose—that until the morning—the ' Saucy Susan '
—be left—(hiccup)—to take care of—herself !'

Another loud chorus of approbation welcomed this
proposition, the shouting and laughter being followed
by the usual outburst of discordant singing and swearing.

'Here be what I like,' vociferated the old sinner, Cole
—'here be true merriment!    Keep it up.    Pitch him
who shirks overboard after the Portuguee.'

'Even so,' says the highwayman ; 'first to go down to
the bottom of the sea, and then to go down ever so far
below that.    The first part of the journey cold and wet,
egad, but the ending of it hot and dry enough.'

'Here's a stave, bullies, here's a stave that they sing in
Bridewell when the jades beat the hemp that hangs their
fancy men.    Give it mouth, bullies—give it mouth !'
And here the miscreant, who had boasted to me of having
broken every gaol in England, sang, with a mellow voice,
for he was not yet quite drunk, having but just come
from the deck—

' Up with your hammers, Bessy and Madge—
   Up with your hammer, Sue ;
Plait their cravats for Joe, Tom, and Jack—
   Cravats they'll grin grimly through !
Never hang head, girls, and never look glum,
   Though they strap for it, all the three,
There's stout fellows plenty are left in the world,
   In spite of old Tyburn tree !'

I would the reader could see the great cabin with all
the drunkards in it, as now it appeared. Some sat in
sodden solemnity muttering to themselves; some rolled,
cursing and fighting, on the floor ; others disputed and
drank, trying, as it were, to outscream their adversaries.
The watch on deck, who had but newly come down, said
not much, but drank off great goblets of spirits, as if it
were a race who should be intoxicated first; and so, in
good sooth, in a very short space of time, the new
comers were as madly drunk as the original revellers.
But in all the insanity of the excitement, Jerry kept
the lead. His face was all flushed and distorted with
the liquor, and he champed foam and saliva from his
mouth—

' Here,' he roared, ' a health—to the—good fellows—
who cry stand and deliver—to the Dons. Bumpers, and
no heel-taps ! Huzza! up yees out !'

And following his example, all the rest drained their
glasses, and flung them in a volley over their shoulders.

' More honour—to that toast,' hiccuped out the brutal
man ; and, suddenly drawing two pistols from his belt,
he fired them right and left into the air.

' Huzza !' shouted the others—' huzza !' and in a minute
knives were flashing, and, amid shouts and yells, the
cabin rung to some half dozen of pistol shots fired in
imitation of the leader of the debauch, in the midst of
which a wild screech rose from the darkest corner of the
cabin, and Josiah Ward staggered out, his face all blood,
and fell at full length on the floor.

' Ho! ho !' shouted Jerry, with an insane roar of
laughter; ' a bullet found its billet. Caulk the shot-hole

with the stopper of a brandy flask ; it will be better in a
man's flesh than in a bottle to-night.'

A scream of laughter answered this proposal, and some
half-dozen of the company getting up, either to aid or
mock the wounded man, fell in a heap, shouting and
swearing above him.

'Nixon—Tommy Nixon—you don't drink—Nixon—
you thief—you are sober,' yelled Jerry. 'There's mischief in it—comrades! mischief! But here, we'll alter
all that—bring hither that tub.'

The tub of which he spoke was an empty bucket, which
rolled upon the floor. It was immediately plucked up,
and trundled along the table to where he stood staggering at the head of it.

'Now fetch me them brandy-bottles,' cries the
mate.

'Go easy, go easy,' says Nixon.

'Easy,' retorted Jerry, in his passion ; 'thou art but a
cur, Tommy Nixon, to shirk the bottle in that fashion ;
but thy throat shall scald for it—there.'

And at the last word the drunken villain caught up a
flask of brandy by the neck, and smashed it into the
bucket. 'There, and there, and there,' he shouted,
dashing in bottle after bottle. 'And now, Nixon, since
you wont drink brandy raw, you shall drink it burning,
my son.'

In a moment, and before any one could interfere, the
savage caught up a candle, burning on the table before
him, and flung it all alight into the raw spirits.

Rumbold and I uttered a cry of horror as the brandy
flashed up in a blue flickering blaze to the very ceiling
of the cabin, but the besotted company only shouted and
cheered.

'Come, Tommy Nixon,' roared the mate, 'dip thy
beak into that snapdragon—come.'

And so saying, he grasped the man with both his
brawny fists.

'Let go, let go your hold, you idiot!' cried Nixon,
'you will have the ship on fire.'

'And what's that to me!' shouted the infuriated man.
'An' you will not drink, by God I shall souse thy head
in the burning liquor.'

At these words they grappled, and yelling and cursing,
they fought for a minute or two, staggering backwards
and forwards, when the brute force of Jerry prevailing,
he dragged Nixon up to the blaze, and dashed him
head first into the flame, falling himself on the top of
the struggling wretch, and upsetting the tub, which
instantly sent a flood of liquid fire surging all over the
cabin.

Oh, then, the oaths, the yells, the frantic strugglings,
which filled that hell upon the waters! Dozens of
bottles had been already broken or spilt, and their contents, surging about, had thoroughly drenched the clothes
of the wallowing brutes, who lay sprawling upon the
floor. The cabin was, in a moment, one blaze of flame,
in which men with their clothes and hair a-fire, and their
faces livid and ghastly in the glare, leaped and staggered,
and sought to clamber on barrels and casks, blas-
pheming, and screaming, and scuffling madly with each
other.

'Up, up!' shouted Rumbold, 'up for dear life!' All
that I have described took place almost in the time that
one sees a flash of lightning. In a moment, without
knowing how I had done it, I was upon the deck, with
my clothes and hair singed, but otherwise unscathed. As
I drew in the first blessed breath of the fresh cool night,
a loud explosion shook the deck under our feet, and we
heard the tinkling crash of the cabin windows as the
glass was blown out of them.

'There went a powder flask!' cried Rumbold; and
then, as if the word appalled him, he staggered back
from me, crying—

'The magazine—the magazine—it is just beneath the
floor of the cabin!'

What I did for the next moment I hardly know. It
is only a vision, of rushing to the davits where a quarter
boat hung—of the rope flying hot through my hand—of

Rumbold searching frantically for oars on the deck, while a blue flame streamed up through the sky-light and cabin stairs, and the shrieks of the burning men mingled in the roar of the fierce fire!

But in that vision, I had one awful glimpse down into the cabin. May I be enabled to forget what I saw! The masses of fat meat, the dry bedding, the clothes scattered on the floor, masses of them being drenched with spirits, were all flaming together, while the drunkards rolled, roaring and scuffling, on the table and the floor, their flesh actually scorching from the bones! I say no more on't. Would I could think no more on't.

Over the side went we with a single leap down into the surging boat. ' Off, off—push off!' And as the pinnace glanced away from the ship, tongues of flame curled and roared out of the cabin windows all round the stern. ' Pull for life!' We stretched to the oars like madmen, and the boat flew over the water. The mizensail, which was as dry as dust, for there was no dew, caught fire from the blaze, roaring up from the sky-light, and in a minute, the scorching element ran all aloft, blazing along the ropes, licking up the broad sails, making the strong canvas tinder, and lighting up for miles and miles the lone midnight sea! There! A bright sheet of red fire shot forth, as if a volcano had burst out under the ocean, the glare showing us for an instant, and no more, a vision of huge beams, and rent masses of timber, flying out and upwards; and then—just as we heard the sound of the explosion, not a loud sharp crack, but a smothered roar, which made all the air shake palpably around us—down with a stately swoop, fell the flaming mizen-mast into the sea!

We sat in speechless horror—unable to move our oars. Then all the fire, low and aloft, disappeared with a loud hiss, and a great white cloud of steam rose boiling from the wreck, loud sounds of cracking and rending timber coming forth from the vapour, mingled with the gurgling rush of water pouring into and sucking down the shattered ship. After this, the white smoke rose and floated like a canopy, all above our heads, and we gazed and gazed, but saw nothing on the midnight sea.

'They are gone—it is all over,' said Rumbold. 'Lord, have mercy on their sinful souls.'

To this I solemnly responded, with **my heart** as with my tongue, 'Amen! am en!'

## CHAPTER XXVIII.

### THE FOODLESS BOAT AND THE ISLAND.

WE sat, for a few moments after the catastrophe, in silence. Then quoth I, 'Let us pull back, there can be no danger now, and try whether there be any floating wreck with any poor wretch clinging to it.'

So we were soon, as nearly as we could judge, floating upon the exact spot where the 'Saucy Susan' foundered. It was Rumbold's opinion, that the powder below the cabin had been so stowed, that the force of the explosion when it took fire was downwards and laterally, rather than upwards—and that the sides of the afterpart of the ship had been actually driven asunder. In such case, of course, the sea would pour like a whirlpool into her, and she would have gone down, as had actually been the case, as though she were a lump of lead. The mizen-mast, with a heap of scorched and blackened wreck floating about, was the sole memorial left of the 'Saucy Susan;' the mast in question having no doubt been broken by the force of the explosion, and so saved from going to the bottom with the ship. We rowed for hours and hours round the spot, returning often to the mast, as it lay all blackened and scorched, weltering in the sea, but no other piece of wreck could we see. Not a box, or cask, or spar, but seemed to have gone right down into the awful depths of the ocean. There was something curiously dreamlike in our situation. My mind seemed wavering and flickering as I thought of what had happened. Sometimes it would appear as though the debauch had taken place years and years ago, so that I remembered it quite faintly. In another moment I would deem that the orgy was roaring around me still.  Then I would see the livid faces and fiery hair of the drunkards so plainly that I pressed my aching eyes with my hands to shut out the vision ; and anon I would deem that it must be all a nightmare, and that I was still keeping the dreary mid watch upon the deck of the ' Saucy Susan.'  But, no ; when under the pressure of such a thought, I started up, my feet would slip on the uneven planks in the boat's bottom, and I would start to hear the plunges of the mizen-mast as it rolled and wallowed beside us in the sea.

And so the grey dawn came, and after it the sun, and we stood upon the seats of the boat, and gazed anxiously all round.  The ocean was landless and shipless.  The fresh morning breeze came merrily down, curling the black summit of the swells and flecking the sombre sea with white bars.  The daylight, however, was a great relief, and we sat and talked of the terrible event of the night before, like two men telling each other sad dreams.

' We could have done nothing to save them,' said Rumbold ; ' nothing. Every man was mad drunk, except Nixon, and Jerry had him clutched as though he were squeezed in an iron vice.  They both went down, I warrant you, grappling each other.  Their bones are lying in the wreck now, with their arms round each other's necks, hundreds of fathoms under the boat's keel.'

I asked him what he thought of Nixon's refusal to drink, which had been the real cause of the mate's mad freak and its consequences, and Rumbold's thoughts jumped with mine, when he said, that he nothing doubted that Nixon had determined, if he could, to fell him, and rob him of the pearls in the drunken riot.  As he spoke this, I produced the shining morsels from the pouch. Rumbold looked sadly at them.

' For these gauds,' he said, ' two poor ignorant Indians have very probably been sacrificed, and now a whole ship's company have gone to the bottom of the sea. True, they were villains almost every man, but the more need was there that they should not be hurried to their last account with all their unrepented sins crimson on their foreheads.'

After some more talk in this strain, we roused ourselves, and began to converse of our own situation, which was bad enough, not having a strip of canvas in the boat to make a sail, and what was much worse, being without a morsel of water or food. By the best calculation I could make, we were near the centre of the Caribbean Sea, about half-way between Jamaica and Curaçoa. The regular trade-wind, blowing nearly from the north-east, might drift us, if we went before it, aided by the gulf stream, to somewhere about Cape Gracias à Dios, the great head-land, west of which the main-land trends away to form the Bay of Honduras. Rumbold agreed with me as to our probable situation, and we computed the nearest point at which we could hope to make land, if we did not succeed in stumbling upon some of the small bushy islands or keys which lie sprinkled nor-east of Cape Gracias—we computed, I say, the nearest land that we could make without sails to be about six hundred miles distant.

'Well,' said Rumbold, 'we must try to get there, that is all; so let us set to work.'

Accordingly, in about two hours, we succeeded in setting, upon one of the oars, a sort of tattered sail only adapted for going before the wind, and patched out of our shirts, by tying the sleeves together. Then pointing the boat's head about west-south-west, as near as we could judge by the sun, we set forth upon our almost hopeless voyage, rowing at the same time to help the boat on, and going about four knots an hour.

'Four knots an hour,' said Rumbold, 'and six hundred miles to be sailed over; that gives one hundred and fifty hours or thereby, if the wind keeps as fair as now, and we row night and day. Now, one hundred and fifty hours make rather more than six days; add two days more—that is a reasonable allowance for resting and times of calm—in all eight days. Can a man live eight days without food, and, in this climate, without water ?'

'No,' says I, tossing aside my oar, and clapping—I confess it—my hands to my face; 'no, we are fools to try it. Better to jump overboard at once among the sharks.'

'Take up your oar, sir,' says Rumbold, sternly; 'God helps those who help themselves. Work, sir, work. There are many chances before us. Perhaps an English ship—at the worst, a Spanish ship; perhaps an island with rain-water in the crevices of the rocks, and turtle sleeping on the sandy beaches, and plenty of birds and eggs.'

The very words put new life into me, and we tugged away for a time as cheerily as, under our circumstances, might be. The wind blew so fresh that we feared it would blow our frail sail right before it. The following seas hove us, as it were, from one to the other, and we made better progress than we hoped for. But the heat of the sun, as the day wore on, was terrible, and we began to thirst. At night, by Rumbold's advice, we washed our mouths with salt water, and afterwards, finding a pebble or two lying in the bottom of the boat, we sucked them to promote the flow of saliva, and keep our tongues cool. We tugged at the oars, but very faintly, until late in the night, and then we fell asleep over them.

The second day was the same as the first—cloudless and hot. We stripped, dipped our clothes in the sea, and then put them on dripping; as soon as the hot sun dried them we plunged the garments into the sea again. It assuaged our thirst a little, but our lips and tongues began to swell, and turn to a horrid blackness. In the afternoon we were hungry for a short space, and directly afterwards sick at stomach, particularly Rumbold, who at length slipped down into the bottom of the boat, where he lay moaning. That night we suffered intensely from the cold, and our skins being irritated by the salt water, every motion was painful to us.

The third day several sea-birds swam near us, regarding us curiously, just as the marrot had done me when I lay drowning, as I thought, upon the spars of the 'Golden Grove,' in the Bay of Biscay. The breeze blew very strong this day, with a heavy sea. Towards noon I, standing on the thafts, holding on by the oar, which was shipped for a mast, descried a sail at a great distance, but, losing it after a few moments, said nothing. Rumbold, who had been by far the stoutest hearted of the twain at starting, grew weak rapidly; and, as his strength left him, his spirits drooped. He was, indeed, an older man than I was, and perhaps naturally not of such a strong constitution. He only rowed a little this day, and towards nightfall sank into a sort of delirious state, and raved.

The fourth day I felt I was in a hot fever, and so weak I could scarce crawl. Rowing was now out of the question, and Rumbold and I lay staring at the sky, and at each other, in the stern sheets. We had suffered very little from hunger, but the thirst was terrible. The night before I had dreamed troubled visions of wells and cool clear pools, and, starting up, I had much ado to refrain from flinging myself in my agony into the sea. Towards the afternoon Rumbold said, with a sad smile—

'Cleopatra, queen of Egypt, drank dissolved pearls. Pity we have not the means to make the beverage here.'

By sundown he was raving again.

The fifth day the morning breeze was long of coming, and we watched it, with longing eyes, ruffling the water astern. Rumbold lay silent, as if worn out; his eyes had a glassy, fixed look, and there were black rings under them. As the forenoon wore on, he pointed to the water around, and I saw the black fins of sharks moving along with the boat.

'They know when death is coming,' he said.

The sixth day Rumbold was alive, and that was all. He took my hand in both of his, and whispered hoarsely, 'I have no wife—and no child—no one who will grieve— that is a great comfort at a time like this.'

2 D

Presently black clouds arose out of the sea to windward, and began to spread over the whole firmament. I pointed them out, and besought Rumbold to take heart. 'Rain is coming,' I said, 'we will live to reach the land yet.' He shook his head, and his eyes grew more and more fixed and glazed. 'I told you—I made you my— legatee,' he muttered, with great difficulty; 'think sometimes of the Peralta who helped you from the Spaniards, or of the Rumbold who died with you in the boat at sea.' All this time the black clouds became heavier, but still no rain fell. The air was like an oven, and the rude linen sail drooped motionless about the mast. I took Rumbold's head on my lap; he was past speaking, but he looked up from time to time in my eyes. At length I felt his heart flutter, and presently the beating stopped. No change whatever took place upon his face, except that it assumed that thin pinched look to which men's features shrink when death lays its hand upon them. He was dead—probably for some time before I was certain of it. When I knew that it was so, I laid the corpse gently down in the stern sheets. In half an hour the windows of Heaven were opened, and the rain poured down in bucketfuls. Oh, those blessed, blessed drops! I knelt, and with my mouth agape swallowed them. I wrung the dripping sail above my wet lips. I licked the water as it trinkled in large drops down the mast. I lapped it up as it accumulated in the little inequalities and hollows in the thafts of the boat. I had soon drunk my fill. The rain gave me fresh strength, fresh spirits, fresh soul. But as for Rumbold, the cool sweet water pattered upon his rigid face—the blessed rain drenched his hair, and great drops ran down his hollow cheeks—but it was of no avail. The manna fell not soon enough, and there lay the corpse, with its white wet face staring starkly up to the sky!

Towards night the rain-clouds broke up, and the sun came slanting in golden bursts down upon the leaden-coloured sea. The breeze also began to blow again—the well-drenched sail caught the first faint puffs of the wind, and we moved forward—the living and the dead, upon our dreary path. It was very terrible, all that long night, to sit alone beside the corpse. The moon rose in all her glory, and the ocean gleamed like molten silver about me. The white sail showed before me like a pale phantom, and at my side lay the stark dead man, with his damp pallid skin glistening in the moonlight. A dozen times I made up my mind to fling the corpse overboard, but I saw those horrible triangular fins, how they glided all round the boat, and my heart failed me. At length, I stripped off Rumbold's doublet and covered his face with the cloth.

The blackness of night faded at length—then came the grey dawn and the red bright sunrise—the seventh I had seen since the 'Saucy Susan' went down. I must have been in a half torpid state, for I lay listlessly, with my face turned to the east, waiting for the breeze to blow, and the morning was already becoming hot, when looking languidly to see if the sail was properly set, I bounded forwards from the stern-sheets, as though all the strength they ever possessed had suddenly come back to my muscles.

Land! yes—land! right ahead—not a mile from me— rocks, with the surf white upon them—sandy beaches glistening in the sun—knolls all green and bushy, and slopes carpeted with Bahama grass. Here and there a feathery palmetta tree rising from the underwood, and clouds of gulls and plovers, ducks and flamingos, pelicans and man-of-war birds, sporting or resting in the air, on the water, or the land. I was close to, as near as I could judge, a group of islets, the principal one being surrounded by many smaller,—some of them indeed mere rocks,—but rocks as I saw teeming with food, and brimming, as I did not doubt, in all their crevices, with fresh, sweet water, from last night's rain.

My heart melted within me, and I sank into the bottom of the boat, and wept, and prayed, and gave thanks. Meantime, the sea-breeze coming on to blow fresh, drove the boat quickly before it, and I had enough to do— steering with an oar to avoid the coral reefs, and spits, and banks of sand, between which I was hurried—and over which the sea went flashing in thunder. Several times the keel of the boat grazed the bottom, and we were swung round and round in the eddies and counter-currents—but still she bore me safely on, until we approached a fair sandy beach, on which the surf broke high. I could see no better landing-place, so let the boat drive, and tied myself, as well as I could, for I was more dead than alive, to an oar, that I might have a last chance of reaching the shore. In a minute or two the boat was in the broken water,—she rode over two or three fierce crests of tumbling seas very gallantly, but then a heavier breaker than common curling up astern of us, fell, as it were, down upon the boat, and I found myself faintly struggling in the white frothy water, which foamed, and buzzed, and roared in my ears, and down into which, at length, losing all sense and consciousness, I sank—a drowning man.

When I opened my eyes again, I knew not where I was, or what had happened to me. I lay in a sort of half-waking torpid state, being dimly conscious that I was stripped and in a bed, and that above me was a roof of wattled branches, and that dark figures of naked men —Indians as I deemed, were moving about me. Then I felt a cup put to my mouth, and some warm liquid, which seemed to revive and comfort me, and flow, as it were, through my poor wasted limbs, warming and re-freshing them, was poured down my throat, my head being raised by some one behind me for the purpose. But all this might or might not be. For all I knew, it was a dream of delirium. I was too weak to speak, and even to think,—consciousness forsook me again, and I fell into a deep dreamless sleep.

I returned again to sense and life. I was in a bed, a hammock, laid upon a cool mat. There was a roof of wattled branches above me, and there were Indians, two very old men, with grey hair and grey beards flowing down upon their swarthy breasts, sitting beside me. Furthermore, I saw that I was in a hut or cottage,

artfully contrived in a recess or split of rock; that part of
the walls were formed of the natural living stone, and
part of very neat and artificial wattle-work, quite wind
and weather tight. The door seemed to open at the end
of the passage, leading upwards from the chamber, which
nestled, as it were, down between the rocks; and through
this door, I saw bushes and long grass waving in the
wind. The light in the hut was somewhat dim and
grey, but I could see around me great numbers of fishing
lines, and bows, and arrows; and, looking more closely,
I saw in little cupboards, or niches, wrought out of the
rock, stores of provisions, with drinking-cups made from
cocoa-nuts and great shells, and rude clay-pots for cooking. But all the attention I could bestow was taken up
upon my hosts. They were so like each other, that I
supposed they were brothers; the same lank grey hair,
the same brown or chestnut hue of the skin, the same
rather flat noses, the same black eyes, so full of cheerful-
ness and kindness, and so completely the same expression
of face, that I could positively see no difference betwixt
their features. In all respects, save one, the ornaments
they wore were also the same. Each had a sort of fillet
of different-coloured pebbles, through which a string had
been passed, placed round his head, and a similar adornment round his neck. Each also wore thin plates of
gold dangling from his ears, but in the fillet of one of
them was fastened a wing feather of the toucan; this was
the mark by which I distinguished one from the other.
Their dress was very simple. It consisted merely of a
sort of bead-embroidered petticoat, or kilt, tied round the
waist, and reaching nearly to the knee, and a sort of
mantle of strange-looking fabric, very soft and fleecy,
which, when they sat down in the hut or cave,
they allowed to fall from their shoulders upon the
floor.

While I gazed at these Indians, they conversed softly
in a language which I had never heard, but which was
very soft and melodious. At length, seeing my eyes
open, and fixed upon them, both rose, and standing over

me, he who wore the toucan's feather said, gravely, and in excellent Spanish—

'Be of good cheer, stranger, for you are among friends.' I was too weak to do aught but take their hands in mine, and try to press them to my breast. Presently the drink I had before taken was again administered to me, and one of the Indians going forth into the open air, returned with a savoury morsel of broiled fish.

'Eat, stranger,' he said, in most sonorous Spanish; 'eat, and be refreshed.'

Thus these kind Indians fed me by degrees, and caused me to sleep with soothing and stilling draughts, I eating, drinking, and slumbering by turns; but all in moderation, so that at length I was enabled to sit up in the hammock, propped against a chest, and to falter forth my thanks, and ask how long I had been lying in that dreamy state? They told me, nigh three days. I asked, if they had found me upon the beach. They replied, the two often speaking together, in a low chanting tone of voice: 'Yes, they had, flung there by the waves, and near me a broken boat. I think my eyes must have told them what I intended for the next question, because, before I had spoken it, the Indian who wore the feather said—

'And also the body of a white man. We buried him beneath a palm-tree, when the moon was in the heavens and the air still. He sleeps well.'

Then the other took up the word—

'Truly he sleeps well; but you have been preserved; for which thank the God of many names and many nations.'

This was towards dusk. When it grew dark the Indians lighted a torch of resinous wood, which burnt bright and clear, and sitting by it, with their cloaks or blankets wrapped round them, smoked gravely from long pipes made of reeds, and drank, but very moderately, the rich juice of the palm-tree—I meantime regarding them attentively, for I was still so weak that to speak was a painful effort. At last, after a long silence, the Indian with the feather, turning to me, said, solemnly—

' I am called Buonahari, and my fathers were caciques.'
The other then said—

' And I am called Behecheco. I am the brother of
Buonahari, born but an hour after him. He is still a
cacique, because our fathers were caciques, and he is the
eldest of our race.'

The first Indian again interposed—

' Our fathers were caciques of Guanhani, where first
white men came. Now, there are none of our people
there, and the island is called St. Salvador.'

The second Indian resumed—

' When we die, the race of the caciques of Guanhani
will be no more. We are the last; but still my brother
Buonahari is a cacique, because the blood of our fathers
is the blood of caciques.'

I here touched my head where Buonahari wore the
feather. He seemed to understand the mute question,
for he replied : ' The feather of the toucan is the crown
of a cacique. If I die first my brother Behecheco will
take it from my head and wear it; when he dies no one
will take it from his head; it will lie flat and rot, because the caciques of Guanhani are no more.'

At this point I became too far exhausted to listen to
more, and the Indians bade me sleep again. When I
wakened in the night they were still sitting beside the
torch, singing, in their melodious language, a low, mournful
chant, which presently sent me to the land of dreams
again. The very next day, however, after a famous breakfast of fish and fowl, for now the Indians allowed me to
eat as much as I would, and that the reader may conceive
was not little, I managed to crawl out of the hut and
sit in the shade of wavy bushes, stirred by the cool sea
breeze. The abode was contrived, as I have said, deep in
a ravine of rocks, half clothed with bushes and rustling
grass, which were disposed partly, as I thought, by
nature, and partly by art, so as artificially to hide the
entrance to the cave—for it was rather that than anything
else—from any except a very curious and a very keen inves-
tigator. But presently the Indians returning from fishing,

they having left me still in the hammock, they led me slowly
and tenderly out of the ravine, and forth upon an open,
breezy space, a sort of terrace, amid the cluster of rocks
in which was their dwelling, and from which I could look
down upon the greater part of the island, which seemed
to be some four or five miles in circumference, uneven and
rocky, with abundance of bays and creeks on the leeward
side, formed by smaller islets and natural indentations in
the coast of the greater.  It was curious to observe, the
trade wind blowing strong, the space of smooth glancing
water left in the lee of the island, and tapering away
towards the south-west.  On the windward side, the sea
broke high upon the rocks, and Behecheco informed me,
that in stormy weather the salt spray flew over and over
the island from beach to beach.  Among the bushes and
trees there fluttered and coo'd countless flocks of pigeons
and other small birds of brilliant plumage ; and down by
the shore, the fowls which wade and swim dotted all the
grey rocks, and glancing shingle beds, and fair beaches of
hard dry sand.

I sat long enjoying the prospect, the Indians being
gravely squatted beside me ; then I asked if there were
other inhabitants of the isle except themselves ?

They replied, ' No.  None else.'

' Did not privateers sometimes come there ?'

' Ships of white men of divers nations sometimes come,'
replied Behecheco ; ' but then we mostly hide closely in
the cave.  The sailors land, and seek for turtle, and perhaps pigeons.  Then they go away again, and we come
forth.'

I then prayed them to tell me how long they had lived
in that solitude, and from what land they came ?  Buonahari replied a follows :—

' Nigh two-score of years have passed away since we
landed upon this island in a canoe.  We fled here from
Hispaniola, where we were slaves to the Spaniards.  It
was when we were slaves that we learned the tongue in
which we now speak to you.  Still we know that you are
not a Spaniard, for your skin is too white, and your eyes

are blue. You are, perhaps, then, one of those nations which come from across the ocean, and make war on the Spaniards?'

Having assented to this conjecture, the Indian resumed thus :—

' We were slaves in Hispaniola, my brother Behecheco and I. We dug in the mines for gold. Our father and mother were also slaves—they also dug in the mines for gold. Their father and mother were likewise slaves, and they likewise dug in the mines for gold. So it was with our family for five descents. We were slaves in Hispaniola. But when our father and mother died, I said to my brother, " We are strong. We know the ways of the mountains. We have found in the woods the plant, which, strewed upon the path of a flying man, causes the blood-hound to lose the scent. Let us be no longer slaves—let us flee." As I said, so we did. We fled from the mines. The Spaniards pursued us, but the blood-hounds lost the scent, and we came to the sea. There we hollowed a tree into a great canoe, according as the traditions of our fathers had taught us—and in this canoe we put to sea, drifting before the wind. We had water, and meal, and cassava, and fruits, and in half a moon we saw this island and landed on it. Here we have continued to live, and here we will die.'

I was much interested in this account, for I conjectured that the Indians were descendants of the race of original inhabitants of the Leeward or Lucayas group, now called the Bahama Islands, which the Spaniards had first discovered, and from which they had, about fifteen years after the first voyage of Columbus, inveigled a great number of the inhabitants to make them slaves in Cuba and Hispaniola. This I say was my conjecture, and it was speedily verified.

' I have said,' continued Behecheco, ' that the blood in our veins is the blood of ancient caciques—the caciques of Guanhani. Though we were slaves, we had that blood still. Our father told us so. His father told him. We speak the old language of Guanhani, for it was taught us in our childhood. We worship the old gods of Guanhani, for we were instructed so to do in our childhood, and we could recount to you the beautiful things of Guanhani, the trees and the rocks, the rivers and the shores, the hills and the streams, the birds and the beasts, although we never saw them. Our father, who taught us, never saw them. His father, who taught him, never saw them. But ever from father to son, and mother to daughter, there flows the knowledge of what our race was once, and what land it ruled over. Now, alas! that knowledge is to perish, even as water sinks in dry sand.'

I thought, as the Indian spoke thus, that both the brothers experienced some kind of satisfaction in recounting to another the secret, which would otherwise die with them, and thus keeping it a little longer floating in the world. Presently, after their accustomed fashion of alternate speaking, Buonahari chimed in—

'Our forefather, who came from Guanhani and Hispaniola, was the son of him who was cacique in Guanhani, when the white men landed upon it, and said, "Here is a New World." Five years after he began to reign, there came many ships with white men. Our forefathers thought that the white men were gods come down from the sun, and they honoured them, and feared them. Then said the white men—" Would you see again your fathers and your mothers, who have died and gone to the happy valleys—to the land of Coyaba—to that land where are cool shades and delicious fruits—where the drought burns not up the ground—and the hurricane tears not up the trees? If you would go thither, come into our ships and we will sail with you to Coyaba, and we will also see your departed friends." So our forefathers believed the white men, and went into their ships, and the white men did not take them to Coyaba, but to Hispaniola and to Cuba, and made them slaves to dig for gold in the mountains. Most of our forefathers died there, and gradually the nation wasted away—but our family did not come to an end, but went on, generation after generation, until we were begotten, and with us our family will die, and the last of the race of Guanhani will be taken from the earth.'

Both the old men spoke as though they had already outlived all sorrow for their lot. Their words and gestures were grave and solemn, but not mournful, for their trust was, that when they died, they would at length go to Coyaba, and see again all their forefathers, those who had been slaves in Cuba and Hispaniola, and those who had borne rule in Guanhani.

In about a week's time I was quite restored, and daily went a hunting and a fishing with my Indian hosts. I had told them my story, to which they listened eagerly, and I had assured them, that if, perchance, there should come to the island a ship manned by my countrymen, and which might carry me away, that I would reveal to none the secret of their habitation, but leave them undisturbed in their solitary abode. I made them lead me also to where Rumbold lay buried beneath the palm. It was a breezy, sunny spot, and upon the turf I piled a little heap, or cairn of stones, such as, in Scotland, where they are found heaped on dreary moors, and among lone hills, are said by the country-people to mark the grave of a hero. Weeks glided away thus. The old Indians were always the same—grave, courteous, and kind. They fished, and set snares for birds, when they wanted them for food, but killed none wantonly. They ever went together, and with the same slow, stately step. Their talk was almost always of Coyaba, and the friends who had gone before them, and who they would meet there. In short, their demeanour and their speech were those of men whose minds were set upon the things of the new world into which they were soon to enter. The space between them and death was short, and their eyes seemed to be able to look beyond it, and to care little for what was on this side of the dark river. Notwithstanding, however, I drew from them many traditionary accounts of their people before white men had visited them; and one night, in particular, I asked whether there had been handed down any remembrance of the first white men who landed

upon Guanhani—they being, indeed, no other than Columbus and his followers.  To this question, Buonahari
readily answered, that he had often heard from his father
the full account of that event, as it had been handed
down, and that, if I pleased, he would narrate it.  Then,
filling his cup with palm-wine, and trimming the torch,
which cast a sparkling glow upon the rock-walls and
wattled roof of the hut—the descendant of the caciques
began the tale.

---

## CHAPTER XXIX.

### THE DISCOVERY OF A NEW WORLD.

THE name of my forefather, who reigned in Guanhani
when white men first came there was the same as mine,
Buonahari.  He was a good cacique, and the people
loved him; he ruled the island, and none disputed his
sway.  Then there was great plenty in the land; the
earth bore her fruits, and the people subsisted upon
them.  There were no fish caught with hook, or spear, or
net; and no birds with snare or arrow.  The people ate
only what grew—the fruits of the ground and the corn,
and about the hut of each man was the field of maize
which he cultivated.  Then were the gods worshipped
piously—the gods who sent the good things the people
enjoyed.  There were songs and dancing through all the
land.  The people met in the evenings, and lighted great
fires upon the altars, and then the young men and the
maidens danced, and the old men and their wives looked
on, and the Bohitos, that is, the priests and the bards,
sang songs in praise of the gods.
    One night there was a great feast of singing and
dancing before the hut where my forefather, the cacique,
dwelt down by the sea.  All the people of the village
were there, for the cacique and the chief of the Bohitos
had caused proclamation to be made that every man and
every woman should come forth from their huts to dance
and sing and praise Zemi, the greatest of the gods.
    Now, when the night was dark, and the songs of the

people were loud, the chief of the Bohitos came to my forefather, the cacique, and said—

' Why are not all the young men at the festival?'

And the cacique answered, ' They are at the festival; they have come from the woods and the sea to praise Zemi.'

But the chief of the Bohitos answered, ' Not so—look! there is a light upon the sea.'

Then my forefather caused search to be made, but all the canoes were drawn up upon the beach above the surf. Still there was a light upon the sea. And the chief Bohito said—

' It is Zemi, who looks at our festival from the sea.'

At these words all the people were glad, and redoubled their songs and their praise. Presently a flash of lightning, and a loud roar of thunder, came across the water, and the chief of the Bohitos and the people were troubled, for they thought that Zemi was speaking in anger. And the Bohito said to my forefather—

' Saw you ever thunder and lightning so close to the ocean?'

And my forefather answered, ' Never.'

Then sad thoughts and ominous whispers began to spread among all the crowd; and the dances ceased, and the songs of praise died away, and the fire went out that was kindled on the altar of Zemi. Still the light burned bright upon the sea; and presently two lights shone; and after that three.

' There are three gods watching us,' said my forefather; but the Bohito answered never a word. None went to rest that night, but tarried sadly on the beach waiting the day. The darkness paled away, and the people saw three mighty shadows on the sea. The grey of the dawn brightened into the day, and the people saw, as it were, three great houses on the sea—houses which floated, and which spread mighty wings to the wind, and glided to-and-fro.

At this the chief of the Bohitos was troubled, and all the people were afraid, and kneeled down upon the beach,

and prayed to Zemi; when, behold, the houses on the
sea thundered and lightened as though they were black
clouds in the air, and a great smoke rose up from them,
and came with the wind down to the beach, and the
people smelt an odour new and strange to their nostrils.
But the prodigies were not over—great canoes came forth
from the floating houses and approached the beach, and,
rising from them upon the air, there swelled a mighty
strain of music and figures, with faces all white, bearing
strange weapons, which flashed in the sun, and clad in
glorious garments, whereof none knew the name, stood
in the big canoes, waving their arms and shouting in
great joy.

But one of the canoes came first, and on the prow of it
was a man of a figure so goodly that he seemed a god.
He stood up towering like a giant.   There was glory on
his forehead—there was holiness on his forehead.   His
eyes flashed like the eyes of the chief of the Bohitos,
when Zemi enters into him and fills him.   He waved in
the air a glittering sword.   He stretched forth his arms,
and his big voice spoke tremblingly, and as if he knew
not what it said.

Nearer and nearer came the canoes.   Then the man,
who was as a god, waved his sword, and they paused, and
he alone walked, with a glorious port, through the surf,
which flashed beneath him, up upon the dry sand, and
there he knelt down, and prayed and wept!

But in a moment more all the white men who followed
him plunged into the water and struggled to the land.
First they knelt, as the foremost of them all had knelt,
and each kissed the sand; then they knelt round about
the leader, and sought to get near him to kiss his hand or
his foot, while he stood erect among them like a palm-tree
above weeds!

This is a description of the cacique of the white
strangers.   He was past the middle age, but erect as a
sapling, and sturdy as a tree.   He had a thin, hard face,
with a long hooked nose, and a mighty forehead, marked
with deep lines like furrows.   His hair was very short,

and quite grey. He had shaggy eyebrows, and under them eyes which pierced, and of a grey or ash colour. He had a scanty beard, which hung in a peak from his chin, with very few hairs on the upper lip. He was not tall, but handsome and strong. On his head he wore a hat looped with golden chains and crowned with feathers, and his garments were all glittering and glorious, and in his right hand he ever held the naked sword! When the white strangers knelt to him, and when my forefathers saw the grandeur and majesty of his face, they felt he was a god, and they knelt likewise—the chief of the Bohitos and also the cacique. So the white cacique stood erect above them all.

Then the white men placed in the sand an upright stick with a shorter stick crossing it, and all baring their heads, sang a loud song very solemn and slow, looking up to heaven, and making a cross with their fingers on their foreheads and their breasts.

Meantime the cacique and the chief of the Bohitos advanced with fear and trembling, and prostrated themselves before the great white cacique. But he raised them with kind looks and gentle-sounding words, and put into their hands treasures—bright flat stones, in which whoso looked saw his own face looking back at him—and hollow vessels like shells, but bright and glittering, which made merry music when they were shaken in the hand. In exchange, the cacique and the chief of the Bohitos gave what they had, maize and the cloth of the cotton-tree. Presently, the white strangers touched the golden plates which hung from our forefathers' ears, and asked by signs where the gold came from? and our forefathers pointed towards where Cuba and Hispaniola lay across the sea. At this the white strangers smiled to each other, and were pleased. The multitudes followed them whithersoever they went, and when the even was come, and the sun going down, the white men passed again in their great canoes to the floating houses with wings, in which they lived on the sea. Our forefathers accompanied them with songs and rejoicings in their small canoes, and the great white cacique, standing high above the ocean, waved them farewell, while the lightning flashed and the thunder rolled from the floating house beneath him.

And this is the story of the first coming of white men, as my forefather, the cacique, who saw them, to'd it to my forefather, the next cacique, who was carried by them a slave to dig for gold in Hispaniola.

---

## CHAPTER THE LAST.

### I MEET OLD FRIENDS.

WEEKS passed slowly away. Twice a day, in the morning and the afternoon, I mounted to the summit of the highest rock in the island, looking anxiously round for sails, and there, by consent of the Indians, who felt secure in their hiding-place, I piled up a great mass of brushwood, ready for firing as a signal, in case of any English vessel approaching. During these long solitary watches I thought much of my life since I had been carried a prisoner to the West Indies. I thought how many great dangers I had undergone, how many narrow escapes I had made, and I began gradually to entertain the idea whether, upon an opportunity offering, I had better resume a buccaneering life, or set out across the Atlantic for home. I said to myself, 'I will not return penniless as when I went forth.' The pearls left to me by poor Rumbold were, as he said, worth fully one thousand pounds, and I doubted not but that my share in the booty captured in the Carthagena galleon, I owning one-third of the schooner which took her, as well as being second officer on board, would come to something very considerable. Here, then, were means upon which I could at once return and bring happiness and wealth to the firesides of Kirkleslie. I brooded over these things much. Lying in the shade of my brushwood pile, watching the buzzing sparkling insects which shot hither and thither in the air—the dragon-fly poising his litho body, and the brightly painted butterflies flitting from flower to flower, I pondered and turned the question in my mind. My old habits of castle-building came back upon me, and I erected two splendid edifices upon the foundation of the subtle air.

The first was of my lot if I remained in the West Indies, or joined the bold adventurers who were pushing across the isthmus of Darien, to launch upon a career of fortune in the South Sea. I pictured myself the commander of a stout ship of war, nay, the admiral of a fleet of stout ships of war, carrying fire and sword into Panama, Payta, or Acapulco, capturing Spanish galleons by the squadron, and dictating terms to the captive governors of overthrown cities. Then, as I lay thinking, and watching the gorgeous proportions of this air-painted dream, it faded away, and another and a humbler vision rose; it represented the green fields and white beaches of the fair coast of Fife—the straggling cottages of Kirkleslie—the pier of whinstone, stretching forth seawards—the little rippling bay, where the Burn of Balwearie poured its frothing waters into the brine—the green bourocks of bent and waving grass, which surrounded it, marked with their brown patches of dry herring nets, and the rocking boats, riding to their grapnels in the bay. Then I saw approaching the shore a stout brig, lofty in her rig and graceful in her form, and I saw the fishers, and their wives, and their bairns, all running down to the beach, and shouting, with joyful clamour, that here was come Leonard Lindsay's new brig, the Royal Thistle, fresh from the stocks at Leith.

And there was another consideration too. It is sad to remember it now, but it was joyful to dream of it then. I had a long tryste at Alicant, and I thought how proud I would be, in my own stout ship, to carry my betrothed from her Spanish city to the northern home which she had chosen and which she would love.

If both of these plans were, in the ending, empty and vain, at least one was built on a less airy foundation than the other. I determined not to grasp at overmuch. I

2 E

decided not to let go the substance for the shadow, and
at length I started up from the grass, and with a heart
light as that of a boy let loose from school, I shouted,
'Home, home! the rough winds and the rugged coasts of
Scotland before all these teeming lands and summer
seas!'

Having once formed this resolution, I was miserable
until I had the means of putting it in execution. From
the grey dawn to the grey eve I sat upon my watch-
tower on the hill; sometimes the Indians accompanied
me, and we talked touching the only subject on which
they cared to converse—the past glories of Guanhani,
and the future happiness of Coyaba. Sometimes I was
alone, tossing restlessly upon the turf in my impatience,
wondering whether all vessels had ceased to sail the sea,
since I saw none,—plucking out my flint and steel every
quarter of an hour, to take care that all was ready for
firing the beacon at a moment's notice; or noting any
change in the slant of the tradewind, which might cause
a vessel to diverge from her course between the islands
and the main. Several times I attempted to patch up
the broken boat of the 'Saucy Susan,' which lay upon a
sheltered bit of beach, with the tide flowing in and out of
her, but she was injured beyond my powers as a ship
carpenter to repair, and besides, had she been afloat and
sound, I had nothing of which I could make a sail. The
Indians possessed a canoe, but only fit for paddling.

During these tedious weeks, I strained my memory in
vain to make out whether I had ever heard of such an
island as that on which I stood. In most of the maps of
the Caribbean Sea, small specks of nameless isles are laid
down in great profusion all round Cape Gracias à Dios,
but I knew that these charts were, for the most part, to
be little depended upon, except as regarded the great
islands and headlands; and I remembered the labyrinth
of rocks, islets, and reefs, in which we found the dwarf
pilot, and which were not even indicated in any one chart
we had on board the 'Will-o'-the-Wisp.' The Indians
said, that the time of ships coming hither was very

uncertain; sometimes two or three passed by in a moon, sometimes two or three moons passed by during which the sea would be sail-less; now a passing ship would keep far off, so that her canvas would show not bigger than the wing of a sea-fowl; anon she would anchor in the lee of the island, and lie there for days, filling her water-casks from the rain ponds in the hollows of the rocks, and allowing the men to scamper at large, hunting pigeons and noddies, or searching for turtles' eggs, all over the island.

But at length my happy moment arrived—the long-looked for came at last. I ought to have mentioned, that the island upon the windward-side was indented by a large bay, which stretched from one extremity of the land to the other. In the centre of this bay, and near the beach, were various rocky islets and sand-banks, amongst which on arriving I had been driven, and upon each horn of the crescent, long points of high and rugged rock jutted forth into the sea, making that appear a deep bay which was in reality a mere shallow coast indentation. My signal-post, as I called it, was near the centre of the bay, and about a mile from each of the jutting and rocky horns which I have mentioned; the hut of the Indians being among the clefts and bushes beneath.

I was wakened early one morning by the howl of the wind through the trees and precipices above us, and, presently going forth, found it blowing a hard gale right into the bay—the rocky islets before the beach being only now and then to be seen like black specks amid the foam. The gale increased as the day advanced, and about noon, a tremendous breaker swept so high up the beach as to catch the wreck of the 'Saucy Susan's' boat, and fairly to drive it to pieces on the shingle. The day was very dark and dismal, the clouds flying fast and low, and the sea-birds making, in flocks, for the cover of the land. The horizon from my look-out was only a few miles in extent, but within it, the seas broke furiously, and the surf upon either horn of the bay was grand to look at. In the afternoon, I wandered forth alone upon the beach

—the Indians, who did not relish such weather, keeping snug at home—and remained for hours in a sheltered nook upon the southern ridge of the bay, watching the great seas rolling in and assaulting the rocks.

The day was wearing away, and the sun was setting behind the island, when I suddenly heard a shout to sea-ward. Starting up to my feet, I saw about a cable's length distant from the bluff, on the outside of the bay, and a little to windward, a small sloop, showing but a rag of sail, and struggling hard to weather the point. The bark, though very small, was decked from stem to stern. Had it not been for that, she would not have lived a moment in such a sea. As it was, she bent over, so that I could see three men lying upon the slanting planks, holding on to the weather-rigging, while the steersman, made fast on the weather side to a staunchion of the light rail, which run round the sloop, worked the tiller by means of blocks and tackling. It was an even chance, so far as I could see, whether the sloop would beat round into the bay, or be shivered upon the head-land, and I rushed as far out as I could upon the rocks to watch the catastrophe. On she came, plunging and tearing over the seas, hove up aloft, so that she was sometimes almost on a level with the ground I stood on, then ducking into the trough, so that I could only see the top of her tiny mainsail, with the spray of the next com-ing sea, torn up by the wind, and pelting over and over it. The figures on board held on to the weather-bulwarks, like grim death ; but as she closed nearer and nearer with the rocks, I saw two of them kick off their shoes, and strip their doublets. A moment would now decide their fate. The sloop was not half-a-score fathoms from the outermost point, over which the sea boiled white. She sank heavily into a deep foaming trough of sea, and her sail flapped in the lull. Up again, as though cast by a sling! She leaped at the next surge—a blast which made me stagger back on the rocks—almost tearing the mast out of her, and lifting her, as it were, bodily over the furiously ridging and tumbling water. The wave burst in milk-white foam beneath, the spray flying round and over me, but from the very centre, as it appeared, of the seething hissing mass of the rebuffed and broken billow, the gallant little bark flew triumphantly round the rock, and into the bay.

'Hurrah,' I shouted; 'bravely done!'

The men on board caught my words, even through the roar of the surf. He who was steering, and who had been hitherto crouching down, watching the run of the seas, looked up. Could I believe my eyes? Nicky Hamstring!

'Lindsay! Will Thistle! Hurrah!' he shouted.

'Comrade—old comrade!' I cried, making a speaking-trumpet of my hands. 'Beach her—run her right through the surf. High and dry—high and dry!'

The sloop was already beyond hearing, but Nicky waved his hand. Up goes the helm, round fly the bows of the bark towards the open white beach of the bay, and shorewards she shoots, leaping from sea to sea!

Leaping indeed from sea to sea, but not faster than I sprung from rock to rock, and bank to bank, striving to be upon the beach before her. It was a grand race. I saw Nicky's crew leap up, as the sloop, now upon an even keel, went scudding like a feather before a hurricane. More sail—more sail! They are shaking out two reefs in the canvas! They will drive her through the breakers in style! Away goes the widened sheet higher and higher up the mast! See how it swells, and tugs, and surges, as though it would pluck the craft out of the water by the very roots, and drag and soar with her through the air! I am running fast, but she heads me. See, Nicky is standing in the stern, and again he waves his hand! Is it in token of hope, or of farewell? A minute will end all. The sloop flies madly into the line of breakers! A sea comes white over and over her! No! she is not down; up she staggers on the crest of the following wave, pouring the water from her sides, and her crew still clinging stedfastly round the mast. On she goes—a dusky spot—a mere tossing

morsel amid the wallowing surf, but the brave mast
still holds on, the stout canvas still bears her
onward, like a bird! There, down into the trough once
more, and now aloft again on the very shoulder of a
breaking sea, which has hove her up, as a strong man
swings a child, and then bearing her recklessly on, dis-
solves beneath her keel, in a tumbling avalanche of
creaming foam, in the centre of which the sloop is carried
triumphantly up, upon the wreaths of sea-weed at the
very top of high water-mark, and there, as the sea re-
cedes, is left high and dry! No Deal boatmen ever
beached a galley more admirably after a wild trip to the
Goodwin Sands.

The next moment I had both Nicky Hamstring's hands
in mine! Such a meeting! It was as if he had fallen
from the moon upon me! And what a world of inquiries
to put to each other. How had I come there? How
had he come there? For five minutes it was nothing but
such rapid question and answer! Then quoth I, ' And
Stout Jem, and the " Will-o'-the-Wisp?" '

' They cannot be five miles to windward,' replied
Nicky, ' and running the same course as we when we saw
breakers ahead, and beat round into the bay. The sloop
is a Spanish craft we wanted to carry to Jamaica, and we
were in company with the schooner all day, until she split
her foresail ; after which we got the start, and lost sight
of her.'

By this time it was getting dark, the gale still blowing
furiously.

' We none of us had the slightest idea of land within a
hundred miles,' said Nicky. ' I would to God that we
had the means of giving Stout Jem notice of what he is
running on, while he has still a mile or two of offing.'

I immediately remembered my beacon of piled brushwood, and thanked heaven that I had collected it. But
as we were all scampering up the hill towards it, we met
the two old Indians coming down to the beach. From a
snug place of espial they had seen the meeting between
Nicky Hamstring and myself, and rightly conjecturing

that they had nothing to fear from one who seemed so much my friend, they had come forth to offer a refuge to the wrecked mariners. Accordingly, leaving them to conduct two of the sailors whom 1 did not know, to the cave, the third being no other than my old shipmate, Lanscriffe, who shook hands with me heartily, he and Nicky and I were speedily standing beside my beacon. It was now quite dark, and seawards we could descry nought beyond the dull white belt of breakers. A light was speedily struck, and in a minute after it was applied; the brushwood being as dry as tinder, a bright blaze, torn and driven by the wind, rose flickering up into the dark night, casting long rays of light over the waving grass and bushes, and the white and tumbling sea. I had made the pile of brushwood so large, that the beacon was nothing but a great bonfire, and presently the two seamen we had left rejoined us with the Indians, carrying between them a small tar barrel which they had made shift to get at out of the stranded bark, the tide having now ebbed considerably back from it. This was a grand addition to our beacon, and, fed by the fat pitchy unguent, the blaze must have been seen leagues away. That it was seen by those for whom we lit it we soon had a satisfactory token, in the quickly following flashes of several guns, fired by a vessel near a league off at sea. Upon this we descended to the beach again. The Will-o'-the-Wisp, for Nicky Hamstring did not doubt but it was she, presently ran up lanterns to her main and topmast heads, and, in a few moments more, she burned a flaring blue light, which showed the beautiful schooner weltering through the seas close hauled under closely reefed fore and mainsails, but, as we all hoped and believed, holding her own very steadily.

As we sat watching her upon the beach, Nicky Hamstring recounted to me the particulars of the attack upon Carthagena harbour after I had been made prisoner, and the subsequent capture of the galleon. My share of the booty was, it seems, lodged in the hands of Mr. Pratt, at Jamaica, and would be at once made over to me. To narrate all the particulars of the cruise of the Will-o'-the Wisp after I quitted her, would be no part of my story, and I dismiss it by simply stating, that so many and so great were the prizes which she took, that not a man who sailed under Stout Jem but was, according to his degree, enriched, and returned to Jamaica with money, and plenty of it, in both pockets.

Talking in this manner, the first part of the night wore away, and, as it waxed late, the gale began to lull. You may be sure in all our converse we never took our eyes from the schooner's lights, which rose and sank regularly upon the seas. But we were soon relieved of our anxiety regarding her, by observing that she rather clawed away from the shore than approached it, and we knew well that not an eye would be closed aboard the schooner that eventful night. About midnight the heavy clouds to windward began to break, and the schooner burnt another blue light, by which we saw that she had a reef out of her sails, and was standing on and off snugly enough, the sea going down very fast.

Thereupon we all retired to the cave, the Indians doing the honours of their abode with such simple grace, that Nicky called them two brown old gentlemen without clothes, and swore that he would run the risk of being wrecked again to be so kindly tended. It was indeed a happy meal! Lanscriffe and his comrades had gone down to the stranded ship, and returned laden with good cheer, and every few minutes, as we ate, and drank, and laughed, one of us would start up and run out to see how the schooner fared, and come back with the news that the wind was going down more and more, and that our friends were all safe, a league from the rocks, and riding as snugly as though the schooner were lying in a mill-pond.

'And all the old faces are still on board?' quoth I.

'Every one of them,' answered Nicky; 'all our old party of the Marmousettes in Hispaniola, from Stout Jem down to Blue Peter, and, indeed, almost every man we shipped in Jamaica, including Mr. Bell, who hath become such a reformed character, that it seems as if that keel-hauling, which you remember, has had the most beneficial effect in washing the roguery out of him.'

' And the negro,' says I; ' the Spanish negro, we captured fishing for pisareros off Carthagena ?'

' Oh! he was sent ashore with the sailors of the galleon, who, I hear, landed at Porto Bello.'

' There was,' says I, ' on board that galleon, one old man, a merchant—'

' He who told Stout Jem that you had escaped from the Spaniards at Carthagena—a grave and reverend old man,' said Nicky. ' He bore his loss so tranquilly, that I thought, and others thought it too, that he went over the side of the galleon into the boat with some of the most precious parts of his goods concealed upon his person. A sly old fox, to be sure.'

To tell the truth, I was not sorry to hear this.

' We got enough from him as it was, Nicky,' I said.

' Humph!' quoth Nicky, ' I must say we did.'

The grey dawn found the schooner anchored in the bay, and before sunrise Nicky and I, having obtained the canoe of the Indians for the purpose, leaped on board.

I almost shook Captain Jem out of his hammock, into which, poor man, he had only just turned, after seeing that all was safe with the ground tackle, and that the weather looked settled.

' Captain Jem! Captain Jem!' I cried; ' you told the merchant on board the galleon, that you loved me as a son, and here is your son come back again to you!'

I will not try to reduce to words the shout of delight with which the hearty old fellow jumped clean out of his hammock, and clutching my hands in both of his, danced me round and round the little cabin. It was a thorough welcome home, and almost induced me to falter in my resolution of immediately returning to Scotland. But the feeling lasted but for a moment. I loved my comrades, but I loved kith and kin more, and now I had that to carry back to them which would bring grateful tears to many an eye.

And now my story is told.

I have bidden a solemn farewell to the representatives of the blood of the old caciques, and the ' Will-o-the-Wisp ' is under weigh, bound direct for Jamaica, from whence I can easily procure a passage home. Her buccaneering cruise, of which I saw so little, is ended. She lies deep in the water, freighted with the spoils of the proud Spaniards, who vainly swore that theirs alone would be the empire and the treasure of the New World. Her merry crew will shortly be dispersed, and never rock in hammocks in one ship again. Stout Jem is bound for Europe, and mayhap we will go together. Nicky Hamstring, true to his opinion, that the New World is a merrier one than the Old, talks of enlisting under the banner of Captain Morgan, to march with him across the mountains to the great South Sea. Each has his plans, and every man's plan is different from his neighbour's. May they all prosper!

And now I bid my readers a kind good by!

I have told them roughly, but truly, as much of my life as was the 'Story of a Buccaneer.' If they have found it stirring enough to while away a leisure hour, I am content. But if from it they have learned something of the real truth concerning Buccaneers, how the order sprung naturally from the greed of the Spaniards to make a monopoly of America—how the Buccaneers lived by sea and land—how they hunted, and sailed, and made war—how there were good and bad, honest hearts and rogues among them—in short, if they have learned what manner of men the Buccaneers were, and what manner of lives they led—then I shall be more than content; I shall think that I have served the memories of my brave countrymen who sleep beneath those western seas, and that I have given to the world some information, not without its uses, touching an interesting chapter of our maritime history.

THE END.

Woodfall & Kinder, Printers, Milford Lane, Strand, London, W.C.